Defining the Jacobean Church

This book proposes a new model for understanding religious debates in the churches of England and Scotland between 1603 and 1625. Setting aside 'narrow' analyses of conflict over predestination, its theme is ecclesiology – the nature of the Church, its rites and governance, and its relationship to the early Stuart political world. Drawing on a substantial number of polemical works, from sermons to books of several hundred pages, it argues that rival interpretations of scripture, pagan and civil history, and the sources central to the Christian historical tradition lay at the heart of disputes between proponents of contrasting ecclesiological visions. Some saw the Church as a blend of spiritual and political elements – a state church – while others insisted that the life of the spirit should be free from civil authority. As the reign went on these positions hardened and they made a major contribution to the religious divisions of the 1640s.

CHARLES W. A. PRIOR is a Research Fellow in the Faculty of History at the University of Cambridge. He is the editor of *Mandeville and Augustan ideas: new essays* (2000).

Cambridge Studies in Early Modern British History

Series editors

ANTHONY FLETCHER
Emeritus Professor of English Social History, University of London

JOHN GUY
Fellow, Clare College, Cambridge

JOHN MORRILL
*Professor of British and Irish History, University of Cambridge,
and Vice-Master of Selwyn College*

This is a series of monographs and studies covering many aspects of the history of the British Isles between the late fifteenth century and the early eighteenth century. It includes the work of established scholars and pioneering work by a new generation of scholars. It includes both reviews and revisions of major topics and books, which open up new historical terrain or which reveal startling new perspectives on familiar subjects. All the volumes set detailed research into our broader perspectives and the books are intended for the use of students as well as of their teachers.

For a list of titles in the series, see end of book.

DEFINING THE JACOBEAN CHURCH

The Politics of Religious Controversy, 1603–1625

CHARLES W. A. PRIOR
University of Cambridge

CAMBRIDGE
UNIVERSITY PRESS

CAMBRIDGE UNIVERSITY PRESS
Cambridge, New York, Melbourne, Madrid, Cape Town, Singapore, São Paulo

CAMBRIDGE UNIVERSITY PRESS
The Edinburgh Building, Cambridge, CB2 2RU, UK

Published in the United States of America by Cambridge University Press,
New York

http://www.cambridge.org
Information on this title: www.cambridge.org/9780521848763

First published 2005

Printed in the United Kingdom at the University Press, Cambridge

A catalogue record for this book is available from the British Library

ISBN-13 978-0-521-84876-3 hardback
ISBN-10 0-521-84876-8 hardback

Cambridge University Press has no responsibility for the persistence or
accuracy of URLs for external or third-party Internet websites referred to in
this book, and does not guarantee that any content on such websites is, or will
remain, accurate or appropriate.

For AFH

CONTENTS

ACKNOWLEDGEMENTS

Like so many others, this book began life as a doctoral dissertation that has been subsequently revised for the present volume. Hence I must record two sets of debts, the first incurred during my two-and-a-half years as a doctoral student, and the second in the period that followed the completion of my degree. Financial support came from the Social Sciences and Humanities Research Council of Canada (SSHRCC), which awarded me a doctoral fellowship, and from various other bodies whose funding made several research trips to Oxford both possible and comfortable. They are: the Timothy C. S. Franks Research Travel Fund, the Graduate Dean's Field Research Fund, the Western Ontario Fellowship, the Dorothy Warne Chambers Memorial Fellowship, the School of Graduate Studies at Queen's University (Kingston), and the Department of History at Queen's, through a series of teaching appointments. The text was greatly revised and expanded in Dallas during November and December 2002, when I held a Visiting Fellowship at the Bridwell Library, Southern Methodist University. I am grateful to Dr Valerie Hotchkiss and her staff for their assistance and hospitality during those weeks. Likewise, I express my thanks to Bill Hodges and his staff at Duke Humfrey's Library in Oxford, where the bulk of the research was completed. Paul Christianson supervised the dissertation with calm and care, and taught me new ways of thinking about the past.

The revision of the text was as peripatetic as was the writing of the thesis: work was carried on in Kingston, Oxford, Herstmonceux Castle (East Sussex), and Cambridge. I am grateful to Queen's University for appointing me to a one-year position that allowed me to teach in my field, and to begin thinking carefully about the process of revision. During those hectic terms, Erik Thomson proved the best of colleagues, and we imbibed together the singular joys of part-time academic employment. A teaching post at the International Study Centre at Herstmonceux Castle offered six comparatively quiet weeks of work, and my colleagues there, especially Nick Pengelley, Giorgio Baruchello, and Stephanie Hall, made sure that I didn't

take myself too seriously. In Cambridge, John Morrill has done for me what
he has done for many others: he has acted as mentor and editor, and I am
pleased that this volume appears in the series edited by him, by John Guy,
and by Anthony Fletcher. The SSHRCC continues to support my work, this
time in the form of a post-doctoral fellowship that has allowed me to
establish myself in Cambridge in order to develop projects that emerged in
the wake of my thesis. I am grateful to the President and Fellows of Wolfson
College for electing me to a Visiting Fellowship; to the Faculty of History for
numerous forms of support; and especially to Michael Watson and his
colleagues at Cambridge University Press for their diligence in seeing the
book into print. Over the past several years, a number of friends and
colleagues have taken the time to discuss aspects of what follows: they
know who they are, and they all have my thanks. I owe a special debt to
my brothers and sister. Life in Cambridge would not be complete without the
cheerful company of my fellow denizens of The Eagle – 'same again?' The
woman to whom this is dedicated stands above all. Annabel Hanson has
witnessed every stage of this work, from conception to completion, and
offered dozens of insights and suggestions as we made dinner and drank
wine at the end of another day's work. Most importantly, she did not once
complain about having to share so much space and time with the project, and
stood by me at a moment when others would probably have not. This book is
for her, with much love and profound gratitude.

NOTE ON THE TEXT

The dates in the text take the year to have begun on 1 January, although in all cases I have given the date of published works as it appears on the title page. I have followed the *ESTC* where attributions needed to be made, and the Bodleian Library *Pre-1920 catalogue of printed books* in cases where the *ESTC* was silent. Unless otherwise noted, biographical information is taken from the *Oxford dictionary of national biography*. I have not supplied biographical details for the writers mentioned in this study, since this information is now easily available in the *ODNB*, and in the thesis from which the present book is derived.[1] Quotations retain original spelling and punctuation. Long omissions and emendations are signalled by square brackets, while shorter omissions are signalled by ellipses.

Throughout, *conformist* is used to indicate those who sought to defend the Church from either Catholic or Protestant critics. I have not found it either useful or strictly helpful to provide, as others have, a further division of this category, whether *moderate* or *avant garde*, nor have I written of either *moderate* or *radical* critics of the Church. Instead, those who were obviously critical are referred to as *reformists*. This was a term widely enough used by writers such as Henoch Clapham, who said of a contemporary that: 'He differs much from the most of our Reformists here at home.'[2] In addition, *reformist* comes the closest to summing up the ecclesiological position of the various writers to whom I have attached the term – the reform, but not the disestablishment of the Church. The word *dissenter(s)* does figure in the literature, but given the associations attached to the term by students of Restoration ecclesiology, I have chosen not to use it. I have, however, employed the term *non-conformity* in cases where the policies and

---

[1] Charles W. A. Prior, 'The regiment of the Church: doctrine, discipline and history in Jacobean ecclesiology, 1603–1625' (Ph.D. diss., Queen's University at Kingston, 2003).
[2] Henoch Clapham, *Errour on the left hand, through a frozen securitie* (London, 1608).

punishments associated with Jacobean conformity are under discussion.³ In no case do I employ the word *puritan*, and I have set out my reasons for not doing so in the appropriate place.⁴ While the term *Anglican* does occur in the contemporary literature, it has subsequently acquired a particular meaning that Jacobean writers did not intend, and hence does not appear here.⁵ *Doctrine* is used in the contemporary sense – the liturgical and scriptural position of the Church – while *discipline* refers to the means – subscription, episcopal visitation, deprivation – by which conformity was enforced; this too was the contemporary understanding of the term.

³ Here I follow Kenneth Fincham, *Prelate as pastor: the episcopate of James I* (Oxford, 1990).
⁴ For a contemporary treatment, see [Thomas Scott], *The interpreter wherein three principall termes of state much mistaken by the vulgar are clearly unfolded* ([Edinburgh?], 1622).
⁵ David Calderwood, *A solution of Doctor Resolutus, his resolutions for kneeling* ([Amsterdam, 1619]), p. 19.

1

Introduction: defining the Church

In 1699, Gilbert Burnet, then Bishop of Salisbury, published *An exposition of the Thirty-nine articles of the Church of England*. The work purported to trace the roots of the English confession from the Reformation forward, and in the preface Burnet lamented that a quarrel over ceremonies and worship, 'and about things that were of their own nature indifferent', had been raging for 'above an Hundred Years'. Burnet certainly knew his subject, having been guided through Elizabethan controversies by Andrew Maunsell's bibliography, and by reading widely in the controversial literature published during the reigns of the early Stuarts.[1] This literature gave him a sense that the general tone and quality of the debate had shifted as the Elizabethan period gave way to the controversies over clerical subscription and ceremonial practice in the early years of James VI and I:

> Our divines were much diverted in the end of that Reign from better Enquiries, by the *Disciplinarian Controversies*; and though what *Whitgift* and *Hooker* writ on those Heads, was much better than all that came after them; yet they neither satisfied those against whom they writ, nor stopt the Writings of their own side. But as Waters gush in, when the Banks are once broken, so the breach that these had made, proved fruitful. Parties were formed, Secular Interests were grafted upon them, and new Quarrels followed those that first begun the Dispute.[2]

It turns out that Burnet was largely right. The religious controversies of the Jacobean age were indeed carried on by lesser lights than Whitgift and Hooker, and as the reign went along we find evidence not only that positions began to harden on matters of doctrine and discipline, but also that these positions had implications for politics. Yet it is also the case that Jacobean controversies took place on a broad scope, which saw the traffic

---

[1] Andrew Maunsell, *The first part of the catalogue of English printed bookes* (London, 1595).
[2] Gilbert Burnet, *An exposition of the Thirty-nine articles of the Church of England* (London, 1699), pp. iii, x.

in ideas move beyond massive treatises governed by the strictures of formal controversy – this was the age of the pamphlet, and the genre expanded in the period that this book surveys.[3] Burnet's reference to gushing water and broken banks reveals the impact of the expansion of print on the process of religious polemic. The premise that justifies the present study, therefore, is the existence of a large body of sources whose contribution to and role in ecclesiological debates has not been fully explored. Burnet's accurate but austere assessment of the Jacobean controversial scene deserves to be revisited.

This book is about religious controversies among English Protestants in the reign of James VI and I. It seeks to address, in part, J. C. D. Clark's call for a 'theoretically articulate history of the Church of England, including its ecclesiology, ecclesiastical polity, and political theory'.[4] Contemporaries regarded these themes as being closely linked, and used phrases like the 'regiment of the Church' or the 'definition of the Church' to refer to a process of deliberation between defenders of the Church and their critics.[5] Regardless of their position on aspects of doctrine and discipline, writers conceived of the English Church as partaking in the history of early Christianity; these perceptions shaped arguments concerning its doctrine and governance, as well as the political implications that attended its status

---

[3] Three genres of religious print have been well studied: sermons, devotional literature, and 'popular print'. For sermons, see Lori Anne Ferrell, *Government by polemic: James I, the King's preachers, and the rhetorics of conformity*, 1603–25 (Stanford, 1998); Peter McCullough, *Sermons at court: politics and religion in Elizabethan and Jacobean preaching* (Cambridge, 1998); Mary Morrissey, 'Interdisciplinarity and the study of early modern sermons', *Historical Journal*, 42 (1999), 1111–23. For devotional literature, see Ian Green's studies: *The Christian's ABC: catechisms and catechizing in England c. 1530–1740* (Oxford, 1986), and *Print and Protestantism in early modern England* (Oxford, 2000). For 'popular' literature, see Tessa Watt, *Cheap print and popular piety, 1550–1640* (Cambridge, 1991). For an interesting treatment of a range of cheap print and seventeenth-century religious culture, see Peter Lake and Michael Questier, *The Antichrist's lewd hat: Protestants, Papists & players in post-Reformation England* (New Haven, 2002). For consumption and readership, see Margaret Spufford, *Small books and pleasant histories: popular fiction and its readership in seventeenth-century England* (London, 1981); Kevin Sharpe, *Sir Robert Cotton, 1586–1631: history and politics in early modern England* (Oxford, 1979); and, more recently, Kevin Sharpe, 'Re-writing Sir Robert Cotton: politics and history in early Stuart England', in his *Remapping early modern England: the culture of seventeenth-century politics* (Cambridge, 2000), pp. 294–341, and *Reading revolutions: the politics of reading in early modern England* (New Haven, 2000). For a summary of the field, see R. C. Richardson, 'History and the early modern communications circuit', *Clio*, 31 (2002), 167–77. With respect to the history of print, while collection and reading are well studied, the production of books has been largely overlooked. Joad Raymond's fascinating study of pamphlets addresses this lack, and is a valuable contribution to the study of a fourth and crucial genre of early modern print. See his, *Pamphlets and pamphleteering in early modern Britain* (Cambridge, 2003), chs. 1, 3.
[4] J. C. D. Clark, 'Protestantism, nationalism and national identity, 1660–1832', *Historical Journal*, 43 (2000), 249–76, at 272.
[5] Henry Jacob, *The divine beginning and institution of Christs true visible or ministeriall church* (Leiden, 1610), sig. B[2v].

as a visible church 'of the realm'. Many works published during the period addressed this theme: Richard Field's *Of the Church*, and Josias Nichols' *Abrahams faith* are typical of the conformist and reformist branches of the literature. Common to all was an interest in how the doctrine, discipline, and governance of the Apostolic church could be carried forth and established in post-Reformation England. In fact, a debate on ecclesiology formed a central theme in pamphlets, sermons, and longer works by writers both famous and unknown.

The context for the debates to be examined here was the introduction of new ecclesiastical Canons in 1604, and the subsequent deprivation of some eighty-five ministers who refused to 'subscribe to' – that is, to affirm by swearing an oath – the directives concerning doctrine and governance contained in them. Similarly, the Perth Articles, which set forth kneeling at communion as part of the 'official' ceremonial practice of the Kirk of Scotland, led to debates between Presbyterians and conformists, and to a deepening of religious tensions in the two kingdoms. In both settings, the introduction of new Canons served as the impetus for a series of debates on ecclesiastical sovereignty, ceremonies, episcopacy, the common law, and the patristic heritage of the Apostolic church. These debates and the literature in which they are preserved help to clarify the political, theological, and historical elements of religious controversy, and are therefore a crucial source for understanding the nature of Jacobean religious conflict.

Since English Protestant thought was based on elements derived from sacred and historical sources, it was inevitable that religious conflict would occur along similar lines. Controversial literature, first examined in studies by Roland Usher and Stuart Barton Babbage, has since become peripheral to the interests of those who study early Stuart religion.[6] This is unfortunate, because the literature of religious controversy sheds important light on the issues and arguments that divided Protestants in the reign of James VI and I, and also points to divisions that would persist into the reign of his successor. One premise of this book is that Jacobean ecclesiology did not consist of pure theology: in both the Henrician and Elizabethan settlements defenders of the Church argued that it was 'dually established', a partly spiritual and partly temporal association that had its being in the Word and in the world. The debates that this book surveys reveal tensions within this blend of spiritual and political elements, and these tensions help us to discern contrasting approaches to ecclesiology and church polity in the writings of those controversialists who participated in printed polemical exchanges. It becomes apparent that writers on both sides were struggling to come to terms with

---

[6] See R. G. Usher, *The reconstruction of the English Church*, 2 vols. (London, 1910); Stuart Barton Babbage, *Puritanism and Richard Bancroft* (London, 1962).

both the nature of early Christian history and their own place within it, for the institution of the Christian Church in which they all claimed communion was distinguished by a contested history and hence the business of religious polemic was always firmly rooted within a vast and complex historiographical tradition. Where writers divided was on the interpretation of that tradition and its implications for post-Reformation ecclesiology.[7] The debates that this book examines were based upon distinct views of the Church's past, which in turn shaped positions on how it should be ordered and governed, as well as the 'language' in which the dispute was carried on.[8] It was a language suited to the examination of the nature of an institution through time, and it served to legitimise aspects of the Church by locating them in the past, or to criticise them by searching into the past to discover alternative modes of doctrine and discipline. This search proceeded in the course of debate, and as time goes on one becomes aware of the development of at least two Protestant historiographical traditions, each with its canon of writers, and each putting forth an argument for how the Church should be ordered and governed.

For example, conformists argued that the English Church was both a spiritual and a political association: a state church founded on a mingling of doctrine and law, and hence able to enjoin conformity among its members.[9] It was also a 'true' and 'ancient' church, not separated from the institution founded by Christ – the church described in the letters of the Apostles, and in the works of the Fathers of the Christian historical tradition. In short, it was a reformed continuation of the Apostolic church, which retained ceremonial practices and episcopal governance, and reserved the right to interpret 'custom' and to establish elements of worship that it deemed 'comely' and 'edifying'. The concept of *adiaphora* – which defined aspects of worship that were essential to salvation as against those that were not – lay at the core of the conformist programme, and on this basis conformists justified the ceremonialism and episcopal governance of the English Church. Disputes over these propositions were central to debates about many aspects of ecclesiology. In defending the Church against their Protestant critics, therefore, conformist controversialists sought to establish

---

[7] See Arthur Ferguson, *Clio unbound: perception of the social and cultural past in Renaissance England* (Durham, NC, 1979).

[8] For the concept of languages, see J. G. A. Pocock, 'Languages and their implications: the transformation of the study of political thought', in *Politics, language and time* (New York, 1971), pp. 3–41, and his, 'The concept of language and the *métier d'historien*: some considerations on practice', in *The languages of political theory in early modern Europe*, ed. Anthony Pagden (Cambridge, 1987), pp. 19–38.

[9] Elsewhere, I have traced these issues into the eighteenth century. See Charles W. A. Prior, '"Then Leave Complaints": Mandeville, anti-Catholicism, and English orthodoxy', in *Mandeville and Augustan ideas: new essays*, ed. Charles W. A. Prior, English Literary Studies Monograph Series, 83 (Victoria, BC, 2000), pp. 51–70.

a sound historical pedigree for doctrine and discipline, and to employ this interpretation to justify ceremonies and governance in the national Church. In doing so, they looked to the record of early Christianity in search of historical precedents, and bolstered these where necessary with testimony from patristic sources and even civil and pagan histories of the Roman and post-Roman polities. The burden of the conformist position, evident in the work of Hooker and many of those who succeeded him, was to establish a usable account of the mingling of sacred and human history, and therefore the mingling of sacred and human authority.

Those Protestants who sought further reformation of the Church grounded their arguments on alternate versions of the history of Christianity, some emphasising Presbyterian government within an established church, and others calling for gathered congregations of free Christians governed by their own 'consent'. They argued that the liturgy, rites, and governance of the Church had to derive from the *iure divino* authority of scripture, and receive confirmation from the sound and uncorrupted testimony of ecclesiastical historians, the Fathers, and contemporary reformed divines. The visible church had to emulate the precepts of true doctrine, and this premise shaped a range of ecclesiological positions from ceremonial practice to governance and discipline. Reformists looked to history in order to discover the point at which the church existed in its purest form, and treated the advent of the Roman church as the beginning of a decline. It was through this lens that they scrutinised the Church of England, arguing that it had not proceeded far enough along the path of reform. From a doctrinal point of view, they argued that ceremonialism and governance by bishops had no pedigree either in scripture or in what the testimony of Christian authorities indicated about the worship and governance of the ancient church. These arguments were based upon painstaking scriptural exegesis, and backed up by a great variety of other theological texts; the use of scholastic methods was not limited to conformists, and William Prynne's catalogue of 'testimonies' exemplifies an abiding interest among reformists in the study of ancient and reformed sources.[10]

There were political implications to these ecclesiological arguments. Conformists emphasised the visible institution of the Church that blended essential and indifferent elements of doctrine, and argued that since the Church was in some sense domiciled within the channels of civil authority, the uniformity of its public doctrine would be maintained by civil measures. This led them to link episcopal government with political stability, and therefore to condemn Presbyterian discipline as a threat to the sovereignty

---

[10] William Prynne, *A catalogue of such testimonies in all ages as plainly evidence bishops and presbyters to be both one, equall and the same in jurisdiction, office, dignity, order, and degree* ([Leiden?], 1637).

of the Crown. By contrast, reformists sought to defend the continuity of a doctrinally 'pure' church over which the Word was sovereign; with respect to human involvement in the Church, they insisted that since the locus of ecclesiastical authority lay with the Crown in parliament, these bodies were charged with the promotion of true doctrine, and hence true governance and ceremonial practice. Yet they also put forth political arguments against the established Church, most notably by suggesting that the deprivation of nonconformist ministers violated the common law and the sovereignty of parliament. Scots writers went a step further, and suggested that the imposition of English worship and governance on the Kirk was both doctrinally indefensible and an assault on the legal and national independence of the Scottish confession. In all cases, a distinct vision of church polity was underpinned by assumptions about the relationship between civil and ecclesiastical authority. Hence, the broad theme that this book seeks to trace is how polemical debates on a range of ecclesiological issues and involving a wide sample of writers led to the development of narratives that sought to strike a balance between civil and ecclesiastical authority. Defining the Church was no easy task, and the question accounted for a profound division among Protestant writers in both the English and Scottish settings, which in turn reveals the first stirrings of the religious conflicts that would emerge in the reign of Charles I.

MODELS OF JACOBEAN PROTESTANT CONFLICT

Polemical debates on ecclesiology and history have haunted the edges of scholarship on early Stuart religion, but have remained largely unstudied.[11] This is despite the fact that a number of direct references to the theme have been made, often by those central to the broad scholarly debate on the nature of religious conflict in early Stuart England. In the late 1980s Peter Lake observed that disagreement about the visible church 'was arguably the crucial divide in English Protestant opinion during this period'.[12] Since then, Lake's work on Stephen Denison and the struggle among London's godly community in the years before the Civil War has supplied a powerful lesson on the importance of polemical sources for our understanding of disputes within English Protestantism.[13] Similarly,

---

[11] Roland Usher correctly identified the principal source of tension inherent in the Jacobean settlement: 'The ultimate object in 1603 was, as before, unity of belief and observance, but it was now to be attained by making the church strong as an institution.' See Usher, *The reconstruction of the English Church*, vol. I, p. 6.

[12] Peter Lake, 'Calvinism and the English Church, 1570–1635', *Past and Present*, 114 (1987), 32–76, at 39. The importance of Lake's message may have been lost in the controversy over Arminianism that dominated the pages of *Past and Present*.

[13] Peter Lake, *The boxmaker's revenge: 'orthodoxy', 'heterodoxy' and the politics of the parish in early Stuart London* (Manchester, 2001).

Conrad Russell has observed that religious conflict resembled 'a custody battle' for control of the Church. Yet, where others have described this contest as one waged between 'Anglicans' and 'puritans', Russell suggested that a sounder approach was to assess the positions of 'rival claimants to the title of orthodox, and therefore between rival criteria of orthodoxy'.[14] J. G. A. Pocock pursued this theme in essays on the nature of 'English orthodoxy' and its relation to politics. The Reformation settlement opened up a tension between an invisible association and the Crown that claimed an admixture of spiritual and secular power over it.[15] Owing to this uneasy balance between spirituals and temporals, neither of which was confined to its own sphere, the history of the Church was dominated by episodes of disruption.[16]

The chapters that follow offer a new interpretation of this disruption in the Jacobean Church, and point to its continuation in early Stuart religious thought. At the heart of the argument is the suggestion that the custody battle over the nature of 'orthodoxy' was more complex than has thus far been shown. However, 'orthodoxy' was not a word that Jacobean writers used with sufficient frequency or consistency to justify its adoption in a study of their theological attitudes. This instability of categories explains why a search for useful terms to describe parties to the dispute has occupied historians of religion since S. R. Gardiner threw down the 'puritan' gauntlet.[17] In writing of 'conformists' and 'reformists', I mean simply to point to a tension between two broad groups, one of which was satisfied with the Church as it stood, and the other anxious to put forth detailed reasons for

---

[14] Conrad Russell, *The causes of the English Civil War* (Oxford, 1990), p. 84.

[15] J. G. A. Pocock, 'The history of British political thought: the creation of a Center', *Journal of British Studies*, 24 (1985), 283–310, at 287–9.

[16] J. G. A. Pocock, 'Within the margins: the definitions of orthodoxy', in *The margins of orthodoxy: heterodox writing and cultural response, 1660–1750*, ed. Roger Lund (Cambridge, 1995), pp. 33–53, at p. 37.

[17] See T. R. Clancy, 'Papist-Protestant-Puritan: English religious taxonomy, 1565–1665', *Recusant History*, 13 (1975–6), 227–53. As was mentioned in 'note on the text', the term 'puritan' has been strenuously avoided in this book. The historiographical scuffle over the term 'puritan' seems to have done little to diminish its place in the conceptual toolbox of the historian of religion, and so the Elizabethan Church as the site of the 'puritan ethos' is now a well-established scholarly convention. Yet 'puritan' has come to mean a group possessed of a shared religious experience, which in turn was transformed into a revolutionary ideology; after all, one could not have the 'Puritan revolution' without 'puritans', and the term has had the unfortunate consequence of eliding the ideas and actions of two groups of people separated by nearly eighty years. See Paul Christianson, 'Reformers and the Church of England under Elizabeth and the early Stuarts', *Journal of Ecclesiastical History*, 31 (October 1980), 463–82, and the response by Patrick Collinson, 'A comment: Concerning the name Puritan', 483–8, in the same volume. Like 'puritanism', the 'Puritan revolution' has consumed a good deal of paper and ink. For a synthesis, see Michael Finlayson, *Historians, puritans and the English Revolution* (Toronto, 1983).

why it should be reformed.[18] It must be stressed that these groups were not uniform as to the specific elements of their case, and that I do not intend to replace one set of binary categories with another. For example, there were variations among conformist defenders of episcopacy: some argued that the office was Apostolic and independent of the Crown, while others regarded bishops in legal and constitutional terms, as 'inferior magistrates'. Further, while their positions may have clashed, writers on both sides of the issue were, on the whole, members of the same theological and intellectual elite, schooled in theology and history at either Oxford or Cambridge, and occupying positions in the English Church, from preachers to bishops; with a few exceptions, all the writers discussed were churchmen when James VI assumed the English throne. This would seem to confirm the aptness of Russell's suggestion that debates between them were part of a contest for control of one Church, and it is this premise that guides the present work.

This book seeks to situate itself within an emerging trend among scholars of early Stuart religion that rejects a 'narrow' interpretation of religious conflict dominated by predestination, Arminianism, and the attack on Calvinist soteriology. The principal focus of scholarly debate has been Nicholas Tyacke's discussion of soteriology and its role in the religious and political conflicts of early Stuart England. Rather than the visible church or problems of conformity, Tyacke focussed on doctrinal debates, on University curricula in divinity, and on evidence of popular attachment to Calvinist teaching on salvation. This led him to suggest that 'by the end of the sixteenth century the church of England was largely Calvinist in doctrine', and that Calvinism 'remained dominant in England throughout the first two decades of the seventeenth century'.[19] Since the doctrinal posture of the English Church was defined predominately by Calvinism, the argument ran, its disruption would result from challenges to this doctrinal 'consensus'. Tyacke's *Anti-Calvinists* was published in 1987, but elements of the thesis were already well established, and remain at the centre of the 'revisionist' interpretation of political and religious conflict before the English Civil War.[20] As early as

---

[18] Again, see my 'note on the text' for an explanation of these terms, and a justification for their use.

[19] Nicholas Tyacke, *Anti-Calvinists: the rise of English Arminianism, c. 1590–1640* (Oxford, 1987; paperback edition, 1990), pp. 3, 5. All citations are from the paperback edition.

[20] See Conrad Russell's *Causes of the English Civil War*, passim; his *Unrevolutionary England* (London, 1990); and his *The fall of the British Monarchies, 1637–1642* (Oxford, 1991). For an endorsement of the spirit, if not the letter, of Tyacke's thesis, see John Morrill's 'The religious context of the English Civil War', *Transactions of the Royal Historical society*, 5th series, 34 (1984), 155–78; his 'The attack on the Church of England in the Long Parliament, 1640–1642', in *History, society and the churches: essays in honour of Owen Chadwick*, ed. Derek Beales and Geoffrey Best (Cambridge, 1985), pp. 105–24, esp. p. 108 n. 14; the introduction to his *The nature of the English Revolution: essays* (London and New York,

1973, Tyacke sought to challenge the explanatory model of the 'Puritan revolution' with what he termed the 'rise of Arminianism'; this doctrine set aside the Calvinist notion of predestination and stressed salvation by works, and Tyacke argued that it signalled the erosion of a Calvinist 'consensus' after 1620.[21] The connection with political life lay in a coterie of Arminian bishops, among them William Laud, who came to enjoy the support of Charles I. This and other issues contributed to the alienation of the House of Commons and a deepening polarisation over the Church, the nature of monarchical rule, and the sovereignty of parliament.[22]

Given the historiographical terrain – the advent of revisionism and the subsequent controversy over the 'origins' of the English Civil War – it was no surprise that Tyacke's thesis came under attack from historians of religion.[23] In a 1983 article, Peter White challenged Tyacke's contention that there was a sudden 'rise' of Arminianism, contended that some measure of debate on the issue could be found in the Elizabethan setting, and denied the presence of a 'doctrinal high road to civil war'.[24] In the following years the pages of *Past and Present* were the site of a series of exchanges between White and Tyacke, and a number of other articles on the issue by scholars such as William Lamont and Peter Lake.[25] Despite this criticism, Tyacke held fast to his argument that the rise of Arminianism after 1620 supplanted Calvinist 'egalitarianism' with a notion of a church and state conceived in 'hierarchical' terms, and that herein lay the challenge to the Calvinist 'world picture'.[26] *Anti-Calvinists* also met with vigorous criticism from G. W. Bernard, who argued that Tyacke had based his analysis upon a poorly developed account of what the English Reformation meant for politics. Bernard therefore stressed the point that any discussion of post-Reformation religion had to be set in the context of a

---

1993), pp. 33–44; and his 'The causes of the British Civil Wars', *Journal of Ecclesiastical History*, 43 (1992), 624–33. See also Mark Fissel, *The Bishops' wars: Charles I's campaigns against Scotland, 1638–49* (Cambridge, 1994).

[21] Nicholas Tyacke, 'Puritanism, Arminianism, and counter-revolution', in *The origins of the English Civil War*, ed. Conrad Russell (London, 1973), pp. 119–43.

[22] Tyacke, *Anti-Calvinists*, ch. 8.

[23] For an assessment of revisionism in its early days, see the editors' essay, 'Introduction: after revisionism', in *Conflict in early Stuart England: studies in religion and politics, 1603–1642*, ed. Richard Cust and Anne Hughes (London, 1989), pp. 1–46. See also Glenn Burgess, 'On revisionism: an analysis of early Stuart historiography in the 1970s and 1980s', *Historical Journal*, 33 (1990), 609–27; and Kevin Sharpe, 'Remapping early modern England: from revisionism to the culture of politics', in his *Remapping early modern England*, pp. 3–37, esp. 15–18.

[24] Peter White, 'The rise of Arminianism reconsidered', *Past and Present*, 101 (1983), 34–54.

[25] William Lamont, 'Comment: The rise of Arminianism reconsidered', *Past and Present*, 107 (1985), 227–31; Peter Lake, 'Calvinism and the English Church'; Nicholas Tyacke and Peter White, 'Debate: The rise of Arminianism reconsidered', *Past and Present*, 115 (1987), 201–29.

[26] Tyacke, *Anti-Calvinists*, pp. 246, 247.

'monarchical' Church, wherein the Crown exercised sovereignty in the interest of preventing religious conflict.[27] Finally, Peter White's full-length study of predestination from the Reformation to the Civil War reprised the argument of his earlier article; that is, that Calvinism and Arminianism were not clearly defined positions set one against the other, but rather that there existed a 'spectrum' of belief on the doctrine of predestination.[28]

This study suggests that critics of the Tyacke thesis have not yet provided the definitive case against it, particularly as it applies to the Jacobean Church.[29] Central to Tyacke's case was the proposition that a Calvinist consensus is what defined the post-Reformation Church, when there is a stronger case to be made for a deeply rooted conflict on the very nature of the visible church itself. This is not to say that the conflict traced by Tyacke is irrelevant – certainly different opinions on the way to salvation entailed different visions of the Church – but rather, the debate over subscription suggests a more broadly based conflict than that described in *Anti-Calvinists*.[30] The debates in question probed a range of topics, from the ecclesiastical sovereignty of the Crown in parliament, the tension between episcopal power and the common law, and the problem of religion in the three kingdoms – the very conflicts that dominated the pamphlet literature of the 1640s.[31] In short, English 'ecclesiastical polity' (as contemporaries called it) was knitted together in a manner whose complexity is not adequately captured by the notion of a Calvinist consensus. In a society where the union of Church and state was a matter of constitutional precept, religious conflict did not turn on the question of doctrine alone, but on the nature of the visible institution in which that doctrine was professed and the links between this institution and other elements of the Tudor and early Stuart political complex. This was the point that Bernard sought to make; however, there is reason to believe that it was overstated. As we shall see, the English Church *did* reflect a strong monarchical component, but just how it was to be used in the service of religion was a source of great tension. In other words, Bernard

---

[27] G. W. Bernard, 'The Church of England c.1529–c.1642', *History*, 75 (1990), 183–206, at 192.

[28] Peter White, *Predestination, policy, and polemic: conflict and consensus in the English Church from the Reformation to the Civil War* (Cambridge, 1992), p. xiii.

[29] Nicholas Tyacke, 'Anglican attitudes: some recent writings on English religious history, from the Reformation to the Civil War', *Journal of British Studies*, 35 (April 1996), 139–67.

[30] Indeed, Tyacke's critics have tended to overlook the fact that he purported to examine 'a particular thread running through the often labyrinthine religious history of the period'. *Anti-Calvinists*, p. xiv.

[31] While Conrad Russell is aware of all of these tensions, his preference has been to side with Tyacke's view that a central plank in English 'orthodoxy' was doctrinal Calvinism, and that the attack on this orthodoxy presaged the Civil War; as Russell put it, 'Charles's abandonment of Calvinist doctrine removed the coping-stone from this edifice.' See *Causes of the English Civil War*, pp. 51–2.

emphasised 'policy' but failed to link it with complex theological debates over points of doctrine and governance, all of which shed light on contemporary perceptions of the Crown's ecclesiastical sovereignty. Here again, what comprised English ecclesiastical polity was a mingling of doctrine and law, and thus an arrangement that was open to attack from either political or theological directions. Peter White's criticism of Tyacke merely rejected the latter's case for a rise of Arminianism, and posited instead a long-term tension over soteriology as a trigger of the English Civil War. Neither Tyacke nor White made a sufficient case for predestinarian doctrine that situated it within other doctrinal issues, namely ceremonial practice and the objections to the Canons of 1604. This study suggests that the political and theological problem was more complex than either proponents or opponents of the Arminian thesis have noted.

In the attempt to skirt the impasse over Arminianism a number of scholars have sought to re-examine religious conflict in the early Stuart Church from the point of view of monarchy, doctrinal history, and conformity. In an influential article, Kenneth Fincham and Peter Lake argued that James VI and I was a deft and subtle 'manipulator' of competing religious factions, and that the English Church under his watch managed to harmonise these potentially divisive groups. The article emphasised statements contained in court sermons, and by James himself, that described him as a 'rex pacificus' dedicated to the imposition of 'peace and unity'.[32] This analytical model served as the impetus for a collection of essays edited by Fincham. In the introductory essay, he noted that 'The search for the causes of the English Civil War has always dominated early Stuart religious history.' The editorial mandate was to re-focus attention on the Church as an institution, on the laity, on the clerical corporation, and on relations between the Church and the Crown. Fincham argued that the Church was so powerful that it became a 'battleground for rival visions of English society'.[33] Hence, an uneasy harmony maintained by a judicious prince rapidly deteriorated, and left the post-Jacobean Church 'riven with friction and disagreement'.[34] The collection also included essays by Nicholas Tyacke and Peter White that clung to the view of a Jacobean peace shattered after 1625, and in fact Fincham conceded the point that 'many of the forces promoting unity in the Jacobean church were dissolved in the 1630s'.[35] *The early Stuart Church*, therefore, retained elements of the model of conflict that it sought to supplant: that the Jacobean Church, while home to conflict, was nevertheless

---

[32] Kenneth Fincham and Peter Lake, 'The ecclesiastical policy of King James I', *Journal of British Studies*, 24 (1985), 169–207, at 169, 206.
[33] *The early Stuart Church, 1603–1642*, ed. Kenneth Fincham (Stanford, 1993), p. 1.
[34] Ibid., p. 11.   [35] Ibid., p. 16.

held together by a consensus that was abruptly shattered in the 1630s and which ultimately contributed to the outbreak of war in the 1640s.

The collection provided a venue for an early version of Anthony Milton's important interpretation of early Stuart religious conflict.[36] In his essay, Milton argued that contemporary perceptions of the past shed important light on the nature of Jacobean religious thought, and proposed the thesis that the early Stuart period witnessed a 'demise' of a 'Jacobean consensus in understandings of the nature of the church'.[37] Much the same sort of analytical model lay at the centre of Milton's *Catholic and reformed*, perhaps the most comprehensive treatment of printed religious controversies in the early Stuart Church. Milton examined how English conformists sought to carve out a confessional identity which rested somewhere between Geneva and Rome, and showed as well how the positions of Protestant controversialists were shaped by their engagement with Catholic writers.[38] It is perhaps this which explains why two-thirds of Milton's book is taken up by Catholic–Protestant controversies.[39] What of the remaining third? In two substantial chapters Milton examined links between the English and Continental reformed churches from the point of view of Calvinism, and portrayed 'Laudianism' as the impetus for the doctrinal alienation of English Protestants from their co-religionists on the Continent. From doctrine, Milton moved to governance and, following Lake's statement noted previously, argued that a 'new emphasis attached to the role of the visible, institutional church in the attainment of salvation, meant that differences over external ecclesiastical polity were more likely to become the main focus of inter-Protestant relations'.[40] As promising as this sounded, Milton's attention was overwhelmingly focussed on tracing the impact of 'Laudian' policy on ceremonies, soteriology, and governance, and the pairing of this impact with the 'demise' of the Jacobean consensus posited in the earlier essay. The problem with this interpretation is that conformists from Whitgift onward were occupied with the task of defining and defending a visible, hierarchical, and ceremonial church, a process which involved stressing its particularly 'English' characteristics; hence, the 'novelty' of Laudianism has to be assessed against the continuity of conformist theories of ceremonies and governance.

---

[36] Anthony Milton, 'The Church of England, Rome and the true church: the demise of a Jacobean consensus', in *Early Stuart Church*, ed. Fincham, pp. 187–210.

[37] Ibid., pp. 187, 210.

[38] This stance was not unique to Milton's work. See Timothy Wadkins, 'Theological polemic and religious culture in early Stuart England: the Percy/"Fisher" controversies, 1605–41' (Ph.D. diss., Graduate Theological Union, Berkeley, CA, 1988).

[39] Anthony Milton, *Catholic and reformed: the Roman and Protestant churches in English Protestant thought, 1600–1640* (Cambridge, 1995), pp. 31–373.

[40] Ibid., p. 449.

Milton's argument may be situated in a broader trend among scholars who seek to draw links between the Jacobean Church and its successor, and who do so by supplanting the 'Arminian' thesis with one emphasising 'Laudianism' or 'Carolinism'. However, a persistent weakness in much of the scholarship on Caroline politics and religion is that the Jacobean Church is treated as a kind of caricature. For example, Julian Davies noted that: 'The religious peace of Jacobean England rested on the promotion of a popular Anglican conformity.' He argued that a distinct 'Caroline' ecclesiology 'undermined a Jacobean consensus' and made 'radicals' out of critics of the Church.[41] Moreover, as some Jacobean scholars have been absorbed with the virulent proponents of 'Anglicanism', Caroline scholars have unduly focussed on William Laud and his circle.[42] Anthony Milton suggested that 'Laudianism' represented a 'gradual movement' away from an earlier 'coherent' view of the Church of England.[43] Here again, the argument emphasised consensus in the Jacobean Church, a condition which in turn gave way to conflict spurred by Laudian policy. In a later essay Milton revised his conception of Laudianism, arguing that, instead of being a movement, it was a 'process' through which English Protestants moved.[44] Yet this transition was examined from the point of view of Peter Heylyn, arguably the most atypical of Caroline divines, whose recollections of the period were coloured either by nostalgia or by harsh indictments of moderate churchmen.[45] What all of these interpretations overlook is that some aspects of churchmanship that appear 'new' in the Laudian context were, as we shall see, deeply entrenched in conformist thought.

The roots of 'Laudian' churchmanship have been probed by a number of scholars, but the effort has resembled a reading of Laudianism back into the Jacobean Church, rather than a study of early conformists in their own setting. For example, Kenneth Fincham and Peter Lake employed a Laudian and 'Arminian' perspective to characterise the positions of

[41] Julian Davies, *The Caroline captivity of the Church: Charles I and the remoulding of Anglicanism, 1625–1641* (Oxford, 1992), pp. 10, 288.

[42] See Peter Lake, 'Lancelot Andrewes, John Buckeridge, and avant-garde conformity at the court of James I', in *The mental world of the Jacobean court*, ed. Linda Levy Peck (Cambridge, 1991), pp. 113–33; Nicholas Tyacke, 'Archbishop Laud', and Peter Lake, 'The Laudian style: order, uniformity and the pursuit of the beauty of holiness in the 1630s', both in *Early Stuart church*, ed. Fincham, pp. 51–70 and 161–85; Nicholas Tyacke, 'Lancelot Andrewes and the myth of Anglicanism', in *Conformity and orthodoxy in the English Church, c. 1560–1660*, ed. Peter Lake and Michael Questier (Woodbridge, Suffolk, 2000), pp. 5–33.

[43] Milton, *Catholic and reformed*, p. 529.

[44] Anthony Milton, 'The creation of Laudianism: a new approach', in *Politics, religion and popularity in early Stuart Britain*, ed. Thomas Cogswell, Richard Cust, and Peter Lake (Cambridge, 2002), pp. 162–84.

[45] Heylyn's verdict on George Abbot, Archbishop of Canterbury from 1611 to 1633, is a case in point; see Susan Holland, 'Archbishop Abbot and the problem of "Puritanism"', *Historical Journal*, 37 (1994), 23–43.

Jacobean clerics such as John Buckeridge and Lancelot Andrewes.[46] In the 1990s, Peter Lake developed this analysis, arguing that in the work of Buckeridge and Andrewes one could detect a 'link in the chain of avant-garde conformist thought which runs between Hooker and Laud'.[47] Finally, Nicholas Tyacke has suggested that, to 'Laudians', Lancelot Andrewes was a 'founding father'.[48] All of these scholars have, on the one hand, sought to establish the roots of Laudianism in the Jacobean Church, while on the other hand emphasising Laudianism's unique character. For example, Peter Lake has claimed that the use of the writings of Doctors, Fathers, and Councils was peculiar to the Laudian episcopate.[49] Julian Davies, who suggested that an interest in the patristic history of the visible church was 'revived' by Caroline divines, has also advanced this notion.[50] Scholars working on the sixteenth-century Church have shown that this was not the case; these studies reveal that scholastic method, patristic scholarship, and engagement with the Fathers permeated learned theological dispute, and was a tactic common to *both* defenders and critics of the Church.[51] As with Laudian 'ceremonialism', the supposedly 'unique' or 'novel' aspects of Laudian or Caroline ecclesiology have to be reassessed in conjunction with a sound portrait of Jacobean theological scholarship.

In the late 1990s there was a renewed interest in theological disputes, which gave rise to an attempt to propose a new model for the study of early Stuart religious conflict. A collection edited by Peter Lake and Michael Questier (2000) promised to grasp the elusive nettle of how contemporaries sought to reconcile a tension between 'outward government and practice' and matters of 'formal doctrinal profession and belief'. The editors announced that they sought to 'problematise' these categories in order to show how 'contemporaries could and did try to gloss and appropriate

---

[46] Fincham and Lake, 'The ecclesiastical policy of King James I', 192–207.

[47] Lake, 'Lancelot Andrewes, John Buckeridge, and avant-garde conformity', p. 131.

[48] Tyacke, 'Lancelot Andrewes and the myth of Anglicanism', p. 32.

[49] Peter Lake, 'The Laudians and the argument from authority', in *Court, country, and culture: essays on early modern British history in honor of Perez Zagorin*, ed. Bonnelyn Kunze and Dwight Brautigan (Rochester, NY, 1992), pp. 149–75. Lake sought to identify the peculiarity of Laudianism by exploring 'the broader ambiguity or tension in the Laudian appeal to the triad of church, scripture, and tradition and the way in which those authorities could be deployed to exalt and defend different aspects of the Laudian view of religion from attack' (p. 171). Yet at no point did Lake seek to examine how pre-Laudian divines employed these sources of authority.

[50] Davies, *Caroline captivity*, ch. 2.

[51] See William Haugaard, 'Renaissance patristic scholarship and theology in sixteenth-century England', *Sixteenth Century Journal*, 10 (1979), 37–60; John K. Luoma, 'Who owns the Fathers?: Hooker and Cartwright on the authority of the primitive church', *Sixteenth Century Journal*, 3 (1977), 45–59; and John Booty, *John Jewel as an apologist for the Church of England* (London, 1963).

them'.[52] The collection therefore set aside nomenclature that described an Anglican / Puritan, Calvinist / anti Calvinist conflict, and sought to 'penetrate the way contemporaries constructed and maintained their religious and political identities'. In some senses, the editorial introduction suggested that Lake had returned to his earlier insight about debate on the visible church and its importance to understanding early Stuart religion. At the root of the problem was a conflict over 'different versions of what the national church was or should be', a conflict located in a 'polemical struggle'.[53] Yet the success of this approach was limited by the fact that polemical sources did not figure prominently in the essays that followed (the footnotes point to some eleven titles), nor was there a treatment of the crucial competition over the 'national' Church as both a spiritual and political association. Instead, essays by Tyacke and David Como reprised the historiographical problem of whether the evaporation of consensus was caused by incipient Arminianism or 'Laudianism'.[54] Here again, the standard model of conflict prevailed.

The influence of the 'new British history' on recent scholarship has led to attempts to incorporate the Jacobean Church of Scotland (hereafter the Kirk) into models of conflict among English Protestants.[55] This makes good sense, since even a superficial glance at the literature of controversy reveals that arguments against episcopacy under Whitgift contained a detailed case in support of Presbyterian discipline, and frequent statements concerning the superior reformed character of the Kirk.[56] David Mullan's studies of the culture of Scottish 'Puritanism' and of the problem of episcopacy reveal a number of fault lines in the Kirk, as well as the existence of conformity and non-conformity.[57] This work built on a small but incisive historiography on the links between the Kirk and the law, and on the traffic in ideas between Presbyterians and Continental reformers.[58] Since the 1990s, following J. G. A. Pocock's dictum that the history of Britain is defined by the interconnected histories of England, Scotland, Ireland, and Wales, scholars have begun to develop perspectives on the unique 'historical consciousness' of the

---

[52] *Conformity and orthodoxy*, ed. Lake and Questier, p. ix.   [53] Ibid., pp. xviii, xix.

[54] Tyacke, 'Lancelot Andrewes and the myth of Anglicanism', and David Como, 'Puritans, predestination and the construction of orthodoxy in early seventeenth-century England', in *Conformity and orthodoxy*, ed. Lake and Questier, pp. 5–33, 64–87.

[55] See *The new British history: founding a modern state, 1603–1715*, ed. Glenn Burgess (London, 1999).

[56] Peter Lake, *Anglicans and Puritans? Presbyterianism and English conformist thought from Whitgift to Hooker* (London, 1988).

[57] David George Mullan, *Episcopacy in Scotland: the history of an idea, 1560–1638* (Edinburgh, 1986); Mullan, *Scottish Puritanism, 1590–1638* (Oxford, 2000).

[58] Francis Lyall, *Of presbyters and kings: church and state in the law of Scotland* (Aberdeen, 1980); Andrew Drummond, *The Kirk and the Continent* (Edinburgh, 1956).

peoples of the archipelago.[59] Work on the 'British problem' has now come to influence work on state formation, religious conflict, and the causes of the crisis that enveloped the three kingdoms at mid-century.[60] This new emphasis on the role of Scotland in particular has meant that emerging scholarship is obliged to incorporate itself within the existing paradigms that seek to identify the 'causes' of the conflict, and at this point we recall Kenneth Fincham's statement about the implications of this for the study of religion. Work by John Morrill, John Ford, and David Mullan has set the study of Scottish religion within the context of existing historiography on the religious 'causes' of the breakdown of the 1640s.[61] It remains to be seen how such perspectives may be reconciled with the Arminian paradigm; Mullan's article on Calvinism in Scotland fell in step with the work of Tyacke, and as a result a range of other areas of conflict were overlooked in favour of Arminianism, evidence of which, he admitted, was difficult to find. Instead, Mullan concluded that Presbyterians divided over topics like ceremonies and the nature of the Apostolic church – suggestive to be sure, but themes too large to treat in a single article.[62] As we shall see, there are strong connections between ecclesiological conflicts in the two kingdoms, connections which suggest refinements to the analyses put forth by Morrill and Ford, and which point to a pattern of religious and political conflict in England and Scotland in the years before the conflict of the 1640s. The emerging paradigm of the Civil War as a 'war of religion' depends on a fuller account of how a very public and broadly based conflict over doctrine and discipline could be a factor in driving Protestant kingdoms to war with each other.[63]

---

[59] J. G. A. Pocock, 'British History: a plea for a new subject', *Journal of Modern History*, 47 (December 1975), 601–28.

[60] *The British problem, c. 1534–1707: state formation in the Atlantic archipelago*, ed. Brendan Bradshaw and John Morrill (Houndmills, Basingstoke, 1996); *The Scottish National Covenant in its British context, 1618–1651*, ed. John Morrill (Edinburgh, 1990); Russell, *Causes of the English Civil War*, chs. 2–5; Kevin Sharpe, *The personal rule of Charles I* (New Haven, 1992), chs. 6, 12, 13.

[61] John Morrill, 'A British patriarchy?: ecclesiastical imperialism under the early Stuarts', in *Religion, culture, and society*, ed. Anthony Fletcher and Peter Roberts (Cambridge, 1994), pp. 209–37; John D. Ford, 'The lawful bonds of Scottish society: the Five Articles of Perth, the Negative Confession and the National Covenant', *Historical Journal*, 37 (1994), 45–64; Ford, 'Conformity and conscience: the structure of the Perth Articles Debate in Scotland, 1618–1638', *Journal of Ecclesiastical History*, 46 (1995), 256–77; David G. Mullan, 'Theology in the Church of Scotland 1618–c. 1640: a Calvinist consensus?', *Sixteenth Century Journal*, 26 (1995), 595–617.

[62] Mullan, 'Theology', 617.

[63] See Russell, *Causes of the English Civil War*, chs. 3–5; *New British history*, ed. Burgess pp. 1–22; Conrad Russell, 'The British problem and the English Civil War', *History*, 75 (1987), 395–415; I. M. Green, '"England's wars of religion"?: Religious conflict and the

THE SCOPE OF THE WORK

A careful interpretation of debates among Jacobean divines allows us both to move beyond narrow interpretations of religious conflict and to lend perspective to the problem of civil and spiritual authority in the early Stuart kingdoms. Where others have frequently noted, but not systematically examined, a debate over the nature of the visible church, as well as debates on doctrine, governance, and ceremonial practice, the present study seeks to reconstruct the debates in which this conflict was played out. Rather than a Calvinist consensus, the Jacobean Church was founded upon a series of propositions that reflected the aspirations of building a national and monarchical Church, but that also invited criticism on a number of political, theological, and historical points. One can only understand the nature of both defences and criticisms of the Church through a measured examination of the texts in which the debate is preserved. The keys to the interpretation set forth here are that polemical exchanges between clerics and other commentators are central to our understanding of religious conflict, and that these exchanges were organised around a complex debate on the nature of the Apostolic church and its applicability as a fund of precept for the ordering of doctrine and governance in the post-Reformation Church of England. Since it is on this axis that the struggle to define the English Church turned, debates on governance and ceremonies are crucial to our understanding of Jacobean religious conflict in both the English and Scottish settings.

That said, it should also be established what this study does *not* aim to do. It makes no attempt to characterise popular religion, nor does it seek to comment on the variations among conforming clergy, or the impact of those variations at the diocesan level.[64] Those readers who are familiar with Richard Hooker's *Ecclesiasticall politie* will detect the dense shadow that work casts over conformist texts; there is not the space here to comment on the nature of their debt to him, or his influence in the debates this book surveys. By setting Hooker to one side and surveying a wider cast of writers, I hope that the reader will gain an appreciation of just how broad the debate

---

English Civil Wars', in *Church, change and revolution*, ed. J. van den Burg and P. G. Hoftijzer (Leiden, 1991), pp. 100–21; Glenn Burgess, 'Was the English Civil War a war of religion?: The Evidence of Political Propaganda', *Huntington Library Quarterly*, 61 (2000), 173–201.

[64] The seminal studies of these issues are Patrick Collinson, *The religion of Protestants: the Church in English society, 1559–1625* (Oxford, 1982), and Judith Maltby, *Prayer book and people in Elizabethan and early Stuart England* (Cambridge, 1998). See also Tom Webster, *Godly clergy in early Stuart England* (Cambridge, 1997); essays in *Religion and the English people, 1500–1640: new voices, new perspectives*, ed. Eric Josef Carlson, Sixteenth Century Essays and Studies, 45 (Kirksville, MO, 1998); and Patrick Collinson, 'The godly: aspects of popular Protestantism', in his *Godly people: essays on English Protestantism and Puritanism* (London, 1983), pp. 1–17.

was.[65] In fact, it was so broad as to necessitate two significant omissions: hence, I have opted not to include a discussion of debates that took place between Protestant and Catholic controversialists, or of those among English Protestant Separatists. In the case of the latter, such debates but rarely intersected with the exchanges on ceremonies and governance that took place between conformists and those writers who remained in the Church despite their misgivings about it. Murray Tolmie's work on the Separatist tradition and Keith Sprunger's on exiled English Protestants are complete studies whose conclusions this book does not seek to challenge.[66] With respect to the Protestant / Catholic debates, the work of Peter Holmes, Alexandra Walsham, Lucy Wooding, and especially Anthony Milton offers a more complete portrait than is possible without making the present book much longer.[67] Here again, with the possible exception of the Oath of Allegiance controversy[68] and scattered works on papal versus episcopal government, the debates that this study surveys were confined exclusively to Protestant writers. Therefore, I have proposed to examine the problem of the definition of the English Church from the point of view of its Protestant critics and defenders. Diocesan or consistory records, or other kinds of unpublished archival material, do not figure among the sources on which this study is based.[69] This is first and foremost a history of ideas, and of controversies whose central themes would have been little understood by the average person.[70] This literature was, for the most part, written and consumed by a narrow segment of English and Scottish society.[71] However, its impact would

---

[65] I am grateful to Anthony Fletcher, whose comments on a draft of this book helped me to clarify this point of interpretation.

[66] Murray Tolmie, *The triumph of the saints: the separate churches of London, 1616–1649* (Cambridge, 1977); Keith Sprunger, *Dutch puritanism: a history of the English and Scottish churches of the Netherlands in the sixteenth and seventeenth centuries* (Leiden, 1982). I should also mention Victoria Joy Gregory, 'Congregational puritanism and the radical puritan community' (Ph.D. diss., University of Cambridge, 2003).

[67] Peter Holmes, *Resistance and compromise: the political thought of the Elizabethan Catholics* (Cambridge, 1982); Alexandra Walsham, *Church papists: Catholicism, conformity, and confessional polemic in early modern England* (Woodbridge, Suffolk, 1993); Lucy E. C. Wooding, *Rethinking Catholicism in Reformation England* (Oxford, 2000); Milton, *Catholic and reformed*, esp. Part 1.

[68] J. P. Sommerville, 'Jacobean political thought and the controversy over the Oath of Allegiance' (Ph.D. diss., University of Cambridge, 1981).

[69] Kenneth Fincham's work has shown how fruitful these sources can be. In addition to his *Prelate as pastor: the episcopate of James I* (Oxford, 1990), see *Visitation articles and injunctions of the early Stuart Church*, ed. Kenneth Fincham, 2 vols. (Woodbridge, Suffolk, 1994–8).

[70] Many of the period's surviving sermons deal with themes that are relevant to this study. For while many were concerned, as they are still, with the wages of sin and the struggle between passion and Christian virtue, others delved deeper into the identity of the faith and how it could be defined.

[71] The contents of the library of Richard Stonley, a Teller of the Elizabethan Exchequer of Receipt, reveal that he owned a great number of works of religious controversy, including works by conformists such as Hooker and Jewel, as well as by their critics Cartwright, Penry,

presumably have been felt among the parishes, for its authors represented the full range of the clergy, from groups of ministers clubbing together to protest their deprivations, to the authors of massive tomes making painstaking use of a range of scholarly sources, themselves the very foundation of the Christian historical tradition.

Very broadly, then, this book seeks to shift the focus of our understanding of religious conflict away from Arminianism and Laudianism, and toward the problem of ecclesiology and its impact on political theory, religious debate, and historical thought. This shift is made possible by the study of polemical sources, and it may emerge that these sources reveal – in a way other sources do not – the central fault lines of the debate among Jacobean Protestants. This is because ecclesiological argument was a dominant aspect of the intellectual culture in the period after the Reformation, in which biblical philology was combined with a humanist interest in the development of Christian history. A Protestant, but still very English, liturgy was grafted onto a visible church whose defenders needed to justify its existence as a reformed continuation of the Apostolic church, but which was nevertheless possessed of modes of doctrine and discipline to which the scripture did not give a clear warrant. The result was that Christian history and the nature of the Apostolic church bulked large in the literature of religious controversy.[72] Rather than Anglican versus puritan, or Calvinist versus Arminian, the principal cleavages amounted to differing schools of thought on how the Apostolic tradition might be interpreted, and what implications these interpretations had for matters of practical ecclesiology. Arthur Ferguson noted as much in his seminal study of historical thought:

They turned for inspiration not so much to classical but to Christian antiquity. Though familiar enough with the standard classical authors ... contestants on both sides sought proof and precedent in the world of the Apostles and church fathers. How they interpreted that world and what relation they believed it bore to their own,

---

and a number of Catholic divines. See Leslie Hotson, 'The library of Elizabeth's embezzling Teller', *Studies in Bibliography*, 2 (1949–50), pp. 49–61, and Raymond, *Pamphlets and pamphleteering*, ch. 1.

[72] Ferguson, *Clio unbound*, chs. 5–6; Patrick Collinson, 'If Constantine, then also Theodosius: St Ambrose and the integrity of the Elizabethan *ecclesia anglicana*', *Journal of Ecclesiastical History*, 30 (1979), 205–29. See also Joseph H. Preston, 'English ecclesiastical historians and the problem of bias, 1559–1742', *Journal of the History of Ideas*, 32 (1971), 203–20; Rainier Pineas, 'William Turner's polemical use of ecclesiastical history and his controversy with Stephen Gardiner', *Renaissance Quarterly*, 33 (1980), 599–608; Robert Dodaro and Michael Questier, 'Strategies in Jacobean polemic: the use and abuse of St Augustine in English Theological Controversy', *Journal of Ecclesiastical History*, 44 (1993), 432–49; M. E. C. Perrott, 'Richard Hooker and the problem of authority in the Elizabethan Church', *Journal of Ecclesiastical History*, 49 (1998), 29–60; and Arthur G. Holder, 'Whitby and all that: the search for Anglican origins', *Anglican Theological Review*, 85 (2003), 231–2.

therefore, became questions of primary importance in estimating the character of Reformation historical thought.[73]

Although the use of ecclesiastical history was a common element in the debate, this book does not attempt to dissect the various ways in which writers employed their sources. Rather, when they were used to attack or justify a particular position, I have noted what texts were employed in either case. One does not find that writers made programmatic statements about why they chose the sources they did; most often, one presumes, the choice was governed by the needs of a given argument. At other times, claims for the accuracy or reliability of historical sources were expressed in negative terms, by way of calling into question their use by an opponent. Instead, I wish simply to show that when matters of doctrine and ecclesiology were in dispute – as they were without interruption in the period the book treats – writers of all stripes appealed to the authority of history in pressing their claims. Those who study early Stuart religious conflict have, in the main, overlooked this aspect of the debate, and it may be that they have fundamentally underestimated their subject as a result.[74] Religious conflict was not driven simply by a debate over soteriology, but by debates about the nature of the Church, its place in Christian history, and its place in the realm. Only when one engages with the problem of ecclesiology in its historical, religious, polemical, and political contexts do the patterns of the problem emerge.

The work begins by examining the intellectual foundations of Jacobean conformity, and concentrates on four related issues: that the stability of Church and commonwealth was predicated upon religious uniformity; that this uniformity was justified owing to the organic conjunction of those bodies; that the ecclesiastical jurisdiction of the Crown was ancient; and finally that the Church itself was both ancient and reformed – which made it unique among Protestant churches. The next chapter examines the printed literature that emerged in the early years of James' reign, and explores a number of tensions that emerged in the wake of the Canons of 1604. Clerical subscription and deprivation led to debates over the jurisdiction of bishops, and over the relationship between ecclesiastical discipline and the common law. The theme of episcopacy is pursued in the fourth chapter, which looks at

---

[73] Ferguson, *Clio unbound*, p. 132.

[74] But see D. R. Woolf, *The idea of history in early Stuart England* (Toronto, 1990), pp. 37–44; and Patrick Collinson, 'Truth, lies, and fiction in sixteenth-century Protestant historiography', in *The historical imagination in early modern Britain: history, rhetoric, and fiction, 1500–1800*, ed. Donald Kelley and David Harris Sacks (Cambridge, 1997), pp. 37–68. J. G. A. Pocock has observed that the Church of England is the 'key' to early modern English history, but thus far we lack a study which shows how this was so. See Pocock, *Barbarism and religion, Vol. I: The Enlightenments of Edward Gibbon, 1737–1764* (Cambridge, 1999), p. 8.

debates on governance. Not only did contemporaries divide on the nature of government appropriate to the Church, but also on the extent of the power, or jurisdiction, of diocesan bishops. Conformists offered doctrinal and historical justifications for diocesan episcopacy, but varied on whether it was Apostolic or divinely ordained. Reformists put forth the case for variations on Presbyterian discipline, and also argued for its divine and Apostolic origins. Debates on governance were carried on alongside others that considered ceremonial practice, and so the fifth chapter presents debates on the doctrinal and historical elements of the ceremonies prescribed by the Canons of 1604. Like governance, ceremonies were crucial hallmarks used to establish how closely visible churches resembled the perfection of the ancient church. Reformists argued that, since Christ had not adopted a kneeling posture at the Last Supper, there was no justification for its continued use. Against this doctrinal and historical argument, conformists offered a case for the 'liberty' of the Church to institute ceremonies according to the standards of 'custom' and 'edification'. Yet they also sought a doctrinal and historical justification for the continued use of 'things indifferent'.

The study concludes by looking at an aspect of Jacobean ecclesiology that has not yet been properly investigated: that is, the conflicts that took place between the two churches over which James claimed sovereignty – the Kirk and the Church of England. The attempt to introduce diocesan episcopacy and kneeling at communion touched off a controversy which, in its latter stages, saw writers urging conformity to a Church of 'Great Britain' as a solution to the clamour over ceremonies and bishops in the churches of England and Scotland. Yet the rift between Protestants in England and Scotland was significant one, defined by controversies in which two historical narratives of the relationship between civil and spiritual authority were ranged against each other. Jacobean ecclesiology was not defined by consensus, but represented a continuation of post-Reformation debates that were animated by the problem of reconciling a definition of the Church as a spiritual association of free Christians with a Church 'established' by statute and annexed to the imperial Crown. Given the fact that the Church continued to draw fire from a range of Protestant critics, the whole enterprise of building, refining, and in some cases tearing down an historical ecclesiology lay at the very root of the problem, and furthermore the language in which it was built, refined, and torn down was central to the way in which contemporary political and religious discourse was carried on.

2

The language of ecclesiastical polity and Jacobean conformist thought

The chief intellectual tension that underlay Jacobean ecclesiological debates is illustrated by disputes about the proper relationship between civil and ecclesiastical authority.[1] These disputes stemmed from the decision – taken first under Henry VIII and subsequently refined under Elizabeth I – to define the Church of England as *the* Church authorised by Christ to continue His earthly ministry; this claim served as the basis for the proposition that since the Church of England was so authorised, it retained within itself power and discretion over matters of doctrine and discipline.[2] This authority did not come solely from the Word, but also from statutes that established the Church. After this initial 'founding', conformists were obliged to make an articulate case for why a Church established in law could also agree with scripture and the practice of the Apostolic church. As later chapters will show, the retention of certain ceremonies and episcopal governance drew, from Protestant critics, arguments fleshed out with doctrinal or historical criticism, and designed to undermine the authority of the Church and its human governors. At the root of the debate was a difficult question: how could a church so evidently grounded in the realm of human creation, of culture and custom, also take part in the world of the divine creation, that is, the community of believers joined to Christ and one another in a spiritual association that was by its very nature free from the direction of human agents?[3] This question absorbed contemporary defenders of the established Church and others interested in the development of a theory of ecclesiastical

---

[1] This point was made, but not systematically explored, by G. W. Bernard, 'The Church of England, c. 1529–c. 1642', *History*, 75 (1990), 191–2. See also Julian Davies, *The Caroline captivity of the Church: Charles I and the remoulding of Anglicanism* (Oxford, 1992), ch. 1; and Patrick Collinson, *The religion of Protestants: the Church in English society, 1559–1625* (Oxford, 1982), ch. 4.

[2] J. G. A. Pocock, 'Within the margins: the definitions of orthodoxy', in *The margins of orthodoxy: heterodox writing and cultural response, 1660–1750*, ed. Roger Lund (Cambridge, 1995), pp. 39–40.

[3] Ferguson, *Clio unbound: perception of the social and cultural past in Renaissance England* (Durham, NC, 1979), pp. 172–4, argued that *adiaphora* lay at the heart of the matter.

polity. The forerunners in this tradition, among them Thomas Starkey, Matthew Parker, John Jewel, and especially Richard Hooker, were all in one way or another engaged in the solution of the tension evident in a Church claiming continuance with the Apostolic tradition, but established by statute and 'governed' by the Crown. Yet there is ample evidence that a wide range of writers explored the theme, and following chapters will present this evidence in detail. For now, we must develop an outline of the language in which this debate was carried on, for it will emerge that this language is central to the polemical debates which this book surveys.

This chapter sets out to examine aspects of conformist thought as conveyed in four works whose authors sought to defend the English Church as a 'political association', and to *define* it as a 'spiritual association'. A central ambition of conformist writers was to reconcile these apparently incompatible qualities; this reconciliation was in many ways at the heart of conformist ecclesiology, and accounts for a major theme in the literature of religious controversy. Conformists acknowledged that the Church was a 'corporation', derived in some sense from human experience and custom, and thus able to alter modes of discipline and worship as its governors saw fit. Yet to be a true church and a vessel of Christ's salvation, it also had to partake in the history of the institution established by Him, while at the same time fitting neatly within the jurisdiction of the secular authority. Hence religion and the question of authority – whether spiritual or civil – were inextricably linked, and this linkage proved rather difficult to define. However, the importance of this theme to the study of political ideas has not been fully appreciated by scholars.[4] This is because they have failed to recognise the manner in which religion and political discourse were blended into a 'language' of ecclesiastical polity. By this is meant a manner of argument and a mode of scholarship which sought to legitimise the authority of the Church by drawing upon scripture and the history of Christianity to account for the Church's connection with the spiritual realm, while also calling attention to historical entitlements to rule, to the tension between public doctrine and private judgement, and to the coterminous nature of Church and realm in order to justify its connection with the political world. We should not forget that the post-Reformation Church was a site of contest because it was a manifestation of Christ's earthly authority.

A very similar case is put forward by Ethan H. Shagan, 'The English Inquisition: constitutional conflict and ecclesiastical law in the 1590s', *The Historical Journal*, 47 (September 2004), 541–65.

[4] Work on Richard Hooker has illuminated some of these themes. See Diarmaid MacCullough, 'Richard Hooker's reputation', *English Historical Review*, 117 (2002), 773–812; W. J. Torrance Kirby, *Richard Hooker's doctrine of the royal supremacy* (Leiden and New York, 1990); Robert K. Faulkner, *Richard Hooker and the politics of a Christian England* (Berkeley, 1981); and Nigel Atkinson, *Richard Hooker and the authority of scripture, tradition, and reason: reformed theologian of the Church of England?* (Carlisle, 1997).

However, since the Church of England intersected so clearly with the institutions of magisterial authority, it was likely that a dispute over the nature of this intersection would blend political, religious, and historical precept.

This blending was the result of the institutional character of the Elizabethan religious settlement. It was an act of state, and represented the birth of a national political association resembling what Jonathan Clark has called a 'confessional state'.[5] The statutes that established the Church as an annex of the 'Imperial crown' defined additional channels of royal sovereignty, and specified the nature of the Crown's ecclesiastical jurisdiction. The Act of Supremacy of 1559 restored the English Crown to its 'ancient' jurisdiction over the Church in its dominions.[6] A long tradition in English ideas likened kings to biblical figures like Solomon and David and it was argued that the power of these ancient figures to order religion and punish heretics descended directly to the Kings of England.[7] The Act of Uniformity proclaimed the Church of England as the sole conduit of English Christianity and enjoined all living within the Crown's dominions to abide by the 'public' worship of the Church.[8] The word 'public' held great importance, for it revealed that the very act of worship had about it a dimension of political loyalty: treason, then as now, most often took place behind closed doors, and hence the Crown proceeded with vigour against both Protestants and Catholics disaffected with the established Church.[9] The legislation of the settlement, therefore, went some way toward defining aspects of a relationship between civil and spiritual authority. However, since the precise nature of this relationship was frequently disputed, the theory of ecclesiastical sovereignty was in constant need of support and refinement.

Definitions of sovereignty were in turn complicated by disputes about the relationship of doctrine and law. As the preamble to the Thirty-nine Articles

---

[5] J. C. D. Clark, *English Society, 1660–1832: religion, ideology and politics during the ancien regime* (Cambridge, 2000), pp. 26–34.

[6] The full title of the Act is revealing: 'An Act restoring to the Crown the ancient jurisdiction over the state ecclesiastical and spiritual, and abolishing all foreign power repugnant to the same'. See *The Tudor constitution: documents and commentary*, ed. G. R. Elton, 2nd edn (Cambridge, 1982), doc. 184, p. 372.

[7] For an example of this genre of literature, see the sermons by William Leigh, *Queen Elizabeth paraleld in her princely vertues, with David, Ioshua and Hezekia* (London, 1612).

[8] Conrad Russell has pointed out that a 'key belief' in Jacobean England was that religious uniformity had to be enforced, and that it was this which brought religion into the realm of politics. See *The causes of the English Civil War* (Oxford, 1990), p. 65.

[9] For details, see Stuart Barton Babbage, *Puritanism and Richard Bancroft* (London, 1962), pp. 147–219; Kenneth Fincham, *Prelate as pastor: the episcopate of James I* (Oxford, 1990), pp. 212–47. For Catholics and the state, see Michael Questier, *Conversion, politics and religion in England, 1580–1621* (Cambridge, 1996), pp. 98–125; Questier, 'The politics of religious conformity and the accession of James I', *Bulletin of the Institute of Historical Research*, 71 (1998), 14–30.

put it, the Crown's duty was 'to *conserve and maintain* the Church ... in the unity of the True religion, and in the Bond of Peace'.[10] Yet as definitive as this sounded, the concept of the 'true religion' in turn depended on a series of complex doctrinal and historical arguments, and so there was constant pressure on the Crown's ecclesiastical authority from those controversialists who promoted alternate doctrinal programmes in the course of polemical debate. Yet conformists did not always feel compelled to address these arguments at length, and emphasised instead the need for civil order; it was this imperative that shaped some accounts of the nature and extent of religious authority, which could prohibit 'unnecessary disputations, Altercations or Questions to be raised, which may nourish Faction in both Church and Commonwealth'.[11] From the point of view of English conformists, the Church was as close to perfection in doctrine, discipline, and governance as was possible for any earthly church. The implication was that all arguments about the rites and governance had been settled, and any remaining critics were dismissed as being motivated by 'opinion', 'private fancy', and 'popularity' – all of them the accoutrements of faction.[12] As Thomas Scott remarked in 1623, the public authority of the Church would be undermined if 'a Man should make his own will the Churches law'.[13] In other words, authority over the Church did not reside in either individuals or congregations – it was a corporate institution over which the Crown and its magistrates (the bishops) were sovereign.[14]

The works to be examined in this chapter were published in the context of debates over the use of oaths to ensure both Protestant conformity and Catholic allegiance. The programme of clerical subscription instituted by Archbishop Richard Bancroft in the wake of the Hampton Court conference led disaffected Protestant ministers to pose questions about whether the Crown or its agents could justly exercise civil power in the name of religion.[15] Yet the conformist case rested on the proposition that there was an

---

[10] *A theological introduction to the Thirty-nine Articles of the Church of England*, ed. E. J. Bicknell, 3rd edn, revised by H. J. Carpenter (London, 1955), ch. 1 (emphases mine).

[11] Church of England, *Articles agreed upon by the archbishops and bishops ... in the convocation holden at London in the year 1562* (London, 1684), n. p. Bodl. 4° Rawl. 277 (8).

[12] Conrad Russell, 'Arguments for religious unity in England, 1530–1650', *Journal of Ecclesiastical History*, 18 (1967), 201–26. With reference to the political message of Hooker's *Ecclesiasticall politie* Russell argued, 'It was easy to deduce from this position that the attempt to withdraw from the Church of England constituted an attempt to withdraw from the commonwealth' (204).

[13] Thomas Scott, *The high-waies of God and the King* (London, 1623), p. 19.

[14] Pocock, 'Within the margins', p. 40.

[15] Fincham, *Prelate as pastor*, ch. 2; Ian Green, 'Career prospects and clerical conformity in the early Stuart Church', *Past and Present*, 90 (1981), 71–115; Peter Lake, 'Moving the goal posts?: modified subscription and the construction of conformity in the early Stuart Church', in *Conformity and orthodoxy in the English Church, c. 1560–1660*, ed. Peter Lake and Michael Questier (Woodbridge, Suffolk, 2000), pp. 179–205.

achievable balance between civil and spiritual authority, and it was this balance that the writers to be discussed below were anxious to clarify. As we shall see, Protestants challenged this authority by arguing that the common law provided a legal check on episcopal jurisdiction, while at the same time seeking to redefine spiritual authority as something that was free from political interference.[16] Many of the same arguments were advanced by Catholics who, at times during the reign of Elizabeth I, and again in the wake of the Gunpowder Plot, were perceived as a grave threat to civil order. James VI and I proposed to deal with this threat via an Oath of Allegiance that reaffirmed the legitimacy of the Crown's power over the Church in its dominions.[17] Yet the oath obliged Catholics to recognise not only the Crown's civil authority, but also the jurisdiction that it claimed over the spiritual life of the Church of England. This could not be reconciled with their loyalty to the Pope, and here again we discover a tension between religion and authority. Both sets of debates from the early years of the reign of James VI and I invited speculation on two tenets that English conformists were anxious to defend: the absolute nature of the Crown's ecclesiastical sovereignty, and the notion that the English Church was, in the words of Richard Hooker, 'truly Christian and duly reformed'. The political language that emerged in the years after the Reformation came to be adopted at points when the ecclesiastical authority of the Crown was subject to challenge, and this language was distinguished by the need to situate the Church within the history of Christianity, and also to reconcile ecclesiastical sovereignty with historical examples of civil power. The purpose of this chapter, then, is to illustrate this aspect of the conformist position in order to provide context for the debates treated in the remainder of this book; the precarious nature of the 'dual establishment' served to drive the debate between defenders of the Church and their critics, and lay at the heart of the attempt to define the Church as a political and spiritual association.

RELIGION THE 'STAY' OF POLITY: PUBLIC DOCTRINE,
HISTORY, AND SOVEREIGNTY

Many of the Jacobean texts to be examined in this study reflected the influence of medieval and late Renaissance habits of mind.[18] Here one

---

[16] For clerical deprivations, see Babbage, *Puritanism and Richard Bancroft*, pp. 147–219.

[17] Michael Questier, 'Loyalty, religion and state power in early modern England: English Romanism and the Jacobean Oath of Allegiance', *Historical Journal*, 40 (1997), 311–29. For the text of the oath, see *The Stuart constitution: documents and commentary*, ed. J. P. Kenyon (Cambridge, 1986), pp. 168–71.

[18] Robert Eccleshall, *Order and reason in politics: theories of absolute and limited monarchy in early modern England* (Oxford, 1978), pp. 47–75.

finds elements of a language suitable for describing a spiritual institution which fell under civil authority, itself responsible for the maintenance of the integrity of the spiritual unit. One of these was to compare the stability of Church and state to the functioning of other bodies, or to conditions such as 'order' or 'harmony'.[19] Among writers of the early seventeenth century, divine providence, the belief not only that God existed, but also that He was active in the affairs of people, helped to shape discussions of political authority.[20] God, argued William Covell in 1595, sought to preserve stability in the realm, in part, by punishing the 'sinnes [of] both the Prince and people'. Covell portrayed both subjects and sovereigns as bound by divine law, the latter in particular owing their station to God's favour. He saw sovereigns as both 'settled' and 'disposed' by God, retaining office so long as they obeyed His law.[21] A similar point was made by Thomas Bilson in his monumental study of Christian kingship: 'A King, because he is the lieutenant of the most High King, was anointed to this end that he should regard and govern the earthly kingdom and the people of God, and above all things his Holy Church, and defend her from wrongs ... which except he do, he can not justly be called King.'[22] Here the authority of the Crown was linked with the preservation and defence of true doctrine.

In the Jacobean mind, religion was central to accounts of how common-wealths fell into disorder, and was spoken of in conjunction with established political metaphors.[23] One of these, 'order', was frequently employed by political writers during the period, as were organic metaphors used to describe the workings of social wholes.[24] Often the metaphor of musical harmony was offered, as it was by Jean Bodin, to describe the necessity of wise rule in a commonwealth. Here Bodin followed Plato, arguing

---

[19] A helpful study of this literature is Kevin Sharpe, 'A commonwealth of meanings: languages, analogues, ideas and politics', in his *Remapping early modern England: the culture of seventeenth-century politics* (Cambridge, 2000), pp. 38–123.

[20] For a thorough elaboration of the theme, see Alexandra Walsham's *Providence in early modern England* (Oxford, 1999).

[21] William Covell, *Polimanteia, or, The meanes lawfull and vnlawfull, to iudge of the fall of a common-wealth* ([Cambridge and London], 1595), sig E^{2r}–E^{3v}.

[22] Thomas Bilson, *The true difference betweene Christian subiection and unchristian rebellion* (Oxford, 1585), p. 251. See Glenn Burgess, 'The divine right of kings reconsidered', *English Historical Review*, 107 (1992), 837–61; J. H. M. Salmon, 'Catholic resistance theory, ultra-montainism, and the royalist response, 1580–1620', in *The Cambridge history of political thought, 1450–1700*, ed. J. H. Burns and Mark Goldie (Cambridge, 1991), pp. 219–53; Conrad Russell, 'Divine rights in the early seventeenth century', in *Public duty and private conscience in seventeenth century England: essays presented to G. E. Aylmer*, ed. John Morrill, Paul Slack, and Daniel Woolf (Oxford, 1993), pp. 101–20.

[23] Richard Greaves, 'Concepts of political obedience in late Tudor England: conflicting perspectives', *Journal of British Studies*, 22 (1982), 23–34.

[24] W. H. Greenleaf, *Order, empiricism, and politics: two traditions in English political thought* (Oxford, 1964).

that it was the mixing together of a 'diversitie and dissimilitude' of voices 'which maketh the sweet harmony'.[25] At other times writers relied on the metaphor of the 'body politic', and argued that its 'order' was superintended by God:

A Commonwealth is a living body compact of sundry estates and degrees of men: this body is composed of two sorts, namely of the soule ... and of the members or parts ... God alone hath so framed the state of the whole commonwealth and the government thereof, by his eternall providence.[26]

An important dimension of the argument that the commonwealth was 'framed' by God was that it was done in order to protect and preserve the 'true' religion. Hence, it became a matter of political wisdom that 'one religion ought to be observed in one kingdom'.[27] Here we detect the link between Church and commonwealth united in a single corporate entity. Since political instability was caused by competing religious factions, often styled as 'infections' of the body politic, conformist writers like William Covell frequently pointed out the dangers posed by Catholics and sectaries: 'I have encountered the Papist, and told him he mistakes the truth: his religion is meere erronious, and whilst I went about soundly to persuade this, Satan raised up the lewde faction of irreligious Brownists.'[28] Both Brownists – the contemporary word for Separatists – and Catholics distanced themselves from the Church established by statute, and, thus, from the English society that it encompassed. It was this problem of religious faction to which William Wilkes' *Obedience or ecclesiastical vnion* was addressed.

On the whole, Wilkes has remained unfamiliar to scholars of Jacobean political and religious culture, in part because they have not attempted to link his work with printed debates on early Jacobean ecclesiology.[29] Perhaps the most important of these was the controversy over aspects of the English doctrine and discipline established at the Hampton Court conference.[30] The reign of James VI and I had begun with Protestant calls for reform and Catholic pleas for toleration, both of which were coloured by the legacy of

---

[25] [Jean Bodin], *The six bookes of a common-weale. Written by I. Bodin*, trans. Richard Knolles (London, 1606), p. 11.

[26] Thomas Floyd, *The picture of a perfit common wealth* (London, 1600), pp. 1, 5–6.

[27] *Six bookes of politickes or Ciuil doctrine, written in Latine by Iustus Lipsius*, trans. William Jones (London, 1594), p. 63.

[28] Covell, *Polimanteia*, sig Bb[3r].

[29] For brief discussions of Wilkes' work, see J. P. Sommerville, *Royalists and patriots: politics and ideology in England, 1603–1640* (London, 1999), pp. 39, 240; Glenn Burgess, *Absolute monarchy and the Stuart constitution* (Yale, 1996), pp. 102–3, at 103; Collinson, *Religion of Protestants*, p. 12.

[30] For a fuller examination of these controversies, see chapter 3, and Babbage, *Puritanism and Richard Bancroft*, pp. 43–73.

Elizabethan debates on ecclesiology.[31] Many English Protestants were disappointed when the higher clergy established a set of Canons that delineated aspects of doctrine and discipline that had been the source of controversy in the late Elizabethan Church. These provisions, set down in the Canons of 1604, were to be enforced via clerical subscription and episcopal visitations; however, many ministers argued that elements of the new liturgy – kneeling at communion, the use of the cross in baptism, and the wearing of the surplice – were of 'human invention' and did not reflect the church left on earth by Christ. Nevertheless, Richard Bancroft proceeded with a programme of subscription, and those ministers who refused to subscribe to the Canons were deprived of their livings.[32] This was done by resorting to the Crown's authority as governor of the Church clearly described by a royal proclamation of March 1604, 'to require and enjoyne all men, aswell Ecclesiasticall and Temporall, to conform themselves unto [the Book of Common Prayer], and to the practise thereof, as the onely Publicke Fourme of serving of God, established and allowed to be in this Realme'. The proclamation also provided a clear statement of the dangers of religious faction, linking it with the business of statecraft:

Neither are We ignorant of the inconveniences that doe arise in Government, by admitting innovation in things once settled by mature deliberation: And how necessarie it is to use constancie in the upholding of the publique determinations of States, for that such is the unquietness and unstedfastness of some dispositions, affecting every yeere new formes of things, as, if they should be followed in their unconstancie, would make all Actions of States ridiculous and contemptible: whereas the stedfast maintaining of things by good advise established, is the weale of all Common wealths.[33]

Conformists dismissed the theological arguments of their opponents as errors that invited social disorder. So much became clear in a proclamation published in July 1604, which warned 'what intractable men doe not performe upon admonition, they must be compelled unto by Authoritie'. Indeed, the July proclamation reinforced its predecessor's statement on the Crown's political intentions in the realm of religion: 'We shall not faile to doe that which Princely providence requireth at Our hands: That is, to put in execution all wayes and means that may take from among Our people, all

---

[31] For treatments of the Elizabethan controversies, see Peter Lake, *Anglicans and Puritans?: Presbyterianism and English conformist thought from Whitgift to Hooker* (London, 1988), chs. 1–3; Peter White, *Predestination, policy and polemic: conflict and consensus in the English Church from the Reformation to the Civil War* (Cambridge, 1992), chs. 2–6.
[32] For details, see Fincham, *Prelate as pastor*, ch. 7. For a discussion of the constitutional and canonical aspects of the late Elizabethan and early Jacobean Church, see R. G. Usher, *The reconstruction of the English Church*, 2 vols. (London, 1910), vol. I, pp. 191–204, 403–23.
[33] 'A proclamation of the authorizing and uniformitie of the Booke of Common Prayer to be used throughout the realms', 5 March 1604. See *Stuart royal proclamations*, ed. J. F. Larkin and P. L. Hughes, 2 vols. (Oxford, 1973), vol. I, pp. 74–6.

grounds and occasions of Sectes, Divisions, and Unquietness.'[34] Among these ways and means was the process of clerical subscription whereby a standard public doctrine was enforced.

Wilkes prefaced his pamphlet with the July proclamation on conformity, and thereby set the theme of the work. Here was a conformist cleric writing about a particular problem then facing the Church of England – how to persuade recalcitrant members of the clergy to subscribe. As others would resort to scripture, councils, and ecclesiastical history to prove that the disputed ceremonies had an ancient pedigree, Wilkes' diagnosis of the political costs of religious dispute was presented in terms of a history of faction. It built upon the central assumption that those who refused to conform to a church governed by the sovereign represented a religious interest that was hostile to the unity of the public profession of the Church. Instead of a history of doctrine, Wilkes furnished his readers with a history of dispute, intended to convey positive lessons applicable to the English context; indeed, Wilkes sought to dispel the charge that the ceremonies adopted at Hampton Court were examples of 'novelty', and did so by situating the conflicts in the Jacobean Church within the broader history of Christianity. The ancient Christian church had itself been divided by internal disputes, and clearly the same condition was faced by its English descendant: 'That which wrought much hurt amongst the auncient Christians, hath greatly troubled the State present, and would dangerouslie hazard the government of both Church and Common-weale, if Princely determination had not prevented it'.[35] This placed the contentions that emerged before and after Hampton Court in historical context, and linked the dangers of faction in the ancient church to the 'present' state of the English Church.

Wilkes emphasised both the antiquity of the Church, and the Crown's jurisdiction over it, which he described as being God-given:

In respect of the *Prince*, for by religion, and workes according thereunto, God is moved to give life unto their councels, perfection to their indeavours, and settlement to their throanes; for which cause, the more eminent they are in regall Authoritie, the more vigilant they ought to be in religious pietie.[36]

---

[34] 'A proclamation enjoyning conformitie', 16 July 1604. *Stuart royal proclamations*, vol. I, pp. 88–90.

[35] Wilkes, *Obedience or ecclesiastical vnion. Treatised by William Wilkes Doctor in Theologie, and one of his Maiesties chaplaines in ordinarie* (London, 1605), sig. B[3]. Wilkes (d. 1634) was educated at Merton College, but dates of attendance and degrees are unknown. Wood reported that Wilkes gained the MA, and then became Vicar of St Peter in the East, where his sermons were popular with Oxford scholars. He was created Chaplain in Ordinary by James I. See Anthony Wood, *Athenae Oxonienses*, 2 vols. (London, 1691–2), vol. I, pp. 298–9.

[36] Wilkes, *Obedience*, p. 6.

In a preface addressed to the King, Wilkes had noted how 'God ... hath put the Globe of this little world into the hands of your rule'; this included the Church, and charged the king with maintaining the integrity of its doctrine and discipline. Indeed, Wilkes linked the King's authority to his competence as an ecclesiastical governor, with the implication that an 'impious' king was less legitimate than one who ruled according to God's law. Chief among the duties of a Christian prince, therefore, was the *preservation* of the Church: 'By his judicial authoritie, made known in his admonitorie declarations, to enrayle those partes of our Christian duties; which noveltie with distaine of Antiquity had licentiously violated'.[37] Wilkes clearly saw the conflict over subscription as taking place between 'novelty' and 'antiquity', and dismissed the criticisms of those who attacked the Canons of 1604. 'Novelists' were depicted as a disruptive faction, who withdrew themselves from the association of the Church: 'I know that Nature has interested every perticular one of you with abilitie to prescribe rules unto yourselves, in your private actions; but those rules are not laws to bind others, because they have respect more to your own private, then reference to the publicke good.'[38] Here again, private judgement had to defer to public doctrine.

Wilkes argued that those who did not partake in the ancient ceremonies of the Church 'must needs be condemned for wicked and ungodly rebellion'. The assumption was clear: given the nature of the Crown's power over the Church, good subjects demonstrated their obedience by conforming to all aspects of doctrine and discipline. Since English conformists stressed the unity of civil and ecclesiastical power, they regarded religious non-conformity as the equivalent of sedition. Yet there were positive elements to the theory, as well. Most often these concerned the nature of the royal power, and the role of religion in the commonwealth; it was thus that Wilkes observed: 'To preserve the peace of the Church is a special prerogative belonging to the supreme power of the highest commander ... the prosperous peace of all well-ordered commonweales, doth acknowledge religion for her chiefest staye.'[39] Both subjects and sovereign were bound 'by conscience' to preserve and encourage the peace of the Church, which was the 'sure conservatorie of the kingdom's happiness'. Unruly members spelt the death

---

[37] Ibid., p. 7. [38] Ibid., p. 13.

[39] Ibid., p. 16. This manner of expression was common among English conformists throughout the period. William Laud noted that the 'State and Church are built upon pillars, neither can stand without the other. The stay of the temple is religion, while that of the state is justice.' Similarly, Roger Maynwaring argued that 'Religion [is] the stay of *Politie*' and the 'foundation of all well-ordered commonwealths'. See William Laud, *A sermon preached on Munday, the sixt of February, at Westminster: at the opening of the Parliament* (London, 1625), sig. B²; Roger Maynwaring, *Religion and alegiance: in two sermons preached before the King's Maiestie* (London, 1627), p. 3.

of the body politic; religious disunity unsettled a kingdom. Unity alone could prevent this threat: 'The united and monochord practice, whereof, hath the happy condition of publicke societie, so closlie woven into it, *that neither can be, where both are not.*'[40]

Wilkes defined the standard of political and religious obedience by public profession and membership in the established Church. In the early modern period, oaths were a common tool for ensuring that subjects adhered to state policies, and the episcopal clergy employed oaths for subscription in the years after Hampton Court.[41] The Canons of 1604 established all aspects of the doctrine and discipline of the Church, and Bancroft implemented an *ex officio* oath to be administered among the ranks of the clergy. The problem was that a number of the lower clergy argued that there was no scriptural or historical warrant for the new liturgy, and on these grounds they refused subscription.[42] To Wilkes, addressing the 'Newfanglists', this argument amounted to the privileging of 'private' opinion over the public constitution of the Church:

Do you not see what opposition, what distraction, what division hath growne from this varietie, what passions have been stirred, what quarrels prosecuted ... what petitions have been framed? what companies assembled? What lawless private subscriptions required against subscription lawfull and publicke?[43]

Part of the conformist emphasis on the unity of public doctrine was a condemnation of independent congregations or individuals who assumed for themselves the spiritual authority that properly belonged to the state. Hence those religious groups – whether reformists or Catholics – that could not (or would not) conform to public doctrine were perceived as threats to the stability of Church and state.[44] In this atmosphere, even apparently minor aspects of the Church's practice could take on tremendous political importance; conformists saw ceremonies, the focus of reformist criticisms, as the elements that bound together the spiritual body politic.[45] Hence, Wilkes could

---

[40] Wilkes, *Obedience*, pp. 9, 15–16 (emphases mine).
[41] Caroline Robbins, 'Selden's pills: state oaths in England, 1558–1714', *Huntington Library Quarterly*, 35 (1971–2), 303–21; David Martin Jones, *Conscience and allegiance in seventeenth century England: the political significance of oaths and engagements* (Rochester, NY, 1999); Shagan, 'English Inquisition', 544–9.
[42] The exact numbers are subject to dispute: Babbage argued that eighty to ninety ministers were deprived of their livings between 1604 and 1610; Kenneth Fincham has revised the figure to a range of seventy-three to eighty-three. See Babbage, *Puritanism and Richard Bancroft*, pp. 147–219, and Fincham, *Prelate as pastor*, Appendix VI.
[43] Wilkes, *Obedience*, p. 17.
[44] Aspects of this problem are treated by Michael Mendle, *Dangerous positions: mixed government, the estates of the realm, and the 'Answer to the xix propositions'* (University, AL: 1985), pp. 63–96.
[45] Wilkes, *Obedience*, p. 71.

write of ceremonies: 'They are the Sinewes, by which religion, and her rites are made of neere neighbours, that the Acts of religion cannot absolutely be performed, if they want the furniture of comely ceremonies, nor the ceremonies accounted sacred, but as by religious separation they serve to holy uses.' Therefore, 'the continuing distance of Ceremonies, will occasion through continuing variation of mindes, continuall hatred, the mother of sedition'.[46]

Wilkes' conception of the Church held that non-conformity bore the 'markes of faction'. This elision meant that conformist writers saw no distinction between religious disobedience and its political counterpart; emphasising the public worship of the Church, conformists dismissed 'toleration' of divers sects as politically imprudent: 'You would not give tolleration to them, who esteeme secret Corners and private Conventicles, (the Schooles of maledictions against princes and rulers) to be of equal use, with Holy Churches, for the publicke performance of divine service.'[47] Hence, Wilkes saw clerical non-conformity as the beginning of a broader erosion of public doctrine. Novelty and private 'fancie' represented wilful acts of separation from the ecclesiastical polity, and an attack on the authority of the Church and its governor:

For if it should be lawfull for every man to cast the frame of religion in the mould of his own fancies, The scruples and inconveniences would be no lesse in the Church, then the suites at the common-lawe, in number infinite, if every man had power to create a newfound estate intaile.[48]

Far from supporting an oppositional model of politics, Jacobean conformists assumed that a stable polity was defined by something like a consensus or identity of religious interest. Individualism or the existence of issue-oriented groups did not come within their intellectual purview, nor did any notion of a separation of religious and political authority.

Wilkes' contribution to conformist thought is defined by his discussion of the links between 'antiquity' and 'authority'. J. G. A. Pocock's pioneering study of the ancient constitution established the premise that the past served to animate the soul of the present, and that to write the history of an institution was also to take a position on its present character.[49] This process of investigation was carried on with respect to both civil and ecclesiastical authority, which, contrary to what Pocock has since argued, were not regarded by contemporaries as being 'differently constructed'.[50] Indeed,

---

[46] Ibid., p. 17.   [47] Ibid., pp. 17, 33.   [48] Ibid., p. 39.

[49] J. G. A. Pocock, *The ancient constitution and the feudal law: A reissue with a retrospect* (Cambridge, 1987), chs. 2–3; Glenn Burgess, 'Common law and political theory in early Stuart England', *Political Science*, 40 (1988), 5–17.

[50] J. G. A. Pocock, *Barbarism and Religion*, Vol. II: *Narratives of civil government* (Cambridge, 1999), p. 29.

the history to which they looked *blended* civil and ecclesiastical authority, and this mirrored the conditions of their own institutions and was therefore useful to them. The English constitution was not a purely secular phenomenon, and nor was English kingship; to the concept of *imperium* contemporaries added that of *sacerdotium*.[51] Indeed, the images of kings and coronations throughout English history adorned the office and the rite with a sacramental quality.[52] Combined with theories of divine right were those of uninterrupted succession, if not of a single family, then certainly of the office of the monarch. In short, kings and queens had ruled both Southern Britain before the Romans, and England for twelve centuries after. Historically, kings had acted as the protectors of the primitive church; Bede's account of Augustine's conversion of the Saxons included an early report of the link between obedience and political unity. Aethelbert I, wrote Bede, 'showed greater favour to believers, because they were fellow citizens of the kingdom of heaven'.[53] For Wilkes and his contemporaries, the relation between the *imperium* and *sacerdotium* had an ancient status, and thus formed the intellectual bedrock of English ecclesiastical polity; it was this history in which they desired to situate themselves.[54]

Both reformists and Catholics sought to undermine and alter this tradition, either by contesting these attempts at linking civil and ecclesiastical history, or by suggesting (in the case of the Catholics) that the Church of England was not *the* true church. In response, conformist writers sought to reinforce the ancient pedigree of both the Church and the office of its ecclesiastical governor. Hence, Wilkes' margins teem with references to scripture, comments on the decisions of ecclesiastical synods and councils, and works of ancient and contemporary history and theology, including Origen, Chrysostom, and Sir Thomas Smith's *De republica Anglorum*. This vast fund of allusion was employed in order to link authority with antiquity and tradition, and oppose 'novelty' to 'innovation'; the result was

---

[51] When one examines the role of *imperium* alone in English thought, the resulting picture conveys the mistaken impression that the primary concerns of politics were humanistic and jurisprudential. This is not to say that these strands of ideas had no influence on English ideas, but rather that the story is incomplete without a sound integration of *sacerdotium*. See John Guy, 'The Henrician age', in *The varieties of British political thought, 1500–1800*, ed. J. G. A. Pocock with the assistance of Gordon J. Schochet and Lois G. Schwoerer (Cambridge, 1993), pp. 13–46.

[52] See Kevin Sharpe, 'Stuart monarchy and political culture', in his *Remapping early modern England*, pp. 201–22.

[53] Bede, *Ecclesiastical history of the English people*, trans. Leo Shirley-Price, intro. D. H. Farmer (Harmondsworth, 1990), p. 77.

[54] For a similar perspective on the Synod of Whitby, see Arthur G. Holder, 'Whitby and all that: the search for Anglican origins', *Anglican Theological Review*, 85 (2003), 231–52.

that Wilkes' concept of public doctrine was underpinned by and combined with the legitimacy of ancient practice:

If it he lawful for every *passionate* spirit carried with an affectation of *Noveltie*, to *repeale* laws which Authoritie hath enacted, to breake *customs* which *Antiquitie* hath commended; to change *Ordinances*, which Experience hath approved, to pervert order which Judgement hath established, and by suiting all occurents to their private *humors*, and to *innovate* that forme of *government* which this *kingdom* has happily followed, and *heaven* richly blessed? where is that so much valued wisdom of the *Auncient*? where is that which time giveth to things profitablie honest? where is that *supremacie* which God hath impropriated to the *Scepter* of *Princes*, as their peculiar right?[55]

Here was a clear defence of the idea that it was the right of the sovereign to preserve the 'custom' of the Church, which was itself an institution whose character changed over time and according to experience; to agitate for reform was to offer a direct challenge to both the antiquity of the Church and the legitimacy of the Crown's jurisdiction over it – it would sever the link of tradition that bound the Church to its history. The position of reformists, Wilkes argued, did 'wrong [to] this body politic', and set the state on an 'unrestrainable and head-long course of violent schisme'. Therefore, the campaign against clerical subscription was dismissed as a dangerous and historically unsound position. Indeed, Wilkes argued – with reference to the Elizabethan reformer Thomas Cartwright – that refusal to subscribe amounted to a dereliction of office: 'That is not a lawfull Ministrie (saith Master Cartwright) that is obstinate, and where the obstinacie is generall, or for the most part, where the State is ruinous, so that the Prince may after due means assayed to bring them home, procure that other be put in their places.'[56] With this statement, we return to the argument of the July proclamation, and the preamble to the Thirty-nine Articles: as defender of the faith, it was the task of the monarch to ensure the unity and authority of the English Church, and to take steps against those who denied these propositions. This concept of unity was central to contemporary understandings of the link between religion and the commonwealth.

One of the most articulate statements of this theory came from the pen of Edward Forset. He is seldom counted among the giants of seventeenth-century ideas; his work – two tracts and a short play – are difficult to relate to the scholarly portraits of Jacobean political thought.[57] Perhaps this is

---

[55] Wilkes, *Obedience*, p. 43. Emphases in original.   [56] Ibid., p. 57.

[57] For brief discussions, see Sommerville, *Royalists and patriots*, p. 53; Glenn Burgess, *The politics of the ancient constitution: an introduction to English political thought, 1603–1642* (University Park, PA, 1992), p. 157. See also Kevin Sharpe, 'A commonwealth of meanings', in his *Remapping early modern England*, pp. 52, 55, 112; and Greenleaf, *Order, empiricism, and politics*, ch. 4.

because of the assumption that truly political writing ought to employ secular language and that all talk of providence marked a peculiar style and is thus irrelevant to the history of political ideas. However, Forset's *Comparatiue discourse* not only began by arguing that the pattern of earthly government was established by God, but was itself a highly developed statement of how good government was established and maintained:

It is beyond the compasse of any contradiction, that in the moral vertues Christ's actions are our instructions; and no lesse may the like rule hold, that in the contriving of prudent government, the impressions and footsteps of God's wisdome ... be in the poynt of regiment our directories for imitation.

Rather than a secular theory of government, Forset envisioned one based upon divine law, 'by marking and matching of the workes of the finger of God'. Indeed, God's laws were not only embodied in the government, and in the relations between subjects and their sovereign, but also in the Church. For this reason Forset styled the Church as a body politic, a comparison which he found in scripture: 'The like comparison is most divinely enlarged by a much better orator, and in a much more important point of the inseparable union of the members of Christ with their head.'[58] That there was a firm union between the communicants of the Church of England and Christ was a point that other writers would develop at length; Forset confined himself to laying out an account of sovereignty that was applied to a society in which Church and commonwealth were conjoined.

There were a number of contemporary accounts on which Forset could draw. James VI of Scotland, writing in 1598, employed the examples of biblical kings to argue that ecclesiastical power was an ancient duty of 'religious princes'. This was an effective response, not only to Catholics who argued that the papacy was of sounder ancient status than kingship, but also to Protestant reformers – with whom James had already dealt – who clamoured for alteration of the settled faith. In putting the case for the Crown as governor of the Church, James repeated the substance of the English coronation oath. In addition, he argued that the coronation oaths of Scotland and other Christian states included a pledge to 'defend' the religion of the realm:

And therefore in the Coronation of their owne Kings, as well as of every Christian monarch they give their oath, first to maintain the Religion presently professed within their countrie, according to their lawes, whereby it is established, and to punish all those that should presse to alter, or disturb the profession thereof.[59]

---

[58] Forset, 'To the Reader', in his *A comparatiue discourse of the bodies natural and politique* (London, 1606).

[59] James I, *The true lawe of free monarchies: or The reciprock and mutuall dutie betwixt a free king, and his naturall subiects* (Edinburgh, 1598). Reprinted in *The political works of James I*, ed. C. H. McIlwain (Cambridge, MA, 1918), p. 55.

In addition to examples from the primitive church, James employed the metaphor of the body politic in order to style the sovereign as the 'head' of the body, charged with 'preventing all evil that may come to the body, or any part thereof'. The corporeal metaphor acted as an effective tool for pointing up the dangers of faction, and as a justification for the use of the civil power to 'cut off some rotten members ... to keep the rest of the body in integrity'. He also argued that the entire commonwealth was superintended by divine law, which served as a check both to tyrants and the possibility of the people rising against their king: 'And therefore in time arm yourselves with patience and humility, since [the king] hath the only power to make him, hath the only power to unmake him; and ye onely to obey, bearing with those straits that I now forshew you, as with the finger of God, which lieth not to you to take off.'[60] Others looked to higher orders, what one writer called the 'Harmonium Coeli' and the 'concordium mundi', in order to argue that it was the task of the sovereign to make order out of chaos, via 'concordia discors' whereby 'contrary factions' were reconciled.[61]

Similarly, Forset began by arguing that all stable commonwealths were based on a relationship of mutual obligation between subjects and sovereigns. Each was bound by either law or duty, and hence 'the ruler should wholy indevor the welfare of his people', and should do so by governing 'by lawes ... the soule of sovereignty'. No apologist for the unlimited power of kings, Forset instead argued that it was unnatural for the sovereign to operate outside the law. Since he saw law as analogous to reason, he argued that it was impossible for the head to act in ways that had the potential to injure the rest of the body: 'the Soveraigne will infringe law, no more than the soule will renounce reason'. Subjects, meanwhile, must leave the process of rule to its proper officers, for,

when any subject shall either deny unto his Soveraigne, or take unto Himselfe, what is it els than if an inferior and ministeriall spirit, who hath no other function in the body, but as an agent or deputy of the soule in the workes to him assigned, shall intrudingly usurpe, arrogate and possesse the place, name and office of the soule itselfe? except we should witlessly imagine two soules in one body, like two sunnes in one firmament.[62]

This not only established the unified and indivisible quality of sovereignty, but also made the point that the state could not persist if there were competitors for power within it. Here we recognise the condition of *imperium in imperio*, or a sovereignty within a sovereignty. Seventeenth-century writers used this idea both as an argument for the necessity of conformity to a single

[60] Ibid., pp. 57, 65.
[61] Richard Eedes, *Six learned and godly Sermons* (London, 1604), p. 2.
[62] Forset, *Comparatiue discourse*, pp. 3–4, 10.

pattern of worship and as a theory of politics. The latter theme animated
Forset's work, underlying not only his injunctions against disobedient subjects, but also those aimed at governors themselves. Hence, 'where the
judgement of the sovereign swerveth from sinceritie ... there his will and
all decrees and executions following the same, must of necessity be culpable
and turne to wrong'. Therefore, prudent governors did not 'take to themselves that absoluteness of sole power in law-giving', but rather relied on
their councils and parliament.[63]

Forset argued at length about the dangers of uncontrolled 'opinion' within
the commonwealth: here again the figure of the body politic proved its
metaphorical worth, for it offered an effective way of accounting for the
existence of a number of political interests within the state.[64] Not only did
this furnish a case against faction, but it also allowed for positive statements
about the nature of sovereignty, frequently styled by Forset as the 'mind' or
soul of the state:

The mind must not suffer itselfe, for want of resolution, to be distracted by diversitie
of undiscussed opinions as wavering and wandering without judgement, having
warre within itselfe: So the governor may not well admit or harken unto different
or factious sectes, tending to the disturbing or instabilitie of his government.[65]

Forset's comments on the danger of faction revealed how many political
writers of the early seventeenth century tended to conceive of their polity in
terms of stability, unity, and order. The burden of rule was less about the
vigorous assertion of power than it was about the reconciliation of competing
interests; in fact, all those interests which diverged from those defined by the
sovereign were seen as social solvents. Transposed to the Church, the additional dimension of religious faction meant that the maintenance of religious
unity was a crucial aspect of governance. Yet, it is also important to remember
that conformist writers posited the concurrence of civil and ecclesiastical
concerns, and so any general expression about the dangers of faction applied
to both aspects of the realm. Forset used the concept of 'regiment' to describe
the civil and ecclesiastical power, and the danger of faction:

So if the Soverraigne in the precincts of his regiment, shall suffer an overgrowing
inequalitie of greatness to get an head, it will quickly gather to it selfe a syding faction
of like disposed disturbers, which will make a shrewde adventure, both of over-
toppling him, and overturning his state.[66]

---

[63] Forset's pages reflected a dominant theme in seventeenth-century ideas: the dangers of 'evil
council' whereby the sovereign was led 'unwittingly by wrong reportes of some neare about
him' (ibid., p. 17).

[64] Hence Thomas Scott: 'Bodys pollotique, are best seene in bodies natural; and what is here
orderly, cannot be there absurd.' *Vox Dei* ([Holland?, 1624]), p. 42.

[65] Forset, *Comparatiue discourse*, p. 17.   [66] Ibid., p. 31.

Evidence of *religious* faction clearly appeared in the Gunpowder Plot, which revived a well-established fear of Catholicism in English culture.[67] Indeed, Catholics represented precisely the sort of faction capable of 'overturning' the state: loyal to the Pope, they had to forswear allegiance to the Crown. To remain Catholics, they had to reject the notion that the Church of England was in any sense a 'true' or 'ancient' church, and of course this statement held implications for the ecclesiastical sovereignty claimed by the Crown. In order for the sovereignty of the Crown in all its dimensions to persist, objections of this type had to be vigorously answered.[68] Forset – who as a JP examined the plotters – defended the Crown and described Catholicism as a 'religion, though never so erroneous or schismaticall'.[69] It had long been a matter of political wisdom, expressed in Matthew 6: 24, that 'no one can serve two masters'.[70] Forset's response to the problem entailed an elucidation of why one master should reign supreme.

Earlier in the *Discourse*, Forset had recounted the 'great giant' described by Hermes Trismegistus in his 'Divine Pymander'[71]: 'whose head was above the firmament, his necke, shoulders, and upper partes in the heavens, his arms and hands reaching to East and West'.[72] Perhaps this was the inspiration for Forset's choice of metaphor (and perhaps too for the title-page of

---

[67] For anti-Catholicism see Alison Shell, *Catholicism and the English literary imagination, 1558–1660* (Cambridge, 1999), and Peter Lake, 'Anti-popery: the structure of a prejudice', in *Conflict in early Stuart England*, ed. Richard Cust and Ann Hughes (London, 1989), pp. 72–106.

[68] The debates surrounding the Oath of Allegiance are helpful in understanding the nature of this problem. In addition to Michael Questier, *Conversion, politics and religion in England*, see Martinus Becanus, *The English iarre: or disagreement amongst the ministers of great Brittaine, concerning the Kinges supremacy* ([St Omer, 1612]). Becanus sought to exploit the disarray among English Protestants in order to make the case for the Apostolic nature of ecclesiastical power over that claimed by 'emperors': '[S]eeing that neither Tiberius or Pilate, nor Herod, nor any other secular Prince, which then lived, did by his favour, authorise the force of the law; but that it came from the Apostles themselves. For that they, by their Apostolicall Authority and power, which they had received from Christ, did decree, and promulgate that law' (p. 31). Forset contributed a tract to the debate on the Oath of Allegiance: *A defence of the right of kings. Wherein the power of the papacie ouer princes, is refuted; and the Oath of Allegeance iustified* (London, 1624). In this work Forset argued that 'every Prince hath *iure divino*, the supremacy of outward preservation of the Church, and Ecclesiastical causes within his Territories and Dominions' (p. 62). In making this claim, Forset was emphasising the point that God had appointed guardians over His Church, whose office was only legitimate if they preserved 'the fayth and Doctrine thereof, from all wronges or corruptions Forraigne or Domesticall' (p. 63).

[69] Forset, *Comparatiue discourse*, p. 51.

[70] A well-known example of this strand of thought is the anonymous *An homelie against disobedience and wylfull rebellion* (London, [1570?]).

[71] Forset would presumably have known the French edition, *Le Pimandre de Mercure Trismagiste*, trans. François de Foix, bp of Aire (Bourdeaux, 1579).

[72] Forset, 'To the Reader', in his *Comparatiue discourse*.

Hobbes' famous work).[73] It allowed Forset – in a manner that anticipated Hobbes – to develop an account of co-ordinate sovereignty:

I wish from my heart (though I show but by a simily) that in the real likewise by such concordance of the parts in each degree, might fasten so their fayth each to each other, as that the *disposing of many to one service*, did tend to a more full & more sure performance of the same: so should both the civil and spiritual side, together with the honourable shoulders on both sides, equally part between them the common care, and much importing worke of upholding the majestie of supreme authoritie, without any fainting or interruption.[74]

The condition that 'disposed' the many to one 'service' corresponded exactly to that solemnification of obedience brought about by the oaths of supremacy and allegiance. Indeed, what Forset described was nothing less than a 'covenant' between subjects and the sovereign, based in equal measure on civil and religious harmony. The success of the covenant depended not only on the unity and indivisibility of civil and ecclesiastical power, but also on the concentration of this power in one person, 'the supreme governing over all ... hath but one head; as if it were utterly impossible, or unsufferablie mischevous, to admit any partnership in the regal dignitie'.[75] Hence, added to the dimension of the sovereignty of the Crown was an account of the structure through which this power was channelled – what William Laud would call the '*Coagmentatio Duplex* ... the double buckling and knitting of the state together'.[76]

Despite his emphasis on the problems and nature of sovereignty, one should be careful in comparing the theories of Forset to those of Hobbes. That the latter posited a link between the ecclesiastical and civil power is well known, if little enough studied.[77] Indeed, Hobbes clearly dealt with the problem of the body politic of the Church and the unity of ecclesiastical authority:

But the Church, if it be one person, is the same thing with a Common-wealth of Christians; called a *Common-wealth*, because it consisteth of men united in one person, their Soveraign; and a *Church*, because it consisteth in Christian men, united in one Christian Sovereign. But if the Church be not one person, then it hath no authority at all.[78]

---

[73] For this see Charles W. A. Prior, 'Trismegistus "his great giant": a source for the title-page of Hobbes' *Leviathan*', *Notes and Queries*, 51 (2004), 366–70.
[74] Forset, *Comparatiue discourse*, pp. 56–7.
[75] Ibid., p. 57.   [76] Laud, *A sermon preached on Munday*, pp. 12, 14.
[77] See, J. G. A. Pocock, 'Time, history and eschatology in the thought of Thomas Hobbes', in his *Politics, language and time: essays on political thought and history* (New York, 1971), pp. 149–201; Patricia Springborg, 'Leviathan and the problem of ecclesiastical authority', *Political Theory*, 3 (1975), 289–303.
[78] Thomas Hobbes, *Leviathan, or The matter, forme, & power of a common-wealth ecclesiasticall and civill* (London, 1651), pp. 205–6. That the word 'ecclesiastical' appears first in the title is worth noting.

Writers of the early seventeenth century would have grasped the importance of this statement: a church riven by schism could not persist as a church, and so it fell to the sovereign to maintain uniformity in doctrine and discipline. We have already seen that contemporaries believed that dereliction of this duty meant that the king fell into sin. Indeed, Jacobean writers consistently argued that faction or 'innovation' in the Church would topple the institutions of state, among them the Crown.

'Absolutism' does not adequately capture the arguments that Forset sought to advance. Contemporaries conceived of social wholes in organic terms in order both to articulate a unitary view of sovereignty and to account for the destructive tendencies of faction in all its guises. Forset's use of the corporate metaphor allowed him to catalogue the divers 'diseases' of the state, 'yet no way comparable for danger to Atheisme, Popery, and disloyaltie'. Moreover, 'innovation' in any form was regarded as a threat to the stability of the Jacobean ecclesiastical polity, and so Forset weighed into the great contemporary debate about reform: 'alterations ... be accounted very perilous, because the imputation of that which is inate and primitive, is intended to tend to the decay and destruction of nature'. Here we might recall the preamble to the Thirty-nine Articles, which held that the sovereign's task was to 'conserve and maintain' religion. Bringing the argument to a close, Forset affirmed this wisdom: 'So the Magistrate's function is either to hold all upright when the state is in a good cause, or to recover and recure all that which shall become unsound.'[79] Once again, the Crown's sovereignty included an ecclesiastical dimension, itself expressed in the preservation of 'custom'. Forset's contribution to the debate amounted to a definition of ecclesiastical and civil sovereignty, united in the person of the king, and mirroring the dual nature of the religious commonwealth.

As we have seen, the sovereignty of the Crown was frequently presented in historical terms, both in tracts and in longer books that sought to trace the succession of religious kings in England. John Hayward's work on sovereignty is a case in point. A prolific antiquary and civil lawyer, Hayward also wrote popular works of devotion; however, despite this clear interest in theological issues, historians most often classify him as a 'secular' political writer.[80] This is particularly surprising given the fact that Hayward penned a powerful defence of the ecclesiastical supremacy during the year – 1606 – when the Church was under vigorous attack by Protestant writers like John

---

[79] Forset, *Comparatiue discourse*, pp. 63, 66–8, 72, 75.
[80] See Burgess, *The politics of the ancient constitution*, pp. 25, 72, 124–5, 227. While Sommerville has noted aspects of Hayward's theories on the nature of the ecclesiastical supremacy of the Crown, these theories have yet to be fully integrated with the substantial volume of contemporary literature on the Jacobean Church. See *Royalists and patriots*, p. 191.

Burges, Henry Jacob, and William Bradshaw. As with Wilkes and Forset, the immediate context for Hayward's pamphlet was furnished by the debates over clerical subscription and the Oath of Allegiance, each having implications for the legitimacy of the royal supremacy over the Church, and thus a spur to renewed statements pertaining to this legitimacy. Hayward devoted a pamphlet to an argument that upheld the ecclesiastical sovereignty of James VI and I.

While the *Discourse* lacked characters designated by name, it was structured *as* a discourse, wherein a wise preceptor, 'N', held forth at a dinner attended by 'persons of most principal note'. The topic was 'the Bill propounded in Parliament against Recusants, and of the Oath of supremacie, which was appointed generally to be taken'.[81] Modelled on the Elizabethan Oath of Supremacy, the Oath of Allegiance (1606) enjoined Catholics to affirm the King's immunity from excommunication or papal deprivation; the implication of the oath was that the papacy retained no jurisdiction in England, and had not since the Elizabethan Act of Supremacy of 1559.[82] However, given the vigorous tradition of Catholic attacks on the royal supremacy, frequent reaffirmations of the Crown's position were necessary. Hayward had already engaged with Catholics in a controversy over the succession, so he was returning to familiar ground.[83]

However, Hayward's argument was not intended to answer Catholic challenges alone, but rather all criticisms of the Crown's power to establish and maintain doctrine and discipline: 'There is but one truth in religion, which is not subject to any humane power: but the discipline thereof, or matters of circumstance and externall form, are held by our Church to depend on the power of the Prince.' While Hayward did not distinguish between the 'visible' and 'invisible' church, he clearly argued that ceremonies and all things that conformists labelled 'indifferent' fell within the jurisdiction of the Crown. Like Edward Forset, Hayward argued that 'order' was the aim of those who were 'appointed for the very head of a society' who 'must give both direction and motion to the principal actions of the whole bodie'. The figure of the body politic was the analogy of choice for those seeking to provide an account of sovereignty, as well as a warning against faction.

[81] John Hayward, *A reporte of a discourse concerning supreme power in affairs of religion* (London, 1606), sigs. A⁵, B⁺. For additional aspects of Hayward's political theory, see Brian Levack, *The civil lawyers in England, 1603–1641* (Oxford, 1973), pp. 89–90, 97, 100–1, 107, 113–15, 116.
[82] For the Elizabethan legislation, see *Tudor constitution*, ed. Elton, pp. 372–7, 410–14.
[83] The writings of Catholic controversialists were crucial to debates in the Jacobean Church. See Peter Holmes, *Resistance and compromise: the political thought of the Elizabethan Catholics* (Cambridge, 1982), pp. 129–165. See also John Hayward, *An answer to the first part of a certaine conference, concerning succession* (London, 1603).

Catholics and reforming Protestants – whom Hayward described as the 'two extremes of religion' – made it 'impossible for that state to stand, much less flourish and thrive'.[84]

Hayward mined history and a range of texts for examples of the dangers of religious competition, and the relationship of religion to political power. The importance of religion in good commonwealths was stressed with a point drawn from Lactantius, who 'affirmeth it the only means to knit and conserve man in mutual societie'. Likewise, in the law code of Justinian Hayward found a pedigree for the role of bishops in the process of maintaining uniformity, and described the episcopate as a conduit of the sovereign power: 'Hereupon also it is necessarilie expedient, that they who beare the sovereigntie of the state, should alwaies manage the affaires of religion; either by themselves, or by some of their appointment within the same State; and never receive direction and rule from a foraine power.'[85] Clearly, Hayward tailored his text to meet the demands of the debates surrounding clerical subscription and the Oath of Allegiance, for not only did he argue that the power of the papacy was subject to *limitation*, but also that the power of the Crown was *extended* through episcopal jurisdiction. It also clearly addressed the political problem created by Catholic recusants – double allegiance: 'That Prince whose subjects soules are in subjection to a stranger for matters of religion, shall neither prevaile more against his enemies, nor beare greater authoritie amongst his own people, then the stranger shall limit him leave.'[86]

The solution to the problems of faction and allegiance was found in the person of the 'Godly prince', whose jurisdiction over the Church was affirmed by a wealth of historical precept.[87] Where others would cite the examples of biblical figures, Hayward reported the findings of ancient authors. Hence, from Justinian we learn 'that it was a custom among the Jewes, to have the same men both Princes and Priests'. At other times, kings 'gave orders in matters of religion, and appointed not only inferior Priests and officers ... but also high Priests'.[88] Included in these orders of religion were ceremonies that, at the time of Hayward's writing, were a topic of debate between and among members of the English clergy; those who refused subscription did so by resorting to the charge that the ceremonies were of recent human invention. Hayward's response was different from the

---

[84] Hayward, *Reporte of a discourse*, pp. 4, 8, 10.
[85] Ibid., p. 11. Often, the argument proceeded with a flurry of classical references: 'For the Church (saieth Optatus) is a part of the State: and (as another said) Religion must be in a commonwealth, and not the Contrarie. Upon which ground Diotogenes in Stoboeus said; A perfect King must of necessitie be a good Commander, and Judge, and Priest' (p. 11).
[86] Ibid., p. 12.
[87] See William Lamont, *Godly rule: politics and religion, 1603–60* (London, 1969), pp. 28–56.
[88] Hayward, *Reporte of a discourse*, p. 15.

standard conformist position, for instead of seeking an ancient pedigree for the ceremonies themselves, he subsumed them within the ecclesiastical jurisdiction of the supreme ruler. In a concession to ecclesiastical history, Hayward illustrated the point with reference to pagan monarchies: 'The Kings of Persia, under whose government the second great empire was founded, are acknowledged by all writers to have been inaugurated to be the princes of their sacred ceremonies.' A citation from Livy affirmed that the Romans followed a similar precept: 'the chiefest in power had authoritie to give order in religion ... for excluding the use of foraigne ceremonies and rites'.[89] Yet there were negative aspects to the theory as well, to the effect that kingly competence depended on the preservation of the true religion; here, Eusebius furnished the example: 'From hence it proceeded, that as the Kings prooved good or evill, so the true religion was either observed or neglected.'[90]

The second half of the dialogue developed the case that the English Church had descended from the Apostles and thus to the Jacobean period. The Apostolic succession was a 'note' put forward by Catholic controversialists in support of the contention that their church had descended directly and without interruption from the Apostles; on this succession they predicated all aspects of Roman doctrine and governance.[91] In response, Hayward sought to recapture the history of the church in the West from Roman Catholicism, and to claim it for English Protestantism. Central to his history was an account of the succession of non-papal governors. Hence, Suetonius' testimony recalled the first Augustan age that would become the model for English society a century after Hayward wrote: 'Augustus annexed the greatest pontificate to the imperiall dignitie, to whom the people by the law of Royalty transferred all their power as well in religion as in civil affairs.' This ecclesiastical covenant was what Jacobean conformists, armed with the proposition that good commonwealths had religion at their foundation, sought to promote in the English setting. The oaths of subscription and allegiance furnished the occasion for precisely the sort of transfer of power that Hayward described. In addition, the Crown claimed a prerogative right to assemble councils – like that held at

---

[89] Ibid., pp. 18, 19. He described the Roman priests as 'Pontifices', which derives from the Latin, *facere*, meaning to 'offer sacrifice'. It is important to note here that Hayward did not seek to present an exclusively Christian history (Chinese and Islamic examples testify to his eclecticism), but rather a history that presented examples in which a relation between political and religious jurisdiction was united in a single officer.

[90] Ibid., p. 15.

[91] For an analysis of this topic, see Anthony Milton, *Catholic and reformed: the Roman and Protestant churches in English Protestant thought, 1600–1640* (Cambridge, 1995), pp. 128–72.

Hampton Court – to debate aspects of doctrine and discipline: 'Now, when any difference did arise in matters of faith; when any greate schisme or disturbance was maintained in the Church; the emperors did use to assemble their Bishops in common council, and those things that were by them decreed, were afterwards confirmed by Imperial constitution.'[92] Citing Socrates Scholasticus, the successor to Eusebius, Hayward found an ancient pedigree for the exercise of imperial religious power: 'When the Emperors began to be Christians, the affairs of the Church depended on them; in so much as the greatest Councels were alwaies assembled by their appointment.'[93] Hence, the kings of England claimed an ancient jurisdiction in spiritual affairs.

Prior to embarking on his discussion of Catholic Rome, Hayward's history of ecclesiastical governors ranged beyond the bounds of Christianity. In the initial stages of the work, he simply described the universal qualities of sovereigns, regardless of religion. In the latter stages of the piece, he united an analysis of the qualities of Christian emperors with a revised history of the Western church; his aim was to integrate the Church of England with this history. Hayward wanted not only to establish James' ecclesiastical jurisdiction as superior to that of the pope, but also to lend legitimacy to diocesan episcopacy and clerical deprivation – the power and jurisdiction of bishops that caused controversy in the Jacobean Church. In places, this became an historical account of the process of clerical subscription: 'The Emperor being both in common estimates, and in very truth a skilful governor, is president strength to synodall sentences; he setteth ecclesiastical orders in forme, he giveth law for the life and civil carriage of those who serve at the altar.' These latter issues pertained to the outward governance and ordering of the 'externall forme' of the Church, which was distinct from the 'essential forme, consisting in the true substance and foundation of faith'.[94] Following St Augustine, Hayward posited that the 'essential form' remained in a state of constant perfection, but was brought into the world via the 'external form' of the Church. Yet this external form could become corrupted, and here Hayward identified the central problem with the Church of Rome.

For Hayward, the Roman church's deviation from the essential form meant that it could not claim to be the 'true' church, descended from the Apostles. The nerve was severed with the rise of the papacy, since which time the 'true' church languished in the wilderness. Rome maintained its supremacy by force and fraud: 'Again, what necessity had the Popes to use force of arms, when the consciences of men were under their command? whilest this rule held good, cloisters and Colleges were instead of Castles unto them; and religious persons were in steed of many armies.' Hayward's

[92] Hayward, *Reporte of a discourse*, p. 30.   [93] Ibid., pp. 23–4, 26.   [94] Ibid., pp. 26, 27.

reference to the English Colleges did double duty, for they were both the point of origin for missionaries bound for England, and the home of efforts on the part of Catholic controversialists to buttress their church's authority with massive works of ecclesiastical history and theology.[95] It was precisely this history that Hayward sought to dismantle, and so he depicted the human holders of the papal office as having become corrupted by 'violence and ambition' which had 'pulled many Bishops of Rome from their owne judgement, in making claim to that authoritie which they never had title to hold'.[96] This led Hayward to conclude that the papacy was not handed to St Peter, but rather to St Linus.[97] An array of ancient writers testified that Christian emperors and kings superintended the ancient church:

> For divers testimonies of St Paul do beare against [Peter's jurisdiction]: St Augustine, S. Cyprian and others of principall authoritie in the Church doe expressly denie it. Whereas the scripture giveth so large and plain testimonie, both for the title and authoritie of Kings, as it seemeth no greater can be added thereunto.[98]

To argue simply that Hayward's tract dealt with the concept of sovereignty would severely neglect the point of the work. Within the context of the debates over clerical subscription and the Oath of Allegiance, Hayward's work emerged as a powerful contribution to the question of the legitimacy of the English Church and the Crown's jurisdiction over it. Recapturing the Church from the Catholic tradition, and designating the Roman Church as 'corrupt', Hayward made a strong case for the Church of England as the descendant of the 'ancient' church – again conjoining antiquity and authority. His second achievement is defined by his use of both Christian and pagan sources to illustrate the link between civil and ecclesiastical authority, suggesting that the discussion of both themes could be carried on with reference to a single historical narrative. Finally, Hayward was not the only conformist with an interest in linking the reformed Church of England with the early Christian church. Most conformists dealt with this issue to a greater or lesser degree, as they used the Church Fathers to bolster their positions, but one – Thomas Bell – dealt with the Christian historical tradition at great length and depth, seeking to unite monarchical sovereignty with the doctrinal identity of the established Church of England.

---

[95] Peter Guilday, *English Catholic refugees on the Continent, 1558–1795* (London, 1989). The Colleges were so unpopular with conformists that William Allen, their founder, sought to defend them. See *An apologie and true declaration of the institution and endeuours of the two English colleges, the one in Rome, the other now resident in Rhemes* ([Rheims], 1581).

[96] Hayward, *Reporte of a discourse*, pp. 38, 45.

[97] The early episcopal lists gave Linus as Bishop of Rome after Peter and Paul. His feast day, 23 September, was suppressed by Vatican II in 1969.

[98] Hayward, *Reporte of a discourse*, p. 47.

THE CHURCH IN HISTORY: BELL'S *REGIMENT* AND THE ANCIENT AND
REFORMED TRADITIONS[99]

In 1610, Bodley's librarian, Thomas James, published the first in a series of
tracts that called for new editions of the works of the Church Fathers. They
were necessary, he argued, in order to 'shew the corruptions of the printed
copies of either Papists or Protestant editions'.[100] What James envisioned
was an authoritative set of texts that would form the core of a controversial
arsenal, to be used by divines in the course of printed religious debates. Yet he
aimed at something more complex, for he realised that in order for the
Church of England to be defended against her Roman and Protestant critics,
links would have to be drawn between her and the 'ancient' church. At stake
was nothing less than the legitimacy of the Church of England, and this
legitimacy demanded that something like an official 'history' be compiled.[101]

James' emphasis on the textual tradition of Christianity provides us with
an important insight into the burden facing English conformists in the period
after the Reformation. Not only did they have to define the Church as a
political or corporate institution, but they had also to explain how it retained
a legitimate spiritual aspect. Put simply, they had to demonstrate that the
Church of England was a 'true' church, that is, that it took part in the
spiritual association which had been established by Christ, and had continued to exist on earth from then onward. The church was to be the embodiment of Christ, and true Christians had to partake in that body in order to
receive the gift of salvation. For Protestants generally, the church was seen to
have continued in the Word, and it was this continuity that they offered in
response to Romanist claims that the papacy represented a sounder link with
Christ. However, English Protestant conformists had a further problem, for
their Church, overseen by the sovereign and a clerical hierarchy, was open to
the charge of not being sufficiently reformed. This question was explored in
the course of debates on ceremonies and governance, themselves the subject of
the following chapters. In short, English conformists had to demonstrate both

---

[99] An abbreviated version of this section is published as Charles W. A. Prior, 'Ancient *and*
reformed?: Thomas Bell and Jacobean conformist thought', *Canadian Journal of History*, 38
(2003), 425–38.
[100] Thomas James, *The humble supplication of Thomas James student in diuinity, and keeper of
the publicke librarie at Oxford, for reformation of the ancient Fathers Workes, by papists
sundrie ways depraued* (London, [ca. 1607]).
[101] Matthew Parker (Archbishop of Canterbury during the Elizabethan reconstruction) worked
to trace the early church from Christ, through Joseph of Arimathea, and thence to Britain.
The result, *De antiquitate Britannicae ecclesiae & priuilegiis ecclesiae Cantuariensis, cum
Archepiscopis eiusdem* ([London], 1572), was still in print in 1729. See Kevin Sharpe, *Sir
Robert Cotton, 1586–1631: history and politics in early modern England* (Oxford, 1979),
pp. 8–9.

that their Church was ancient, and also that its mode of hierarchical government and laws against non-conformity did not violate the tenets of
Protestantism or the laws of England.

As we shall see, English conformists were reluctant to dispense altogether
with the textual tradition – the Doctors, Fathers, and Councils – which, prior
to the Reformation, had been the sole possession of Rome.[102] Indeed, it was
partly the burden of answering the attacks of Roman controversialists that
led post-Reformation conformists to engage with the Fathers and Councils
on an epic and exhaustive scale. For example, the Catholic/conformist
controversy over Christ's descent into Hell led to an exchange that lasted
until the end of the reign of James VI and I. Yet the theological problem –
whether Christ had suffered in Hell – was only the issue via which a more
compelling problem was revealed. Both sides drew upon a common textual
tradition, and this made answering one's opponent a tricky business. Most
often, writers attacked each other on the basis of faulty scholarship: unreli-
able translations of key passages from the Fathers, the use of discredited
editions, bias, and the glossing of passages in a manner that distorted their
true meaning.[103] In other cases, it was the distortion of contemporary controversialists that was at issue. Hence, in the course of a protracted exchange
between Theophilius Higgons and Thomas Morton, then Dean of
Gloucester, the latter remarked of his adversary's text that 'there are many
hundreds of testimonies alleged out of the Romish writers, wherein they are
found to contradict one another in almost every question'.[104] Morton's work
took the form of an extended animadversion, or line-by-line response,
wherein a passage from Higgons' text was reproduced and then followed
by a painstaking criticism. While Higgons attacked English conformists for
depriving ministers for 'trifles' like 'crosse, cap, and surplice' at the expense
of the far more important matter of Christ's putative meeting with the Devil,
Morton retorted that, concerning Christ's descent into Hell, the Roman
church had failed to offer sound testimony 'either from the Apostolical
tradition, or from perspicuous places of Scriptures', and so side-stepped
Higgons' original criticism that English conformity was unsound on major
theological questions.[105]

There were others, however, who were unwilling to let Morton off the
hook so easily. One of these was the prolific Catholic controversialist

---

[102] For a discussion, see John K. Luoma, 'Who owns the Fathers?: Hooker and Cartwright on
the authority of the primitive church', *Sixteenth Century Journal*, 3 (1977), 45–59.

[103] This aspect of religious dispute remains to be adequately explored, but see Anthony Grafton,
Forgers and critics: creativity and duplicity in Western scholarship (London, 1990).

[104] Thomas Morton, *A direct answer vnto the scandalous exceptions, which Theophilus
Higgons hath lately obiected against D. Morton* (London, 1609), sig. A³ʳ.

[105] Morton, *Direct answer*, pp. 20, 22.

Richard Broughton, whose defence of Higgons appeared shortly after Morton's book. Broughton focussed on the inconsistencies that he found in the writings of Morton's peers, the defenders of English conformity; in a strange twist that would often be repeated, Broughton sided with Protestant reformists in suggesting that conformists had engaged in a deliberate mis-interpretation of the standard authorities in order to bolster the argument for the English Church:

If I could produce no other presumption, or argument of wilful corruptions, falsifica-tions, slanders, and other enormous dealings of that kinde, in the published writings of M. Doctor Morton, Protestant Dean of Gloucester (as I am informed) then only his ministerial function and calling itselfe: yet the late (and present also) Protestant Professors, Doctors, and chiefest handlers of Divinity, of his own profession, and the publickly authorised Examiners and Approvers of their printed bookes, doe testifie it to be so usual and agreed a custom between them, to corrupt, falsifie, slander and abuse the holy Scriptures, Councels, Fathers, and all Sacred Authorities.[106]

This sort of argument was nothing new for Broughton, whose works suggest an excellent feel for English Protestant controversies that exceeded the capabilities of many of those writers who would have counted themselves among the defenders of the English Church.[107] Indeed, not only did Broughton make every attempt to side with English reformists, but he also suggested that they too sided with him, for Broughton knew very well that English conformists altered their posture depending on which group – Catholics or reformists – they were addressing. This, he argued, subverted the conformist case:

And thus I might alleage from others, especially triumphing in this manner, either when they write against Puritans ... as the Bishop of Wincester is cited: or when they speak in generall, and the authorities of Fathers are neither to be answered, as produced by Catholics, or alleaged for Protestants; as it appeareth in those places of Dr Sutcliffe, and M. Willet's great and glorious speaches of the Fathers. But when these men are either to answer those primitive Fathers, cited for our cause; or stand upon their testimony in particular for themselves, *the case is altered*, as is objected to the Bishop of Wincester, by his Puritan opposite.[108]

---

[106] Richard Broughton, *A plaine patterne of a perfect Protestant professor* ([S.I.: English secret press, ca. 1608]), p. 7.

[107] Broughton (d. 1634) was a Catholic historian, who was briefly at Oxford, from where he transferred to the English College at Rheims, where he studied Hebrew, English antiquities, and theology. Wood mentions that during 1626, Broughton 'was entered a student into the publicke library [the Bodleian]', where he had 'formerly studied ... to gain materials for the publishing of certaine books'. This may explain Broughton's grasp of the writings of his opponents, and suggests also that the Penal Laws did not stringently apply to the republic of letters. See Wood, *Athenae Oxonienses*, vol. II, p. 854.

[108] Richard Broughton, *The first part of Protestants proofes, for Catholickes religion and recusancy* ([Printed by the English secret press], 1607), pp. 32–3. Bilson's opposite was the

In another example, published by the Catholic writer Edward Maihew in 1608, we find a similar use of Protestant writers. Writing in response to William Crashaw on the authority of the Catholic church to devise its own manner of governance, Maihew observed that English conformists – among them Richard Field, Thomas Hutton, and Gabriel Powel – were putting forth a *Catholic* vision of governance: 'our English Protestants themselves disputing against the Puritans, are forced to acknowledge that the Church hath authority to proscribe orders for her government, which everyone is bound to obey'.[109] Both Catholics and Protestants knew that the Church was vulnerable on the issue of human authority and 'custom'.

At the root of the debate was a problem as old as Christianity itself. It is useful to recall that Christianity was built upon the theological and doctrinal foundations of an already ancient faith, through which God spoke to His people. One of the burdens of early Christian theology, therefore, was to establish that the Messiah had come in the manner foreseen by the prophets, and that while His coming entailed a shift in theology, it did not sever the links with the covenant made between God and Abraham.[110] In other words, in the link to that covenant lay the legitimacy of the faith itself, and the 'denominations' of contemporary Judaism, whether Sadducee, Pharisee, or Essene, tended to divide on how strict interpretations of the Abrahamic tradition and the Mosaic law could be reconciled with Hellenism or the influences of Roman culture and imperial rule.[111] The tension between early Christians and other adherents to the Jewish tradition was fuelled by a dispute about which group could claim possession of the covenant. In a

---

Hebraist Hugh Broughton (no relation to Richard) whose writings against Bilson paid particular attention to the latter's scholarship, especially biblical history. In one example, Broughton averred that perhaps the blame could not be laid exclusively on Bilson, but also on his amanuensis: 'a certain helper who can assiste him to marre all learning and religion'. See Hugh Broughton, *Declaration of general corruption, of religion, Scripture, and all learninge: wrought by D. Bilson* ([Amsterdam?], 1604). Again, the topic of controversy was Christ's descent into Hell, which Broughton discounted in a clever way: 'As Britanie contayning England and Scotland, a Scot is not born in England because he is borne in Brittanie: So Hades conteyning Heaven and HEL, our Lord his Holy soule going to Hades to his Holy Joy, can not be said to go to Hell, because his went to Hades.' See Hugh Broughton, *Two little workes defensiue of our redemption* ([Middelburg], 1604), n. p.

[109] Edward Maihew, *A treatise of the groundes of the old and newe religion* ([Printed by the English secret press, 1608]), p. 50.

[110] My understanding of this aspect of early Christian theology owes a great deal to Henry Chadwick, *The early Church*, vol. 1 of *The Pelican history of the church*, ed. Owen Chadwick, 6 vols. (London, 1967), pp. 9–18.

[111] Modern scholars of English religion have missed a golden opportunity to trace the roots of a debate on predestination to its earliest times. Paul's Letters to the Corinthians dealt with the question of inherent grace versus justification, and this problem may have been inherited from the Essenes, authors of the Dead Sea Scrolls. See A. Lange, *Weisheit und Prädestination: Weisheitliche Urordnung und Prädestination in den Textfunden von Qumran* (Leiden, 1995).

similar way, post-Reformation controversialists offered rival interpretations of the 'doctrine' of the Church: how could it be distinguished? What was the nature of its doctrine and mode of governance? The Reformation was, in essence, a challenge to the Roman church's claims to be the sole earthly embodiment of the ancient church, but with the repudiation of Roman authority, the question was not decisively settled. Protestantism, therefore, was defined too by disputes over the link between the ancient church and its earthly embodiments, and English conformists were anxious to claim that their Church was such an exemplar.[112]

At this point we return to Thomas James, Bodley's Librarian during the Jacobean period. James I's policy of textual production was part of a broader campaign to locate the English Church in both the ancient and reformed traditions.[113] As we have seen, the first was essential for any church seeking to claim legitimacy for its rites and governance, as well as its descent from the church left on earth by Christ. The second ground of legitimacy concerned the agreement of the Church of England with the work of contemporary reformed divines, and here controversialists would emphasise the peculiar character of the English Reformation. Indeed, for conformists the Reformation not only entailed the restoration of the purity of doctrine, worship, governance, and discipline that characterised the church before the rise of Rome, but also, as the Act of Supremacy stated, the restoration of 'ancient jurisdiction' of the Crown over the Church in its dominions. Each of these propositions was challenged: the first, concerning the purity of doctrine, by reformers who questioned aspects of the Church's rites and governance, while the second, concerning the ecclesiastical supremacy of the Crown, was attacked by Roman Catholics who argued that reformation entailed a severing of all Protestant churches from the universal church of Christ.[114] The result of these debates was the emergence of competing

---

[112] S. L. Greenslade, *The English reformers and the Fathers of the Church* (Oxford, 1960).

[113] The bulk of the scholarship on this topic is concerned with debates between conformists and their Catholic opponents. See D. H. Willson, 'James I and his literary assistants', *Huntington Library Quarterly*, 8 (1944–5), pp. 35–57; J. P. Sommerville, 'Jacobean political thought and the controversy over the Oath of Allegiance', (Ph.D. diss., Cambridge University, 1981). A crucial aspect of the Jacobean campaign against Roman Catholicism was Chelsea College, which was founded in 1609 in order to concentrate the polemical activities of those helping to maintain 'the religion professed' in England. See Milton, *Catholic and reformed*, pp. 32–3; D. E. Kennedy, 'King James I's College of controversial divinity at Chelsea', in *Grounds of controversy: three studies of late 16th and early 17th century English polemics*, ed. D. E. Kennedy (Melbourne, 1989), pp. 97–119. Neither Milton or Kennedy consulted what may be the best early contemporary account of the College and its activities, John Darley, *The glory of Chelsey Colledge revived* (London, 1662).

[114] For the Protestant branch of this controversy, see Lake, *Anglicans and Puritans*. Both are treated by Milton, *Catholic and reformed*, and T. H. Wadkins, 'Theological polemic and religious culture in early Stuart England: the Percy / "Fisher" controversies, 1605–41', (Ph.D.

historical narratives of the development of the church: rival accounts of the antiquity and character of Catholic, reformed, and English churches, each of which was informed by a particular reconstruction of the textual tradition of Christianity.[115] Further, these reconstructions were employed in the course of religious controversy, for the ultimate burden of these controversies was to show an uninterrupted and immemorial connection with the ancient church.

Yet the English controversies which form the subject of this study took on a further dimension. For in answer to the charge, put about by reformers, that the Church of England was 'not rightly reformed', English conformists had to defend their Church as being agreeable and superior to that of the reformed churches. Although their texts referred to the testimonies of Bucer, Calvin, or Luther, they argued not only that the Church of England was agreeable to the Word, but also that it enjoyed the power to make determinations in matters of doctrine and discipline. An articulate statement of this position came from Peter Heylyn, looking back on the writings of Jacobean controversialists from the point of view of the Restoration:

> In the managing of which great business, they took the Scripture for their ground, according to the general explication of the ancient Fathers; the practice of the Primitive times for their Rule and Pattern, as it was expressed to them in approved Authors: No regard was had to Luther or Calvin, in the procedure of their Work, but only to the writings of the prophets and Apostles, Christ Jesus being the cornerstone of that excellent structure.[116]

As we shall see with reference to the debate on ceremonies, the theological implications of suggesting that the scripture contained only a 'general' rule for the establishment of rites was a question that concerned many writers. And this was because English controversialists sought to distinguish between points of doctrine and practice enjoined by scripture, and those left to the judgement of the Church. Moreover, the notion that the Church could 'judge' for itself entailed also that it could define both modes of governance and ceremonial practice, and also what constituted heresy; this in turn led to an argument about the practical need for religious conformity. The English Church was thus defined by conformists in terms of antiquity, hierarchy, and sovereignty: it was descended from Christ and the Apostles, possessed of an hierarchy of clerical officers surmounted by a supreme governor, whose ultimate power could be used to impose sanctions on those who disagreed with one or more of its tenets. There was more to the position than a bland assertion of what modern scholars have called 'Erastianism'; rather, the

diss., Graduate Theological Union, Berkeley, CA, 1988), ch. 2. For a bibliography, see Peter Milward, *Religious controversies of the Elizabethan age: a survey of printed sources* (London, 1977).

[115] Milton's *Catholic and reformed* addressed the broad implications of this debate.

[116] Peter Heylyn, *Cyprianus anglicus* (London, 1671), p. 3.

legitimacy of the English Church as a spiritual and political association depended on its being firmly established as partaking in the history of the church left on earth by Christ.[117]

The fluidity of the textual traditions that defined post-Reformation English ecclesiology is well demonstrated by the example of Thomas Bell (fl. 1573–1610). Priest, scholar, and most crucially, a Catholic apostate, Bell brought his considerable talents to bear on the question of the antiquity of the English confession. It might seem that Bell was an unlikely defender of the historical pedigree of the English Church, until one reflects that both Roman and English confessions laid claim to the same textual tradition, that is, the same Fathers of the Church, and the same Councils. Hence, Richard Walpole could argue that the 'Holy fathers' testified to the legitimacy and succession of the 'Catholicke, ancient, and true Church which was left and established by Christ as the true pillar and stay of truth'.[118] In the same year, 1603, Robert Parsons argued that the writings of English Protestants substituted a tradition of heresy for sound doctrine and the 'tradition of the greatest and most ancient Church'.[119] Similarly, Matthew Kellison, Professor of Divinity, and from 1613 head of the English College at Douai, challenged English Protestants to: 'Shew us the origin of their Churches, let them unfolde the order of their bishops which successors, so runneth on from the beginning to the Apostles or apostolical men who lived in the Apostles time'.[120] Indeed, the opening years of the reign of James I abounded with Catholic tracts whose purpose was to challenge the historical pedigree of the English Church.

Bell's work treated with great clarity the themes that form the subject of the debates surveyed in the following chapters. He wrote at a time when the Jacobean settlement was the subject of vigorous debate, and therefore provided excellent insights into the basic tenets of the conformist position. He was interested in the relationship between religion and the political structure of the state, in the nature of obedience and loyalty, and in finding an historical pedigree for the power of the Crown as governor of the Church.

---

[117] See D. Alan Orr, *Treason and the state: law, politics and ideology in the English Civil War* (Cambridge, 2002), pp. 102–3. Dr Orr argues that the seventeenth-century definition of 'Erastianism' entailed an affirmation that the power to 'determine doctrine and exercise discipline' lay with the 'secular magistrate, whether that be king, parliament, or king-in-parliament, rather than with any ecclesiastical body'. As we shall see, the existence of High Commission served to complicate the definition.

[118] Richard Walpole, *A briefe, and cleere confutation, of a new, vaine, and vaunting chalenge, made by O. E.* ([Antwerp], 1603), p. 4.

[119] Robert Parsons, *A treatise of the three conuersions of England from paganisme to Christian religion* ([St Omer], 1603), pp. 127, 129.

[120] Matthew Kellison, *A suruey of the new religion, detecting manie grosse absurdities which it implieth* (Douai, 1603), p. 9.

Second, he considered the question of tradition, and argued that Bancroft's policy of subscription was one of the marks of a sovereign church; this in turn linked with the next theme, which considered the sources of authority by which ceremonies were defined. Reformists argued that the rites of the Church had to be found in scripture, whereas Bell suggested that in certain questions dealing with 'things indifferent', the Church had the power to order its liturgy as it saw fit. A further debate on Bancroft's policy of clerical deprivations defined the fourth theme, concerning the power of the bishops as civil and ecclesiastical functionaries. Finally, he followed Bancroft's example, set forth in works like *Daungerous positions* and *A Suruay of the pretended holy discipline*, and considered the problem of Presbyterian discipline; the shared opinion between the two was that here was a form of church governance that proposed itself as a rival to the mode of government established by the Canons of 1604. Bell's arguments on the 'sovereignty' of the Church were therefore central to the English–Scots controversy that forms the subject of the final chapter of this book.

Bell's *Regiment of the Church*, published in 1606, was not his first contribution to debates on English ecclesiology, and some of his earlier work furnishes a useful guide to the development of his views. In 1593 Bell published an account of his conversion, which he defended on historical grounds: the Roman church, he argued, was merely 'in error', having been propped up by scholars who misrepresented the testimonies of Fathers and Councils. Bell argued that the Reformation in England was, in reality, a *restoration* of the doctrine and governance that had defined the ancient church: 'The religion this day established by Godly laws in this realme of England, is the ancient Christian, catholicke and apostolic doctrine, which was taught by Christ [and] practiced in the primitive Church.'[121] The *Motiues* therefore established the method that would shape the remainder of Bell's work: he engaged with the textual authorities held up by the Roman church as evidence of the legitimacy and antiquity of that institution, and furnished his own translations in order to demonstrate the depth of Roman corruption. Indeed, Bell argued that Protestant theologians treated the tradition with greater respect: 'The Protestants, speaking of the wiser and discreeter sort, do highly reverence the holy fathers and ancient writers, dilligently reade their works, and gladly use them as ordinary helpes and ordinary meanes under God: for and concerning the exact explication of Holy Writ.'[122] In other words, Protestant theologians used the Fathers to

---

[121] Thomas Bell, *Thomas Bels motiues: concerning Romish faith and religion* (Cambridge, 1593)), p. 9.
[122] Bell, *Motiues*, p. 126.

interpret and draw out the message of scripture, whereas their Roman opponents supplanted the Word with a corrupt scholarly tradition.

One of the key Roman corruptions identified by Bell was the argument that the succession of popes beginning with the Apostle Peter was a principal 'note' of the antiquity of the church.[123] Indeed, the schisms experienced in the church had long since broken the line of direct succession, which meant that a more certain badge of antiquity had to be found. Like a good Protestant, Bell suggested that the 'Church doth not consist in men' but in the Word, and offered the concurring testimony of Augustine and Dionysus Areopagatica – himself purportedly converted by Paul (Acts 17).[124] Yet the Word needed an interpreter, and so Bell put forward an argument that would later be developed by Thomas Hobbes: the 'Christian Emperor' was sovereign over his Church, and a mark of this sovereignty was the interpretation of scripture.[125] The argument that Bell employed looked back to the tradition of Christian princes – of whom Constantine was the pioneering exemplar – and argued that this office was far older than the Papacy. Examples of biblical figures like David, Solomon, and Hezekiah were offered as evidence that God sought to establish 'nursing fathers' for His church, and this point allowed Bell to suggest that the hierarchical organisation of the English Church was ordained by scripture, as were those measures needed to combat problems of religious plurality. The argument was fleshed out with a passing reference to Luther's attack on the three 'walls' of Romanism, and principally that policy whereby temporal princes were prevented from calling Councils.

[W]hen any controversies shall arise to the disturbance of the Peace of the Church, then every absolute and Independent Magistrate, must command his Archbishop, Bishops, and other learned Ministers within his territories and dominions, to come together, and celebrate a National council or synod, and then there to debate, discuss, and decide the controversie in religion ... This done, the one civil Independent Magistrate, must call together his wise and grave councellors, and after mature deliberation had with them, confirme whatsoever shall tend to the advancement of God's glory, and the peace of His Church. And withall, he must publishe sharpe penall statutes against all such, as shall with disloyal contumacy violate and transgresse the same.[126]

---

[123] Anthony Milton has argued that, in debates between Roman and Protestant controversialists, the central issue was 'not the question of antiquity, but that of succession'. This misses the point that Roman controversialists believed that the succession of the Popes was indeed a mark of the antiquity of their church – the two were not separate categories. See *Catholic and reformed*, p. 277.

[124] Thomas Bell, *The golden ballance of tryall* (London, 1603), pp. 6, 9, 28.

[125] 'For, whosoever hath a lawful power over any Writing, to make it Law, hath the power also to approve, or disapprove the interpretation of the same.' Hobbes, *Leviathan*, p. 207.

[126] Bell, *Golden ballance*, pp. 37–8.

Here, Bell's task was less to discredit the Roman church than to demonstrate the ways in which the English Church enjoyed the sovereignty transmitted through its 'national' synods, and the Crown in parliament. Also note that Bell did not distinguish between Protestant and Catholic critics of the Crown's ecclesiastical policy – a uniformity of confession and the 'peace' of the Church were matters enjoined by scripture and carried out by the magistrate.

Bell's attacks on the Roman confession were not simply academic exercises intended to justify his own conversion; instead, they represented part of a larger process of controversy in which English writers sought to develop a history of their Church that accounted for the rise of Rome, and the subsequent 'eclipse' of the true church. For Bell, the English Church represented the re-emergence of that eclipsed church, a point that allowed him to downplay the novelty of the Reformation, and instead to depict it as a process which *restored* the true church. In his *Downefall of poperie*, Bell furnished the reader with a chronology of the rise of the papacy in order to show that the popes had once been subservient to emperors, established by God to preserve His 'law and rule'.[127] In other words, Bell contended that it was God's will that popes and other 'bishops', should remain subordinate to supreme civil rulers, a point which drew a quick response from the Jesuit Richard Smith:

> The true difference therefore betwixt Catholiques and English Protestants ... would not be whether the prince or Pope or Ministers ought to be head of the Church, wherein I appeale to any indifferent mans judgement, whether it be more agreeable to God's word, that the successor of S. Peter, upon whom Christ built his Church ... should be head of the Church, or they who are successors to none but beginners of them selves who (as S. Ciprian writeth) no man enacting them Bishops, made themselves Bishops.[128]

Smith's argument exemplified the Catholic position: the scriptures gave firm and irrefutable evidence that the 'true' church descended from Peter, having been 'established' in the first instance by Christ. Hence, the Roman church best represented the 'first institution' – the act of God (*iure divino*) rather than the establishment of men (*iure humano*). A further response to Bell's *Downefall* condemned the author for a corruption of the textual tradition of the Roman church, and particularly his use of Roman theologians to undermine the premises of the Roman confession: 'what treacherous tricks also he practiseth concerning Doctors and Fathers, Councells and Scripture'.[129]

---

[127] Thomas Bell, *The downefall of poperie* (London, 1604), p. 53.

[128] Richard Smith, *An answer to Thomas Bels late challeng named by him The downfal of popery* (Douai, 1605), p. 14.

[129] Philip Woodward, *The fore-runner of Bels downefall* (Douai, 1605), p. 20. See also pp. 23–4.

Common to both responses was an attack on Bell's scholarly method, and the suggestion that the claims of the English Church to legitimacy could only be maintained by a deliberate falsification of the textual tradition.

Clearly the tide of the argument turned on the problem of scholarship. In response to his Jesuit critics, Bell tried a new strategy that sought to reverse the charge that the Church of England was *iure humano* by pointing out that the Roman church was itself founded upon a corruption of the textual tradition. Bell sought to isolate that point in history at which the popes claimed an overwhelming supremacy. Hence the examples of Gregory 'the Great' (ca. 540–604) and the Greek church served as evidence of the subordination of popes to political rulers, while the corruption of Roman theologians was exposed as manufactured props for the papal supremacy: 'Legists and Canonists, doe now and then so wrest and writhe the holy scriptures, to that sense which themselves like best.'[130] The rise of the papacy entailed a departure from the foundations of the church left on earth by Christ, and this process was abetted by the 'invention' of new 'unwritten' traditions not sanctioned by the standard textual authorities. Hence, Roman theologians 'cannot defend and maintaine their poperie by the authoritie of Scripture, but by some other way and meanes. Viz. By mans forged inventions, and Popish unwritten vanities, which they term the Churches traditions'.[131] By 1606, therefore, Bell was able to summarise his position against the Roman confession as a vast corruption of the scholarly tradition, at the expense of man-made traditions 'which the Pope and his Romish schoolemen have brought into the Church'.[132]

It was the articulation of the historical and doctrinal identity of *the* Church with which Bell's *Regiment of the Church* was concerned. This work was in many ways the culmination of Bell's controversial career, and it was the first systematic defence of the English confession to appear since Hooker's *Lawes of ecclesiasticall politie*. While brief in comparison – the *Regiment* ran to 225 pages – it was considerably denser and more confined in its interests; chief among these was a defence of the Church of England in a year in which it was beginning to come under vigorous attack by those who argued that English doctrine had no sound historical pedigree. Yet it differed from Bell's previous works in that it was not directed at Catholic critics of the English Church, but rather at those Protestants who argued that the terms of the Jacobean settlement did not meet the standard which the Crown was anxious to promote.

---

[130] Thomas Bell, *The woefull crie of Rome. Containing a defiance to popery* (London, 1605), p. 5.

[131] Ibid., p. 6.

[132] Thomas Bell, *The popes funerall, containing an exact and pithy reply, to a pretended answere of a shamelesse and foolish libell, called, The forerunner of Bells downfall* (London, 1606), sig. F^r.

Indeed, Bell dedicated the work to Richard Bancroft, and pointed out that his purpose was to defend the Church from its Protestant critics: 'They beare the simple people in hand, that our Temples are prophaned; our Doctrine corrupt, our Sacraments impure, our Byshops anti-Christian, and our kind of Church-government repugnant to that Sacred form and order, which our LORD JESUS prescribed in his holie worde.'[133]

Bell began by discussing aspects of civil and ecclesiastical governance, and employed the Aristotelian doctrine of the 'normal commonwealth' to describe the public good. This was essentially an argument against faction, and one which was rooted firmly within the tradition, evident in Wilkes' pamphlet, which sought to contrast public doctrine with private duty: 'If the common good be sought and intended, the government is godly; but if private gain or pleasure be either wholly or principally intended, the government is wicked.' However, Bell sought to apply this wisdom to all members of the commonwealth, and thus furnished a caution to those civil rulers who sought 'private lucre'; should this happen, then 'so farre from being a king indeed, he is become a flat tyrant, and his government changed into plaine tyrannie'. Similarly, the best form of *ecclesiastical* polity was grounded on the universal obedience of all subjects to the public worship, an act that recognised the ecclesiastical authority of the sovereign:

> We reprove in like manner all those, who yeeld and give authoritie in religion unto Magistrates, onely in capital matters touching death, whilest they denie them authoritie to call Synods and consult of religion, to reforme Churches, and to appoint out of God's word, the things that pertaine to the salvation of their subjects: and will only have them to be the mere exequtors of those things, which the Bishops doe decree.[134]

Just as he identified the Crown in parliament as the legitimate authority over the Church, Bell firmly supported the freedom of the Crown's prerogative from the influence of the bishops – as we shall see, this would become a crucial issue in the Jacobean Church.

Yet this does not mean that Bell saw no place in the Church for the episcopal office: rather, he sought to map the historical pedigree of a hier-archical system of ecclesiastical governance. Against the attacks of those who argued that bishops were condemned by the reformed tradition, Bell offered the example of Calvin's account of the Council of Nicaea (325): 'Thus writeth Maister Calvin of the antiquitie of degrees and superioritie, amongst the Ministers of the Church.' The purpose of the hierarchy was to ensure the 'preservation of discipline', and the reformed tradition lent 'consent' to a

---

[133] Thomas Bell, *The regiment of the Church: as it is agreeable with Scriptures, all antiquities of the Fathers, and modern Writers, from the Apostles themselves, vnto this present age* (London, 1606), sig. A³ʳ.

[134] Ibid., pp. 1, 2, 13.

church distinguished by degrees of ministers, and hence to the idea that superior ministers retained the power to censure their inferiors. This was precisely the issue raised by Bancroft's policy of clerical subscription. As we shall see, the opponents of this process argued that such episcopal jurisdiction was an innovation and a 'politique' device, having no ancient history and thus no legitimacy. Hence, part of Bell's purpose was to defend the antiquity of the episcopal office: 'our Archbishops and Metropolitans in the English Church, have no new Ministrie, nor other authoritie, then was had and practised by the holy Fathers in ancient time, even in the primitive Church'.[135]

Moreover, the question that emerged in the debates over episcopacy concerned the civil jurisdiction of ecclesiastical officers – clerical livings fell into the category of 'property', and hence were protected by common law. Deprivation of beneficed ministers was therefore depicted as a violation of English common law and the provisions of Magna Carta, and so Bell sought out authorities that *predated* sources of legal precedent. Citing church Fathers such as Hermas, Eusebius, and St Callistus, Bell argued that 'Noah, Abraham, Isaac and Jacob, and others, did rule over those who were committed to their charge, as well in ecclesiasticall as civil causes [and] God himself made a general law [that] the priests and the civil magistrate should jointly determine, judge, and decide all controversies.'[136] Suddenly, the English common law became a layer of human invention whose tenets violated the older precedents supplied by the history of God's people. The message that Bell sought to extract from the older tradition was a simple one: the Crown and bishops were sovereign over the affairs of the Church. This sovereignty, defined by scripture, was of greater antiquity than the common law, and therefore superseded it.

This last point allowed Bell to proceed to the question of ceremonies, for part of Bancroft's programme of subscription included ceremonies that, to some, smacked of 'popery' and were thus ill-suited to a 'reformed' church. Bell's response to this problem was to become a hallmark of the conformist position: the Church, he argued, had the power to enjoin observance to ceremonies that were in themselves *adiaphora*, or 'indifferent': 'The Church may make decrees, Lawes, ordinances and constitutions, in all Things *Adiaphorus*, which are of their own nature indifferent; so the same tend to edification, comliness or peaceable government of the Church.'[137] The concept signalled one of the deepest rifts in post-Reformation English Protestantism, for it defined an epistemological division that underlay many of the polemical controversies in the Jacobean Church. Briefly, reformists

---

[135] Ibid., p. 40.   [136] Ibid., p. 44.   [137] Ibid., pp. 56–7.

argued that there was no difference in kind between the ceremonies practised
by the Church and the divine warrant of scripture: hence the rites of the
Church were strictly confined to the example and teaching of Christ and
could not blend these divine precedents with any elements of human invention, or 'custom'. Conformists argued that in addition to those things warranted by scripture, there were the accrued 'traditions' and 'customs' of the
early church, and the needs of circumstance that made it necessary to alter
the practices of the Church; so long as these were 'helps' to edification, and
did not lean toward the idolatrous practice of the Roman church, then all
subjects were bound to obey them as they would any decree of the supreme
magistrate.

This leads us to a further aspect of the conformist position developed by
Bell – the elision of religious uniformity and political obedience. It was along
this line that he sought to defend the ceremonies set forth in the Canons of
1604 as *adiaphora*:

> If our bretheren would seriously ponder, and duly weigh this golden advise of this
> Holy Father [St Ambrose], they would abandon all contentions doubtlesse, about the
> sign of the Cross, the Surplesse, and such like Indifferent Things, and for that dutie
> which they owe unto the Magistrate, whom they are bound to obey in all lawfull
> things, even for conscience sake; they would conform themselves to his lawes and
> their bretheren, and not to scandalise the whole Church as they do.

Part of Bell's purpose in citing the testimony of Ambrose was to answer the
reformist complaint that the argument for 'things indifferent' was simply a
device to skirt the charge that the prescribed ceremonies were *iure humano*,
of human invention. Bell countered by arguing that in the absence of a
specific scriptural rule, there remained a 'general rule' which offered a certain
latitude to churches in the ordering of their ceremonies: 'For we knowe, that
every Church hath her freedom and Libertie, to institute and ordaine such a
kind of policie (and discipline) as shall be thought meet and profitable for the
same; because our Lord prescribed no certain rule therein.'[138] Ceremonies in
general were a 'support' to worship and an aid to 'increase reverence'; taken
singly, they conveyed no grace and presumably had no role in the process of
salvation. However, Bell argued that they should be enjoined nevertheless: 'It
is therefore most prudently and right Christianly provided in the Canons of
Anno. 1604 that none shall be permitted to preach without licence', for 'it is
not every private man's part to define, decide, and appoint what is order and
comlinesse in things indifferent, and the externall government of the
Church'.[139]

[138] Ibid., pp. 58, 60.   [139] Ibid., pp. 89, 92.

From the elision of uniformity and obedience, Bell proceeded to the matter of conformity and clerical subscription, and their relation to the reformed 'tradition'. Indeed, Bell posited a further elision, between tradition and reformation, in order to show how the doctrine of the Church of England could be reconciled with tradition (and hence antiquity), as well as the judgement of reformed divines. Bell cited the Calvinist theologian Girolamo Zanchi (1516–90): 'Let this therefore be the summe and conclusion, that such traditions as agree with the word of God, and serve for the Churches use, and to stirre up mens mindes to pietie and true worship of God, may this day be still retained and used, so it be done without superstition and opinion of merite.'[140] The endorsement of this reformed divine served Bell's purpose by answering the reforming charge that old ceremonies must necessarily be idolatrous, and this allowed him to argue that the Church had the power to preserve the uniformity of its doctrine via the 'election' of ministers. Here Bell offered examples drawn from scripture (Matthew 10; Luke 10; Acts 1, 6, 14; 1 Timothy 5; Titus 1), the Council of Laodicea, and Calvin's *Institutes* in order to argue that the election of ministers was not based on the 'consent' of the people. Instead, Bell continued, 'the Church may change the manner of election, and consequently, that no one certain kind of election, is *de iure divino*, decreed by God's law to be perpetual'. Hence, like the settling of rites, the ordaining of ministers was a mark of the sovereignty of the Church.[141]

The concept of the sovereignty of the Church was a crucial aspect of English conformist thought, for it was used to account for not only deprivations, but also the existence of an office of superior clergy whose task it was to ensure a uniformity of doctrine and discipline. During the Jacobean period, this power would come to be challenged by divines writing in support of the Scottish Kirk, when, in 1618, the Crown ordered the imposition of English ceremonies in Scotland, and defended the policy by appealing to the sovereign Church of 'Great Britain'. Likewise, Bell argued that a Presbyterian mode of government consisting of pastors, deacons, and elders 'is not compatible with a Christian Monarchie; but must perforce despoyle her, and bereave her of her royall soveraigntie. I prove it, because the said Presbyterie challengeth unto her selfe, all authoritie in causes ecclesiasticall; the supreme over-sight of which causes, pertaineth to the civill Magistrate.' Bell clearly recognised the problem that ensued from competing modes of governance within a single church; here he found an ally in Heinrich Bullinger (1504–75), Swiss reformer and an active opponent of Anabaptism. One aspect of Bullinger's doctrine that aided Bell's cause was the suggestion that there was no difference in kind between the Christian state and the

---

[140] Ibid., p. 101. [141] Ibid., pp. 106–7.

Christian church; hence Bell could speak of the 'whole Church' and the mode of governance appropriate to it: 'it is most apparent and cleare, that all power is granted unto the whole Church, who to avoyde confusion and for order sake, committeth her authoritie to certaine chosen persons. Which persons are the Bishops and Prelates of the Church, say I, and all antiquitie will confesse the same with me.'[142]

Bell brought the work to a close with a lengthy discussion of the 'Discipline of the Church', whose purpose was to account for the Church as a political association. Again Bell employed the elision between political obedience and religious uniformity. A frequently cited scripture which captured this idea – and appeared on Bell's title-page – was 1 Corinthians 14: 40, 'Let all things be done decently, and in order.' In fact, the verse was employed in defence of two propositions: 'decency' was a synonym for the use of those ceremonies defined as 'indifferent' and signalled that they were employed for edification. The second proposition concerned the unity of true faith and the implications of this condition for the body politic of the Church; dissent and schism were examples of disorder, and a violation of the warrant of scripture. When combined, these propositions furnished the foundation of a theory of the sovereignty of the Church to adapt to the needs of circumstance:

Againe, if the Church had not power to displace, suspend, and prohibit Ministers from Preaching, as their demeanours, and circumstances of times, places and persons shall require; then doubtlesse would the Church abounde with schismes, confusion, and all *ataxia* contrarie to the Apostolic canon, which prescribeth all things to be done decently, and in order.[143]

Hence the peace and order of the Church, as well as the means to ensure their promotion, were warranted by the scripture, and were therefore *iure divino*: 'whoever rejecteth such lawes and ordinances of the Church, contemneth the authoritie of God and not of men'. The cement of this theory of order was 'conscience', and the concluding section of the work considered the damage that could be done to the Church by 'malefactors' – that is, critics of the sovereignty of the Church and its foundation in the laws of God. In a political sense, the argument turned on the concept of 'jurisdiction':

[T]he Church hath authoritie to impose every lawful ordinance and constitution, which she deemeth profitable for the Church, upon every person subject to her jurisdiction ... if it be Adiaphora, a thing of its own nature indifferent, then it is likewise in the power and libertie of the Church, to impose the same uppon every member within her jurisdiction.[144]

As we shall see, Protestant critics of the Church argued that an ordinance not derived from scripture could not be passed off as 'indifferent'. The challenge

---

[142] Ibid., p. 132.   [143] Ibid., p. 165.   [144] Ibid., pp. 200, 201.

in subsequent debates was to close the gap between the express law of scripture and the accumulated traditions of the Church, while reconciling both within the secular and mutable institutions of state.

We are now in a position to assemble the various elements that comprised the vision of ecclesiastical polity espoused by Wilkes, Forset, Hayward, and Bell, and thus to establish the outlines of Jacobean conformist thought. It was dominated by two propositions, each of which was defended with reference to scripture and the traditions of civil and ecclesiastical history. First, the Church of England was a legally 'established' church, founded in law and within the jurisdiction of the English Crown, its 'ancient' governor. This meant that the English Church was a political association defined by a public mode of worship to which all English subjects were required to conform. Those Protestants and Catholics who did not conform were seen to have withdrawn their loyalty from the political and spiritual association that the English Reformation had established. The second proposition portrayed this Reformation as a *restoration* of the spiritual association that defined the church established by Christ and descended through the Apostles. This restoration represented the re-emergence of the 'true' church after a period during which it had been eclipsed by the errors of Rome. Moreover, the English Church was taken to be an exemplar of the 'reformed' churches, a spiritual and political church militant.

The political ideas that sustained English conformity must be appreciated as responses to a particular set of problems, which were moreover shaped by a pattern of assumptions about the workings of social wholes. Neither Wilkes, Forset, nor Hayward wished either to abolish monarchy or to establish a broadly defined programme of religious toleration. Rather, these defenders of the monarchical Church of England are part of a larger group of writers who tried to come to grips with the institutions of state, and to put forth a theory of governance that was based on the nature of those institutions. Where it will be the business of the remaining chapters to analyse debates between defenders of the Church and their critics, the present chapter has been confined to an examination of the conformist language of ecclesiastical polity, for in the writings of defenders of the Church one finds a strand of ideas that would prove crucial to the politics of religious polemic in the years before the Civil War. The burden faced by defenders of the Church was to ensure that there was agreement between the religious ends of the state and those of its people;[145] this meant that great emphasis

---

[145] A little-known paper by Christopher Hill put this point very nicely; see 'Archbishop Laud and the English Revolution', in *Religion, resistance, and civil war*, ed. Gordon Schochet, Proceedings of the Folger Institute Center for the History of British Political Thought, 3 (Washington, DC, 1990), pp. 127–49.

was placed on unity, conformity, and public worship, and precedents for these conditions were sought in the example of history. This in turn elevated a definition of the Church to a position of great importance for political ideas. Yet, Thomas Bell's contributions to the debate reveal that there was more to the question than could be addressed by politics or a political theory of obedience. His three contemporaries – a chaplain, a jurist, and an antiquary – all predicated political stability on a uniform mode of worship, but they did not seek to contribute to the debate on the doctrinal identity of the Church. Citing a tradition of Doctors, councils, and scripture, both Catholics and reformists posed challenges to this identity. Against criticisms of this type, assertions of the conjoined nature of civil and ecclesiastical sovereignty did not go far enough. Bell's work situated the English Church in the textual and doctrinal history of Christianity, and defended the terms of the Jacobean settlement as the appropriate means by which the true faith was to be preserved.

English conformists sought to emphasise that their Church was both ancient and reformed, both a spiritual and political association in possession of sovereignty over its own doctrine and discipline, and reinforced by the authority of the Crown. However, between these propositions there existed a great deal of disagreement, and so it is the case that all religious controversy from the Reformation to the mid-nineteenth century was, to some degree, shaped by the need to engage with the problem of civil and spiritual authority.[146] The task facing conformist writers was defined, therefore, by the need to defend the English Church as a spiritual association not separated from the church established by Christ, and as a political association established by law and in possession of the authority to employ the civil arm of the state against those who refused to conform. In comparison to other political units – whether boroughs, guilds, or the venerable wreckage of feudalism – the English Church has claims to being, or at least striving to be, the first truly *national* political association, of a scope unique in the English experience, and this meant in turn that political ideas in England were profoundly influenced by religion. The language of ecclesiastical polity was a language steeped in the historical investigation of ancient states, whether pagan or Christian, and driven by the need to situate the experience of the post-Reformation English Church within a series of historical narratives that testified to the prior existence and flourishing of religious commonwealths.

---

[146] For this see Clark, *English society*, pp. 43–124.

3

Doctrine, law, and conflict over the Canons of 1604

Immediately before and after the Hampton Court conference, English Protestants debated how the Church should be ordered, and while conformists advanced the arguments discussed in the previous chapter, their opponents offered an alternative definition of the Church as a *purely* spiritual association, patterned on scripture and confirmed in the writings of approved Fathers of the Church. It was this proposition that led them, in turn, to attack the programme of clerical subscription that followed Hampton Court.[1] Subscription, the argument ran, was a political means to enforce a spiritual end; it was a policy of human devising, carried out by bishops whose offices themselves had no scriptural warrant; the imperative of civil order was being promoted at the cost of the purity of doctrine, and this moved the Church away from its proper form. Against these claims, conformists advanced arguments that emphasised the freedom of the Church, under the Crown, to regulate governance, worship, doctrine, and discipline, and situated the case within Apostolic and common law interpretations of history. In short, the debate was a continuation of the theme, examined in the previous chapter, of the compatibility of the historical narratives that testified to the relationship between civil and ecclesiastical authority.

This chapter examines the tension between doctrinal and legal conceptions of the Church of England, and situates them within the larger question of the nature of authority over the Church. Principally, it will examine issues of tension in the late Elizabethan Church, notably, the court of High Commission, diocesan episcopacy, and the enforcement of ceremonies by clerical subscription. These issues were not fully settled when James VI arrived in England as a celebrated peacemaker, and convened the Hampton Court conference. The Conference has been interpreted in various ways, and it has

---

[1] Ogbu U. Kalo, 'Continuity in change: bishops of London and religious dissent in early Stuart England', *Journal of British Studies*, 18 (1978), 28–45.

been suggested that its aim was to pacify 'puritan' opposition to the Church, and to balance 'moderate' and 'radical' factions. Hampton Court has also figured in the work of those scholars who see in Arminianism the central conflict of the early Stuart Church.[2] What these interpretations tend to overlook is the wider question of doctrine and governance that both preceded and followed Hampton Court, and the way in which these questions were treated in the context of religious and legal historiography. Indeed, Bancroft's ecclesiastical policy generated a great deal of debate, and the period is defined by a flurry of printed works that treated themes associated with doctrinal and legal conceptions of the Church.[3] Official pronouncements and a number of published works of controversy form the bulk of the material on which this chapter is based. This literature suggests that conflict over governance and the enforcement of doctrinally controversial ceremonies dominated debate after Hampton Court. These debates served to define tensions between rival conceptions of the doctrine of the Church, and led many writers to probe into the legal implications of some conformist defences of ecclesiastical polity. Where conformists emphasised a state Church allied to the temporal power of the Crown, their opponents argued for a doctrinal Church, wherein discipline could be reconciled with both the scripture, the practice of the ancient church, and the English common law. At the heart of the matter was a dispute over the extent and nature of human authority in the spiritual realm. The conformist vision, as has been shown, stressed the point that although the Church was subject to the will of human agents, it remained within the ambit of the spiritual. To this reformists replied that the established Church reposed too much authority in the hands of its governors, and that this came at the expense of sounder patterns of discipline and governance, themselves evident in the scripture and practice of the ancient church.

[2] See Kenneth Fincham and Peter Lake, 'The ecclesiastical policy of King James I', *Journal of British Studies*, 24 (1985), 169–207; Frederick Shriver, 'Hampton Court revisited: James I and the puritans', *Journal of Ecclesiastical History*, 33 (1982), 48–71; Nicholas Tyacke, *Anti-Calvinists: the rise of English Arminianism, c. 1590–1640* (Oxford, 1987), ch. 1; Peter White, *Predestination, policy and polemic: conflict and consensus in the English Church from the Reformation to the Civil War* (Cambridge, 1992), pp. 140–52.

[3] A clandestine book trade and an active overseas press foiled the efforts of Jacobean censors. For censorship, see Cyndia Clegg, *Press censorship in Jacobean England* (Cambridge, 2001); Sheila Lambert, 'State control of the Press in theory and practice: the role of the Stationers' Company before 1640', in *Censorship and the control of print in England and France, 1600–1900*, ed. Robin Myers and Michael Harris (Winchester, 1992), pp. 1–32; Anthony Milton, 'Licensing, censorship, and religious orthodoxy in early Stuart England', *Historical Journal*, 41 (1998), 625–51. For the book trade, see Kari Konkola, '"People of the Book": the production of theological texts in early modern England', *PBSA*, 94 (2000), 5–33; W. W. Greg, *Some aspects and problems of London publishing between 1550 and 1650* (Oxford, 1956). For printing, see Denis B. Woodfield, *Surreptitious printing in England, 1550–1640* (New York, 1973); Keith Sprunger, *Trumpets from the tower: English puritan printing in the Netherlands* (Leiden, 1994).

JUS ANTIQUUM: SCRIPTURE AND LAW, CA. 1580–1604

When James I arrived in his new kingdom in the spring of 1603, England had been in the throes of religious debate for over seventy years. The settlement of 1559, with its Acts of Supremacy and Uniformity, established royal governance over the Church and enforced a vernacular Book of Common Prayer based upon that of 1552. The Injunctions of 1559 unleashed an official attack on Roman Catholic piety, including the removal of images and the replacement of stone altars by wooden communion tables. The Thirty-nine Articles, passed at the Convocation of 1563, defined the Protestant doctrine of the newly reformed Church.[4] Far from 'tolerant', the Elizabethan regime set a strong precedent for the punishing of non-conformity, first of Roman Catholics, and then of Protestants, promising not to molest clergy and subjects 'either by examination or inquisition ... as long as they shall profess the Christian faith, not gainsaying the authority of the Holy Scriptures and the Articles of our Faith'.[5] The High Commission, a prerogative court that could, controversially, administer punishments independently of the common law, was the instrument by which religious uniformity would be enforced.[6] Contemporary evidence suggests the presence of a conflict over the origins of the High Commission itself: common lawyers maintained that the body owed its life to statute, while civil lawyers argued that the court was an aspect of the royal supremacy.[7] The Elizabethan Act of Supremacy provided for action against 'errors, heresies, and schisms' by ensuring that 'any spiritual or ecclesiastical power or authority [which] hath heretofore been or may lawfully be exercised or used for the visitation of the ecclesiastical state and persons ... shall for ever by the authority of this present Parliament be united and annexed to the imperial crown of this realm'.[8] This established the governance of the Church of England through the Crown in parliament. However, the Act also implied that the ecclesiastical sovereignty of the

---

[4] See Judith Maltby, *Prayer Book and people in Elizabethan and early Stuart England* (Cambridge, 1998), pp. 1–30; Eamon Duffy, *The stripping of the altars: traditional religion in England, c.1400–c.1580* (New Haven, 1992); and Michael Questier, 'Practical antipapistry during the reign of Elizabeth I', *Journal of British Studies*, 36 (1997), 371–96.

[5] *State Papers* (Domestic) Eliz. I, vol. LXVI.

[6] The standard study is Roland G. Usher, *The rise and fall of the High Commission*, with a new introduction by Philip Tyler (Oxford, 1968). The work was first published in 1913, and since that time some of Usher's conclusions and assumptions have been revised; details of the debate are given by Philip Tyler in the introduction to the most recent edition, and in *The Tudor constitution: documents and commentary*, ed. G. R. Elton, 2nd edn (Cambridge, 1982), pp. 221–6. Conflict between common lawyers and clerics over the power of the High Commission, and writs of prohibition and consultation, is a topic in need of further study.

[7] See Henry Gee, *Documents illustrative of English church history* (London, 1910), and Stuart Barton Babbage, *Puritanism and Richard Bancroft* (London, 1962), pp. 259–61.

[8] Act of Supremacy, in *Tudor constitution*, ed. Elton, doc. 184, pp. 372–7, at p. 374.

Crown could be transferred via letters patent to others, who might 'execute any jurisdiction, power or authority spiritual'.[9] As we shall see, rival interpretations of what the Act of Supremacy allowed drove debate on the governance of the Church of the realm.

It is this that explains why discussion of the nature of the 'realm' and its laws was uppermost in those publications that sought to defend a divine standard of discipline against that envisioned by John Whitgift, Archbishop of Canterbury from 1583 to 1604. An anonymous pamphleteer noted the 'lamentable contention' in the Church that had resulted from a policy of clerical subscription to the Three Articles – the centrepiece of Whitgift's ecclesiological vision, and the forerunner of the controversial 36th Canon introduced by Whitgift's successor, Richard Bancroft.[10] The doctrine and governance of the Elizabethan Church had been a source of continued debate, and Whitgift struggled to establish a mode of public doctrine that had the weight of law behind it. However, his policy of clerical subscription represented an affront to what contemporary reformists called the divine 'pattern of regiment'. An anonymous pamphleteer put clearly the case for following the commands of Christ above the laws of the land:

I conclude that a Minister bound, as you have seene before, to minister the Discipline of Christ, ought to Minister the same, as the Lord hath commanded, though the lawes of the Realme should not have received the same. For no discipline in truth can be said to be the Discipline of Christ, unlesse it be indeede ministered, as the Lord Christ hath commanded the same to be ministered. And therefore, as no Bishop may or ought to correct or punish any transgressor, any otherwise then according to the Lawes of God: so no minister ought to exercise any discipline, then such as the Lord hath commanded.[11]

---

[9] Ibid., p. 377.

[10] The articles read as follows:

  1. That her Majesty, under God, hath and ought to have the sovereignty and rule over all manner of persons born within her realms and dominions and countries, of what estate ecclesiastical or temporal so ever they be. And that none other foreign power, prelate, state or potentate hath or ought to have any jurisdiction, power, superiority, preeminence or authority ecclesiastical or temporal within her Majesty's said realmes and dominions.
  2. That the Book of Common Prayer, and of ordering bishops, priests and deacons, containeth nothing in it contrary to the Word of God. And that the same may be lawfully used; and that he himself will use the form of the book prescribed, in public prayer and the administration of sacraments, and none other.
  3. That he alloweth the book of Articles of Religion, agreed upon by the archbishops and bishops in both provinces, and the whole clergy in the Convocation holden at London in the year of our Lord 1562, and set forth by her Majesty's authority. And that he believeth all the articles therein contained to be agreeable to the word of God.

      Tudor constitution, ed. Elton, doc. 207, pp. 455–6.

[11] [William Stoughton], *An abstract, of certain acts of parliament: of certaine her Maiesties Iniunctions: of certaine canons, constitutions, and synodalles prouinciall* ([London, 1583]), pp. 35–6.

The assumption that underlay this position was that all aspects of the doctrine and discipline of the Church had to be derived without alteration from the divine pattern found in the scriptures. The 'laws of the realm' were the laws of men, and their jurisdiction did not apply to the spiritual association over which Christ alone was sovereign.

The civil lawyer Richard Cosin quickly answered the pamphlet.[12] Clearly, a tension arose between the authorities that could be invoked to justify the doctrine and discipline of the Church; reformists based their position almost entirely on scripture, while conformists emphasised the earthly institution, structure, and range of offices and clerical roles that defined the early Christian church. Cosin argued that the ceremonies and government of the Church did not fall exclusively within the ambit of the scripture, and this meant that each national church was free to determine its own edifying practices:

Not that it is to be thought that everie ceremonie, forme or circumstance about these ... things are either in particularitie delivered in scripture ... or that therein either this church or anie other is or can be tied to any certaine exact forme *in hypothesi* as we term it: but that certaine generall rules for ceremonies and government, being there set down, everie church is to follow the said rules, in such particular manner as they shall judge ... to be fit for edifying and governing of that people.[13]

Cosin sought to defend the authority of the Church by modifying the notion that the scriptures set forth a complete pattern for the establishment of doctrine and discipline, proposing instead that they established only general rules which individual churches were free to follow as they saw fit.

Not surprisingly, Cosin's work prompted a number of replies, among them a tract by Dudley Fenner, himself recently deprived for refusing subscription to Whitgift's articles. Fenner argued that Christ's 'heritage is to be governed and protected' from corruption by 'uncertayne ... human constitutions' and on this basis rejected the policy of clerical subscription:

it is not in the power of man to alter or change these offices by addition or detraction, because they can not give nor take away members to and from Christ's bodie, but all the gyfts are from one spirit, the faculties from one God, the administration from one Lorde: and finally all Church ministries must be from Heaven and not from earth.[14]

Other works from the period sought to dismiss the machinations of bishops and civil lawyers as fomenters of schism leading to the alienation of the Church

---

[12] Brian Levack, *The civil lawyers in England, 1603–1641* (Oxford, 1973), pp. 158–95.

[13] Richard Cosin, *An answer to the two fyrst and principall treatises of a certaine factious libell* (London, 1584), p. 55.

[14] [Dudley Fenner], *A counter-poyson, modestly written for the time, to make aunswere to the obiections and reproches, wherewith the aunswerer to the Abstract, would disgrace the holy discipline of Christ* (London, [1584]), pp. 11–12.

of England from the true church. In one dialogue, a bishop 'Orthodoxos' and a lawyer 'Philodoxos' held forth against an incredulous chaplain and an inn-keeper who lamented clerical deprivations as the chief cause behind the collapse of his tavern's profits.[15] Another anonymous tract argued that to depart from doctrine and discipline as ordained by scripture was to risk the ruin of the Church: 'The doctrine and discipline of God, are the two pillars of the kingdom of Christ, so twisted together, that the one can not stand without the other. For as discipline containeth an order for fit men to be ordained to [the] ministrie ... so doctrine is a continual nurse ... And where either one or both faile, there must needs follow the ruin of the whole Church.'[16]

Under Whitgift, the High Commission became the principal arm by which ecclesiastical authority was exercised over the ministry, and Richard Cosin, in his *Apologie*, defended its activities.[17] Cosin's substantial and deeply learned work was directed to the analysis of a single problem: how the ecclesiastical sovereignty of the Crown was channelled through 'inferior magistrates', bishops, and ecclesiastical commissions. Critics of the process argued that the Act of Supremacy did not clearly state that the Crown could transfer its ecclesiastical sovereignty to other officers; Cosin argued that the wording of the Act could be interpreted to give authority to bishops for executing the ecclesiastical law.[18] The problem was that presentation to clerical posts (advowsons) was considered as 'property' and, therefore, came under the jurisdiction of the common law; the question that emerged in the context of the debate on Whitgift's Articles was whether the jurisdic-tion of the parliament could supersede that of the Church. Hence, Cosin argued that Magna Carta granted the Church power over its own affairs, and situated this interpretation in the context of the rise of the papal supremacy. He styled the Reformation as a restoration of ancient English ecclesiastical jurisdiction, and suggested that the temporal and spiritual jurisdiction flo-wed from the Crown:

I will object these words of Magna Charta, where it is not a newe granted, but confirmed only, *That for evermore the Church of England shall be free, and shall have her whole rites and liberties inviolable.* And this is a conformation of their rites and liberties, before any graunt was made to the rest of the realme besides: being yeelded at such time, when as (through generall ignorance) it was untruly holden, that the state Ecclesiasticall (signified by those words, the Church of England) had not their

---

[15] [Anon], *A dialogue, concerning the strife of our churche* (London, 1584).

[16] [Anon], *The unlawfull practises of prelates against godly ministers, the maintainers of the discipline of God* ([London, 1584]), sig. 2^v–3^r.

[17] Ethan H. Shagan, 'The English Inquisition: constitutional conflict and ecclesiastical law in the 1590s', *Historical Journal*, 47 (2004), 541–65.

[18] Richard Cosin, *An apologie for sundrie proceedings by iurisdiction ecclesiastical, of late times by some chalenged, and also diuersly by them impugned* (London, 1593).

jurisdiction from the Prince, but from God alone, derived down to them by the means of the Pope: and therefore that the Courtes and lawes … were not in any respect to be accounted for Courts holden by the Kings auctoritie, or their lawes the Kings lawes. Whereupon arose that untrue and prejudicial phase of severance of a Court Christian from a Kings Court. So that if they were confirmed to them when their Jurisdictions (in facte) were not holden by the Kinge, as now they be, and ought to be by God's lawe: is there not then more just cause so to continue them at this time, seeing they be not so much as a diverse course from the Customes and lawes of the Realme in Courts Temporall?[19]

This complex paragraph put forth the argument that Magna Carta upheld the independence of the Church, denounced the 'severance' of Church courts from royal jurisdiction, and defended their continuance after the Reformation as once again holding their jurisdiction from the Crown. Central to the argument was that the High Commission could be reconciled with the 'ancient' custom of the common law. Such a claim allowed for it to be defended both as a legitimate extension of the ecclesiastical sovereignty of the Crown, and as a mode of jurisdiction that did not violate the laws of England. Cosin also sought to defend the exercise of ecclesiastical discipline:

Furthermore, it is well and notoriously knowen, that proceedings and condemnations Ecclesiastical in ordinarie courts were never made by the judgement of a mans peers, viz. By a Jurie: and therefore those words rehearsed, can not be so farre extended, as to include that jurisdiction. Yet as institution unto a benefice, both before and after Magna Charta, belonged alwaies to ecclesiastical persons and jurisdiction; so did also the destitution and deprivation of a benefice by the common lawe.[20]

Here was a defence of the most controversial legal aspect of post-Reformation discipline: deprivation of clergy without trial by jury did not conflict with the common law, but was guaranteed by it. Cosin therefore sought to establish the right of the Church to exact discipline over its clergy as a power more ancient than the common law, and hence free from its strictures.

In addition to the formal interpretation of the law, the conformist tendency to treat non-conformity as the activity of 'associations' rather than individuals clearly acted as a spur to the debate. Thomas Bilson developed a complex case for the elision of the civil and spiritual authority of the Church, and following the Elizabethan Act of Supremacy suggested that these powers came from the Crown:

Wee teach, that God in delivering the Sword to Princes, hath given them this direct charge to provide that as well true religion be mayntayned in their realmes, as civil justice ministered: and hath to this end allowed Princes full power to forbid, prevent, and punish in all their subjectes, be they laymen, Clerkes or Bishops, not only murders, thefts,

---

[19] Ibid., pp. 73–4.   [20] Ibid., p. 104.

adulteries, perjuries, and such like breaches of the second table; but also schisms, heresies, Idolatries, and all other offences against the first table pertayning only to the service of God and matters of religion.[21]

Bilson equated spiritual crimes with sins, breaches of the first and second tables of the Ten Commandments. He argued that all power to punish these crimes emanated from the Crown: sins against God (schisms and heresies) fell under the jurisdiction of the Church courts, while sins against human subjects fell under the jurisdiction of the common-law courts.

In response to such reiterations of the royal power and its putative responsibility for the Church, reformists sought to emphasise the importance of parliamentary statute. Josias Nichols' *Plea of the innocent* was a fine example of this genre of controversial literature. He suggested that the means to align the Elizabethan church with that known in the Apostles' times were ready to hand, in the form of 'statutes, Articles, Canons and Injunctions'. Here we find evidence of the fluidity of the reformist position, for Nichols, in attacking the bishops, invoked the legal apparatus of the Reformation put in place by parliament, convocation, and the Crown. The bishops, he argued, had failed to adhere to the laws that 'established' the Church, and operated instead according to upstart laws of their own; they had ceased to be 'pastors' and had become instead 'Lords'.[22] Hence, part of Nichols' complaint concerned the nature of ecclesiastical governance that, he suggested, was rightfully exercised by the Crown in parliament. In this context, the bishops comprised a 'faction' which sought to undermine the legitimate channels of ecclesiastical authority.

For Nichols, the doctrine of the Church was also a topic of contention. He argued that the liturgical aspects of the Elizabethan settlement signified that the Church of England departed from its restored ancient perfection, and tilted toward the Church of Rome. For reformists did not perceive three churches – Roman, Reformed, and English – but two: Roman and English, the latter of which more closely approximated the 'true' church. On the topic of the 'errors of Rome', many English Protestant writers agreed. The issue that divided them was which Protestant group most clearly embodied the continuation of the ancient church. That the higher clergy had forsaken the traditions of the 'reformed' church lay at the foundation of Nichols' argument. Citing with approval a host of Elizabethan defenders of the Church of

---

[21] Thomas Bilson, *The true difference betweene Christian subiection and unchristian rebellion* (London, 1585), p. 129. See also Francis Oakley, 'Jacobean political theology: the absolute and ordinary powers of the king', *Journal of the History of Ideas*, 29 (1968), 323–46.

[22] Josias Nichols, *The plea of the innocent: wherein is auerred; that the ministers and people falslie termed puritanes, are iniuriouslie slaundered for enemies or troublers of the state* ([London], 1602), pp. 40–1, 43, 51.

England, Nichols argued that the ceremonies and programme of subscription would not have garnered the support of such champions of the faith as John Jewel and Thomas Bilson:

And I hope the plaine appearance of this contradictorie writing doth show, what mens consciences do deeme of the truth we call for: so that we are not to be condemned as men singular, and divisions of new platforms of discipline. And that in dutie to the very bookes themselves, to the Canons, and proceedings of the good and learned defenders of our Church, we ought not to subscribe: but rather use all dutifull means by petitions and otherwise as we have done, that things may be reformed. [23]

The programme of reform put forth by Nichols was intended to *restore* rather than innovate: the removal of 'popish' ceremonies, the end of 'Lordship and civil jurisdiction' by bishops, and the purging of 'accessorie additamentes, brought into the Church by humane constitution'. All of these things, argued Nichols, added nothing to essential matters of faith, and so could be 'clean taken away [and] the religion, faith, administration of Christ and the true worship of God, as it is now in the Church of England, might and would remain whole without them'.[24] In place of these elements, Nichols envisioned a process of clerical reform that included increased preaching. Since the scripture constituted the crucial link with the ancient church, the clergy should ensure that its message was conveyed to the people. This criticism had a good deal to do with the state of the Church as an institution at the time of Nichols' writing: variation in terms of wealth and education of the clergy meant that many of England's thousands of parishes were in a state of decline.[25] The problems associated with lay preaching, non-beneficed or non-resident clergy meant that many parishes lacked a competent minister.[26] Nichols' argument was driven by the assumption that there was no doctrinal justification for depriving ministers who refused to subscribe, and that this process of deprivation only served to weaken the Church.

Nichols' objection to subscription consisted of two main points: the ceremonies set forth and the manner in which they were enforced could not be found in scripture, and so to enjoin clergymen to subscribe condemned them to be 'false witnesses of God'. Furthermore, to deprive them of their livings threatened to 'bring evil upon this land and Church', by depriving the realm of able preachers. He also opposed the Book of Common Prayer as a contradiction of both scripture and the Thirty-nine Articles: 'In the said booke of

---

[23] Ibid., p. 53.   [24] Ibid., pp. 87, 90–2, 93.

[25] See Patrick Collinson, *The religion of Protestants: the Church in English society, 1559–1625* (Oxford, 1982), pp. 69–70, 95, 117, 130–1.

[26] See Eric Josef Carlson, '"Practical divinity": Richard Greenham's ministry in Elizabethan England', in *Religion and the English people, 1500–1640: new voices, new perspectives*, ed. Eric Josef Carlson, Sixteenth Century Essays and Studies, 45 (Kirksville, MO, 1998), pp. 147–98; and Kevin Sharpe, *The personal rule of Charles I* (New Haven, 1992), ch. 6.

Articles we build, "That the visible Church of Christ, is a company of faithful people, among whome the pure word of God is preached." Then in the booke of Common Prayer, we destroy that againe. Because we preech some chapters which containe untruths, and absurdities'.[27] Nichols challenged several aspects of the conformist programme: first, the conformists' understanding of the complex nature of the Church's traditions and 'customs', conveyed not only through scripture, but also through the writings of their defenders, both ancient and contemporary. Second, Nichols condemned the stewards of the Church, the bishops, for turning away from their ancient and reformed traditions and erecting a programme of rule that constituted an opening to 'popery' and thus a threat to the Church and commonwealth. Finally, Nichols criticised the Book of Common Prayer for its non-scriptural form and contents. This involved a reinterpretation of the Church's history since the Elizabethan settlement, an interpretation that saw a gradual reversal of the English Reformation by a return to Catholicism.

Given the searching nature of Nichols' criticisms it is not surprising that William Covell, a staunch defender of the conformist position, quickly answered the tract. Covell based his argument on the conformist interpretations of ecclesiastical supremacy and antiquity, the former stressing conformity and condemning non-conformity as a threat to political order, the latter answering calls for reform by linking the Church of England with the ancient church. Looking back to the Admonition controversy, Covell observed that religious infighting served only to turn the branches of parliament against one another, an action that trespassed on the authority of the legislature, and hence on that of the Crown, to pass and enforce laws pertaining to the Church.[28] Hence non-conformists 'have taken from them one of the three Estates and from all that Authoritie, which they ascribe to a number of ignorant and sillie artificers'.[29] Naturally, Covell included the bishops as Lords Ecclesiastical among the estates, but what is most important about his observation is that it provided a clear case for religious faction as a disruption of the workings of government. We have seen already that contemporaries conceived of the state as having tightly knit ecclesiastical and 'politique' parts, and so Covell situated Nichols' attack in that context: 'Nay whilst some of late have been earnest, though ignorant refusers of subscription, they have showed in their actions, how uncharitably they have thought of their late sovereign's sincere religion.'[30]

For Covell, an attack on any part of the ecclesiastical hierarchy amounted to an attack on the Crown; therefore, he dedicated much of his response to Nichols

---

[27] Nichols, *Plea of the innocent*, pp. 196, 198, 200.

[28] William Covell, *A modest and reasonable examination, of some things in vse in the Church of England, sundrie times heretofore misliked* (London, 1604), p. 4.

[29] Ibid., p. 5.   [30] Ibid., p. 3.

to defending the sovereignty of the Church, and particularly the power of the Crown to summon meetings and to prescribe means by which doctrine and discipline might be uniformly maintained. Historical examples of this were furnished by 'Scriptures, by Historie, By Fathers, and by the Testimonie of some of the Popes themselves; who have earnestly entreated the Christian emperors to call Councels'.[31] Moreover, Covell argued that solutions for problems like plurality and non-residency could only be found if all members of the clergy willingly followed the dictates of the Crown and, in spiritual causes, the 'inferior magistrates' or bishops: 'For what indifferent man can think it unmeete, that when the Prince, and the Parliament have made Orders, Canons, Injunctions, Articles, or anything of that Kinde, for the Uniformitie of Church Government, that a Bishop having authoritie to institute into spiritual livings ... should require by subscription a consent unto these things, before he be admitted to that charge?'[32] Although Covell saw the enforced ceremonies as *adiaphora*, mere 'virtuous furtherances' to worship, he defended them 'as sinewes to hold all and every several member of the Church', and as a badge to distinguish the faith.[33] Near the end of his argument, Covell alluded to an 'intemperate petition' issued by 1000 ministers (the Millenary Petition), and argued that those among the clergy who refused to subscribe to articles and ceremonies drawn from the ancient church aimed at nothing less than the subversion of the contemporary embodiment of that church:

In the meantime, those false conjectural effects, for which subscription was required, are but uncharitable devices of their owne, only to make those in authority to be more odious; that contempt of their persons, breeding disobedience to their government, either a general dissolution may bring a palsey into the Church, or else we must only be ruled by orders of their making.[34]

BEATI PACIFICI?: THE JACOBEAN SETTLEMENT

The arrival of James VI and I was celebrated in sermons and larger tracts that looked forward to a reign of peace.[35] The new King was clever enough to have advertised his position on questions of governance in a new preface to his *Basilikon doron*.[36] John Fenton expressed in verse the sentiments shared by many, the King included:

---

[31] Ibid., p. 9.   [32] Ibid., p. 79.   [33] Ibid., pp. 51, 60.   [34] Ibid., p. 91.

[35] See Peter McCullough, *Sermons at court: politics and religion in Elizabethan and Jacobean preaching* (Cambridge, 1998), pp. 101–6.

[36] James I, King of England, *Basilikon doron. Or, His Maiesties instructions to his dearest sonne, Henrie the prince* (London, 1603). See also Jenny Wormald, 'James VI and I, *Basilikon doron* and *The trew law of free monarchies*: the Scottish context and the English translation', in *The mental world of the Jacobean court*, ed. Linda Levy Peck (Cambridge, 1991), pp. 36–54.

> For all the hopes which Papistry expected,
> Or else the triumphs to revenge erected,
> Roisters and murtherers are cleere put downe:
> Dispayring, when they hear James wears the Crown.[37]

Sermons on the Union of the Crowns likened James to biblical figures, most often noted defenders of the faith, and celebrated his arrival as an opportunity to put an end to religious divisions. Writers celebrated the benefits of unity, and drew increasingly solid links between religion and politics. John Thornborough pointed out that religion was 'the chiefest band of hearty union' in which each subject might 'participate, in the common Obedience, transferred unto all, under the Government of One'.[38] Another Union sermon, preached by John Gordon, argued that 'the contrary vertue to Division (which is Union) is the basis of the preservation of all spiritual and Temporal felicity', and that the instrument of this union was religion. What both sermons had in common was the use of a corporate metaphor to point out the dangers of religious factions within the state. Where Thornborough had likened the state to a 'little world', Gordon wrote of a little kingdom composed of diverse members and surmounted by a head, which he designated as 'the sovereign governor of the whole body'.[39] John Thornborough once again stressed the importance of unity in a sermon that celebrated the Union of the Crowns as the best way to diminish the threat of 'divers laws and customs' which 'do oft times beggar the common good & peace of the weale publique'.[40]

Since the Church was conceived as inextricably joined with the body politic of the state, the idea of sovereignty had a religious dimension. William Willymat argued that the king charged both civil and spiritual magistrates to govern the people:

All such both supreme and inferior civill Magistrates are ministers armed with both laws and sword, to be nursers to Gods church or people, and Fathers to the commonwealth, to guide, governe, and order the people within their seuerall circuites and charges ... to execute justice and discipline, as well in Ecclesiasticall, as in all other causes, for the benefit, and good of the good, and punishment of the bad.[41]

---

[37] [John Fenton], *King Iames his welcome to London* (London, 1603), sig. B^v.

[38] John Thornborough, *The ioifull and blessed reuniting of the two mighty & famous kingdomes, England & Scotland into their ancient name of great Brittaine* (Oxford, 1604), pp. 8–9.

[39] John Gordon, *Enotikon or A sermon of the vnion of Great Brittainie* (London, 1604), pp. 1, 8.

[40] John Thornborough, *A discourse plainely prouing the euident vtilitie and vrgent necessitie of the desired happie vnion of the two famous kingdomes of England and Scotland* (London, 1604), p. 29.

[41] William Willymat, *A loyal subiects looking-glasse* (London, 1604), sig. C^{3v}.

Precisely this connection between the civil and spiritual authority made English sovereignty complete. Preaching a sermon before James I in 1604, Henry Hooke argued that the unity of the civil and spiritual power served to strengthen the commonwealth as a whole; England could boast the best of a 'religious commonwealth' combined with a 'civil societie whose constitution is wholly framed of humane policie'.[42] Yet there were limits to the nature of the power exercised over this arrangement, and the added complication of the influence of external actors. Hence, John Stockwood argued that it was the duty of the Christian prince to prevent the rise of undue influence at the hands of those who 'conceyve hope of some private benefit'.[43] While this was some way off from the mature language of interests, whether public or private, it was obvious that contemporaries saw faction and competition as threats to religious peace.[44] In the course of statements of this type, contemporaries voiced justifications for the Crown's jurisdiction over the Church.

Some sermons on the Union likened England's new peacemaker to biblical exemplars. Andrew Willet therefore conjured up the images of Solomon and David in the course of a lengthy excursus on the 122nd Psalm ('Pray for the Peace of Jerusalem'). The central point of Willet's tract was to exhort both King and subjects to strive for unity and peace in religion: 'Wherefore masters, fathers, and governors should rather seeke by their Godly care to win those unto God, that belong unto Him, then pull them by their negligence from God, for whom they are accomptable.'[45] Yet Willet also sought to respond to a specific challenge to the Church as a political association; he did so by stressing the connection between the Church and the Crown. Willet, whom some[46] have called a 'moderate Puritan', displayed a coolness toward conformists such as Hooker, but also celebrated the Church of England as the 'true' religion, James as the embodiment of the 'Christian prince', and unity as essential in church and commonwealth:

A vertuous king then is a most excellent means to draw people distracted in opinions and sectes, to one true worship of God: they that live in one kingdom, should have one Christendome, be all of one faith and religion: as they obey one King in earth, so they should adore one God in heaven: and as they are subject to one law for civill

---

[42] Henry Hooke, *A sermon preached before the king at White-hall, the eight of May 1604* (London, 1604), sig. A⁵.
[43] John Stockwood, *A verie godlie and profitable sermon of the necessitie, properties, and office of a good magistrate* (London, 1584), sig. A²ʳ.
[44] J. A. W. Gunn, *Politics and the public interest in the seventeenth century* (London, 1969).
[45] Andrew Willet, *Ecclesia triumphans: that is, The ioy of the English church, for the happie coronation of the most vertuous and pious prince, Iames* ([Cambridge], 1603), pp. 26–7.
[46] Anthony Milton, *Catholic and reformed: the Roman and Protestant churches in English Protestant thought, 1600–1640* (Cambridge, 1995), p. 129.

administration, so they should walk after one rule, concerning their Christian profession.[47]

Willet's exhortations to unity and uniformity in doctrine (and presumably discipline) were pitched in softer language than usually found, for example, in the sermons of 'avant-garde' conformists such as Lancelot Andrewes.[48] However, Willet clearly suggested that the Church should remain established, and that monarchy and some measure of ecclesiastical hierarchy had a crucial role in promoting unity in doctrine and discipline.

On the subject of Separatists, Willet struck a conciliatory note: 'Now, as for them which stand apart, and separate themselves from us, swelling with an opinion of their owne greater holiness, if they will be counted among the tribes of the Lord, let them also come to Jerusalem: if anything hath grieved them in our Church.'[49] As for the 'notes' of the Church – that is, the historical and doctrinal marks by which the true church could be recognised – Willet argued that the principal three were 'the word of God, the next the sacraments, the third is discipline'. He had no doctrinal quarrel with the Church of England: 'We teach no doctrine but concluded out of Scriptures, we receive no sacraments, but those instituted by Our Saviour.'[50] Yet Willet did not go so far as to say that sacraments must be drawn literally from the scriptures, and so he argued that they were acceptable so long as they were 'edifying'. This was a standard argument among conformists, who styled sacraments as 'helps' to understanding one's religious duty, but not instrumental in the process of salvation.[51]

Although Willet and his contemporaries looked to the past, they also examined the present and sought in it signs of order and stability. Many saw the peaceful accession of James I as an act of divine providence.[52] It is in this language that Willet celebrated the arrival of James, and expressed his hope that the King would preside over a final, binding, and peaceful settlement of English religion:

That whereas all things before were confused, there was no order, no justice, no redresse of errors, no correction of offenders, now David hath constituted an exact

---

[47] Willet, *Ecclesia triumphans*, pp. 56–7.

[48] For 'avant-garde' conformity, see Peter Lake, 'Lancelot Andrewes, John Buckeridge, and avant-garde conformity', in *Mental world of the Jacobean court*, ed. Peck, pp. 113–33. Lake rightly argued that conformists tended to favour things 'indifferent' and frequently stressed the need to obey the Christian prince; Hooker, meanwhile, emphasised a 'Christian community' (p. 133). Willet exhibited a strong preference for two of these three elements; still in question is his attitude to things 'indifferent', which is hard to judge, but which is discussed below.

[49] Willet, *Ecclesia triumphans*, pp. 60–1.   [50] Ibid., pp. 62–3, 65.   [51] Ibid., pp. 71–2.

[52] Alexandra Walsham, *Providence in early modern England* (Oxford, 1999); Peter Lake and Michael Questier, *The Antichrists's lewd hat: Protestants, papists and players in post-Reformation England* (New Haven, 2002).

politie and government, he appointed thrones of justice, where everyman's complaint might be heard. We see then, what an excellent benefit it is, when the Lord giveth unto a nation a settled and established government.

The authority to institute 'polity' and 'government' was lodged in the person of the King, compared here to the great biblical King David. Willet concluded with the hope that the 'Ecclesiastical and Civil state of this kingdome ... may never be parted and pulled asunder'.[53] This statement showed how he shared the contemporary view of the need for a conjoined state to uphold political and religious stability, and as well his confidence that James would preside over the Church as a 'godly' prince.

Chief among the powers of ecclesiastical sovereignty was the assembling of councils and synods to consider the state of the Church. That James I summoned such a conference early in his English reign was partly an assertion of his authority, and partly a response to the Millenary Petition, which claimed to represent the state of opinion among the ordinary clergy, who had subscribed to the Elizabethan Book of Common Prayer 'some upon protestation, some upon exposition given them, some with condition[s]'.[54] This range of response to the Prayer Book hardly defined a single 'puritan' movement. The petition called for a number of reforms: the simplifying of clerical dress, including the removal of the cap and surplice; that a sermon be preached prior to communion; and the moderation of music for 'better edification', 'that there may be a uniformity of doctrine proscribed'. At the heart of the problem, and clearly what united this disparate group of clergymen, was the apparatus of Elizabethan conformity and its putative victims, the clergy: 'who shall be no more suspended, silenced, disgraced, imprisoned, for men's traditions'. The complaint was not with the Church of England *per se*, but rather with a small number of ceremonies, and especially the power of bishops and the court of High Commission. The authors concluded that, if given the opportunity, they would be able to 'show' that the ceremonies in question were not 'agreeable to the scriptures'.[55] Hence, the Petition offered criticism of the two central propositions that underlay the conformist position: that the Church as a corporation retained the freedom to exact standards of discipline and establish modes of worship, and that this mixture of the human and mutable with the spiritual and immutable did not entail the Church's deviation from the pattern of scripture or the practice of the ancient church.[56]

---

[53] Willet, *Ecclesia triumphans*, pp. 75, 80.
[54] The text cited here is reproduced in *The Stuart constitution: documents and commentary*, ed. J. P. Kenyon (Cambridge, 1986), doc. 39, pp. 117–19.
[55] Ibid., pp. 117–19 passim.
[56] Arthur Ferguson, *Clio unbound: perception of the social and cultural past in Renaissance England* (Durham, NC, 1979), pp. 130, 172.

While it is true that ceremonies and governance were, on the surface, minor issues, it is also the case that they cut to the core of a profound ecclesiological problem concerning the definition of the Church. It is this rift that drove the debate in the early stages of James' tenure. The first articulation of the conformist position came in a royal proclamation, published on 24 October 1603, announcing the King's intention to call a conference of the clergy. It condemned those who zealously sought reformation of the Church, and *twice* stated, as if anticipating an attack upon episcopacy, that 'the estate of the Church here established, and the degrees and orders of Ministers governing the same [is] agreeable to the worde of God, and the forme of the Primitive Church'.[57] The conference at Hampton Court was set to meet, but the governance of the Church was not on the agenda. The first book-length response to the Millenary Petition took issue with the statement that the ministers could 'show' that the liturgy of the Church conflicted with scripture. Coming from Oxford, and confirmed by divines at Cambridge, the *Answere ... To the humble petition* marked the opening stage of a series of controversial exchanges that would last for the remainder of the reign. Firmly rooted within the textual tradition that defended the English Church, it referred to some of the foundational literature of the conformist position, including the October proclamation, as well as works by Thomas Bilson, Richard Bancroft, Matthew Sutcliffe, and Richard Hooker.[58] In short, the *Answere* reiterated the antiquity of the Church as defined by its late Elizabethan conformist defenders, and condemned the petitioners for having ignored this history:

The idle vaunt that the Petitioners make of being able to shew that these and other such abuses (as they call them) remaining and practiced in the Church of England are not agreeable to the Scriptures, doth appear to be the more ridiculous; because they have passed over in deep silence many Learned tracts published long since; wherein their vaine fancies, and illiterate objections, are refuted at large; If they will needs argue and dispute, there are [writers] ready that will either satisfie them, or by argument silence them. And were it not in regard that we would not seem as undutifull in accepting, as they have been in the offering of this challenge; it is a thing we would urge and instantly entreat, that these matters might be debated between us in writing.[59]

---

[57] *Stuart royal proclamations*, ed. J. F. Larkin and P. L. Hughes, 2 vols. (Oxford, 1973), vol. I, pp. 60–3 passim.

[58] *The answere of the vicechancelour, the doctors, both the proctors, and other the heads of houses in the Vniversity of Oxford ... To the humble petition of the ministers of the Church of England, desiring reformation of certain ceremonies and abuses of the Church* (Oxford, 1603).

[59] Ibid., p. 26.

The *Answere* took one part of the Elizabethan tradition, claimed that it retained a definitive status, and heaped scorn on those who departed from the judgements of the principal defenders of the English Church. This attack on the apparent lack of learning of the petitioners may have had some substance. The controversial apparatus of the average signatory to the Millenary Petition would probably have consisted of a small private library, whereas an Oxford divine, seated in the revivified library above the Divinity School, could draw on a vast and unparalleled collection of histories and commentaries. Antiquity, as conveyed in the works of the early Church Fathers, was much more accessible to Oxbridge divines than to parish clergy, and they invited a debate 'in writing' in which they held a considerable advantage.

Coupled with the charge that the reformist position was based on a thin grasp of the church's scholarly tradition, the Oxford *Answere* sought to trace the links between ecclesiology and political life: 'Church government is doubly supported unto the supreme civil state, and withal doth mightily support the same.' The relation between the ecclesiastical and 'politique' parts of the state that we saw articulated in the previous chapter also informed the position of the Oxford divines. The arguments of reformists were not carefully considered in terms of their theological propositions, but rather were briskly dismissed as threats to stable polity: 'the things they seeke are so prejudicial, both to the civil state in general, and in Particular, to so many of the very best in the Ministry'. The Oxford divines criticised this call for reform because they felt that the Church as it then stood was, as the October proclamation had put it, 'agreeable to God's word, and neere to the Condition of the Primitive Church'. This defence stressed the ancient roots of doctrine, episcopal polity, and clerical learning of the established Church. From the point of view of the Oxford divines, the Church of England exemplified 'the Purity of Religion, perpetually supported by an uniform most Ancient kind of commendable Church government; and the plenty of all manner of good Learning, abundantly derived from the Wellsprings thereof, into all the Parts, both of the Church and Commonwealth'.[60]

Also early in the reign of James VI and I, some reformists proposed to examine the ancient church, and to point out those matters on which the Church of England seemed to depart from its example. In the Elizabethan setting, the Marprelate controversy turned on the question of whether episcopacy was of genuine ancient status, or whether the ancient church had been governed by other means. The argument resumed in 1604: Henry Jacob, one of the architects of the Millenary Petition, argued that the

---

[60] Ibid., 'To the Christian Reader', p. 30.

Church of England did depart from Apostolic traditions, since the ancient church was not diocesan but comprised of 'particular and ordinary congregations'. He argued that the scriptures confirmed this congregational mode of governance, and the alteration of this purity deformed the Church of England.[61] Perhaps sensing the need to broaden the case, Jacob put forward evidence to refute the conformist argument that patristic authors supported diocesan episcopacy. Thus, passages from St Ambrose, St Jerome, St Augustine, Eusebius, and Pseudo Dionysius were analysed in order to show how conformist writers had deliberately misinterpreted their texts: 'Wherefore the common accompts and catalogues of the succession of Bishops from the Apostles times to our dayes is very deceiptfull and false'.[62] At the crux of Jacob's argument was a question central to the religious controversies of the period: the nature of the validity of the Church's 'traditions'. For Jacob, there was an important difference between traditions, and what he defined as 'circumstances': the former were evident in the scriptures, and via unadulterated readings of the Fathers, while the latter were the result of human 'policie'. There was a further difference between circumstances and things indifferent: 'So that it remaineth sure, that all Church Traditions without God's word (& therefore all invented forms of Visible Churches using government, offices of Ministrie and Ceremonies) are simply evil and unlawful, and therefore of necessity ought to be reformed.'[63] Jacob did not see the Church as the product of time and experience, but as an immemorial institution.

   Although the issue of governance was not on the Hampton Court agenda, the problem of episcopal jurisdiction and its relation to the royal supremacy was a common theme in controversial literature published in the early months of James' reign; moreover, it led writers to consider the problem of 'jurisdiction' and ecclesiastical sovereignty.[64] Francis Bacon warned the King that, given the emerging power of the bishops, there might be reason to expect that the ecclesiastical jurisdiction of the Crown could clash with that of the higher clergy if they continued to seek 'sole and unassisted' power.[65] The civil lawyer

---

[61] Henry Jacob, 'Epistle Dedicatory', in *Reasons taken out of Gods word and the best humane testimonies prouing a necessitie of reforming our churches in England* ([Middelburg], 1604).

[62] Jacob, *Reasons taken*, pp. 8–9. Jacob argued that St Timothy, whom Eusebius regarded as the first Bishop of Ephesus, fulfilled the scriptural definition of an 'evangelical' bishop. Cf. Kenneth Fincham, *Prelate as pastor: the episcopate of James I* (Oxford, 1990), ch. 8; Keith Sprunger, *Dutch puritanism: a history of the English and Scottish churches of the Netherlands in the sixteenth and seventeenth centuries* (Leiden, 1982), pp. 32, 68, 136, 137, 233.

[63] Jacob, *Reasons taken*, pp. 11, 13.

[64] For a treatment of this issue in the Caroline context, see D. Alan Orr, 'Sovereignty, supremacy, and the origins of the English Civil War', *History*, 87 (2002), 474–90.

[65] [Francis Bacon], *Certaine considerations touching the better pacification and edification of the Church of England* (London, 1604), sig. C[2v].

William Stoughton argued that 'a reformation of the Church, can not but infer a desolation of the state', and suggested that it was a matter of political prudence to ensure that the 'estates' of parliament did not fall victim to the condition of *imperium in imperio* – that is, the preponderance of one estate above the others. Indeed, Stoughton argued that parliament consisted of King, Nobles, and Commons gathered together without the presence of any members of the clergy:[66]

And that the King, the Nobles and the Commons of this realm, without Prelates, Bishops, or Clerkes, do make up all of the members, and parts of this body, and of this state; and may therefore ordaine, promulge, and execute, all manner of lawes, without any consent, approbation, or authority yielded unto the same, by the Bishops spiritual, or any other of the clergie.[67]

Indeed, Stoughton alleged that, in pursuing a programme of subscription and deprivation, the bishops were 'entermedlers ... by reason of schisme ... they have so farre encroached upon the perrogatives of the Prince, and the privileges of the people, by forcing the choice of pastors on the people'.[68] Stoughton repeatedly expressed his satisfaction that the Crown was supreme over the Church, and that the Church of England agreed with the 'true' church – save on the matter of governance. For him, episcopacy compromised the purity of the ecclesiastical supremacy of the Crown, and ran contrary to the Presbyterian polity practised in the ancient church. It was this assumption that underlay his suggestion that all ecclesiastical courts should be abolished, and all matters of governance committed to courts of the common law.[69] On the question of rites, Stoughton was almost silent; rather, his interest lay in the questions of organisation and authority, and their ancient warrants.[70]

The issue of the rites and liturgy appropriate to the Church was the focus of the Hampton Court conference, held in January 1604.[71] Some of the debates waged between 'reformers' and members of the higher clergy have

---

[66] For a discussion of Stoughton's anti-episcopal career in the context of the Marprelate controversy, see Michael Mendle, *Dangerous positions: mixed government, the estates of the realm, and the 'Answer to the xix propositions'* (University, AL, 1985), pp. 98–102.

[67] William Stoughton, *An assertion for true and Christian church-policie* ([Middelburg], 1604), pp. 14–15, 170.

[68] Ibid., pp. 206–7.

[69] Usher, *Rise and fall of the High Commission*, pp. 187–8.

[70] Almost. 'And as touching rites and ceremonies, we affirme not, that every rite, ceremony or circumstance to be used in the externall execution of Church government, is precisely sett down in the holie Scriptures.' *An assertion*, pp. 434–5. Stoughton argued that it was for 'church governors' (i.e. the Crown) to decide these matters.

[71] See Patrick Collinson, 'The Jacobean religious settlement: the Hampton Court conference', in *Before the English Civil War*, ed. Howard Tomlinson (London, 1983), pp. 27–51; Kenneth Fincham, 'Ramifications of the Hampton Court conference in the Dioceses, 1603–1609', *Journal of Ecclesiastical History*, 36 (1985), 208–27; and Babbage, *Puritanism and Richard Bancroft*, pp. 57–73.

survived in two contemporary sources.[72] In royal proclamations published before the conference, the King had expressed his satisfaction with the Church, particularly on the fundamental matters of doctrine and governance. Dismissing the reformists, William Barlow, the author of the most detailed 'account' of the conference, suggested that instead of genuine debate, the aim of the meeting was 'to cast a sop into Cereberus his mouth'. Indeed, the King's caution about opening the door to a reversal of the Elizabethan Church's position was evident in Barlow's account. James ordered that the debate be confined to the Prayer Book, ecclesiastical courts, and the Irish Ministry, and that predestination 'might be verie tenderly handled'. A prominent theme in the debates was the problem of uniformity, and how it was to be maintained. Even John Rainolds – President of Corpus Christi, former tutor to Richard Hooker, and chosen by the King to speak for the remonstrant side – called for a new edition of the Bible, 'that no marginal notes should be added, having found ... them which are annexed to the Geneva translation ... very partial, untrue, seditious, and favouring too much of dangerous and trayterous conceits'. As an example, Rainolds cited Exodus 1: 19, which furnished, he argued, an exhortation to 'disobedience to kings'; Rainolds of course was anxious to make it known that reform did not entail disobedience.[73]

The conference was also the site of a renewed debate over the widely criticised programme of subscription to ceremonies whose theological grounds were disputed by the remonstrants. Rainolds characterised the Elizabethan programme of subscription as a 'great impeachment to a learned Ministry'. By 'learned' he meant university-educated ministers who preached from the Bible. It was this statement that furnished the broader context for Rainolds' complaint about 'seditious books', and his attacks on the composition of the Prayer Book.[74] The liturgy of the Church, he suggested, was not faithfully adapted from the Word, and was thus cluttered with elements of human devising. The conformist response to Rainolds was that, always and everywhere, the Church had the power to 'institute and retaine' rites and ceremonies of its own choosing – its sovereignty was not confined to a literal interpretation of scripture. By way of illustration, Barlow related the dispute over the antiquity of the cross:

[72] William Barlow, *The summe and substance of the conference ... at Hampton Court, January 14. 1603* (London, 1604). Also see the 'Anonymous account', printed in R. G. Usher, *The reconstruction of the English Church*, 2 vols. (London, 1910), vol. II, pp. 341–54.
[73] Barlow, *Summe and substance*, pp. 6–7, 30, 43, 45.
[74] See W. B. Patterson, *King James VI and I and the reunion of Christendom* (Cambridge, 1997), pp. 46–7.

And here the king desired, to have himselfe made acquainted about the antiquitie of the use of the Crosse. Which Doctor Reynolds confessed, to have been ever since the Apostles times, but this was the difficulty, to prove it, of that ancient use in Baptisme. For that, at their going abroad, or entering into the Church, or at their Prayers and benedictions, it was used by the Aunciens, desired no greate proofe: but whether, in Baptisme, Antiquitie approved it, was the doubt cast in.[75]

At this point the Dean of Winchester furnished references from Tertullian, Cyprian, and Origen, proving the antiquity of certain 'signes', and the Church's right to enjoin the clergy to observe them. Satisfied, the King agreed that the wearing of the surplice and the use of the cross in baptism would remain, given their ancient warrant; joined to these was the ancient power of the Crown to ensure that those of 'unquiet humour should presently be enforced to a conformity'. Indeed, the King concluded his statements to the assembly by pointing out that, having fulfilled his duty as defender of the faith, he was not prepared to tolerate dissent in his Church: 'we have taken here paines, and in the end have concluded of an unity and uniformity, and, you forsooth, must prefer the Credites of a few private men, before the generall peace of the Church'.[76] To be noted is James' emphasis of the public nature of the worship of the Church of England – it was an association joined together with the state, and the two could not be divided.

Immediately following Hampton Court there appeared a series of statements that outlined the Crown's position on 'dissent', and restated the case for the disputed ceremonies. A royal proclamation issued in March 1604 lent the terms to the debate between English Protestants that came to be used to describe religious cleavages in the seventeenth century: 'conformist' and 'dissenter'. It also established that the higher clergy, the 'Archbishops, Bishops, and all other publique Ministers, as well Ecclesiastical as Civill' should ensure conformity to the Book of Common Prayer; the same proclamation announced that a new edition of the Prayer Book was pending.[77] The resulting edition, the so-called 'Hampton Court Book', contained incidental changes that were intended to iron out issues of inconsistency raised at Hampton Court. Both the March proclamation and the Elizabethan Act of Uniformity were included at the front of the 1604 edition of the Prayer Book; in addition, it included a new preface and a short explanation of

---

[75] Barlow, *Summe and substance*, pp. 59, 68–9.

[76] Ibid., pp. 100, 102; and 'A proclamation for the authorizing and uniformitie of the Booke of Common Prayer to be used throughout the realme', 5 March 1604, in *Stuart royal proclamations*, ed. Larkin and Hughes, vol. I, p. 75.

[77] The Proclamation contained a very forceful statement against those who worshipped outside of the Church: 'For both they used forms of publique serving of God not here allowed, held assemblies without Authoritie, and did other things carrying a very apparent shew of sedition, more than of Zeale.'

ceremonies.[78] The preface dealt with the 'original of Divine service', which, according to the ancient Fathers, was established for the 'great advancement of Godliness'.[79] However, during the Middle Ages this ancient perfection had fallen into decline: 'this godly and decent order of the ancient Fathers hath beene so altered, broken and neglected'. Like the Church, the service itself was plagued by disunity, and the Prayer Book was proposed as a solution that *restored* the 'old way' of the Fathers.

The brief section 'Of Ceremonies' proposed to offer a clear explanation of a complex doctrinal point: *adiaphora*, or 'things indifferent'. Again, the corruption of the ancient tradition became the means of explaining not that mediaeval ceremonies were 'devised by man', but rather that they injured rather than edified. Well-worn conformist arguments were used to justify the approved ceremonies now listed in the Book of Common Prayer: 'And although the keeping or omitting of a Ceremonie, in itself considered, is but a small thing: yet the willful and contemptuous transgression and breaking of a *common* order and discipline, is no small offence before God.'[80] The remark sought to provide an historical and scriptural justification for the uniformity of discipline. Moreover, in the manner of Richard Hooker, the passage defended the power of the Church to order worship in a manner that maintained a 'seemly and due' public sense of decorum:

Let all things be done among you, sayeth S. Paul, in a seemly and due order. The appoyntment of which order, pertaineth not to private men: therefore no man ought to take in hand, nor presume to appoint or alter any publicke or common order in Christ's Church, *except he be lawfully called or authorised thereunto.*[81]

The critics of the ceremonies of the Church were portrayed as being motivated by private 'opinion', while their defenders were identified as the 'lawfully called' maintainers of 'publicke or common order'. Like the Jacobean proclamations, the passage stressed a view of the Church as an 'association' which demanded concord among its clergy.

A second proclamation, issued in July, reiterated the Crown's continuing intention to 'settle the affairs of this Church of England in an Uniformitie as well of Doctrine, as of Government, both of them agreeable to the Word of God, [and] the Doctrine of the Primitive Church'. Hence, the position of the

---

[78] There were five variants of the Prayer Book published during 1604; the Hampton Court version was distinguished by a title-page printed in red and black within a border. The text was based upon the edition of 1601, and leaves were added at fols. D and S to accommodate the additional text. See David Griffiths, *The bibliography of the Book of Common Prayer, 1549–1999* (London, 2002), p. 89.

[79] Church of England, 'Preface', in *The booke of common prayer, and administration of the sacraments, and other rites and ceremonies of the Church of England* (London, 1604).

[80] 'Of Ceremonies, why some be abolished, some retained', in *Booke of common prayer*, n. p.

[81] Ibid., passim.

Crown had not changed as a result of the Hampton Court conference, but had rather hardened. The conformist position on ecclesiastical sovereignty, antiquity, and uniformity was now reinforced by the civil power of the Crown: '[O]ur duetie towards God requireth at our hands, that what untractable men doe not performe upon admonition, they must be compelled unto by Authoritie, whereof the Supreme power resting in our hands, by Gods ordinance, Wee are bound to use the same in *nothing more*, then in preservation of the Churches tranquillitie.'[82] This echoed a long line of pronouncements, analysed in the previous chapter, that dealt with the King's power as an ecclesiastical governor.

Perhaps the strongest conformist statement appeared in the *Constitutions and canons ecclesiastical*, which emerged in the wake of the Convocation held during May 1604. The Canons set forth an interpretation of the Church of England that would stand throughout the Jacobean period, and reiterated the conformist position on the disputed issues of the surplice and the sign of the cross in baptism, as well as long-standing issues of plurality and non-residency. Not only were clergy required to subscribe to these articles on pain of deprivation, but they also had to affirm the doctrinal and ancient perfection of the liturgy and governance of the Church:

Whosoever shall hereafter affirm, That the Church of England, by law established under the king's majesty, is not a true and an apostolical church, teaching and maintaining the doctrine of the apostles [and] Whoever shall hereafter affirm, That the form of God's worship in the Church of England, established by law, and contained in the Book of Common Prayer and Administration of Sacraments, is a corrupt, superstitious, or unlawful worship of God, or containeth anything in it that is repugnant to the scriptures; let him be excommunicated *ipso facto*, and not restored.[83]

Crucial among the 141 clauses that comprised the Canons was number thirty-six, which contained three articles. The first article was derived from the Elizabethan Oath of Supremacy, and concerned the King's status as 'supreme Governour' in 'all Spiritual or Ecclesiastical things or causes'. The second article affirmed the soundness of the Book of Common Prayer, and 'of ordering of Bishops, Priests and Deacons', and stipulated that the service would be based on the Prayer Book and 'none other'. Finally, the third article reiterated that 'all and every' of the Thirty-nine Articles were 'agreeable to the Word of God'.[84] It was these articles to which the oath of subscription was attached:

---

[82] *Stuart royal proclamations*, ed. Larkin and Hughes, vol. I, p. 76; 'A Proclamation Enjoyning Conformitie', 16 July 1604, pp. 88, 89. Emphasis added.

[83] *Stuart royal proclamations*, ed. Larkin and Hughes, vol. I, pp. 249–50.

[84] See *Constitutions and canons ecclesiastical* (London, 1604), reprinted in *Synodalia: a collection of articles of religion, Canons, and proceedings of convocations in the province of Canterbury*, ed. Edward Cardwell, 2 vols. (Oxford, 1842; repr. 1966), vol. I, pp. 245–329.

To these three Articles whosoever will subscribe he shall for the avoiding of all ambiguities subscribe in this order and forme of words, setting down both his christen and surname, viz. *I N.N. doe willingly and* ex animo *subscribe to these three Articles above mentioned, and to all things that are contained in them.*[85]

Richard Bancroft was instrumental in pressing the Canons through Convocation, and his policy was clear: the Church would uphold the supremacy of the Crown, episcopal governance, and the Protestant doctrine put forward in the Thirty-nine Articles. Long a central figure in Whitgift's struggle against the Presbyterians, Bancroft would employ the political tools available to him to ensure the uniformity of the public doctrine of the Church of England.[86]

A letter from the Privy Council sent to Bancroft soon after his consecration as Archbishop of Canterbury (10 December 1604) noted that the deadline for conformity set by the July proclamation had passed, and expressed the hope that 'your lordship throughout your province ... will have regard to the execution of the said laws and constitutions ... as is meet and necessary for the uniformity of the church discipline'. The members of the Council then pledged their assistance: 'as we cannot omit both to assist your own readiness with our advice and concurrence of judgment, and that which is much more, to give you knowledge of the expectation his majesty hath of your proceedings herein'.[87] In short, Archbishop Bancroft had received an order, and moved to issue orders of his own. These came in a letter that set forth his directions concerning subscription: all new ministers were to be given the oath of subscription, and those that refused but showed signs of reversing their positions were to be given time to do so; still, the Archbishop was to be given their names. Concerning those that 'utterly refuse', Bancroft ordered that they be deprived according to the Elizabethan Act of Uniformity, and that all questions concerning the procedure be directed to the Chancellor of the Diocese in the first instance, and to Canterbury after that. He concluded by noting that,

I have not hitherto greatly liked of any severe course; but perceiving by certain instructions lately cast abroad, that the present opposition so lately prosecuted, doth rather proceed from a combination of sundry factious, who in the pride of their mind are loath to be foiled ... than of any religious care or true conscience; I have thought it very necessary, for the repressing of such irregular designments, earnestly to commend to your Lordship the careful execution of these directions.[88]

---

[85] Ibid., sig. F^{2v-r}.

[86] For details, see Babbage, *Puritanism and Richard Bancroft*, pp. 74–102.

[87] Lambeth Palace Library, Bancroft's Register, fol. 127a. 'The Council's Letter from Proceeding Against the Non-Conformitans of the Clergy' (1604).

[88] Lambeth Palace Library, Bancroft's Register, fol. 127b. 'The Archbishop of Canterbury's Directions to the Same Purpose' (1604). In his sermon preached at Paul's Cross in February 1588, Bancroft had suggested that 'there is no reformed church in Christendome which doth

The initial optimism of the Jacobean settlement gave way to tension over the doctrine and discipline of the Church. These tensions were set against two issues left over from Elizabethan debates: the jurisdiction of the High Commission and the problem of clerical subscription. The Hampton Court conference was primarily concerned with liturgy and doctrine, but it met in a climate of increasing tension over the doctrinal and legal elements that defined the conformist position, and which were a lasting source of reformist disaffection.

DISSENTING PETITIONS

The new orders contained in the Canons of 1604 were rapidly put into effect, and given that they reinforced aspects of doctrine (especially kneeling at communion) and discipline (subscription enforced by the bishops) that had raised considerable contention in the previous decades, a debate about these provisions got quickly under way.[89] A broadside petition submitted to the Crown by a group of twenty-two London ministers put the elements of the dilemma facing reformists in succinct form: they wished to express their loyalty to the Crown, and to make a point of theological principle. Therefore, the petition covered the principal grounds of politics and scholarship; on the former, they affirmed their loyalty, but made a point to remind the King that both he and they were bound by a higher authority: 'If anythinge were commanded us by Your Magestie, which we might doe, without offence to the Highest Majestie, there is not one man among us, that would not willingly obey the same.' The statement takes some unpacking, but at bottom what was being said was that the laws of God would govern the minds and actions of the ministers before the laws of the Crown. From this point, the authors went on to suggest that, since the King himself had expressed his desire that all questionable points of doctrine should be debated, then they, like the authors of the Millenary Petition, were prepared to make the case against the official liturgy: 'your Majestie hath often said, that if any can shewe the things required to be unlawfull, your highness will not have them urged. And except we are able, by the evidence of the Holy Scripture, to prove the same, we will present yeeld to conformitie required.'[90] Here again, the profession of loyalty was qualified by reference to the *iure*

---

not in this case require subscription (at the least) of their ministers'. See Bancroft, *A sermon preached at Paules Cross the 9. of Februarie, being the first Sunday in the Parleament, anno. 1588* (London, 1588), p. 47.

[89] For details see Babbage, *Puritanism and Richard Bancroft*, pp. 103–23; Fincham, *Prelate as pastor*, pp. 35–67.

[90] *To the Kinges most excellent Majestie the humble petition of two and twentie preachers in London and the suburbs thereof* ([W. Jones' secret press?, 1605?]).

divino authority of scripture, itself the sole ground for judging issues pertaining to the doctrine and governance of the Church.

In another petition, a group of parishioners in the Diocese of Lincoln complained that the deprivation of their minister opened the door to popery; they expressed their loyalty to the Crown and suggested 'good doctrine and example . . . safely contain ye common people in the duties of their Subjection and Loyalty to the Supreme Power'.[91] In Hereford, Bishop Francis Godwin published his visitation articles, which included provisions for the removal of 'hainous offences [that] are daily committed against the Lawes Ecclesiastical of his Majesty'.[92] Kenneth Fincham's collection of these articles reveals the ways in which conformity was policed, virtually on a parish-by-parish basis; standard queries included whether copies of the Prayer Book, the Thirty-nine Articles, and the Canons were prominently displayed in the church's porch, whether anyone 'quarrelled with the minister', or if the latter was ever to be seen 'conversing with recusants'.[93] References to both 'puritans' and 'papists' dominate some of the early treatments of the Canons and their enforcement. A Star Chamber Assembly in 1604 pondered the question of whether the High Commission overseeing ministerial deprivation was a lawful entity, or whether it constituted a new and unprecedented power. The judges concluded that the court did 'not confer any new power, but explaine . . . the Ancient power'. This reinforced the idea that the ancient constitution of England placed ecclesiastical jurisdiction in the hands of the monarch, who could in turn delegate it to 'inferior magistrates'.[94]

Other contributions to the early stages of the debate sought to persuade members of the clergy that the rites and ceremonies established by the Canons were marks of the 'true' church. John Panke put the case in a dialogue whose preceptor offered evidence of the ancient status of the disputed ceremonies to an opponent who demanded, 'shew me I pray you what times the Primitive Church . . . used to celebrate'. The preceptor argued that the ceremonial use of the cross was a mark of the visible church, and connected the faithful to God: 'it is the spirit of the living God, that living secretly hid under the shadow of these crosses, which doth purifie, correct and comfort'. Panke's purpose was to diffuse the common charge that the symbol was that of the anti-Christ; it was

---

[91] Bodl. Carte MS, fol. 77, n. 590. Earl of Huntington Papers.

[92] [Francis Godwin], 'To the Parson, Vicar or Curate of [blank] . . . orders for the reformation of abuses', (1603). Bodl. B.4.3. (13) Linc.

[93] *Visitation articles and injunctions of the early Stuart Church*, ed. Kenneth Fincham, 2 vols. (Woodbridge, Suffolk, 1994–8), vol. I, pp. 7–9. Quotes are from 'Abp. Bancroft's Articles for His Metropolitical Visitation of ten Dioceses, 1605.'

[94] Bodl. Carte MS, fol. 59, n. 427. Misc. Ormonde Papers. 'A Narrative of Proceedings by the Judges of England and Others Concerning Papists and Puritans' (1604). There is already an abundant literature concerning oaths, yet the bulk of scholarly attention has been fixed on their use against Catholic recusants. The MSS cited here referred to Elizabethan precedents.

instead a badge and a sign of what it meant to 'be a true member of the mystical body of Christ, whereof he is the head'.[95] Citing a range of Apostolic examples, and the testimony of St Anacletus, St Thomas Aquinas, and Dionysius Areopagatica, Panke argued that the ancient church distinguished itself by ordering its public worship in a manner that provided the pattern for the English Church.[96] 'Outward profession' and 'essential marks' were symbolic customs, and 'in not receiving you are neither joined to Christ the head, nor to the members of the faithful; for hereupon is the receiving of this sacrament called a Communion: a knitting together of many in one'.[97] Here Panke invited his reader to consider the Church as a united spiritual body – an association – in which ceremonies and sacraments acted as ties binding the people one to another, and the whole to the ancient church.

Another dialogue, between the aptly named 'Irenaeus' and 'Antimachus', also pondered how the body politic of the Church 'hath been disquieted with home-born crossbiters'. The dialogue format allowed the author to treat the positions of conformists and their critics side by side, a tactic that produced a printed version of a formal clerical dispute. It also answered a number of practical concerns: in the absence of actual reformist tracts, the dialogue offered the controversialist the opportunity to enter the debate merely for the price of inventing an opponent. Hence Samuel Gardiner's dialogue featured a thorough treatment of the problem of ceremonies, notably the wearing of the surplice and the use of the cross in baptism.[98] Yet the interlocutors shared a common enemy, the Church of Rome, which they exploited in unique

---

[95] John Panke, *A short admonition by way of dialogue, to all those who hitherto ... with-held them-selues from comming to the Lordes table* (Oxford, 1604), sigs. C[8v], B[2r–3r].

[96] St Anacletus, or simply 'Cletus', followed St Linus as Bishop of Rome in the first century. Both he and Linus were often used by conformist controversialists to dispute the Catholic position that the church proceeded from Christ to Peter and Paul, and hence to the succession of popes. Both saints' feast days were rescinded after Vatican II. Dionysius the 'Pseudo-Areopagite' was a mystical theologian of the fifth century, who emphasised the union between God and the whole of creation, and promoted the use of symbols and the edifying power of sacraments. Perhaps owing to the tendency among reformists to challenge the use of non-scriptural authorities in either preaching or works of controversy, some conformist writers made a point of downplaying their importance. Hence, Henry Jacob argued that 'In ordinarie Preaching unto Christian congregations to Allege Authorities of Men whether Philosophers, Poets, or Divines; or to use Latin, or other languages besides the vulgar, is unprofitable, unreasonable and unlawful.' Egeon Askew, meanwhile, appealed to reformist concerns by pointing out that unity of ceremonies and confession were an excellent block to popery, and while he chided 'Pamphleteers' whose unsound use of the Fathers left them 'wounded by their own quills', he conceded that as sound as these authorities were, scripture remained a useful guide. [Henry Jacob], *A position against vainglorious, and that which is falsly called learned preaching* ([Middelburg], 1604), sig. A[3v]; Egeon Askew, *Brotherly reconcilement* (London, 1605), ¶3.

[97] Panke, *Short admonition*, sig. B[5v].

[98] Samuel Gardiner, *A dialogue or conference betweene Irenaeus and Antimachus, about the rites and ceremonies of the Church of England* (London, 1605).

ways. For Antimachus, the dissenter, Rome served as the example of what the Church of England, with its use of 'Popish trash' like the surplice and cross, was beginning to resemble. However, Irenaeus argued that the use of ceremonies in the Roman church departed from the ancient purpose of ceremonies as aids to devotion; hence superstition and idolatry had subsumed sound learning and 'usage':

> It will be so that the outward ornaments of the Church be but such, or commonly have been used, especially if they be plaine as the surplesse, rochet, and the habit of our ministers and Bishops is. For the use, and plainest of them prevent and take away all manner of admiration. I would also think it more likely, that the people, whilest in wonder they behold such things, would fall into further and deeper meditations of divine matters.[99]

To some reformists, this would have sounded a good deal like the observance and ceremony of Roman Catholicism, and hence Gardiner employed the standard conformist defence that sacraments were aids to 'edification': 'In themselves they are indifferent, but the Christian magistrate commanding them, whom we stand bound to obey for conscience sake, I hold them necessarie to be observed: Lawes and obedience are the feete that beare up the bodie, both of the politique and spiritual state, and the two arms that feed it and defend it'.[100] Less concerned with the ancient status of ceremonies, Gardiner stressed instead the political need for obedience, portraying the Church as a political association governed by the Crown and demanding the loyalty of all English Protestants. Yet he did find use for ancient examples, much in the manner of Hayward's *Report of a discourse* – both shared the tendency to portray faction as a problem faced by the church in all ages, and in the present Church a divisive force which the 'Papists would choak us with'.[101]

Anti-popery was a common theme in the Jacobean literature of religious controversy, for it offered a portrait of the very worst that could happen to the English state. Beyond their considerable rhetoric, contemporaries regarded Catholicism as both a rival confession with its own claims to antiquity, and also – like Presbyterianism – a rival conception of ecclesiastical governance. Not surprisingly, writers on both sides of the debate found it a useful device for pointing up the dangers of the position of opponents. While some drew connections between the doctrinal positions of Rome and Canterbury, some reformists found another way of employing the shibboleth to press their own cause. They depicted ministerial deprivations as policies that fundamentally weakened the Church and left the door open to popish tyranny. This argument appeared in a pamphlet written by a group of disaffected ministers, who

---

[99] Ibid., sig. C^{2r}. [100] Ibid., sig. E^{4v}. [101] Ibid., sig. E^{3r}.

argued that 'the least of the commandments and traditions of men' was an insufficient ground to deprive 'learned, grave and Godly ministers' - especially when the Church still contained a great number of 'scandalous' ministers, whose greed for wealthy benefices took precedence over their doctrinal scruples. The result was that the people were led into error, and invented traditions supplanted the sounder guide of scripture, and 'infect the whole Church, and by consequence, lay wast the commonweale, as a prey to the popish faction'.[102]

The statement about 'invented traditions' opened up the question of *which* traditions – those of Christian antiquity or that of English law – ought to be followed. The reformist authors of this pamphlet offered scriptural proofs in support of the claim that 'schism' had a particular meaning: not simply a sundering of the Church, but rather a digression from the perfection of the ancient church: 'For it must be an unlawful discession, by inobedience, from the unitie of the first and mother Church of Jerusalem'. They argued that the rites and ceremonies codified by the Canons, as well as the liturgy set forth in the Prayer Book, caused the Church of England to depart from the ancient model. In addition they argued that the High Commission compromised the ecclesiastical supremacy of the Crown, by proceeding '*ex officio* to punish these defaultes', and asked 'their Lordships to resolve us, by what law, beside this statute, they may so proceed'.[103] The Canons of 1604 and the High Commission not only constituted a departure from the ancient church, but also from the tradition of English law and ecclesiastical governance. What began to emerge in the debate after Hampton Court, then, was a conflict over the role of the Crown in parliament in ensuring the uniformity of the Church. According to these ministers, the enforcement of ceremonies through the High Commission challenged the law-making function of parliament:

From whence it seemeth to follow, that whatsoever subject shall take upon him, full and plenarie power to deliver justice in any cause to any of the king's subjects, or to punish any crime and offence within the King's dominions by virtue of these lawes . . . that the same person denyeth the Parliament, to have full power to allow and disallow lawes in all causes, to all the King's subjects, and consequently, that the high court of Parliament is not a compleate Court for the whole and entire body of the realme.[104]

The political understanding of English reformists showed considerable sophistication as they applied the English constitutional tradition to the current dispute. From the point of view of the Midlands ministers, the High Commission was neither an extension of the Crown's sovereignty nor a body authorised by statute – it was an upstart power that subverted the

---

[102] *Certaine considerations drawne from the canons of the last Sinod, and other the Kings ecclesiastical and statue [sic] law* ([Middelburg], 1605), sig. A^{3r-4v}. See also Babbage, *Puritanism and Richard Bancroft*, p. 263.
[103] Ibid., sig. B^{v}, pp. 26–7.   [104] Ibid., pp. 30–1.

laws of England. This position was developed even further in an attack on the Book of Common Prayer whose authors portrayed clerical deprivation as a violation of the laws of nature, nations, and England:

> Are they not oppressed when they are deprived of their benefices (which bee their free-holdes) altogether without law? Are they not oppressed, when by the canon (contrary to Magna Charta, the law of nations, the light of nature and all reason) they are not suffered to prosecute their appeales? If Bishops might by law deprive Ministers of their benefices, for not subscribing or not conforming according to the late Canons, why doe they not suffer the law (which your Magestie at your Coronation, did sweare to maintaine) to have due course?[105]

Even the Coronation Oath figured in this appeal to the King to 'defend' the faith enjoined by scripture. Where conformists like Richard Cosin had cited Magna Carta in support of the position that the Church had 'libertie' to establish doctrine and governance, reformists maintained that the common law condemned this activity, and instead served to protect non-conforming ministers from unlawful deprivation.

A tract addressed to Richard Bancroft and other members of the high clergy used the format of a mock dialogue to depict the deprivations as the casting away of sober and learned ministers and the toleration of 'light, lascivious and unlearned Preachers'. At issue were the surplice and the use of the cross in baptism, ceremonies not found in scripture, and therefore improperly enforced. The authors emphasised those aspects of the liturgy that were of human invention, in order to make the case that the divine law of scripture was supreme: 'We demand what good proofe your Lordships can make out of holy writ, that Ministers of the Gospel may be commanded, not to pray, not to preach, and not to administer the sacraments without Ministerial garments, not appointed by God, but by man in the time of the Gospel.'[106] Once again, the reformist argument was guided by the assumption that scripture took precedence over ceremonies of human devising, for only God's law could order God's church. To bring home the point, they applied to the enforced ceremonies the warning against idolatry found in the books of Exodus and Revelation: 'it is by these Scriptures commanded that the children of Israel should not so much as once hearken after or inquire ... unto Idols'.[107]

---

[105] *A suruey of the booke of common prayer, by way of 197. quaeres grounded vpon 58. places, ministring iust matter of question, with a view of London ministers exceptions* ([Middelburg], 1606), pp. 6–7.

[106] *Certain demandes with their grounds, drawne out of holy writ, and propounded in foro conscientiae by some religious gentl.* ([Middelburg], 1605), p. 8.

[107] They cited Exodus 20: 4 (against graven images); and Revelation 13 (anti-Christ), 14 (chaste and uncorrupt followers of God), and 17 (judgement of the Whore of Babylon). *Certain*

The implication of this argument was that the episcopal clergy had allowed the Church to be led into error, by adopting practices without sufficient scriptural warrant, and then depriving those 'learned' members of the clergy who might have spoken out against them.[108] The authors of the petition offered a clever inversion of a Jacobean shibboleth, 'No Bishop, No King', chiding the bishops for linking ceremonies to the continued existence of episcopacy and monarchy to uphold their illegal laws:

> This is your Lordships gradation therefore, made upon the first day [of the Hampton Court conference] from the not being of a ceremonie, to the not being of a Bishop, to the not being of a King: And this your protestation made upon the next day, of the being of a King, to the being of a ceremonie, what ells doeth the one and the other argue and imparte, but a fear and a suspicion ... that the lawes of your Lordships likewise would of themselves, soon after fall to the ground.[109]

There was no pretension to disloyalty here, nor was there any indication that the ministers felt that the problem lay in monarchical absolutism. Instead, they wrote decidedly in favour of the monarchical jurisdiction over the Church, and portrayed an encroaching episcopal jurisdiction as the real threat. As we have seen, it was not the sole preserve of the conformist clergy to liken the King to biblical figures and stewards of the church. Reformists just as strongly upheld the power of the godly prince over the Church, and emphasised ecclesiastical jurisdiction exercised by the Crown in parliament.[110]

Talk of the law also furnished reformists with a powerful weapon with which to attack the legal 'establishment' of the Church. Another multi-authored tract, addressed to the parliament, argued that the deprivation of ministers both opened a door to 'popery' and also undermined the legal precepts of the Elizabethan settlement.[111] The authors drew upon that political precept that predicated the stability of the commonwealth upon the unity and 'practice' of true religion, for 'they cannot be faithful to Kings and kingdoms, neither to themselves that Neglect the true worship of God

---

demandes, p. 23. For other instances of the use of apocalyptic imagery in connection with questions of jurisdiction, see Paul Christianson, *Reformers and Babylon* (Toronto, 1978), p. 121.

[108] The concept of 'tradition' was employed to question the use of the cross in baptism: 'For if it be partly traditional, and partly divine, we still urge your Lordships to prove unto us, by the Holy Scriptures, whether it were ever lawful in any act of God's worship, to act a thing merely traditional, or partly traditional, and partly divine' (*Certain demandes*, (p. 33).

[109] Ibid., p. 47.

[110] For an influential contemporary opinion, see Francis Bacon, *Certaine considerations*, sig. C²ᵛ. This is not to say that bishops were never celebrated as defenders of the Church: Thomas Churchyard portrayed Whitgift as the epitome of learning and a staunch defender of the Church. See *Churchyards good will* (London, 1604), sig. B³.

[111] *Certain arguments to perswade and prouoke the most honourable and high court of Parliament now assembled* ([London:, W Jones' secret press], 1606), pp. 2–9, passim.

and the means thereof'. Indeed, the ministers in this case agreed that religion was surely a 'stay' of polity, and hence to deprive sound ministers of their livings was a violation both of the law of God and of political prudence. Yet the problem went deeper, and so the authors appealed to the common law: 'For it is absolutely of late proved, that all the Late proceedings, against the Ministers, in repressing of their Ministry, and in depriving them of their free holds, is contrary to the lawes of this kingdom, both to Charta Magna, and also to many statutes.'[112] Bancroft's Canons threatened both the practice of 'true religion' – howsoever it was defined – and also the sanctity of the common law, the chief bulwark of peace, order, and stability:

It is also against reason, that the basest Cobbler and Tinker can not be ejected from his free hold of but 10 shillings by the yeare, but by a Jury of 12 men, and before some of his Magesties judges in sollemne form of law, and that the Ministers and Ambassadors of Christ Jesus, in the matters of eternal life, should be cast out of their free hold, of what worth soever, by one man only, and not only without any jury, but also without any complaint or accusation against them.[113]

Indeed, the crux of the argument turned on the point that the breeding of 'controversie and contention' by enforcing ceremonies created rifts in the fabric of the Church, and boosted the 'courage of the common adversaries, the Papists ... Because as the concord, peace, and good agreement is a principall part of the strength of a King and kingdom, so their discord and contention, cannot be but dangerous for King and kingdome'.[114] Clearly, arguments in support of order could cut in more than one direction.

   Given the level of agreement among writers on both sides that religion was the foundation of political order, the dispute inevitably returned to the question of how religion related to questions of governance. When Gabriel Powel addressed the various pamphlets that we have been surveying, he found in them a common affront to the theory of ecclesiastical polity. His case depended on the point that the disputed ceremonies constituted 'things indifferent', and that enforcing them through subscription did not constitute either the unlawful promotion of heretical ceremonies, or a violation of common law. Powel portrayed the reformists as disturbers of the temporal and spiritual peace: 'For otherwise it cannot be denied, but that presumptuously and willfully they contend with the Magistrate, impugning his authoritie in things indifferent, and sovereignty in ecclesiasticall causes ... and also they make a faction and manifest schism in the Church of God.'[115] In citing the example of Magna Carta, Powel suggested that the ministers had mistaken the point that

[112] Ibid., pp. 9–10, at p. 10.   [113] Ibid., p. 11.   [114] Ibid., p. 19.
[115] Gabriel Powel, *A consideration of the depriued and silenced ministers arguments, for their restitution to the vse and libertie of their ministerie* (London, 1606), p. 11.

the ecclesiastical supremacy of English Kings *predated* 1215, and was therefore immemorial in a way the common law was not:

And now seeing all Jurisdiction and authoritie in this realme, as well Ecclesiasticall, as
Temporall, was ever in right, but now is absolutely acknowledged, and is in fact,
united and Incorporated into the Crowne of this realme: therefore that judgement is
duely given by the Jurisdiction Ecclesiasticall, is given by the Law of the Land, and not
contrarie to Magna Charta.[116]

For this interpretation, Powel cited the ultimate juridical authority, Edward
Coke, rather than scripture or patristic sources, because he sought to address
head on the argument that the High Commission violated provisions of the
common law. The ministers, he argued, were not proceeded against for
anything having to do with liturgy, but rather for 'noveltie, for faction,
schisme and impugning the Magistrates authority, or disturbing the peace
and quietness of the Church'.[117] In response to the charge that deprivation of
ministers was carried out by an extra-legal authority, Powel countered that
the High Commission was simply an extension of the ecclesiastical sovereignty described by the Elizabethan Act of Supremacy; this allowed him to
argue that the deprived clergy had broken the statute which enforced the
Crown's power over the Church.

The first phase of the debate opened up the tension inherent in the conformist theory of ecclesiastical polity, and particularly the nature of human
authority over the Church. Not only did reformists argue that this authority
was in all cases bounded by the common law, but also that when it impinged
on the spiritual realm it was obliged to serve the ends of true doctrine. What
becomes apparent is the way in which doctrinal dispute could also raise
questions ordinarily confined to the realm of secular politics, and vice
versa. The Jacobean settlement served to bring to the fore a range of positions
which had the potential to disrupt the peace of ecclesiastical polity.

WILLIAM BRADSHAW AND HIS OPPONENTS

Central to Gabriel Powel's *theological* case against the ministers was the
argument that the ceremonies enjoined by the Canons were 'indifferent' –
mere helps to edification, and hence not central to the process of salvation.
This allowed conformists to suggest that no doctrinal error was being committed in their enforcement, itself defended as a matter of civil 'policie'. By
downplaying the doctrinal aspect, they portrayed ceremonies and subscription as matters of obedience to the Crown, and those ministers who refused
subscription as disturbers of the state. Reformist writers, on the other hand,

---

[116] Ibid., p. 42.   [117] Ibid., p. 48.

demanded that things 'indifferent' be defended on a doctrinal level (justified by scripture), and suggested further that the 'civil' power of bishops was evidence of innovation, and of an office with no scriptural, legal, or historical precedent. Reformist writers who resorted to legal categories in order to trump the claims to authority and tradition made by conformists often exploited the confusion or conflation of the political languages posited by Glenn Burgess.[118] In a series of pamphlets published during 1604 and 1605, William Bradshaw pursued precisely this line of argument, and offered one of the most articulate attacks on English conformity of the Jacobean period.

It was disingenuous, Bradshaw argued, for conformists to portray the deprived ministers as schismatics, for they only sought to execute the 'Ministry of the Gospel ... with a good conscience'. Bradshaw organised his work around the explication of the theme that the enforcement of illegitimate ceremonies represented a far greater crime than simply refusing to subscribe to them. In an early tract, he argued that genuine schism represented the attempt to shift the Church away from its basis in scripture and the example of the Apostles – by this standard, it was the conformists who were guilty of measures that moved the Church away from the ancient exemplar. This effectively directed the blame away from the deprived ministers, and toward the higher clergy: 'But if all the prelates cannot give one Argument soundly concluded from the Word, to prove, that the Ceremonies in question may be prescribed by authority, and yielded unto by the Ministry, without sinne, then they are Schismatickes, according to the judgement of the Apostles.'[119] One of the crucial reasons why the bishops could be thought of as 'schismatics' was that they elevated their own opinions above the sounder guide of the Word, thus: 'All religious ceremonies or ceremonies of religion, are spirituall, that is, ordained for spiritual uses and endes, and not for civil or temporal.'[120] Bradshaw even went so far as to close off the common escape open to conformists concerning the rites of the Church. For conformists could resort either to the expression of the sovereignty of the Church set down by the Canons of 1604, or to the concept of 'tradition', invoked in the course of an alignment of the English Church with an ancient exemplar. Bradshaw countered the Canonical argument by offering the warrant of scripture, and argued that all aspects of Church government should be patterned *iure divino*, from scripture. To evidence drawn from the Fathers

[118] See Glenn Burgess, *The politics of the ancient constitution: an introduction to English political thought, 1603–1642* (University Park, PA, 1992), p. 130–6.
[119] William Bradshaw, *A consideration of certain positions archiepiscopall* ([London: W. Jones' secret press?, 1604–05]), pp. 10, 11.
[120] William Bradshaw, *A treatise of divine worship, tending to prove that the ceremonies imposed vpon the ministers of the Gospell in England, in present controversie, are in their vse vnlawfull* ([Middelburg], 1604), p. 25.

he offered countering evidence from the Fathers, and he borrowed Thomas Bell's tactic of mounting a reinterpretation of their texts. Hence, Bradshaw devoted a separate work to the cross in baptism, and based its argument on a reading of patristic authors, 'From whence I conclude, that if the godly Fathers were so vehement against erecting images of Christ', they would also have opposed the ceremonies enjoined by the Canons of 1604.[121]

This use of the Fathers prompted a vigorous attack on Bradshaw by Leonard Hutten, an Oxford divine and one of the translators of the Authorised Version of the King James Bible – a scholar on familiar terms with a range of controversial tools. Hutten's purpose was to defend and offer refinement to aspects of the conformist definition of ceremonies and governance. The response open to him was to offer a counter-interpretation of Bradshaw's reinterpretation; the attack focussed on Bradshaw's frequent use of a syllogism to criticise the official liturgy and to dismiss the disputed ceremonies as being of 'human invention'.[122] Not so, countered Hutten amid a flurry of citations from St Ambrose and St Augustine, as well as reports of the Councils of Chalcedon and Toledo, for 'out of these premises, we may gather this firme and sure Conclusion, That therefore Ceremonies of those Times were certainly of humane ordinance: or, to Speak more Properly, of Ecclesiastical Constitution'. The reason that the writings of the Fathers failed to confirm Bradshaw's position, Hutten argued, was because his interpretations of them 'over-reacheth upon [their] words', and hence the conclusions he drew from their writings were based in error.[123]

Part of the purpose of Hutten's reinterpretation of the texts was to suggest that the liturgy of the English Church restored to sound usage elements of worship previously marred by error. As had Thomas Bell, Hutten portrayed the English Church as ancient and reformed: a restored, true embodiment of the church as it had existed before the rise of Rome. Hutten wished to suggest that – regardless of antiquity and scripture – the Church of England always retained sovereignty over itself. Using a biblical precedent, if only by analogy, Hutten argued that: 'our Reformers did the same thing in their reformation, of the Crosse in Baptisme, which Ezekiah did in his reformation of the Brasen Serpent: for what was that which Ezekiah did? Surely it was, that he took away the abuse, wherein it was faulty, not the right use.' Reformation in this sense entailed *restoration* of proper usage. Yet the real

---

[121] William Bradshaw, *A short treatise, of the crosse in baptisme* ([London: W. Jones' secret press], 1604), p. 6.

[122] '1) No humane ordinance becoming an Idol, may lawfully be used in the service of God / 2) But the sign of the Cross being an human ordinance is become an idol; ergo: / 3) The sign of the Cross may not lawfully be used in the service of God.' See Ibid., title page.

[123] Leonard Hutten, *An answere to a certaine treatise of the crosse in baptisme* (Oxford, 1605), pp. 14, 44; [Ambrose], *Sancti Ambrosii . . . opera, ex editione Romana*, 2 vols. (Paris, 1603).

question between Bradshaw and Hutten concerned the sufficiency of antiquity as a guide to the ordering of the Church. Hutten dismissed Bradshaw's
criticism that arguments from antiquity were needed to promote doctrine and
discipline that were not confirmed by scripture – a common Protestant attack
against the Church of Rome.[124] It was here that Hutten resorted to the
conformist notion of things indifferent to salvation providing edification:
'our Church by examining those reasons, that caused the Fathers to institute
and use this Ceremony of the crosse in Baptisme, hath found, that it was then,
so may be still a ceremony of decencie, and profitable Admonition in the
Church'.[125]

Yet Bradshaw was unwilling to concede that anything done contrary to
the scriptures could be in any way 'edifying', for to act contrary to this
authority was to follow a pattern of worship that had no scriptural or
Apostolic warrant. Although he was clearly comfortable with the works of
the Fathers, the bulk of Bradshaw's arguments were based on scriptural
exegesis. Indeed, Bradshaw employed the New Testament in two ways: as
an 'eyewitness' to biblical events involving Christ, the Apostles, and other
figures, and as a literal account of the sayings of Christ, which in themselves
constituted elements of divine law. Taken together, these scriptural patterns
conveyed a complete account of the practices of the early church. Bradshaw's
exegetical strategies were employed to refute the practice of kneeling at
communion as an 'invention of man'. He cited an 'eyewitness' account of
scripture to describe the posture of Christ at the Last Supper ('And when the
hour was come, he sat down and the Apostles with him' [Luke 22: 14]), and
also used scripture as a source that conveyed divine commands for ordering
the church ('Now I praise you, brethren, that ye remember me in all things,
and keep the ordinances, as I delivered them to you' [1 Cor. 11: 1]).[126] Taken
together, these constituted the 'first institution' of Christian rites, practice,
and doctrine in the church, and any deviation from or alteration of them
amounted to a departure from the true church. Bradshaw's ultimate aim was
to link – via the scripture – the doctrinal and ceremonial programme that he
promoted with the idea of the Church as established *iure divino*.

Bradshaw's emphasis on the divine law of scripture entailed a criticism of
the 'laws of men' which he saw at the foundation of the Church established by
the Canons of 1604. Indeed, Hampton Court and the Canons were evidently

[124] 'True worship both for matter and manner, ought to be according to the prescript rule of
Gods word only: neither doth any mortal or man [have] authoritie to frame according to his
own conceit, any forme or fashion of God's service or worship.' Bradshaw, *A treatise of
divine worship*, p. 30.
[125] Hutten, *An answere*, pp. 115, 116.
[126] William Bradshaw, *A proposition. Concerning kneeling in the very act of receiuing howsoever* ([London: William Jones' secret press], 1605), p. 8.

the result of 'custom' and Bradshaw sought to expand the debate to capture aspects of governance, as well as doctrine. From Bradshaw's perspective, there was a gulf between the two types of authority – civil and ecclesiastical – that applied to the debate on ceremonies. In early tracts, Bradshaw dealt with the problem of the jurisdiction of bishops by offering scriptural evidence, but in later work the question received a different treatment. This came in the form of a criticism of the conjoined jurisdiction over temporals and spirituals, 'for there being an opposition in reason between things CIVIL and ECCLESIASTICAL, though they have some things common to both, yet it is ridiculous to affirme that those things are civil, that are merely ecclesiasticall, and are actions peculiarly appropriated and tied to Divine Worship'. Here Bradshaw sought to drive a wedge between the civil and ecclesiastical powers of the Crown as described by the Elizabethan Act of Supremacy. The terms of Jacobean conformity meant that, in order for a minister to observe the present law of the state, he 'should sinne against God', whereas to follow his conscience meant also to break the law.[127] This left the conformist argument that it was no sin to observe a ceremony that was in itself 'indifferent', an objection which Bradshaw answered by pointing out that there was no indifferent act of religion: 'No action of Religion whether Morall or Ceremoniall grounded only upon the Will of Man, and not Upon the Word of God, can bring any special glory to God, and therefore no such Act can be an Act of Religion, but of Superstition, and therefore cannot be Indifferent.'[128]

A final pair of tracts from 1605 indicates that Bradshaw was beginning to develop an argument on governance. This was perhaps owing to the fact that the time to dispute matters of doctrine had, for the moment, passed. The times also placed a certain pressure on the development of arguments that, if exchanged in a climate where ministers were *not* being deprived of their livings, would ordinarily have been more measured. For Bradshaw, the programme of subscription and deprivation opened up questions of authority and jurisdiction, the definition of the government of the Church, and the nature of the authority of that government over individuals.

[T]he governors of the Church ought with all pacience and quietnesse, hear what every offender can possiblie say for himself, either for qualification, defence, apology or Justification of any supposed crime or error ... it [is] an evident character of a

---

[127] William Bradshaw, *Twelve generall arguments, proving that the ceremonies imposed upon the ministers of the gospell in England, by our prelates, are unlawfull* ([Middelburg], 1605), sig. B^{5r}, C^{3v}.

[128] William Bradshaw, *A treatise of the nature and vse of things indifferent. Tendinge to proue that the ceremonies in present controuersie amongst the ministers of the gospell in the realme of Englande, are neither in nature nor vse indifferent* ([London: W. Jones' secret press], 1605), p. 23.

corrupt Ecclesiastical Government, where the parties covenanted may not have full libertie to speak for themselves.[129]

In stressing the liberty of covenanters, Bradshaw seemed to call for a return to congregational governance – a Presbyterian model. Further, Bradshaw argued that those to blame for the deprivations – the bishops – violated the King's ecclesiastical sovereignty: 'we hold it plaine anti-Christian for any Churche or Church officers whatsoever, either to arrogate or assure unto themselves any part or parcel thereof, and utterly unlawful for the king to give away or alienate the same from his own Crown and dignitie to any spiritual poten-tates or rulers whatsoever *within or without* his dominions'.[130] Here Bradshaw modified those sentences of the Elizabethan Act of Supremacy that dealt with the jurisdiction of foreign 'popes and potentates', and applied its message to the domestic setting; the bishops sought to arrogate the ecclesiastical sovereignty to themselves. Bradshaw completed the argument by affirming the loyalty of the deprived ministers who 'renounce and abhore from their soules all such Ecclesiastical Jurisdiction or policie, that is in any way repugnant and derogatorie ... to the Monarchical State'.[131]

This last statement was briskly answered by Oliver Ormerod, who had little interest in untangling the niceties of Bradshaw's argument as it related to the questions of authority or things indifferent. Rather, in the latter's position he recognised only the voice of one bent on dismantling order in both Church and state. In some ways, Ormerod's tract hardly belonged in the category of controversial literature, for unlike the vast majority of the works that form the basis of this study his made no attempt to engage with the argument of his opponent, but merely branded him as an enemy of the state, plotting with his like in 'private conventicles': 'It is most apparently known to all men, that they have never ceased since His Magesties most happie entry into this realme, untill this day, to meet together in private houses, and there to meddle with matters too high for them.'[132] By 'too high' Ormerod meant

---

[129] William Bradshaw, *English puritanisme containening* [sic]. *The maine opinions of the rigidest sorte of those that are called Puritanes in the realme of England* ([London: W. Jones' secret press], 1605), p. 28.

[130] William Bradshaw, *A protestation of the Kings supremacie. Made in the name of the afflicted ministers, and opposed to the shamefull calumnations of the prelates* ([London: W. Jones' secret press], 1605), p. 2, emphasis added. For the latter statement: 'We hold that in all things concerning *this life* whatsoever, the Civil Jurisdiction of Kings and Civil States excelleth and ought to have preheminence over the Ecclesiasticall, and that the Ecclesiasticall neither hath or ought to have over the bodies, lives, goods, or liberties of any person whatsoever, much less of the Kings and Rulers of the Earth' (ibid., p. 4).

[131] William Bradshaw, *English puritanisme*, p. 11.

[132] Oliver Ormerod, *Picture of a Puritane: or, a relation of the opinions, qualities, and practises of the Anabaptists in Germanie, and of the Puritanes in England* (London, 1605), sig. C[3r–4v].

matters of formal controversy, aspects of which were extensively treated in the margins of his text. [133] Beyond the rhetoric, Ormerod's tract revealed that the debate involved competing definitions of English ecclesiastical polity: the one envisioning a sovereign political and spiritual association wedded to the state, the other a spiritual association deriving from the Word and confirmed by Apostolic practice, and thereby resistant to the meddling of human agents.

Ormerod defined the Church and state in terms of a single body and a single sovereignty. Seen in this light, non-conformity reflected a theological error that translated into a political problem, for to quarrel with English conformists amounted to withholding one's loyalty to the body of the Church. This meant that things indifferent to salvation could become necessary for political order: 'Laws made without contradiction to Positive Lawes in Scriptures, and received by a Whole Church, are such, as they that Live within the Bosom of that same Church, must not think it a matter indifferent, either to yield or not to yield obedience.' Yet Bradshaw and Ormerod had more in common than either (perhaps) would have admitted: both invoked the 'positive law' of scripture, but parted ways on how far it should be applied to doctrine and discipline. Ormerod's tract provides no evidence that he was convinced that Bradshaw was motivated by anything resembling 'principle'. To some conformists, the writings of their opponents were simply ill-conceived attempts to stir up disaffection toward the legitimate government of the Church: in other words, to propose a form of governance other than that sanctioned and defended by the Crown was to propose a revolution in ecclesiastical government. But Ormerod also queried Bradshaw's use of scripture: 'It hath been the tricke of Heretickes and Schismaticks in all ages, to fill the margents of their bookes full of places of Scripture, that by this means they might more easily deceive the simple people, and make them thinke their whole Bookes to be Scripture, and nothing else but Scriptures, when indeed they wring from the Scriptures that sence, which the words themselves would not beare.' [134] Bradshaw was labelled a fomenter of schism, of erroneous doctrine, and indeed of heresy, even though Ormerod did not attack the doctrine of salvation that his opponent held. Instead, Ormerod engaged with the implications of Bradshaw's argument as it applied to the widely accepted definition of the Church as a spiritual and political association.

---

[133] See, for example, ibid., sigs. G–H, where the literature of the Admonition controversy was surveyed. Ormerod found the body of reformist literature a potential source for the dissemination of errors about the Church: 'Neither did our Puritans therewithall content themselves; but that their poyson might ranckle the farther, to the disturbance and peril both of Church and commonwealth, they have published a great number of Bookes, which are as fit for the fire as books of curious arts' (sig. D^{4v}).

[134] Ibid., sigs. E^{2v}, G^{4r}.

A further conformist response to Bradshaw appeared in 1606, written by John Dove, Oxford divine and rector of St Mary Aldermary, London. The tract resembled contemporary sermons, headed by a line from scripture intended to set the tone of the piece; in this case, Dove chose 1 Corinthians 1: 10, 'That we knit together in one minde and judgement', which seemed to suggest the irenic stance evident in John Panke's *Admonition*. However, Dove's argument against Bradshaw was a vigorous one, and singled out for attention those two questions that seemed to demand a firm and definitive answer – episcopacy, and the question of antiquity as it applied to things indifferent. On the former, Dove cited a collection of Fathers all of whom spoke in favour of 'patriarchal bishops'. To these authorities Dove added that of English tradition. Here again he enunciated the conformist vision of the Church as both spiritual and political. Dove took this a step further, explaining how the English Church with its hierarchy of bishops still satisfied the standard of being ancient and reformed. This entailed a certain amount of explanation concerning its organisation and hierarchy, which had to be integrated with the claim that the Church of England enjoyed an uninterrupted connection with Christ and derived its powers from the monarch: 'With *us* Bishops are the Kings Lieutenants in Ecclesiastical causes, and all Ecclesiastical courts are the Kings courts, they be held immediately under the King, his authority in Causes ecclesiastical, being subalternate, and immediately subordinate to our Saviour Christ.'[135] Here Dove provided an explanation of how the High Commission could function without a derogation of the royal supremacy, and in a manner which suggested that it reflected the ancient pattern.

Indeed, Dove offered 'order' and 'antiquity' as evidence for the legitimacy of episcopal governance. Where Bradshaw had attempted to sever the sovereignty of the Church from that of the state, Dove countered with the examples of biblical kings and Christian princes, whom he styled as 'Magistrates of the Church [who] command the judges to execute what theirselves would have done'. Dove, therefore, was clearly not persuaded by Bradshaw's use of scripture, and invited him to restate his case: 'Therefore I demand *other* sound reasons, or place of Scripture, to prove why it should not continue among us who are also God's people, especially our Ecclesiasticall persons being more honourable under the Gospel, then they were under the Law?'[136] Sensitive to Bradshaw's dogged insistence on scriptural proofs, therefore, Dove continually emphasised the testimony of the Word above all other sources. Hence the crux of his answer to Bradshaw's tract on the

---

[135] John Dove, *A defence of church gouernment. Dedicated to the high Court of Parliament* (London, 1606), pp. 23, 32.
[136] Ibid., pp. 33, 40.

Canonical injunction concerning the use of the cross in baptism was the argument that it formed part of a 'scriptural tradition'. Where Bradshaw's case revolved around the recent enforcement of a point of doctrinal error, Dove privileged examples from scripture and included testimony from ancient sources. Hence, rather than a novel policy of Bancroft's, the cross 'hath been commended to use from antiquitie of the Primitive Church ... we allege antiquity against the novelty of they which slander us, shewing that antiquitie in point of Religion is to be preferred before novelty'.[137]

In 1606 William Bradshaw published a defence of the 1606 petition to the parliament (*Certaine arguments*), and included too an attack on Gabriel Powel's response to that petition. Bradshaw's *Myld and iust defence* was itself a petition, addressed to the parliament and asking for a reconsideration of the legality of the programme of clerical subscription. This renewed the controversy over ceremonies and subscription, and also touched off a debate about the power and authority of bishops. Since the reformist position refused to accept any pattern of governance or practice save that set forth in scripture, there was little left to Bradshaw but to restate the argument against the antiquity of the required ceremonies. In sum, he returned to the suggestion that the antiquity of scripture made a sounder guide than the human inventions of the Fathers or later Christians:

Besides, the things in controversie which we desire to be removed, may much more justly be called both Noveltie and Forrayne, because they were not of Apostolical institution ... as both been shewed in divers other books written on our side, not yet answered: especially in the Abridgment made by the Ministers of Lincoln Diocese.[138]

The 'Abridgment' to which Bradshaw referred was a petition published by the ministers of Lincoln diocese in 1605 (to be examined in the succeeding chapter), and the allusion revealed the extent to which this literature was known and employed in the course of controversies. This in turn indicates how broad was the debate on authority, Apostolic tradition, and 'custom'.

Yet Bradshaw's principal target was Gabriel Powel, who had gone to great lengths to demonstrate the antiquity of the rites and governance of the Church, as well as the powers of the Church to censure those of its ministers who refused to conform to that arrangement. In response, Bradshaw pointed his criticism at the higher clergy who, for those closely involved with the subscription debate, were the most visible agents of the state's programme of ensuring conformity:

---

[137] Dove, 'An Answere to the Treatise of the Cross in Baptism', in *A defence*, pp. 59, 68, 72.
[138] William Bradshaw, *A myld and iust defence of certeyne arguments, at the last session of Parliament directed to that most Honourable High Court, in behalfe of the ministers suspended and deprived* ([London: W. Jones' secret press], 1606), p. 5.

The author might well cry out, that the gospel is in part banished, by the suppression of so many able, godly, faithful and paynfull ministers; that God's worship is in fact corrupted, both in the doctrine ... especially ... this late vehement stryving by our Prelates for conformitie ... and also in the other publicke exercises of religion by mixture of human inventions, Ceremonys and Traditions.[139]

Bradshaw recognised that the dispute among English Protestants was not about predestination, but about subscription, rites, and their precedents ancient or scriptural. Combining the notion of 'publicke exercises' with that of 'human invention', Bradshaw was able to argue that Jacobean conformists emphasised the institutional aspects of the Church, rather than the true pattern of scripture. Indeed, Bradshaw argued that the testimony of the 'ancient Apostolicall Churches, and also the present Churches reformed' demonstrated that the enjoined ceremonies had no basis in doctrine and would not naturally have continued were it not for the episcopal clergy.

Bradshaw compared the rule of English bishops with the way in which the Church of Rome defended its supremacy through the ages, and he wondered whether future generations of the faithful would view the subscription debate in similar terms:

[Catholics] have fallen away from the doctrine and ancient simplicitie in the worship of God, that at the beginning was in the Ancient Roman Church, and in other true Churches, planted by the Apostles. In like manner therefore let our accusers in the feare of God consider, whether the blame of schisme doe not for the causes before expressed, more aptly belong to them, then to us.[140]

Indeed, for reformists, Rome epitomised the transformation of a church from a doctrinal and spiritual association, into a political institution. It was natural, then, that they should try to apply the analogy to England. This Bradshaw did with reference to the *ius pontificum*, a power which he likened to the degree of sovereignty sought by the English bishops, but which the statutes that defined the Elizabethan settlement had labelled as a 'foreign' ecclesiastical jurisdiction.[141] Yet there was still the matter of professing one's loyalty to the Crown, and so with respect to the ecclesiastical polity of England, Bradshaw upheld the King's ecclesiastical supremacy as a power defined by Magna Carta, but argued in turn that this supremacy was bounded by the law: 'we again assume from this statute of the Great Charter [i.e. Cap. 29] that sundry sentences of deprivation of Ministers, from their benefices, for causes before specified, are unlawful'. The problem

---

[139] Ibid., p. 9.   [140] Ibid., p. 48.

[141] Bradshaw argued that, since the time of Henry VIII, '[T]he *ius pontificum* ... was altogether (excepting the tyme of Queen Mary) abrogated, anulled, and made voyd, by an Act of Parliament; and consequently it is but a meere Alien, Forraigne and strange law, and of no municipal law of England, and therefore not of the King's ecclesiastical law.' See ibid., p. 92.

was that episcopal jurisdiction struck at the sanctity of trial by jury, itself the very heart of the common law:

The question is not whether jurisdiction Ecclesiastical by the law of the land doth belong (under the king) unto the ordinaries: nor whether the ordinaries in the exercise of the Kings jurisdiction Ecclesiastical, and Constitutional trialls, ought to proceed by virtue of peers, etc. but whether some Ordinarys, exercising the Kings ecclesiastical jurisdiction, have proceeded in their Ecclesiastical Consistories, against some ministers, without authority of the King's ecclesiastical law: & therefore in that respect, contrary to Magna Charta, which reqyreth nothing to be done without the King's law.

For conformists, the deprivation of ministers by bishops was merely an extension of the Crown's sovereignty, clearly set forth in the thirty-sixth Canon and further justified by the Act of Supremacy. Yet this was of no interest to Bradshaw, who maintained that the ordering of the church was set forth in scripture, and hence the power adopted by the bishops was a law unto itself, alienated from both divine and English law. He thus upheld the King's divine authority over the Canons of the Church, and 'if these two pillars of His Magestie's prerogative Royal (namely his grace and his power) be thus shaken by this Canon, must it not necessarily follow that the Lords and Commons in Parliament are prejudiced thereby?'[142] For Bradshaw, the Canons sapped power from both the Crown and parliament, and placed it in the hands of the bishops.

A rare bit of support for Bradshaw's position came from the pen of Robert Parker, himself arrested by the High Commission and subsequently exiled in Holland.[143] Parker sought to set forth a doctrine of the Church based on ancient and scriptural proofs. To counter conformist arguments about enforcing indifferent ceremonies, Parker questioned the doctrinal purity of the sign of the cross, and sought to separate it from public worship in the Jacobean Church. For Parker, the cross was a remnant of pagan idolatry, roundly condemned by both the Old Testament and the Fathers, as well as by reformers like Calvin and Peter Martyr; hence, it could not be legitimately enjoined 'to the end of Civil Obedience'.[144] Indeed, Parker singled out claims of the antiquity of the cross for special scrutiny, arguing that this antiquity was far from self-evident, leaving conformist churchmen to 'strive, as much as in them lieth, to draw the antiquity of the Cross immediately from Christ'. Parker dismissed the use of patristic authorities, and argued that such texts were fraught with error and misinterpretation. Traditions ascribed to the

---

[142] Ibid., pp. 93, 107, 110.
[143] Sprunger, *Dutch puritanism*, pp. 59, 95, 136, 263.
[144] Robert Parker, *A scholasticall discourse against symbolizing with Antichrist in ceremonies: especially in the signe of the cross* ([Middelburg], 1607), pp. 11, 12, 37, 51; Sprunger, *Dutch Puritanism*, pp. 116, 136, 263, 282, 344, 367.

Apostles were really the innovation of a later time, and the history of the church since Apostolic times was depicted as a history of gradually accumulating error: 'For the Church ceased to be a chaste virgin immediately after the death of the Apostles, even as of old she ceased to be chaste immediately after the death of the Elders who saw her Deliverance out of Egypt. They who succeeded the Apostles, came greatly short of them.'[145] Hence, Parker's notion of Apostolic perfection was very simple: the scripture reported the activities and words of Christ, and the letters of the Apostles provided details of the earliest Christians. This record – provided the text was not corrupt – was far superior to any written after it. The argument depended upon placing the history of the church as an institution governed by human agents alongside the history of the 'purity' of doctrine, in order to point out how human invention only served to corrupt the Word. The Church as a purely doctrinal entity was independent from human agents; to guard against the corruption of doctrine, reformists found it convenient to emphasise the need to pattern the Church exactly on scripture.

Conformist writers attempted to get around this objection by arguing that scripture left open the possibility that the Church was free to follow 'custom' in establishing a pattern of liturgy. In a contribution to the doctrinal question of kneeling at communion, Thomas Rogers argued that: 'The maner of our Countrie is to receive our corporall food sitting; the order of our Church, that we receive the spiritual food of our soules at the Communion kneeling.'[146] Rogers continued by distinguishing between the good and pernicious use of customs, and cited Catholics as examples of the latter. The rule of the English Church was to institute modes of worship that were 'fit and profitable' and not 'repugnant to the Word of God'. These orders he styled as 'the customs and manners of our Church', and argued that it was a mark of the Church's sovereignty that it should make 'constitutions'.[147] Therefore, Rogers sought to establish a distinction between what Christ had ordered to be done, and what He had left to the discretion of His church – this accumulated tradition was 'custom': 'And here the wisdom of our Lord and Saviour shewth itself most admirable, who having prescribed and instituted what he would have done; hath not prescribed yet the form and manner of how he would have the sacraments administered.'[148] The conformist emphasis on

---

[145] Parker, *Scholasticall discourse*, pp. 126, 127–8.

[146] Thomas Rogers, *Two dialogues, or conferences ... Concerning kneeling in the very act of receiuing the sacramental bread and wine, in the Supper of the Lord* (London, 1608), sig. C^{2r}.

[147] Ibid., sigs. D^{3v-4v}.

[148] Ibid., sig. H^{2r}. Parker's response to this sort of argument resembled his rejection of the textual authority of the Fathers: customs, like texts, could become corrupted. Alternatively,

the sovereignty of the Church over its visible aspect was designed to subject a broadly defined notion of worship to the rule of ecclesiastical authority; in other words, all things that were *adiaphora*, that is, not strictly enjoined by scripture, were left to the jurisdiction of the governors of the Church.

The final contribution to this debate linked Bradshaw's *Myld and iust defence* with the petition presented to the Commons in 1606 by deprived ministers. The work was another product of the busy pen of Gabriel Powel, a bulldog among conformist controversialists. In *De adiaphoris*, published in 1607, Powel had offered a lengthy refutation of the reformist argument concerning 'things indifferent'.[149] In his *Reioynder* to Bradshaw's work, Powel touched briefly on that question, before moving on to the theme of obedience, order, and episcopacy. For all of the controversy between them, Bradshaw and Powel had very similar approaches to the scripture. Bradshaw divided the New Testament into those portions that directly reported the words of Christ (the Gospels) and those that were witnesses to His actions. In much the same fashion, Powel referred to 'essential' and 'accidental' elements of scripture. The first covered those aspects necessary to worship, and 'without them, a man could not communicate rightly according to the institution, commandment, and example of Christ'. Accidental aspects of scripture comprised actions that 'do not signifie any mysterie, neither did Christ say *do this*'.[150] The argument was as clever as it was simple: to define accidental aspects as not signifying mystery was an excellent foil for the frequent portrayal of the disputed ceremonies as badges of idolatry. Since the scriptures did not forbid these ceremonies, Christians who used them did not violate an ordinance, because one had never been established. While Bradshaw had distinguished between Christ's words and His actions, both had for him the status of divine law; Powel severed this link between Christ's words and actions, and assigned to the latter the label 'indifferent', and left the enforcement of 'indifferent' ceremonies to the 'liberty' of the Church.

This argumentative shift removed modes of worship from the realm of divine law to the law of the Magistrate – once a particular rite was declared 'indifferent', it became a political and temporal matter, rather than a strictly spiritual one. Powel, therefore, made a point of emphasising a disjunction between doctrine and ceremony that reformists argued could not be legitimately accomplished. Severing the link between matters of doctrine and the

customs could be 'imitations' of rites practised by the Jews; yet, Parker observed, since the Jews were not Christians at the time, the custom was not properly Christian. See Parker, *Scholasticall discourse*, pp. 131–2.

[149] Gabriel Powel, *De adiaphoris. Theological and scholastical positions, concerning the nature and vse of things indifferent* (London, 1607).

[150] Gabriel Powel, *A reioynder unto the mild defence, iustifying the consideration of the silenced ministers supplication vnto the high court of parliament* (London: Felix Kyngston, 1607), p. 110.

powers of the Church and its officers freed conformists to define the duties of these officers in a variety of ways. Hence, where Bradshaw complained bitterly about the episcopal power of deprivation, Powel defended it as a measure necessary for combating schism:

As touching the Prelates, I answer, that in inflicting the punishment he speaketh of, they doe but their dutie, by executing the law upon offenders, in obedience toward the Superior magistrate, for the peace and quietnesse of the Church: and let all the World Judge, whether it be more meet and fit, that these self-conceited refractories should dutifully conform themselves, or that the Magistrate to satisfie their wrangling and restlesse humour, should dissolve the whole frame of so well settled Government.[151]

Powel did not regard bishops endeavouring to ensure the peace and stability of the Church as being engaged in a spiritual exercise, save in enforcing what the scriptures enjoined with respect to 'order'. Instead, the bishops were the channels through which the supremacy of the Crown flowed.

It will be remembered that Bradshaw argued that the deprivations violated the provisions of Magna Carta, and that in the process the bishops claimed for themselves a power that rightfully belonged to parliament. Powel saw the ministers' petition to the parliament in a similar fashion, and accused them of trying to turn the legislature against the rest of the commonwealth. The ministers were guilty of 'most impudently challenging that Honourable Assemblie, not onely to favour their seditious faction, but also as a partie in their schisme, to have entermeddled and dealt on their behalfe, contrarie to the knowledge of the whole kingdome'.[152] Indeed, Powel's political assumptions reflected those of his age, especially the approach to social wholes that emphasised the qualities of order and harmony. Operating on the presumption that 'all good is united, not divided', Powel argued that subscription was merely the extension of the political precepts that assured the stability of corporate states into the realm of the Church:

Have the reverend and wise Prelates any reason, to admit such to labour in the Ministrie: who they know will disturbe the peace of the Church? Yea who plainly professe that they will never be conformable unto the Discipline established. None at all. Especially seeing the Superior Magistrates hath reposed such trust in their fidelitie and diligence, that they would carefully, to their utmost abilitie, endeavour to preserve pure religion and unitie among His subjects.[153]

---

[151] Ibid., p. 114.   [152] Ibid., p. 115.

[153] Ibid., p. 173. Similarly, John Batt argued, 'Magistrates, likewise that have auctoritie either in Church or commonwealth, should labour to gather good testimonies of their regeneration of that zeal which they show for the benefit of the republick, and the Church of God. They ought to be mouthes to speak for the Church and God's people, as Moses was unto Pharo: they ought to defend to good cause of God's Church as Jephiah did against the Amonites, first in disputation by words, and after in battaile with the sword.' See John Batt, *The royall priesthood of Christians* (London, 1605), p. 57ᵛ.

Here again, there was no concession made to the doctrinal arguments of reformists. Instead, they were depicted as the chief obstacles to that solemn endeavour to preserve the Church in a unity of faith. As we have seen, writers like William Bradshaw held a very similar position with respect to the bishops, and argued that clerical deprivation not only sundered Protestant unity and opened a door to 'popery', but also served to shift the Church away from its ancient and godly foundations.

By now it will be clear that a tension between doctrine and law underlay religious debates before and after the Hampton Court conference. The late Elizabethan Church could rely on champions such as Richard Cosin to defend the jurisdiction of the High Commission, but in the early years of the reign of James I reformists sought once again to criticise the doctrine and governance of the Church – the two questions which Hampton Court had not settled. Not only was diocesan episcopacy a mode of governance that could not be reconciled with the evidence of the ancient church, but the court of High Commission seemed to present a threat to the jurisdiction of the common law and the ecclesiastical sovereignty of the Crown in parliament. From the point of view of doctrine, reformists argued that the Prayer Book and Thirty-nine Articles enjoined ceremonies and modes of worship that could not be reconciled with scripture or the practice of the ancient church. Central to this argument was the proposition that there could be no separation of belief and practice: the scripture and the actions and words of Christ represented divine law, and a pattern by which the church was to be ordered. In response, conformists defended episcopacy as an Apostolic office, and offered a broad definition of doctrine based on 'things indifferent' and the need for order and stability in the Church. Their interpretation of the law and its history stressed both the 'liberty' of the Church and the free operation of its sovereignty, and defined the operation of that sovereignty as descending from the Crown to inferior magistrates. With respect to doctrine, they maintained that the Word did not contain a complete pattern for the ordering of doctrine and discipline, and it was on this ground that they predicated the case that the Church was free to establish modes of worship and 'customs' based on necessity and experience.

In both cases, the burden of demonstrating a certain mode of authority over the Church depended on historical argument. Conformists needed to show that the Canons of 1604 were neither novel nor political, but rather a continuation of a restored pattern of worship that was itself ancient and scripturally sound. Discipline was a note of the English Church that had to be defended on doctrinal grounds. Yet reformist attacks on the High Commission exposed a tension in the conformist case: could civil power be used to enforce purely spiritual ends, and was the Church a political or spiritual association? Here history was used to show that the common law curtailed the power of bishops, while ancient authorities were cited in support of Presbyterian discipline. In response, conformists argued that the political and spiritual capacities of the Church were not novel and had precedents in the ancient context; moreover, the Church's sovereignty over temporals was a legitimate manifestation of the Crown's sovereignty that did not violate the provisions of the common law or the testimony of the Christian textual tradition. At a very early point in the life of the Jacobean Church, therefore, one detects the beginnings of a profound difference of opinion on the nature of the Church as a spiritual institution, and on its proper relation to the civil polity. It remains to be seen how continued ecclesiological debate served to further shape these positions.

4

Apostoli, episcopi, divini?: *models of ecclesiastical governance*

The theme of governance was explored in controversies in which writers considered the issue of episcopacy based on minute examinations of the governance of the ancient church.[1] In addition, the *civil* power of the bishops, that is, the power to deprive clergy of livings, continued to raise questions of a legal and constitutional nature, and represented a continuation of the conflict over conformity and the High Commission examined in the previous chapter. There were therefore two planes on which the debate took place. On one hand, episcopacy was a practical issue: it involved claims to rule the Church and to exercise discipline in order to preserve doctrinal uniformity. As an institution, the Church was ordered as an hierarchy, from Convocation down to visitations and injunctions on the level of the diocese; bishops were the channels through which the Crown's sovereignty over the Church was exercised.[2] On the other hand, episcopacy also invited speculation on matters of ecclesiology, and specifically on how well the Church of England emulated the mode of governance that obtained in the ancient church.[3] Did the Apostles and their successors rule over the church as a whole, or were they merely charged with guidance and instruction? The debates on governance, therefore, exposed to scrutiny the tension inherent in a church defined by its advocates as a blend of civil and spiritual elements, and attacked by its critics as an unholy alliance of doctrinal precept and political expediency.

[1] For Hooker's treatment of Apostolic origins, see Stanley Archer, 'Hooker on Apostolic succession: the two voices', *Sixteenth Century Journal*, 24 (1993), 67–74. Two early and still relevant studies are A. J. Mason, *The Church of England and episcopacy* (Cambridge, 1914), ch. 1; and Norman Sykes, *Old priest and new presbyter* (Cambridge, 1956), chs. 2–3.

[2] See Stephanie Mary Langton, 'Bishops as governors: diocesan administration and social organisation among the late Elizabethan and Jacobean episcopacy', (MA diss., University of Alberta, 2002).

[3] Kenneth E. Kirk, *The Apostolic ministry: essays on the history and doctrine of episcopacy* (London, 1946).

What links the present chapter with that previous is the question of how modes of revivified Apostolic governance impacted on the ecclesiastical rule of the Crown in parliament, as well as on the common law. Here again, the debate was carried on in the context of competing historical arguments. The question of governance was central to the identity of all Christian churches, since it provided evidence of continuity with the ancient church, evidence that was in turn derived from historical interpretation and used to attach legitimacy to a particular pattern of rule. In other words, governance best illustrated the problem of the relationship between civil and spiritual authority that some were anxious to clarify and others to dispute. Hence, conformists defended their right to govern the Church, to define it, and to settle its doctrine and liturgy. As the Church of Rome traced its links with the ancient church through the succession of popes, so English conformists sought to link Canterbury and the other sees with the Apostles and their successors.

Yet the historical record was ambiguous, and a dispute emerged over whether bishops were 'pastors' or 'prelates'.[4] That is, was their function defined by preaching the Word, promoting a 'godly' ministry, and the administration of the diocese, or were they officers charged with rooting out heresy via visitations, subscription, and the deprivation of non-conforming ministers?[5] This power, which contemporaries described as 'discipline', was employed to describe the power of the Church over its members, and the measures by which this power was employed. What one side defended as an indelible mark of ecclesiastical sovereignty, the other condemned as a vestige of human invention, and the mark of a church tilted too far toward Rome.[6] Reformists argued that there had to be a firm link between 'doctrine' and 'discipline' – that any mode of governance adopted by the Church had to be shown to have a sound warrant in scripture; if it did not, then it was merely of 'human invention', and a political device applied to a spiritual end.

JURISDICTION, SOVEREIGNTY, AND SUCCESSION

Elizabethan debates on episcopacy furnish the background for the conflict that would emerge in the next reign. At first, the question had been largely confined to a debate between Catholic and Protestant members of the high clergy, yet there was a further spur to the development of ideas on

---

[4] This theme was central to Fincham's examination of 'rival forms of churchmanship'. See Kenneth Fincham, *Prelate as pastor: the episcopate of James I* (Oxford, 1990), ch. 8.

[5] Ibid., pp. 112–46, 248–93, and 304.

[6] See D. Alan Orr, 'Sovereignty, supremacy and the origins of the English Civil War', *History*, 87 (2002), 474–90. Dr Orr's interesting article suggests that it was a struggle over the 'definition' of the concept of sovereignty in both its civil and ecclesiastical guises that led to a polarisation of opinion during the Personal Rule.

episcopacy, in the form of those debates among Elizabethan Protestants on the manner of government appropriate to the newly reformed Church. Hence, episcopacy became a catalyst for a conflict over what defined the governance of a reformed Church, and this debate expanded to encompass another on the definition of the Church. In response to Presbyterian charges that the episcopal power was 'novel' and 'political', conformists traced the history of the office back to its Apostolic origins. The historical case that they proposed did double duty, for while it answered the Protestants, it also offered a reinterpretation of the literature that traced the Apostolic tradition. One of the consequences of controversy between English Protestants was that conformist divines were led to make new and well-developed statements on the place of bishops in the English Church. Like John Rainolds' anti-episcopal tracts, Thomas Bilson's *Perpetual gouernement* and Richard Bancroft's controversial Paul's Cross sermon preached in February 1588 enjoyed a life after their immediate context, and came to influence debate on the question of governance in both the English and Scottish settings.

As we saw with reference to debates on the High Commission, reformists argued that both the laws of God and the laws of the 'realm' bound the earthly minders of the Church. William Stoughton could therefore argue that: '[T]he Bishop, by virtue of the order and force appointed by Act of Parliament bindeth him, as well to minister the Discipline of Christ, within his cure, as the doctrine and sacraments of Christ, as the Lord hath commanded it, as this realme hath received it, according to the commandments of God.'[7] Indeed, early controversies over the High Commission invited speculation on the nature of episcopal authority and its relation to a conception of the Church that emphasised modes of doctrine and discipline established on the divine pattern. Another writer argued that the governors of the Church could not rightfully institute new modes of doctrine and discipline; 'Pastors, Doctors, Governors, and Deacons' were confined by what was established *iure divino*, rather than what might be established *iure humano*:

By which the church of God may, according to his worde, be directed in all matters, which are commonly called Ecclesiastical. And therefore as it is unlawful, so it is uneedful for men, following the devises of their own brayne, without the warrant of God's worde, to institute and ordayne any other offices or kindes of ministerye besides those, appointed and approved by God himselfe.[8]

It would be a mistake to suggest that opinions like this were confined to reformists. Scholars have made much of the fact that bishops claimed to hold

---

[7] William Stoughton, *An abstract, of certain acts of parliament* (London, 1583), p. 34.

[8] [William Fulke; Dudley Fenner; Walter Travers?], *A briefe and plaine declaration, concerning the desires of all those faithfull ministers, that haue and do seeke for the discipline and reformation of the Church of Englande* (London, 1584), p. 7.

power *iure divino*; yet this did not mean an unfettered, absolute form of power.[9] Rather, the phrase signified that God granted the office for the governance and protection of His Church. Thomas Bilson, a leading voice among English conformists, was very clear that episcopal power was inferior to that of the Crown. Bilson drove the point home by invoking the 'rock' that the Roman church claimed as its foundation, and by offering a distinction between the functions of prince and priest: 'This distinction between them is evident by their severall commissions which God hath signed. The prince, not the priest is God's minister to revenge malefactors. Peter himself was sharply rebuked by Christ for using the Sword, and in Peter all Pastors and Bishops are straightly charged not to meddle with it.'[10] In addition Bilson agreed with William Fulke in his conception of bishops as 'pastors' rather than 'prelates'. While Bilson did not deny that bishops had a function in the Church, he argued nevertheless that the nature of this function was defined by the law of scripture: 'Their function is limited to the preaching of the Word, and dispensing the sacraments, which *have no kind of compulsion in them*, but invite men only by sober persuasions to believe and embrace the promises of God.'[11]

In 1593 Bilson released a further work on episcopacy, but this time he sought to defend the episcopal function as a necessary block to religious conflict and disorder. Part of this argumentative shift had to do with the polemical context: the *Perpetual gouernement* was aimed specifically at 'Martin Marprelate' and other Presbyterian writers, from Thomas Cartwright to John Penry. At the heart of Marprelate's position was the argument that the power of bishops as defended by English conformists was 'novel' and 'political'; that is, it could not be defended on the basis of the warrant of scripture, and was employed in a manner that violated a further scriptural ideal, that of the bishop as pastor rather than prelate.[12] Against the charge of novelty, conformists offered the example of the history of the spiritual function of bishops: not only had they existed in the ancient church, but their duties were defined by the need to maintain uniformity of doctrine, and this entailed the enforcement of 'discipline'. In the Jacobean setting this argument was employed not only to defend the ceremonies enjoined by the

---

[9] See J. P. Sommerville, 'The royal supremacy and episcopacy "jure divino", 1603–1640', *Journal of Ecclesiastical History*, 34 (1983), 548–58.

[10] Thomas Bilson, *The true difference betweene Christian subiection and unchristian rebellion* (London, 1585), p. 127; William Lamont, 'The rise and fall of Bishop Bilson', *Journal of British Studies*, 5 (1966), 22–32.

[11] Bilson, *True difference*, p. 127. Emphasis added.

[12] Peter Milward, *Religious controversies of the Elizabethan age: a survey of printed sources* (London, 1977), pp. 86–93.

Canons of 1604, but also to provide a justification of the means whereby these ceremonies were enforced.

Bilson's text furnished a broad-ranging consideration of all of these issues. Yet there was more to the work than an historical exegesis of the episcopal office: it also made a statement of political precept, and can therefore be situated within the literature whose aim was to defend the public doctrine of the Church. Conformists sought to draw links between episcopal government and the stability of the Church as an institution. One of the conformist participants in the Marprelate controversy, Robert Some, argued that:

It is the Princes duetie to provide for the safetie of the bodies, therefore much more for safety of the soules of his subjects. If for the safety of their soules, then they may not suffer them to poyson their soules. True religion is the foode of the soule. It is but one. To swarve from that, is the bane of the soule. It leadeth to hell. The Shipmaster and shepeard must keep his shippe and sheepe from rock and wolfe. *Qui non servat si potest periturum, occidit.*[13]

At the root of conformist conceptions of ecclesiastical authority, therefore, was the proposition that it was the chief task of the governors of the Church to ensure the preservation of order. Hence, like many in that tradition, Bilson emphasised the virtue of order and the danger of 'discord': 'Profane writers could tell me, By concord, the weakest things grow strong: by discord, the mightiest states are overthrown: and that made me loath to increase or nourish the dislikes and quarrels that have lately fallen out in this Realme, betwixt Professors and Teachers of one and the Same Religion.' Here was a comment on the state of conflict between Elizabethan Protestants, a condition that violated a need for order that even pagan writers recognised. Since religion was the stay of polity, the argument ran, a divided faith meant also a divided state.[14] The antidote for disorder was sound governance, and one could not have government based on parity, and here we discover the root of Bilson's attack on Presbyterianism:

Order, saieth Nazianzene, is the Mother and preserver of all things ... If order and discipline be necessarie for all persons and ages in the Church of Christ; the government of the Church must not cease with the Apostles, but endure as long as the Church continueth ... and consequently, so much of the Apostolic power, as it is

---

[13] Robert Some, *A godly treatise containing and deciding certaine questions, mouued of late in London and other places, touching the ministerie, sacraments, and Church* (London, 1588), p. 6.

[14] Even Bilson's putative targets recognised this point: 'The Church and Commonwealth indeed, as the Elme and the Vine, rejoyce and flourish together, and in a sort, mourne and pine together. And if by this lacke of teaching, the Church loose as it were her life; shall not the commonwealth languish?' See [Anon], *The unlawfull practises of prelates against godly ministers, the maintainers of the discipline of God* ([London, 1584?]), sig. B^r.

requisite for the perpetual government of the Church, must remaine to those that from time to time supply the Apostles charge & succeed in the Apostles rooms.[15]

Bilson's book therefore set out to do two things: to argue that the necessary form of Church government was one defined by hierarchy, and that this form of government was established by the Apostles and had persisted since then. Yet there was more to tracing the succession of bishops than an argument on governance, for implicit in Bilson's position was the claim that between Peter, Paul, and Canterbury there was a succession that demonstrated the connection between the Church of England, and the church established by Christ.

This is why Bilson also sought a pedigree for the disciplinary aspect of English governance, the duties which were signified by the simultaneous possession of spiritual and political power: 'All of these duties, I often reduce to two branches, which are, Doctrine and Discipline. Comprising in doctrine, the dividing of the Word, and dispensing of the Sacraments, and referring the rest, I mean the *publicke* use of the keis, and imposition of hands, to the discipline or Regiment of the Church.'[16] This notion of 'public' authority was precisely what reformists dismissed as the seizure of political power by members of the clergy whose role was defined already by scripture. The spiritual office, they argued, did not consist in the enforcement of discipline, but rather in preaching and guidance. Bilson and other conformists therefore sought to demonstrate that the spiritual or pastoral office *was* resident in the function of diocesan bishops, and this point defined the purpose of Bilson's work.[17] Indeed, Bilson had no reservation about portraying the Church as an institution, and employed this element to counter Presbyterian parity and the notion of bishops as pastors: 'for if all should be Teachers', he asked, 'who should be Hearers?' Moreover, he suggested that the textual authorities that his opponents offered in support of their position failed to confirm that 'lay elders' had ever existed in the church. Bilson held up the Apostles themselves as evidence of a mode of governance whose aims could be reconciled with diocesan episcopacy – that is, the promotion of discipline and unity: 'The externall unitie and perpetuitie of the Church depend wholly on these. As to avoide schismes, bishops were first appointed, so to maintaine the Churches in unitie, the singularitie of one

---

[15] Thomas Bilson, *The perpetual gouernement of Christes Church* (London, 1593). The work was republished in 1610. Gregory of Nazianzus (329–89) was one of the Cappadocian Fathers who helped to restore the Nicene faith. Bilson was likely citing his *Epigrams and spiritual sentences*, trans. Thomas Drant (London, 1568).

[16] Bilson, *Perpetual gouernement*, pp. 207, 208.

[17] The *Perpetual gouernement* itself is situated within what Milward called an 'appendix' to the Marprelate controversy. See *Religious controversies of the Elizabethan age*, pp. 100–3.

Pastor over each flock is commended in the scriptures.'[18] Here Bilson identified episcopal governance as a 'note' of the Apostolic church.

Bilson's work suggested that English conformists realised that at stake was the definition of a mode of ecclesiastical governance, and by extension the definition of the Church itself. This was not a debate between rival confessions, Catholic and Protestant, but rather a debate within a single confession, split between proponents of two modes of governance, each with its own history. In other words, it was a battle for the reformed Church in England, and Bilson devoted entire chapters to the refutation of the historical and scriptural claims underpinning the Presbyterian position. Hence he turned the charge of 'novelty' back on its source, and dismissed the historical case for Presbyterian governance:

You frame churches to your fancies, and then you straightaway thinks the scriptures doe answere Your devices. If we give Bishops anything, which the ancient and Catholic Church did not first give them, in God's name spare us not, let the world know it: but if we professe the universal judgement of the Primitive Church in expounding the scriptures touching the power and function of Bishops, before your particular and late dreames, you must not blame us. They were nearer the Apostles times and likelier to understand the Apostles meanings than you, ye come after 1500 yeares with a new plot of Church government never heard of before.[19]

Part of the debate within the reformed tradition concerned the sources of authority that were employed to justify aspects of doctrine and discipline, and the Marprelate controversy was exemplary of this tension. Given the atmosphere of conformist / Presbyterian conflict, it is not surprising that we should find works that addressed the episcopal system in the context of the political dangers of religious discord. Richard Bancroft's sermon of February 1588 reflected this strand of ideas, in that it depicted an hierarchical mode of Church government as both a demonstrated historical necessity and a practical political expedient. Like William Wilkes, Bancroft constructed a 'history' of religious discord in order to make the case for the necessity of an ecclesiastical hierarchy. It will be remembered that the political aspects of Jacobean ecclesiology were characterised by an approach to associations whose signal concepts were order, hierarchy, and stability, and that this manner of analysis was often applied to the Church itself. Moreover, the political and ecclesiastical parts of the realm were interrelated, and hence religion was the 'stay' of polity. Bancroft could cite early Christian apologists such as Irenaeus, Tertullian, and Epiphanius in support of the proposition that 'schismatics' had long been and continued to be a threat to ecclesiastical polity: 'They are bold and stand in their

---

[18] Bilson, *Perpetual gouernement*, pp. 209, 224, 245. [19] Ibid., p. 285.

Owen conceit: they despise government and Fear not to speake evil of them that are in dignitie and authoritie.'[20]

Bancroft depicted the episcopate as having an Apostolic pedigree, yet he did not wish to demonstrate the point for its own sake. Rather, the case was directed against those critics of episcopacy – Marprelate being the most vocal – who mined the scriptures for evidence to reject the antiquity of bishops, and to define Presbyterianism as a more legitimate form of governance. Bancroft answered these criticisms by examining the history of the church, and arguing that episcopacy had a sounder claim to antiquity than did Presbyterian government. He observed that 'I cannot choose but account these Interpreters to be in Truth perverters of Christ's meaning: and do hold them among the number of those of whom Tertullian speaking saith: *Caedem scripturarem faciunt as materium suam.*'[21] Therefore, the reformist case against the government of the Church was an attempt to define a false, rival form of government; since heresy and 'false' government went hand in hand, Presbyterian discipline entailed a rejection of the 'true' church. Bancroft argued that episcopacy characterised the governance of the historical church that could not be racked by schism, for God was the author of peace, not disorder. The burden of maintaining an harmonious confession became the central part of Bancroft's case in support of bishops:

For unto them as S. Jerome saith ever since Saint Marks time the care of the Church government hath been committed. They had authoritie over the rest of the Ministrie, *Vt schismatum semina tollerentur:* That seede of schisms might be taken away. And againe, *Ne unusquique ad se trahens Christi ecclesiam rumperet.* Least every one drawing to himselfe by a severall way, should rent in pieces the Church of Christ.[22]

To cite Jerome reporting on the example of St Mark was to assemble power-ful authorities in aid of the argument. In addition, the example addressed the two most pressing issues of Bancroft's time: the need to find a pedigree for the episcopal mode of governance, as well as an argument for why, beside its antiquity, such a mode of governance was necessary. Schism was, in essence, the unravelling of the ancient confession, and a process whereby the ancient and historical elements of the 'true' religion were supplanted by the opinions of men. Schism was therefore proven to justify episcopacy and the institution of extra-scriptural checks against the fragmentation of the Church.

However, the response to Bancroft reversed these categories: in the work of John Penry, a central figure in the Marprelate controversy, human authorities – the bishops – had supplanted the authority of scripture. The 'first institution', the pattern for governance contained in the scripture, was

---

[20] Richard Bancroft, *A sermon preached at Paules Crosse the 9. of Februarie, being the first Sunday in the Parleament, anno. 1588* (London, 1588), p. 5.
[21] Ibid., p. 11. 'They murder the scriptures to serve their own purpose.'   [22] Ibid., pp. 14–15.

iure divino; yet the bishops had impinged upon this pattern, and sought to shape the Church to their own designs:

> The Office of Christ as he is a King, is boath to teach and to governe his Church by his owne lawes. Our bishops do professe themselves to robbe the Church of the scepter of government; which they have tyrannically wrested to themselves, and therefore we truly say, that they suffer Christ to have but halfe a kingdome at the most, under their Jurisdiction.[23]

Penry's tract had to do with *both* the civil and the ecclesiastical jurisdiction of the bishops. In the first case, he argued that it was 'intolerable' that the bishops 'should intrude their subscriptions' among the people 'whereas no such things are warranted by statute'. The true governors of the Church, he continued, were the parliament and the Crown, 'unto whose hands the Lord hath committed' the Church.[24] But there was more to the argument than a glib statement about the immemoriality of the first institution. Indeed, Penry argued that it was the responsibility of the Crown in parliament to ensure that the mode of governance adopted and practised in the Church of England was compatible with the warrant of scripture, and the example of the first institution. Like William Stoughton, therefore, Penry sought to promote the alliance between the laws of scripture and the laws of the realm, and to portray both as the pillars supporting the continuation of the 'true' church in England:

> This indeede we affirme. Moreover, that her Magesty and the parliament are bound to establish and erect among their subjects, all such lawes and ceremonies, as the True Ministers of the Word, shall prove by the Scriptures of God, to be meete and necessary for the government of the Temple and House of the Lord, within this Kingdome: And that they are bound to see, that no forme of religion or Church government be in force among the subjects, but that alone which by the word of God may be proved lawful, and so they are bound to see, that the Church of God be clensed and purified of all Idolatrous, popish, superstitious, and superflous government and ceremonies. And furthermore we say, *that they are to provide by law* that all persons, both Ministers and others, doe submit themselves without contradiction, unto all such things as shall be Godly established in the Church.[25]

From the point of view of the English constitution, this argument bound the Church's legitimate governors to their task, and this squared exactly with that part of the Coronation Oath that enjoined the sovereign to 'defend' England's religion. Penry's case amounted to a plea to Crown and parliament

---

[23] [John Penry], *A briefe discouery of the vntruths and slanders (against the true gouernement of the Church of Christ) contained in a sermon, preached the 8. [sic] of Februarie 1588. by D. Bancroft* (Edinburgh, 1590), pp. 16–17.

[24] Ibid., p. 40. 'Ministers, we say, are not to deal in civill causes, and therefore in that point we ascribe unto the Magistrate both *Potestate juris & facti*: that is, power to make lawes, and to execute them' (p. 45).

[25] Ibid., p. 41. Emphasis added.

to defend and promote the religion of the first institution against the machinations of the bishops. It was they, rather than the High Commission, who were the sole legitimate bearers of ecclesiastical sovereignty, and this power had to be exercised in the service of true doctrine. Moreover, should they fail in this duty, they could consider themselves to have violated God's law that enjoined them to defend the faith. It is worth noting that Penry was anxious to defend those elements of the Church that defined it as a sovereign political association, while excluding episcopacy from among those elements. In other words, he did not deny the proposition that the Church had a connection with civil authority, but rather sought to reaffirm that political power in the Church should be confined to those bodies to whom it had been given in 1559. Furthermore, Crown and parliament had to ensure that the Church remained firmly planted on its scriptural foundations. This meant that the legislature had to act to ensure that the bishops did not wholly capture its ecclesiastical sovereignty, diverting the Church away from reform.

A further theme that emerged in the debate on episcopacy was a dispute about who among English Protestants could claim a connection with the 'best reformed' churches of the Continent.[26] Some writers, such as Francis Mason, argued that the reformed tradition was no tradition at all, merely a congeries of churches that had only Protestantism in common.[27] He and others emphasised the claims of the English Church to uniqueness within the broader reformed confession.[28] This was the position taken by Francis Godwin, Bishop of Llandaff, in his treatise on the episcopal succession. Like Bilson, he argued that the defence of the faith required sound government. Yet the scope of the case was broadened to include the reformed churches generally. It was thus that Godwin depicted England as the strongest friend of reform:

Those countries that heretofore have yeelded great plenty of able worke-folkes for the Lords vineyard; now that brood is spent which attayned learning, the rewards yet standing whole; they hardly can shew a man able to set pen to paper in defence of the truth. Yea, even amongst us, although the godly and excellent care of her Maiestie hath preserved the state of this our Church in such sort, as I think no other reformed Church of Christendome anything neere comparable unto it; yet the example of others, the knowen greediness of so many sacrilegious cormorants as await daily the destruction of the same, and the doubt least it will decay, for that we cannot hope for the like piety in all succeeding Princes.[29]

[26] For aspects of this problem, see Anthony Milton, *Catholic and reformed: the Roman and Protestant churches in English Protestant thought, 1600–1640* (Cambridge, 1995), ch. 8.

[27] Francis Mason, *The avthoritie of the Chvrch in making canons and constitutions concerning things indifferent* (London, 1607). Mason rejected the jurisdiction of 'foreign churches' and argued that the sovereignty of the Church of England was complete.

[28] See Milton, *Catholic and reformed*, pp. 448–528.

[29] Francis Godwin, 'To the Reader', in *A catalogue of the bishops of England, since the first planting of Christian religion in this island* (London, 1601).

In the short term, Godwin's fears would not be realised, for in James VI and I the Church gained an advocate whose broader mandate was to unite the reformed churches, with England as the natural locus of scholarly power. This furnished part of the context for the Hampton Court conference and the impetus behind the new edition of the Bible.[30] Yet Godwin was also prescient, for he knew that the reformed aspect of English doctrine was in a precarious position, and that under a king not actively disposed to its preservation a conflict within might ensue. As it turned out, the first articulate development of this theme in conjunction with a criticism of English conformity came in the course of debates about the office of bishops.

THE WATCHMEN OF THE CHURCH: EPISCOPACY AND CONFORMITY

In the Elizabethan setting, the question of episcopacy turned on the definition of the office in terms of its spiritual versus political elements. A very clear statement about this problem as it applied to the Jacobean Church came from the semi-Separatist Henry Jacob.[31] Writing at the height of the controversy over clerical subscription, Jacob argued that the bishops had not fulfilled the task set them by the King, that is, to prove via disputation that the contested aspects of rites and governance had a scriptural warrant. Instead, the bishops had turned out ministers by force, and in the process had promoted forms of worship that were of human devising:

The prelates have left no means of rigour and extremitie unessayed, for the suppressing of this cause and for the discouraging and daunting of all those that either speake or write for it; and yet the glorious evidence of the truth is such, that it wanteth no witnesses, there being at this day many hundreds of the most painful and profitable Preachers in this Kingdom (besides those already turned out) which are readie to lose both their Ministry and their Maintenance, and to expose themselves and theirs to all manner of misery, rather then they will renounce this cause, and conform themselves to the corruptions of the times.[32]

---

[30] See W. B. Patterson, *King James VI and I and the reunion of Christendom* (Cambridge, 1997), pp. 31–74.

[31] See Keith Sprunger, *Dutch puritanism: a history of the English and Scottish churches of the Netherlands in the sixteenth and seventeenth centuries* (Leiden, 1982), pp. 23, 32, 68, 136–7, 233, 345–6; and Murray Tolmie, *The triumph of the saints: the separate churches in London, 1616–1649* (Cambridge, 1977), who gives details of the 'Jacobean' church established by Jacob in London. See also Victoria Joy Gregory, 'Congregational puritanism and the radical puritan community in England c. 1585–1625' (Ph.D. diss., University of Cambridge, 2003).

[32] Henry Jacob, 'Epistle dedicatory', in *A Christian and modest offer of a most indifferent conference, or disputation, about the maine and principall controversies betwixt the prelats, and the late silenced and deprived ministers in England* ([London: W. Jones' secret press], 1606), *3.

That learning had failed the bishops was taken as evidence that their case could not be defended by the divine warrant of scripture. Jacob sought to defend the combined ecclesiastical sovereignty of Crown in parliament; in addition, he maintained that the divinely ordained pattern of Presbyterian government was a better friend to monarchy: '[T]he Government of the Churches of Christ by Pastors, Teachers, and Elders, is much more agreeable to the State of a Monarchy, then is the present Government by Archbishops, Bishops, Archdeacons, Commisaries and the rest of the Romish hierarchy.' Jacob's elision of episcopacy and 'popery' merely addressed the problem of ecclesiastical jurisdiction in metaphorical terms: Rome was a foreign church, and so Jacob sought to depict the bishops as similarly foreign. He did so not only by condemning the 'ungodly' practice of subscription, but noted as well that Bancroft's programme of conformity came at the expense of the common law and the independence of parliament: 'Only the prelats, having many voices of their cause in the Upper House, have, by their gross flatteries and fayned promises ... ever CROSSED the holy endeavours of the parliament, for the removal of these burdens, grievous to both Church and commonwealth.'[33]

This battle was traced to the early history of the church in Thomas Whetenhall's examination of 'abuses' present in the Church of England. Indeed, antiquity was attached to the concept of corruption in order to show the long history whereby the church fell away from its founding and toward corruption and error. Whetenhall plied the standard argument that the pattern of governance left in the scriptures should be 'restored' – all elements of human 'custom' had to be purged:

[M]any excellent men have already by manifold reasons grounded and taken out of the Word of God, proved that there ought to be a full reformation both in doctrine and discipline, according to that order in the Church, which Christ and his Apostles left; which must be acknowledged to be the only sure ground and proofe for all points of controversie in the Church of God.[34]

Whetenhall proposed a definition of a reformed Church that included the element of the Apostolic pedigree; yet rather than defining a church that was traced through the works of scholars and theologians, he envisioned a continuity in the Word, and through its immemorial character in history. Standing in the way of 'reformation' was the scholarly arsenal employed by the bishops to maintain the rites laid forth in the Canons, which in turn were based not on the Word, but upon 'custom, antiquitie and auncient Fathers'. Turning this interpretation against itself, Whetenhall argued that if examples from antiquity proved anything, it was that the 'pride and

---

[33] Jacob, 'Epistle', in *Modest offer*, pp. 16–17, 26.

[34] Thomas Whetenhall, *A discourse of the abuses now in question in the churches of Christ* ([London: W. Jones' secret press], 1606), p. 5.

ambition' of the bishops were concealed beneath the pretence of 'unitie, conformitie and Peace in the Church'.[35] In other words, where conformists mined history for evidence of the antiquity of the episcopal office, their opponents conducted similar researches in order to demonstrate the manner in which the bishops had undermined the Church. This rejection of modes of rites and governance that were of 'human invention' was extended to the Canons of 1604: devised by clerics, they reflected not the perfection of doctrine (*iure divino*) but the work of earthly agents. This alone justified that they be ignored: 'And therefore, touching all constitutions of bishops, without the express warrant, we ought to take them for lyers and deceavers, and by no means subscribe unto them.'[36] The assumption was clear: a church based on the Word was doctrinally pure – its rites and governance did not have to be defended by complex scholarly arguments. Indeed, Whetenhall's strong condemnation of episcopacy was based on the assumption that there existed a divine and perfect pattern by which the Church was to be ordered, and that this pattern could not be combined with human ordinances.[37]

Yet conformists did not embrace the principles behind the positions of their opponents, for to do so would have been to concede that the institution of the Church was somehow flawed. Instead, they translated theological positions into political ones: schism and clamour were condemned as threats to the Church and state.[38] It was thus that Anthony Maxey styled the English Church as a 'lilly amongst thorns ... oppressed with enemies, Molested with Schisme, Contention and Heresies'.[39] Perhaps no writer put it more clearly than Francis Bacon, writing to advise the King early in the reign. Bacon touched upon a theme that recurred in his essays, that is, the dangers of religious faction, which he linked to the question of 'obedience':

[U]ntil Your Magestie doth otherwise determine and order, all actual and full obedience is to be given to ecclesiastical jurisdiction, as it now stands, and when Your Magesty hath determined and ordered, that every good subject ought to rest satisfied and apply his obedience to your Magesties laws, ordinances and Royal Commandments.[40]

---

[35] Ibid., pp. 6–7, at p. 7.   [36] Ibid., p. 68.

[37] On reading Whetenhall's tract, Bancroft ordered that his lodgings be searched and his library seized. See Stuart Barton Babbage, *Puritanism and Richard Bancroft* (London, 1962), p. 145.

[38] Anti-Catholicism exerted a powerful influence on conceptions of the political dangers of religious competition. As Edward Coke noted with reference to Catholics, '[T]hey were enjoyned to work his Magestie's overthrow, unlesse he would reconcile himself to Rome, hold his Crown of the Pope, and conform himself and all of his subjects to the Religion of the Roman Church.' See Edward Coke, *The preface to his charge given at the assize holden at Norwich* (London, 1606), sig. G^{r-v}.

[39] Anthony Maxey, *The churches sleepe, expressed in a sermon preached at the court* (London, 1606), sig. A^3.

[40] [Francis Bacon], *Certaine considerations touching the better pacification, and edification of the Church of England* (London, 1604), sig. A^{4v}.

Bacon combined obedience with ecclesiastical authority, and placed adherence to ecclesiastical orders on a par with obedience to the temporal laws of the realm. Elsewhere Bacon had treated the evils of religious faction, which he styled as akin to wounds in the natural body: 'Therefore it is most necessary that the Church by doctrine and decree; princes by their sword ... damn and send to hell ... those facts and opinions.'[41] This political necessity was determined, Bacon argued, by the fact that Church and commonwealth were bound together: 'It is not possible in respect of the great and neere sympathy between the state civil and the state ecclesiasticall to make so mayne an alteration in the Church, but it would have a perilous operation on the Kingdom.'[42] Joseph Hall, writing against the Brownist sect in 1610, noted that the alliance between the 'civil politie' and the 'divine politie' meant that religious peace was to be desired. In the same year Robert Abbot suggested that the possibility of sound members of the Church being led into error by sectarians 'pretending ... to be the right way' justified a strong clerical hierarchy charged with the preservation of uniform doctrine.[43] What these examples suggest is that, apart from doctrine and history, there was a *political* case available to those who sought to defend episcopacy.

The summoning of representatives of the Scottish Kirk to Hampton Court in September 1606 furnished conformist clerics with an opportunity to reinforce aspects of the authority of the Church – namely the sovereignty of Convocation and the role of bishops in the process of ecclesiastical governance.[44] William Barlow, our principal source for the 1604 assembly at Hampton Court, preached before the unwilling Scottish divines, and argued that, far from being the enemies of the Church, the bishops were among its most vigorous defenders. Indeed, their 'reverence of antiquitie' and 'ornaments of learning' were evident in the synods of the Church, themselves so much 'physic' for an ailing body spiritual. Clearly, the times shaped Barlow's thinking on this point, for one of the themes of the sermon was a denunciation of those who 'prefer their owne fancie before all

---

[41] 'Of Unity in Religion', in *Essays*, by Francis Bacon, ed. John Strachan (Hertfordshire, 1997), pp. 9, 12.

[42] Bacon, *Certaine considerations*, sig. B^{4v}.

[43] Joseph Hall, *A common apologie of the Church of England: against the vnjust challenges of the over-just sect, commonly called Brownists* (London, 1610), p. 21. Robert Abbot, *The old waye. A sermon preached at Oxford, the eight day of July, being the Act Sunday. 1610* (London, 1610), p. 8.

[44] The English–Scots controversies form the subject of the final chapter, and while the sermons to be discussed here bear on that topic, I have chosen to treat them in the context of the present chapter, since as a group they aimed to defend aspects of the governance of the Church that were being challenged in print more strenuously by English reformists. For a discussion of the 1606 discussions at Hampton Court within the context of James' broader ecclesiastical policy, see Patterson, *James VI and I*, pp. 113–17.

antiquity'.[45] The Presbyterians, the argument ran, were guilty of doctrinal error fomented by misguided leaders like the Melvilles.[46] Here again we find the tension between antiquity and human invention that underlay the controversy between Bancroft and Penry. For Barlow, Presbyterian parity bred contention and disorder within the Church, and this furnished the point of his argument. Citing St Jerome, Barlow argued that the stability and unity of the Church was predicated upon some form of clerical hierarchy: '[T]hose effects which use to follow Parity and Plurality, viz. Dissention and confusion, it was generally decreed, as Hierome confesseth ... that one should be placed above the others to governe both presbyters and flocke [and] he should be stiled by the name of Bishop'. Yet it was commonly maintained by reformists that since no ancient pedigree for the episcopal office – not to mention the word 'bishop' – could be found in scripture, the office was the mark of 'popery'. Barlow answered these charges and refuted the Roman interpretation of episcopal succession in the patriarchal sees founded by the Apostles:

Surely, we are no Arcadians, to fetch our Pedigrees from beyond the Moone: shall Histories of fact, or the Testimonies of the Ancient, be our heralds for record? Eusebius, the most ancient of the Historiographers, that we have for 300 years succession nameth the persons & calculateth the times of the Bishops of the four principal Churches of the world, Jerusalem, Antioch, Rome and Alexandria.[47]

Yet over time the office became corrupted, as the Roman church sought precedence among the churches in the West. In the wake of Rome's decline with the Reformation, Barlow argued, it was up to the particular churches to restore bishops to their ancient status. This explained the position of the Church of England, which, as with 'disused' Roman ceremonies, had also restored the episcopal office to sound 'usage'. Hence, Barlow provided an historical case in response to the charge that the episcopal office was 'novel'.

Other sermons preached before the sceptical Presbyterian visitors (and their Episcopalian countrymen) established the authority of the bishops by linking it with that of the King. To set forth this argument was to suggest that, whatever powers the bishops employed, they did so legitimately as extensions of the Crown's ecclesiastical sovereignty. James I's famous maxim, 'No Bishop, No King' represented the essence of the case – taken

---

[45] William Barlow, *One of the foure sermons preached before the Kings Maiestie, at Hampton Court in September last. This concerning the antiquitie and superioritie of bishops* (London, 1606), sig. B[r].

[46] That is, Andrew Melville (1545–1622), Presbyterian controversialist and scholar, and his nephew James Melville (1556–1614), Professor of Hebrew – both were summoned to London by James I after careers in which they gained and lost a number of clerical and academic posts and professed throughout a principled opposition to English ecclesiology.

[47] Barlow, *One of the foure sermons*, sig. E[r].

jointly, these offices constituted the bulwark of the Church against schism, and could command the obedience of individuals. John Buckeridge argued that conscience, the 'forum internum', enjoined obedience to both superior and inferior magistrates in civil and religious causes, 'And these causes concurring, the matter being lawfull or indifferent, the forme due, the efficient potent, and the end publicke and good, the laws of Man must be obeyed, not only for wrath, but for Conscience, which is the greatest obligation on earth.'[48] Indeed, acknowledged Buckeridge, subscription *was* the result of the laws of men, but this was defensible because these laws were conceived to protect God's church, and fulfilled the scriptural injunction that 'all things be done decently and in order'.[49] Yet Buckeridge's argument had less to do with obedience to bishops than it had with obedience to the King: the sermon can thus be situated within that tradition which extolled the virtues of the 'religious prince', who acted as a 'nursing father' to the church. Not only were examples of Christian princes to be found in the scriptures, but a definition of the powers of the office was set forth in the Act of Supremacy. In Buckeridge's sermon, then, we find an example of the argument that maintained that the bishops acted as the legitimate channels of the ecclesiastical sovereignty of the Crown. Buckeridge surveyed centuries of ecclesiastical history, and provided dozens of examples wherein princes charged their inferior clerics with the maintenance of discipline. Thus the 'precept' of the King's authority, concluded Buckeridge, 'extends not only to civil causes ... but also religion'.[50]

It will be remembered that contemporaries depicted this extension of the Crown's sovereignty in historical terms, most often in connection with a reference to biblical monarchs or other Christian princes. Lancelot Andrewes combined this strand of thinking with a case for the historical right of the Church to summon councils for the purpose of strengthening its liturgy: 'Assemblies being ever a speciall means to revive the Law, (as occasions serve) and to keep it in life; As if the law itselfe therefore lacked yet something, and were not perfect and full without them.'[51] The purpose of these laws was to 'restrain and redress abuses', meaning both a restoration of the liturgy and the implementation of means whereby its future deviation from the standard applied by the Church might be prevented. Moreover, the sovereignty of the assembly was linked to that of the Crown, and hence synods and

---

[48] John Buckeridge, *A sermon preached at Hampton Court before the Kings Maiestie, on Tuesday the 23. of September, anno 1606* (London, 1606), pp. 5, 8.

[49] 1 Corinthians 14: 40. This line comes up frequently in conformist sermons, but was less frequently chosen as the text on which the sermon was based.

[50] Buckeridge, *A sermon preached at Hampton Court*, pp. 16–17.

[51] Lancelot Andrewes, *A sermon preached before the Kings Maiestie at Hampton Court, concerning the right and power of calling assemblies* (London, 1606), p. 4.

councils were conceived to be natural extensions of the power of the magistrate in the ecclesiastical sphere; this Andrewes defined as the 'Rectitudo Regis. A Power Regall ... Thus, from Moses to the Maccabees, we see in whose hands this power was.' This sort of historical exercise explained why kings were seen as having a divine office – they were seen to partake in a long succession of non-papal rulers chosen by God to defend and maintain His earthly church, 'and so it hath been holden in all nations, as a special power belonging to Dominion'.[52]

A contrasting point of view was put forward by John King, who argued that while it was the magistrate's God-given task to protect the 'Ancient apostolique Church', his power over the Church was nevertheless inferior to that of the bishops. This did not entail disobedience to the Crown, and so King was anxious to point out that: 'the King that ruleth his people well, and laboureth the Good both of Church and commonwealth, is worthy of double honour, both of allegiance and allowance of his subjects'.[53] King did not pursue the full implications of this statement, which suggested that a king who failed in his duty to Church and commonwealth no longer warranted the allegiance of his subjects. However, he did explain in very clear terms what the notion of the king as 'nursing father' to the Church implied, and indicated that a lapse in this duty had consequences: 'Princes, themselves, though they bee the nursing-fathers of the Church, yet they are her servants too, and therefore must ever remember to submit themselves, subject to their scepters, & caste downe their crownes before her.' King implied that the governance of the Church by kings was divinely preordained, and also part of the natural order of things: comparing the Church to a vineyard, King cast James in the role of vintner whose job it was to cause all to thrive with judicious discipline. Presbyterian 'parity' represented 'the world turned upside downe, where the people commandeth all'.[54] King took the tension between the laws of God and the actions of men posited by many writers, and turned it against the Presbyterians by depicting their discipline as *iure humano*; this allowed him to justify episcopacy as *iure divino*. For King, the role of the prince was diminished from that upheld by Andrewes, and this reveals a point of disagreement among conformists.

With reference to debates among English Protestants, conformists claimed that while scripture did indeed enjoin aspects of doctrine and discipline, it did not do so with the rigidity implied by their critics. Samuel Collins addressed this question by arguing that in scripture could be found two 'levels' of

[52] Ibid., pp. 11, 19, 31.
[53] John King, *The fourth sermon preached at Hampton Court on Tuesday the Last of Sept. 1606* (Oxford, 1607), pp. 27–8.
[54] Ibid., pp. 22, 24.

doctrine: 'not only the written word of God, but everie doctrine that is not dissenting or swarving therefrom; not only that which is expressed, but that which is inferred'. This notion of 'inference', which included ceremonies and other *adiaphora*, was left to the interpretation of the Church, and its implementation by the 'interposition of lawful authority'.[55] By this Collins meant bishops and the programme of subscription, which he sought to situate within the traditions of the ancient church: 'So ancient is the custom of requiring subscription at the hands of Churchmen, to prevent faction once a-foot'. The ancients, Collins argued, had not been obliged to contend with opponents as strident as William Bradshaw, and so where the scriptures were silent, God had ensured that in the wisdom of the prince, means could be devised to ensure the stability of the Church: 'So, the Christian Magistrate and Regent of the Church, whom God hath indued with the spirit of wisdom ... supplies in this case, that which was no imperfection of the scripture to leave out, but rather an impossibility for the scripture to comprehend.'[56]

Gabriel Powel in *De adiaphoris* offered a link between the duties of the prince and the nature of doctrine. Powel upheld the 'libertie' of the Church to 'use those things which are truly indifferent', as well as the power of the magistrate armed with the 'external sword' to punish 'violators and contemners of Discipline, whether they be ministers or common people'.[57] By 'things indifferent' Powel, and indeed all conformists, meant those aspects of doctrine and discipline that were not strictly enjoined by scripture and hence were left to the discretion of the Church. This approach shifted the emphasis away from the vexed question of doctrinal purity toward the practical problems of achieving some measure of stability in the visible church – the institution. Powel grouped the office of the ecclesiastical magistrate under three main headings: as 'David', ensuring that the Church is 'rightly settled and governed'; as a public authority charged by God to preserve order; and as one who acts to 'assist and defend the ministrie'.[58] Both magistrates and their 'inferiors', therefore, were concerned with 'outward discipline', a point that left open the crucial question posed by reformists, notably Henry Jacob, who argued that 'belief and practice cannot be separated'.[59] Indeed, central to Powel's position was the assumption that there was no necessary connection between belief and practice. From the

[55] Samuel Collins, *A sermon preached at Paule's- Crosse, vpon the 1. of Nouember, being All-Saint's Day, anno 1607* (London, 1607), pp. 3–4.
[56] Ibid., pp. 16, 41.
[57] Gabriel Powel, *De adiaphoris. Theological and scholastical positions, concerning the nature and vse of things indifferent* (London, 1607), pp. 31, 42.
[58] Ibid., pp. 42–4, passim.
[59] [Henry Jacob], *A collection of sundry matters ... appointed by God for his visible church spiritually politicall* ([Amsterdam], 1616), sig. B8v–r.

point of view of his opponents, however, the disputed rites were a corruption of matters of belief and faith that were themselves plainly evident in scripture. Given this, the conformist notion of 'things indifferent' was mere rhetorical sleight of hand, for everything done contrary to the scripture was sin, and therefore not indifferent.

In response to the call for 'consent', the right of individuals and individual churches to refuse the imposition of ceremonies and modes of governance not found in scripture, Powel offered a two-fold description of law – that of God and that of nations. The latter, essentially the same as 'custom', covered things indifferent: 'For it is most certaine that the GOSPELS HATH NOT ORDAINED ANY EXTERNALL OR CORPOREAL POLICIE: but permitteth us freely to use the policies of all nations.'[60] The law of God, meanwhile, had nothing to do with matters of faith, but rather with an ideal of order: God's church should be the site of peace, and so to quarrel with aspects of rites and governance was to violate this ordinance: 'For it is the commandment of God, that we submit ourselves unto the Magistrate, and this precept of God toucheth the conscience.'[61] Powel enjoined obedience to the ordinances of God's earthly steward over His Church, for that steward and his inferiors acted only in the interest of peace, order, comeliness, and edification:

[T]he direct and proper end of the Prelates and Pastors ecclesiasticall, is that they may edifie, governe, informe and teach by the Word of God, the consciences of the Citizens of the Church [and] they that conferr not their obedience unto the Ecclesiasticall lawes, they hurt the faith, manners and consciences of other men, they rayse scandals, and rashly and schismatically disturbe the peace and quietness of the Church.[62]

Note that Powel referred to members of the Church as 'citizens', a term applied to the freemen of urban places in early seventeenth-century England and which suggested that he viewed the Church as a political entity. This perspective may well have angered those who argued that the ordering of the 'visible church' could not come at the expense of divine law – the institution of the Church had to proceed directly from doctrine. Yet, given the peculiarity of the English situation, with its blending of civil and ecclesiastical offices, ecclesiology was dominated by the practical needs of a vast earthly institution. To acquiesce on the point of governance would mean the surrendering of sovereignty, which may help to explain the tendency among conformists to elide the positions of their Protestant opponents with disobedience.

---

[60] Powel, *De adiaphoris*, p. 49. Upper case in original. Powel speaks of the 'regiment' of the Church in civil terms: 'according unto the externall and politique Regiment, every Christian is necessarily subject to all humane lawes … whether they be made by the civil Magistrate, or by the Church' (p. 50).

[61] Ibid., p. 51.   [62] Ibid., p. 54.

It also helps to explain reformist arguments against those civil punishments meted out in the name of religious conformity. Often these came from laymen, and so to Thomas Whetenhall we may add Nicholas Fuller, a prominent common-law advocate who defended two non-conformists against deprivations ordered by the High Commission.[63] Fuller's argument – published by sympathisers after his own imprisonment – was arranged under the heads of ecclesiastical jurisdiction and the legal precedents for it offered by the common law.[64] In order for Church and commonwealth to 'agree', there had to be a 'right distribution of the Jurisdiction of the Church of England, and jurisdiction of the Common lawes of England'.[65] Fuller's purpose, therefore, was to ask whether subscription and deprivation by the High Commission could be reconciled with the common law. Like William Bradshaw, Fuller argued that deprivation at the hands of the High Commission violated the 29th article of Magna Carta, which stipulated that seizure of property and imprisonment could only be enforced by jury.[66] Since the High Commission removed ministers from their livings without either a jury trial or reference to the common law, deprivation clearly violated Magna Carta. The Elizabethan Act of Supremacy that returned the Crown to its 'ancient jurisdiction' over the Church supplied a more recent precedent. Here, Fuller argued that the High Commission imposed upon the sovereignty of the Crown; moreover, the Act of Supremacy could not be seen to have described a transfer of sovereignty from the Crown to the ecclesiastical courts:

> [T]his Act of an I Eliz. neyther doth, nor can give life to this Commission, by any right construction, in these parts above rehearsed, but contrarywise doth expressly abolish their Jurisdiction to imprison subjectes, fyne them, and force them to accuse themselves, as repugnant to the Ancient Ecclesiastical Jurisdiction, which, by this Act, is restored to the Crowne.[67]

This 'forgotten exponent of English liberty' was, in reality, a firm defender of the Crown's ecclesiastical prerogative against various competitors, whether bishops or judges. Like William Fulke and William Bradshaw, Fuller sought to defend the role of parliament in the establishment of ecclesiastical discipline, and to ensure that this process was guided by the common law.

---

[63] For details, see R. G. Usher, 'Nicholas Fuller: a forgotten exponent of English liberty', *American Historical Review*, 12 (1907), 743–60, esp. 749.

[64] For a discussion of Fuller's position in the context of later conflicts over the High Commission, particularly under Laud, see D. Alan Orr, *Treason and the state: law, politics and ideology in the English Civil War* (Cambridge, 2002), pp. 132–3. For general accounts, see R. G. Usher, *The rise and fall of the High Commission*, with a new introduction by Philip Tyler (Oxford, 1968), pp. 170–9, and his *The reconstruction of the English Church*, 2 vols. (London, 1910), vol. II, pp. 134–54.

[65] Nicholas Fuller, *The argument of master Nicholas Fuller, in the case of Thomas Lad, and Richard Maunsell, his clients* ([W. Jones' secret press], 1607), p. 2.

[66] Ibid., p. 14.   [67] Ibid., p. 23.

Although he was an opponent of subscription, Fuller nevertheless exemplified a body of writers who looked warily at units – whether Crown or parliament – that compromised ecclesiastical sovereignty.[68]

Despite the depth of Fuller's attack on the High Commission, it did not answer the main question, which concerned not the ecclesiastical jurisdiction of *civil* officers, but rather the civil jurisdiction of *ecclesiastical* officers; for we will recall that clerical livings were considered as 'property', and hence fell under the jurisdiction of the common law. Thomas Ridley argued that the problem of competing jurisdictions demanded careful handling: 'where there are two divers jurisdictions in one Commonwealth, unlesse they be carefully bounded by the Prince ... as the advancement of one increaseth, so the practice of the Other decreaseth'.[69] It was this problem that led writers like William Bradshaw to argue that in enforcing deprivations the bishops were also contravening the common law of England; they had, in other words, assumed superiority in a constitutional sphere where the common law was claimed to be sovereign. Given this attack, conformist writers had to explain how bishops could retain power to deprive ministers, and to do so in a way that did not violate the common law. As we have seen with reference to both Hayward and Gabriel Powel, one way of doing this was to argue that the superiority of bishops over their clergy predated English law, and was hence independent of it. Thomas Rogers therefore traced episcopal superiority to the Apostolic church:

Albeit the terms and titles of archbishops we find not, yet the superiority which they enjoy, and the authority which the bishops and archbishops do exercise, in ordering and consecrating of bishops, and ecclesiastical ministers, is grounded upon the word of God. For we find that in the Apostles days how themselves both were in dignity above the Evangelists, and the seventy disciples, and for authority both in and over the Church, as twelve patriarchs, saieth Beza, and also established an ecclesiastical hierarchy.[70]

Yet there was a problem with this argument, for in between the Apostles and the Jacobean Church lay that period when the true church languished in the wilderness. Here Rome reigned supreme, and its supremacy was maintained by a rank of superior ecclesiastical magistrates. Rogers explained this away

---

[68] This is not to say that Fuller was a champion of James I: as an MP he voted in favour of delaying subsidies, opposed the King on Bate's case (concerning the King's right to impose duties on goods for the purposes of controlling trade), and on the Union with Scotland. See Usher, *The reconstruction of the English Church*, vol. I, p. 137; and Babbage, *Puritanism and Richard Bancroft*, pp. 272–4.

[69] Thomas Ridley, *A view of the ciuile and ecclesiastical law* (London, 1607), p. 108; Brian Levack, *The civil lawyers in England, 1603–1641* (Oxford, 1973), pp. 29, 128–9.

[70] Thomas Rogers, *The faith, doctrine, and religion, professed, & protected in the realme of England, and dominions of the same* (Cambridge, 1607), p. 328. Citations are from the Parker Society edition, ed. J. J. S. Perowne (London, 1854; 1968).

by pointing out that while there was an uninterrupted 'succession of bishops', there had also from 'time to time ... been both mar-prelates and mock-prelates' who abused their God-given estate over the church. Despite these abuses, Rogers claimed that the episcopal function was enjoined by divine law, and that the bishops of the English Church stood in line of succession with the Apostles: 'The church's authority to decree rites and ceremonies is warranted in the word of God; first, by the example of the Apostles, who did ordain rites and ceremonies.' Hence, the bishops and the Apostles were linked in their functions: they were conduits for God's will that 'everything in the Church be done unto edifying, honestly and by order'.[71] Given this, how could subscription and deprivation – God's commandments – not be carried out? Indeed, translated into the categories we have been surveying, Rogers' argument established subscription and deprivation as modes of discipline that were of a greater antiquity than the laws of England, and in this point lay the independence of the Church and its governors.

Clearly, the conformist position was moving toward a statement about the sovereignty of the Church that depended on an account of episcopal power that, to some, implied a diminution of other sources of authority in the English state. Following Rogers, John Tichborne outlined aspects of that sovereignty, and in the course of his argument attempted to shift emphasis away from deprivation as a civil punishment, and toward excommunication as an historical punishment practised by the church. Hence his 'triple antidote' against scandal consisted of subscription and excommunication, rather than 'deprivation', a term which implied a loss of property, and a punishment that was seen to fall within the jurisdiction of the common law.[72] Tichborne's strategy for diminishing the strength of legal objections to deprivation was to stress the powers of the clergy and to posit a strong relationship between religious order and civil concord. Bancroft had argued vigorously that the danger of schism authorised the Church to take steps to ensure the stability of the faith, a process that was in turn emphasised in terms of its relationship to political stability.

[T]hose proceedings herein which are merely civil, or mixt sometimes of both, according to their several ends, authors and originals, doe principally, and for the most part, respect the common policy of the whole state, and that which is Civil as well and more particularly many times, as that which is Ecclesiastical, albeit they ought to agree in all things together as Hippocrates his Twinnes.[73]

---

[71] Ibid., p. 184.
[72] John Tichborne, *A triple antidote, against certaine very common scandals of this time* (London, 1609). Tichborne wrote of 'excommination ordinii', that is 'by some orderly proceeding and under some course of law and constitution Just or unjust any are removed from any such company and privileges belonging thereunto' (p. 5).
[73] Ibid., p. 8.

While this positing of the conjoined nature of the corporate state was a common theme in the literature of religious controversy, the clericalism of some conformists seemed to threaten the Crown's jurisdiction over the Church. In Tichborne's pages, this theory received further refinement: in essence, he proposed two 'levels' of authority, the one 'immediately' over the Church 'for the determining of all controversies, and expounding of Scriptures according to the rule of faith and manners'. The second level of authority concerned the conjoined state, ecclesiastical and civil, and 'this entercourse of politique administrations, Ecclesiastical and Civill ... neither may the proper orders and proceedings of the one be truly saide to be any more prejudiciall or contrary to the other'.[74] While Tichborne was careful to point out that critics of the Crown's ecclesiastical sovereignty sought to erect a 'Macedonian throne', he nevertheless described episcopal power in a manner which seemed to privilege it over all other authorities: 'that the Bishops being put in trust by God and man with the government of the Church, and all state occasions depending thereupon, they do no more here-in ... then that which the common lawes of the Kingdom, and the chief governors of our whole state do enjoyne them, and require at their hands, and none other'.[75] In other words, Tichborne subscribed to the argument that the bishops were merely conduits for the ecclesiastical authority of the Crown, rather than an 'upstart' power that trespassed on the authority of parliament, the Crown, and the common law.

Henry Jacob led the reformist attack on episcopacy. Having already pre-sented a case for reform of the Church of England, Jacob came to write a plea for 'toleration' in 1609. The *Humble supplication* made the case that the deprived ministers intended no disloyalty by refusing to subscribe, and pointed out that there were other groups in the state who posed a greater threat to the Church and the royal prerogative. The bishops, argued Jacob, represented an extra-scriptural and extra-legal power: 'the Prelates, our Professed adversaries, and their Officers, have not either the nature of their offices, or for the Qualitie of their Proceedings any warrant from the Word of the Lord Jesus, or the Lawe of this Kingdome'.[76] From Jacob's point of view, the government of Christ's church by human agents served to sever it from the ancient and Apostolic church. Yet it also stood as an affront to the King's supremacy over the Church in his dominions because the authority of bishops derived 'not from any authority domestical or proper to the state':

---

[74] Ibid., pp. 18, 19.   [75] Ibid., pp. 23, 50.
[76] Henry Jacob, *To the right high and mightie prince, Iames by the grace of God, King of great Britannie, France, and Irelande defender of the faith, &c. An humble supplication for toleration and libertie to enioy and observe the ordinances of Christ Iesus in th'administration of his churches in lieu of humane constitutions* ([Middelburg] 1609), pp. 7–8.

Wherein they greatly prejudice your Imperial Crown: so they offer no meane indigni-
tie and injurie to the temporal state, by intercepting and seizing upon the
Magistracy ... usurping upon the Supremacie of the Civil Magistrate, in whose
power only it resteth to enact and ordaine laws ecclesiastical.

Among Jacob's principal complaints were those ecclesiastical laws made at
Hampton Court which allowed bishops to 'assume to themselves the power
of enacting laws'.[77] Of course he referred here to the High Commission, the
very agent of the misfortunes of those ministers whom Jacob was eager to
defend.

In addition to an extensive political argument against rule by bishops,
Jacob offered a doctrinal case against subscription and conformity. Here he
sided with those conformists who argued that 'order' and 'peace' were
divinely ordained for the Church; yet, where his opponents employed these
categories to justify subscription and conformity, Jacob employed them to
condemn the policy: 'And forasmuch as the inferior Law ought to give place
unto the superior: the Law of *unitie* & peace in the Churches being of a
nobler discent and ranke, then that of outward Conformitie in humane Rites
and Ceremonies the Canon for the said Conformitie ... ought so farre to
yeeld to the said Law of *unitie*.'[78] Jacob rounded out the argument by
suggesting that 'toleration' should be extended as a matter of political
prudence; eliding the 'humane ordinances' of the English bishops with
those of the Church of Rome, Jacob argued that the doctrine of the reformed
community of churches should stand as the model for the Church of England.
He therefore urged James to grant his 'approbation and protection', making
it 'lawfull for us to worship and honour the Lord Jesus according to the
directions only left in his holy worde and after the manner observed in the
reformed Churches'.[79]

In a subsequent work Jacob developed the case for the doctrine of
the Church.[80] Clearly, he understood the English debate as being driven by
competing versions of just what constituted the 'true' church. The institution,
ceremonies, and government of the Church were, he argued, *iure
divino* – established by Christ and thus unalterable by human agents.
However, the controversy over subscription and deprivation revealed a deeper

---

[77] Ibid., pp. 9, 12–13. Following this line of argument, Jacob went so far as to criticise
Presbyterian discipline: '[R]uling Synods and united Presbyteries exercising
government and imposing lawes and Decrees upon Severall Churches, and the Pastors of
them, are not onely human inventions, but in regarde of the said government and authoritie of
imposing laws, altogether unlawfull, and usurping upon the supremacie of the civil
Magistrate, in whose power only it resteth to enact and ordaine laws ecclesiastical for and
over all the Churches within his dominions' (p. 13).

[78] Ibid., p. 34.   [79] Ibid., p. 35.

[80] Henry Jacob, *The divine beginning and institution of Christs true visible or ministeriall
church* (Leiden, 1610), sig. A^{3r-v}.

problem, for the bishops had taken it upon themselves to impose modes of governance on the Church, and thus aimed to alter its very nature: 'If Christ's true Ministeriall Church be not now and allways under the Gospel, a speciall divine institution, but is left at some time to the discretion of men, then there are many and divers Definitions, or else there is no definition at all of Christ's said true Visible and Ministeriall Church.' The bishops sought to transform the Church from a 'spiritual body politicke' into a 'civil body politicke', thereby capturing it for themselves, and shunting aside the divinely ordained form of government 'appointed' by Christ and the Apostles.[81] At the heart of the controversy was a dispute over which mode of governance was truly Apostolic, and which could claim legitimate jurisdiction over individuals:

Christ and His Apostles have by speciall institution appointed ... Visible and Ministeriall Churches in the New Testament; and those not Naturall or civill societies and bodyes politicke (such as the Adversaries in this cause doe conceive them to be) but proper spirituall and supernaturall societies having proper spiritual and super-naturall power over mens soules.[82]

Here we find Jacob offering the contrast between a church defined as a political association, and one defined, *iure divino*, as a spiritual association. Also to be noted in this passage is the suggestion that a church so defined was Apostolic, and this served to counter the aspect of the conformist argument that sought to develop an Apostolic pedigree for bishops.

In response to arguments that questioned whether the Apostolic pedigree supported diocesan jurisdiction, defenders of episcopacy sought to bolster the historical case. Some conformist statements about the role of the bishops in the governance of the Church attempted to diffuse the question as to whether they represented a sovereignty to rival that of the Crown in parliament. As was also the case in the debates on ceremonies (to be discussed in the next chapter), the charge of 'novelty' was answered with that of antiquity; to combat the notion that bishops represented an upstart power, one might resort to an interpretation of the history of the church that traced the episcopal 'function'. Francis Holyoake therefore pointed out that there had always been an hierarchy of ecclesiastical officers, grouped under a central figure:

---

[81] Ibid., sig. B^{2v}. Jacob employed an Aristotelian argument to make the case for a broadly based form of ecclesiastical governance: 'Democratie, Aristocracie and Monarchy do differ formally and essentially one from the other. Now the Christian churches true and right government (in this regarde that the whole company of the people do give their free consent therein) is a certaine Democratie. The Diocesan, Provincial and Catholicke governments are monarchical, or at best they are Aristocratical. Therefore the Churches true and right government doth differ formally and essentially from the government Diocesan, Provincial and Catholicke' (sig. A^{3r-v}).

[82] Ibid., sig. B^{8r}.

In the Apostles times it is plaine there were prophets, and Apostles, Pastors, Teachers, Priests or Elders, Deacons, Bishops, Evangelists and divers others. In the ages succeeding the Apostles, the general consent of All Antiquitie and the Churches of God easterne and Western in all ages hitherto have kept a difference in degrees in the Church; some besides labouring in the Word of God to rule and governe, and others that also labour in the worde and are subject to be governed by others.[83]

God Himself enjoined this right and pattern of governance for the better ordering of His Church. Citing Zanchi, Holyoake observed that 'he proveth that ecclesiastical Tradition and constitutions, are not merely human, but divine'.[84] Reformists would have endorsed half of this proposition, and would have added the point that those aspects of 'human ordinance' that were present in the Church only served to transgress the divine law of God. For Holyoake, however, to impugn the Church as it stood 'is to clip God's coine [and is] treason against God himself', as well as against the authority of the Church to determine the 'general rule' of rites.[85] Similarly, Hooker had noted that 'The Ministry of things divine is a *function* which as God did Himself institute, so neither may men undertake the same but by authority and power given them in a lawful manner.'[86] For the conformists we have been surveying, the Act of Supremacy was the channel via which divine authority had been conveyed to the bishops.

An account of the divine authority left to the Church was a principal theme in a work written by George Carleton to counter Catholic attacks on the Crown's supremacy over the English Church, or rather the church *in* England. Indeed, we must not forget that there was a concurrent debate being carried on with Catholic controversialists, which led conformists to refine their positions in ways designed to answer the Catholics, but which also led reformists to question their opponents' commitment to the reformed tradition. Yet this tradition was defined most often in terms of doctrine rather than governance. It was the conformists' emphasis on discipline over doctrine that fuelled the conflict with their co-religionists; indeed, to emphasise the elements of the Church that defined it as a political association was also to privilege elements in a definition of the Church that seemed to run counter to reformed ecclesiology. Conformists therefore sought to argue that, while scripture did contain a pattern concerning doctrine, it also established the need for order and unity in the faith, so that this doctrine might be clearly understood and followed. It was this last point that Carleton was keen to address:

[83] Francis Holyoake, *A sermon of obedience especially vnto authoritie ecclesiasticall* (Oxford, 1610), p. 5.
[84] Ibid., p. 22. Girolamo Zanchi (1516–90) was a Calvinist theologian.   [85] Ibid., p. 22.
[86] Richard Hooker, *Of the lawes of ecclesiastical politie eight bookes by Richard Hooker* (London: Printed by Will Stansby [for Henrie Fetherstone], 1618), Bk. V, ch. lxxvii, §I.

Concerning the Jurisdiction which Christ left to His Church, let all the Scriptures be searched and there will nothing be found of externall Jurisdiction consisting in power co-active: but all that Christ left was partly, yea principally, inward and spiritual power, partly external for establishing doctrines of faith and good order in the Church, by councels, determinations, judicature, spiritual censures, excommunication: deposing and despatching of the disobedient.[87]

While the office of bishops may not have been clearly set forth in scripture, both testaments did contain general statements about the need for 'order' in the church; how this order was to be achieved was left to the national churches. Yet Carleton was not about to leave the door open whereby his own office might be undermined, hence 'the Ancient Fathers deliver it as a truth never questioned, nor doubted, that in the Government of the Church, the Bishops are the undoubted successors of the Apostles'.[88] Nothing too controversial there, but Carleton went a step further, and opened up an issue that would define religious controversy after 1610:

For the preservation of the True doctrine of the Church, the bishops are the great watchmen. Herein they are authorised by God. If Princes withstand them in these things, they have warrant not to obey Princes, because with these things Christ hath put them in trust.[89]

This introduced a new sentiment that could not be reconciled with earlier positions, notably Bilson's. Many English Protestants on both sides of the debate on episcopacy had argued that God established the King as the defender of the Church. The central problem in the debate we have been examining had less to do with the relation between king and bishops than with the authority exercised by the bishops over the inferior clergy and its relation to the divine and common law. Those who argued against episcopacy often expressed reservations about the derogation of the King's sovereignty, while many conformists saw bishops primarily as 'inferior' magistrates. Yet Carleton went further and argued that there was an ecclesiastical sovereignty, bestowed by God, in which the King did not partake and which in some cases was not answerable to his law. This reversed a number of statements by English conformists which explained, as had Bilson, that the 'prince' was in all cases superior to the 'priest'.

FUNCTION VERSUS JURISDICTION: THE DOWNAME CONTROVERSY

Among the questions raised in the Jacobean controversies over bishops, two were of particular concern to contemporaries. The first dealt with the historical

---

[87] George Carleton, *Iurisdiction regall, episcopall, papall* (London, 1610), p. 39; Patterson, *King James VI and I*, pp. 264, 265–6, 270–1, 280–1.
[88] Carleton, *Iurisdiction*, p. 43.   [89] Ibid., p. 44.

pedigree of the office itself: were there bishops in the ancient church, and if so, what role did they play in terms of the administration of doctrine and discipline? Related to this question was that of the jurisdiction of bishops in the Church of England: did they have power over other members of the clergy, and did this power extend to the deprivation of non-conforming ministers? Perhaps the most controversial element of this question concerned the origin of episcopal authority: did it issue from the law, and hence the sovereignty of the Crown, or was it Apostolic in origin, prescribed and set forth in the scripture and the example of the ancient church? Elements of these questions were treated in connection with an emerging debate over the proper relationship between the ecclesiastical jurisdiction of the bishops and that of the Crown. The principal tension in this debate concerned rival historical accounts of episcopal authority, and hence the definition of the office itself. One perspective on these questions was offered by George Downame, Bishop of Derry, in a pair of sermons preached during 1608. The first concerned the state of the ministry in general, and seems to have attracted little attention, which is surprising in light of the argument that Downame put forth. The second, to be examined a little further along, provoked a debate that lasted until the final year of the reign.

Downame's first sermon treated the ministry, and argued that its principal function was to safeguard the Church. At one level, the bishops were called by God to ordain and censure ministers, while the ministers themselves,

are set over the Church, [and] are called ... stewards of God set over His household. And whereas the authoritie of a steward is signified by the keyes committed unto him: our Saviour Christ therefore to his stewards hath committed keyes, *The keis to the Kingdom of Heaven*, that both by preaching the Gospel, and by Ecclesiastical Discipline, they might open to some the gates of heaven, and shut them to others.[90]

This statement clearly defied the Calvinist doctrine of absolute predestination, which posited a lesser role for the ministry in the salvation of the elect, namely the preaching of the Word and the right administration of the sacraments. Moreover, Downame observed that the ability to 'bind and loose the soules of men' signified that the 'authority' of the ministry was more 'glorious' than that of the Crown, whose power was limited to the 'earthly kingdome'.[91] While this was not the same as saying that the ministry had a

---

[90] George Downame, *Two sermons, the one commending the ministerie in generall: the other defending the office of bishops in particular* (London, 1608), pp. 7, 30.

[91] Ibid., p. 39. A very similar argument was made by Catholic controversialists in the course of works that exhorted marooned English Catholics to have courage in the face of state persecution. The King, they argued, could not exact the ultimate punishment. See Thomas Hide, *A consolatorie epistle to the afflicted catholickes, set foorth by Thomas Hide Priest* (Louvain, 1579); Robert Southwell, *An epistle of comfort, to the reverend priestes & to the honorable, worshipful, & other of the laye sort restrayned in durance for the Catholicke fayth* ([London, 1587?]).

civil power that was superior to that of the Crown, it did imply an alternate view of the conformist doctrine of grace, and a role for the ministry that was not often described in the literature of the period. Indeed, Downame made several statements concerning the function of the ministry in the attainment of grace: 'For in that the true Christian hath attained to grace, he hath obtained it by the helpe of the Ministrie, whereby he was reconciled unto God, enlightened with the truth, begotten unto God, etc.'[92] Instead of the Calvinist doctrine of absolute predestination and unfailing grace, Downame's position looked back to the Augustinian dictum of subsequent grace, whereby the spirit of God worked in the individual after conversion, as well as a notion of regeneration conveyed via baptism.

From this point, Downame left matters of theology and turned to consider the status of the ministry in relation to temporal affairs.[93] While he made an effort to profess his agreement with the King's sovereignty 'over all persons, as Ecclesiastical as Civil', his sermons contained compelling reasons to believe that he envisioned a special episcopal jurisdiction. Indeed, he stated that since the ministry possessed the power of salvation, 'the Ministrie in dignity doth excell the Magistracie'. Moreover, given that the ministry bore 'the image of God's authoritie before men in forgiving or retaining sines, you are to honour and obey them as God, whose viceregents they be'.[94] At this point we recognise Downame's revision of the *iure divino* claim: where previous writers described 'discipline' as a function defined by divine law, Downame argued that the jurisdiction of bishops over all the clergy was also so defined. The problem with this statement would have been clear to contemporaries: if the bishops were to be obeyed before others because they alone acted on God's behalf, then the Crown's jurisdiction over the Church must be inferior, since its authority was confined to the temporal realm. In case any doubt remained as to the direction of his argument, Downame supplied an historical example: 'Yea the Emperor Justinian acknowledging, that the Ministrie, & the Magistracie, were two principall gifts of God, giveth the precedence to the Ministrie. And the like preeminence do our lawes give to those of the spirituality before them of the temporality.'[95] The use of a non-English example only partly diffused the statement,

---

[92] Downame, *Two sermons*, p. 43.
[93] Downame's sermon also included an extensive treatment of tithes, which he argued were due to the ministry *iure divino*; yet, like his statements on the doctrine of grace, the discussion of tithes received no response, despite the existence of a healthy contemporary debate on that subject. Here, it seemed, was a topic that invited speculation on the relationship of the Church to the law, the civil powers of bishops, as well as the historical pedigree of the Church's self-jurisdiction.
[94] Downame, *Two sermons*, pp. 54, 58.   [95] Ibid., pp. 66–7.

which implied that those who exercised spiritual jurisdiction were independent of the common law and, presumably, the Act of Supremacy.

For all of Downame's potentially controversial talk of grace, it was his account of the superiority of bishops that provoked the most vigorous response. The second of his two sermons, defending the 'honourable function of bishops', was published with its own title-page in 1608, and offered an historical argument for both the pedigree and the ecclesiological necessity of the episcopal office. In the preface, Downame expressed frustration at those who 'protest to all the world, unless their assertions bee graunted, they see not how our separation from the Church of Rome can be justified'. Among these critical texts he counted Henry Jacob's *Christian and modest offer*, which was examined earlier in this chapter, and to which Downame offered a prolonged response.[96] There were two principal contexts for Downame's sermon. The first was the continuing debate over clerical subscription. Downame likened non-conformity to a desire 'To place the height of religion in disconformity, turning zeal into faction, godly conferences into bitter invectives against Bishops, & odious censures of such as they call formalists'. Linked to this debate was that over the rival forms of church governance – episcopal versus Presbyterian – in the recently joined kingdoms. According to Downame, the ancient precedent revealed that bishops were 'not parishional, but diocesan'; rather than parity among ministers, 'the Bishops ... of the primitive Church, were superior, as well as ours, in degree to other Ministers'.[97]

This superiority was demonstrated with reference to the history of the church, and indeed could only be defended in that context. For the office of bishops had to be shown to have been plainly evident in the practice of the ancient church, having been first established by the Apostles themselves: 'Neither can anything be more evidently proved out of the monuments of Antiquitie then this, that bishoppes continued their regency for term of life ... and so throughout the succession of Bishoppes from the Apostles to the Council of Nice, and so downward'. On the question of Presbyterian discipline, Downame argued that the Apostolic pedigree of the bishops justified their superiority over all other clergy:

But the Bishops doth govern also *in soro externo*, not one particular flocke, but the whole diocese; and not the people onely, but the Presbyters also, having authoritie both to direct, and also to correct them. And that authoritie is derived unto them from the Apostles, as to their successors in the government of the Church. For which cause, as we will hear anon, Bishops were called Apostles.

---

[96] George Downame, *A sermon defending the honourable function of bishops* (London, 1608), sig. A3v. This was issued with a separate title-page and pagination.
[97] Ibid., sig. 2r, pp. 5, 10, 28–9.

Citing St Jerome, Downame continued by observing that 'in the true Church, Bishops do hold the place of the Apostles'.[98] In fact, there was more to the argument than the ancient pedigree of the bishops, for the broader context which Downame sought to evoke concerned the identity of the 'true' church left on earth by Christ and handed to the Apostles; it also concerned the definition of its mode of governance. Thus, Downame dismissed Presbyterian discipline as a 'new-found opinion', as a mode of governance that was of human origin, rather than an example of the uninterrupted succession of the church since the times of the Apostles.

The argument for the antiquity of episcopacy required Downame to distinguish between the 'function' and 'jurisdiction' of bishops, for the critics of diocesan episcopacy argued that, while officers *resembling* bishops might be found in the ancient church, they nevertheless exerted no authority over other clergy. Moreover, Downame had to account for the fact that nowhere in the ancient record did the word 'bishop' appear. In response he described the office in terms of jurisdiction, to which the name 'bishop' was added in later times:

the Episcopall power, which consisteth specially in the right of ordination, and in the sway of ecclesiastical jurisdiction committed to one, the Apostles each of them retained in their owne hands ... All which while, bishops were not so needfull; the Apostles providing for the necessity of those Churches, either by their presence, or by their letters or messengers.

This description allowed Downame to posit the English episcopate as the continuation of the ecclesiastical jurisdiction of the Apostles, who 'left substitutes, and at their death appointed successors, to whom they committed the government of the Churches'.[99] This notion of a direct connection to the Apostles, and hence to Christ, informed the argument of the sermon. By *iure divino*, therefore, Downame did not mean that bishops could exercise 'absolute power', or even that episcopal government was the only form of government permissible in the churches of the West. Rather, he meant that it was the best form of ecclesiastical government simply because it could be traced to Christ; in other words, it was of 'first institution', meaning that it had been established by Christ and could not be altered or removed. Bishops were 'of God's ordinance, and as it were from the Lord's hands'.[100]

The first response to Downame came in the form of *Informations: or a protestation* – a series of anti-episcopal arguments by John Rainolds.[101] In fact, Rainolds had died the year before Downame's sermon was preached,

---

[98] Ibid., pp. 35–6, 41, 45.   [99] Ibid., pp. 69–70.   [100] Ibid., p. 93.
[101] The original tract was [John Rainolds], *The summe of the conference betwene Iohn Rainoldes and Iohn Hart* (London, 1584). The work was re-issued in 1588, 1598, and 1609. The tract was ostensibly the result of a debate between Rainolds and Hart (d. 1586) held in Oxford in 1580.

and it is likely that the printer sought to cash in on the weight of Rainold's name, by binding a number of new items together with the text of a manu-script of Rainolds' notes on Richard Bancroft's sermon of February 1588.[102] The author of the additional material is unknown, but following Rainolds he argued that Church polity had to be derived from scripture and confirmed by the authorities of the early church. Where he differed from Downame was on how ecclesiastical government should be defined, especially as it concerned the nature of episcopal jurisdiction over what the author portrayed as a sovereign church – the Scottish Kirk. In 1606, a group of Presbyterians submitted a 'Protestation' to the Scottish parliament, arguing that Christ's word was the sole authority in the determination of matters of rites and governance.[103] Following a line that would be more fully developed by Henry Jacob, the author argued that the mode of governance to be observed in the Church was of divine warrant, and that it was the business of parliament to 'mayntayne and advance by your authoritie that Church which the Lord hath fashioned … but not that yee should presume to fashion, and shape a new portrature of a Kirke, and a new forme of divine service, which God in his worde hath not before allowed'.[104] Note that both Downame and his oppo-nent suggested that the type of Church government that they wished to defend possessed a divine sanction, and that they condemned holders of the opposite position as adherents to 'novel' forms of governance. Hence where Downame described Presbyterian government as a human invention, his opponent styled episcopal government as *iure humano*, exhorting the Scottish parliament to reject it: 'if ye should (as God forbid) authorise the authority of Bishops and their preheminence above their bretheren, ye should bring into the Kirke of God the Ordinance of Man'.[105] As we shall see in the final chapter, arguments over ecclesiastical governance involved more than one of the three kingdoms.

Clearly, the disagreement concerned which aspects of discipline were of human origin and which were not, and hence at the foundation of the question was the historical and doctrinal identity of the Church itself. This identity was described via a particular reading of both the scriptures and the

---

[102] J. P. Sommerville criticised William Lamont's 'ludicrous' suggestion that the first response to Downame came from John Rainolds. However, Sommerville was unaware of the tract in question – *Informations*, which consisted of five items, including copies of letters from Rainolds to Francis Knollis – and assumed Lamont to be referring to Sherwood's *An answere to a sermon*, to be discussed below. Sommerville, 'The royal supremacy and episcopacy "jure divino"', p. 555. See also Peter Milward, *Religious controversies of the Jacobean age: a survey of printed sources* (London, 1978), pp. 17–18.

[103] See David George Mullan, *Episcopacy in Scotland: the history of an idea, 1560–1638* (Edinburgh, 1986), pp. 105, 229 n. 120.

[104] *Informations, or a protestation, and a treatise from Scotland* ([W. Jones' secret press], 1608), sig. A^{2r}–A^{3v}.

[105] Ibid., p. 4.

historical record of Christianity. The problem was that there was only one textual tradition on which to draw, and so the argument took on the character of exegesis ranged against exegesis. Each writer had to interpret the narrative in a way that favoured his position. Of course, Downame's opponent knew this, and went further to suggest that the ancient pedigree of the Kirk had been ratified by parliament:

And we are able, by the grace of God, and will offer ourselves to prove, that this Bishopprick to be erected, is against the Word of God, the Ancient Fathers, and Canons of the Kirke, the modern most learned and godly divines, the Doctrine and Constitution of the Kirke of Scotland since the first reformation of religion, within the same Countrie, the lawes of the realme ratifying the government of the Kirk by the general and Provincial assemblies, Presbyteries and Sessions.[106]

The argument was a clever one, and it satisfied the burden of ancient proof by replicating all of the aspects of the English conformist case, and then applying these elements to another form of church polity. Indeed, the author's task was less to deny the historical legitimacy of the Church of England than to advance that of the Kirk; yet the case was nevertheless arranged around the topics brought to the surface in the broader controversy. Hence, he countered the notion of an ancient episcopacy with that of an ancient presbytery, for at stake was 'the true Discipline and Gubernation of the house of God'. For our anonymous author, the entire question rested on the determination of what mode of governance was of 'first institution'. Once this was established, it was a short step to arguing that any departure from this institution represented a 'corruption' of the divinely ordained doctrine of the Church.

Indeed, the anonymous writer suggested that at the heart of the conformist position was the belief that the ancient church was somehow imperfect, and in need of man's help. '[T]his supreme Governor, *Isai 9:6*, Christ Jesus; hath not left his Kirke which is His body, maimed or imperfect, destitute of right government, Lawes and Office, needful for the same ... let no man thinke, that Christ hath left his Kirke to be ruled at the lust and arbitrement of men.'[107] Like Downame, our author sought to distinguish between the function and jurisdiction of bishops, and cited scriptural references in support of the case. It has been mentioned that critics of episcopacy argued that,

---

[106] Ibid., p. 11.
[107] Ibid., pp. 17, 18–19. This position borrowed heavily from an earlier tract by Marprelate: 'That the Lord, in His Word, hath left the Church perfect in all her members, which He should not have done, if He had not ordained all the officers, namely, the members thereof; and so He should have the building of His Church unperfect.' See *Theses Martinianae* ([Wolston, Warks., 22 July 1589]), p. 307.

while one might find reference to officers resembling bishops, in no case did they exercise a superior jurisdiction. It was thus that 'Rainolds' cited the Acts of the Apostles (5: 1–2; 20: 17) in support of the contention that: 'The name of Bishop being common to Pastors, Teachers, and Rulers, it is not to be appropriate to any one with title power, or prerogative above the rest.' Therefore, 'the Regiment of the Kirke, cannot be claimed by Papal Bishops or Prelates by scripture, or by Christ his Institution'.[108] In other words, the doctrine of the church established by scripture and the Apostles was immemorial and incorruptible – and Presbyterian.

The final stage of the argument put forth by Downame's opponent concerned the civil power of bishops. For, while having proved that there was no ancient warrant to justify their jurisdiction in the Church, he still had to contend with the fact that they remained in positions of power in their dioceses, at Court, and on the High Commission. It was thus that he closed the argument by pointing out that through these channels the bishops violated the sovereignty of the Crown in parliament, and sought to impose their own government independent of this authority: 'Whosoever doth participate with the Anti-Christ in usurping a Civil Power, and practising the same in the Kirke directly against the Word, and Institution of Christ, they are of that Anti-Christ, and their usurpation anti-Christian.' Indeed, not only did the bishops violate the divine provisions of church government, but also the advice of the Council of Chalcedon, which defended the proposition 'to keepe rightly the distinction that is betwixt Civil and Ecclesiastical Office and function'.[109] It is important here to note that our author's opposition to the civil power of bishops was not expressed in terms of a violation of the law, or with reference to any sort of constitutional precept. Rather, the argument was that episcopacy constituted an imposition on the divine jurisdiction of Christ, as expressed in the scriptures, and embodied in the directions concerning the governance of the Kirk. In circumventing these precepts, the bishops were styled as 'anti-Christ': that is, a self-proclaimed alternate government of the Church that usurped the divine sovereignty of Christ.

A further answer to Downame's sermon appeared in 1609; its author may have been Richard Sherwood, rector at Thurlaston, and deprived of that living in April 1605.[110] This anonymous contribution also dismissed the proposition that episcopacy was *iure divino* as '[a] doctrine utterly false, verie hurtful and obnoxious, necessarie indeed, to be confuted, at no hand to be believed: doctrine repugnant to the truth, the word of the truth, scripture

---

[108] *Informations*, pp. 51, 52–3.   [109] Ibid., pp. 55, 62.
[110] Babbage, *Puritanism and Richard Bancroft*, pp. 179–82; Fincham, *Prelate as pastor*, p. 324.

of the truth, contrarie to the judgement and practyce of the prime Churches next after Christ and his Apostles, and all Reformed Churches'.[111] Instead, the tract portrayed episcopacy as a 'politicke device', employed for the convenience of human governors rather than for the good of the Church. Here again the question of scriptural warrant was raised. In order for an office so obviously lacking support from scripture to persist, it must have involved the deliberate subversion of the textual tradition of the 'true' church:

> consider who they are that arrogate the title of the Church of England; the uncertainty of the doctrine they holde, altering and varying as it is expounded and interpreted at their pleasure, especially that sitt in the see of Canterburie, and the impugning of divers parts of the Truth by preaching and printing, the cheefe prelates winking, if not approving, and in a sort providing [that] it may be done impure.[112]

To attack the 'doctrine' of the Church of England was also to question its claim to the status of a 'true' church; rather than a doctrinally pure spiritual association taking part in the heritage of Christ, the Church was here depicted as a political association, shaped by the actions of its human governors. Once again we find the attack on the pretended antiquity of the episcopal office presented in tandem with an argument concerning the civil jurisdiction. Those with such impure motives toward God's church could not be expected to be loyal subjects, and so it was partly with the aim of so styling the bishops, and partly with the hope of acquitting the non-conformists of the same charge, that the anonymous writer pointed out that the bishops had 'gotten an inche of his Magestie'. One might easily overlook statements like this as special pleading on the part of the 'deprived brethren', among whom we may possibly number our anonymous writer. However, the argument allowed for speculation on the relationship between the authority of the Crown in parliament and that of the upstart bishops, 'not to content themselves to hold their sovereignties of the civil magistrate, as their predecessors before them have done, but must needs enjoy it now by a new found pattent, even *iure divino*'.[113] This contrasted the arguments of Downame with those of his Elizabethan predecessors. Indeed, the argument continued, the genuine political threat came not from the critics of diocesan episcopacy, whom the bishops had branded with 'false imputations of combination, faction, sedition, puritanisme and odious termes of schismatiques', but rather from the bishops themselves.

---

[111] [Attrib. to Richard Sherwood], *An answere to a sermon preached the 17 of April anno D. 1608, by George Downame* ([Amsterdam: Printed by Jodocus Hondius and Giles Thorp], 1609), pp. 3–4.
[112] Ibid., p. 21.   [113] Ibid., p. 36.

Downame directed a massive reply to this and another anonymous pamphlet.[114] In four separate books totalling over 400 pages, his *Defence* was far out of proportion to the attacks on his earlier sermon. This fact reminds us of the variety that defines the literature of religious controversy, as well as the importance – in the minds of some conformists – of mounting effective answers to their critics. Downame opened his book by invoking Thucydides, whom he felt had anticipated the plight of the Jacobean conformist, 'assayled on both sides: The Romanists on the one side blaming us for departing too farre from the Church of Rome; our innovators accusing us on the other side, for coming too neare to the same'.[115] The polemical trope of the Church of England as caught between Rome and Geneva has been usefully explored by Anthony Milton, although not in the context of the controversies surveyed in this study.[116] However, conformists rarely sought to engage with both sides in a single treatise, for to do so would have required works of vast size and range of reference. Instead of a rival confession, Downame addressed a rival Protestant church, the Kirk, and hence revisited the question of antiquity. No church on earth, he argued, 'doth come so neere the pattern of the prime and Apostolical Churches' as the Church of England, and for this he credited James VI and I for establishing its 'Ancient and Apostolical government'. In his earlier sermon, Downame had devoted little attention to the Crown's ecclesiastical supremacy; perhaps sensitive to the charges of his opponents, he made that provision of English conformity abundantly clear in the *Defence*. In the process, he evoked the wording of the proclamation of October 1603, to the effect that the Church was 'agreeable' to the Word of God, and 'neere to the condition' of the primitive church. His purpose, therefore, was to restate the antiquity of the Church of England via a restatement of the antiquity of the episcopal office. This marked a direct attack upon all but governance by diocesan bishops, for he sought to demonstrate that 'the Presbyterian discipline is a meere human

---

[114] George Downame, *A defence of the sermon preached at the consecration of the L. Bishop of Bath and Welles, against a confutation thereof by a namelesse author* (London, 1611). Peter Milward (*Religious controversies of the Jacobean age*, p. 18) has suggested that Downame's response was confined to the *Answere to a sermon*. While Downame did refer to the 'Answerer' – it was common for writers to label their anonymous opponents according to the first principal word of the title – he also made reference to a 'Refuter'. Even where Downame did not distinguish between the two in the text, he nevertheless inserted marginal references to the pagination of the work under discussion; since the *Answere* was only fifty-eight pages in length, Downame was clearly referring in Bk. IV, ch. 1, p. 3 to a second work, with its note to '*Ad pag.* 108'.

[115] Downame, *Defence of the sermon*, sig. A³ʳ.

[116] See Anthony Milton, 'The Church of England, Rome and the true church: the demise of a Jacobean consensus', in *The early Stuart Church, 1603–1642*, ed. Kenneth Fincham (Stanford, 1993), pp. 187–210. See also Peter White, 'The *via media* in the early Stuart Church', pp. 211–30 in the same volume.

invention, and new divise, having no ground either in the Scriptures, or other monuments of antiquitie: but also that the Episcopal function is of Apostolical and divine institution'. When it came to the government of the church established by the 'first institution', the evidence of antiquity proved that the 'governors of the primitive Church ... were Diocesan bishops'.[117]

In order to show that bishops were indeed present in the ancient church, Downame had to engage with two types of evidence: that set forth by the scriptures, and that subsequently incorporated into the practice of the ancient church. The burden of the argument was to disarm writers who criticised those aspects of doctrine and discipline as 'politick' devices of human invention. Hence Downame took care to posit the antiquity of episcopal jurisdiction, which he designated as 'custom': 'It is evident that the B.B. were diocesan before they were actually metropolitans; and upon the consociation of provinces, were Patriarches ordayned, and yet long before the council of Nice the Patriarches were in use, and the customs of subjecting diverse provinces to them, are called ... ancient customs.' Hence, he presented a pedigree not only for the organisational structure of the Church – diocesan versus provincial – but also for the particular powers of the individual sees over the diverse congregations within them. This was precisely the question that had arisen in the debates over subscription, in which conformists defended the particular 'custom' of the Church of England to establish its own doctrine and enforce its own discipline. Yet Downame made no great effort to reconcile 'custom' with matters of divine law, for, as we have seen, it was a hallmark of the conformist case to sever the link between the two in order to defend the legitimacy of custom and the liberty of the Church to establish its own rites and liturgy. Downame's treatment of the problem involved positing two levels of 'divine ordinance', the one originating from Christ, the second from the Apostles:

> Though in respect of the first institution, there is a small difference betweene an Apostolical and Divine ordinance, because what was ordained by the Apostles proceeded from God (in which sense and no other, I doe hold the Episcopal function to be a divine Ordinance, I meane in respect of the first institution), yet in respect of perpetuitie, difference by some is made betweene those things which be *Divini*, and those which be *Apostolici jurii*: the former, in their understanding being generally, perpetually and immutably necessary, the latter not so.[118]

Critics of diocesan episcopacy would not have accepted this likening of Apostolic and divine 'ordinance', for it elevated matters of human tradition to the status of God's revealed will. What was worse, these traditions often represented a corruption of divine law, itself complete and sufficient for

---

[117] Downame, *Defence of the sermon*, sig. A^{5r}, Bk. IV, ch. 1, p. 2.
[118] Ibid., Bk. IV, ch. 6, p. 139.

determining the fitness of points of governance. This was one of many ways in which the conformist case was shaped in the course of debate. Downame's attempt to posit a divine ordinance for the mode of governance instituted by the Apostles was shaped by the need to rebut the charge that episcopacy was a human invention, part of the history of the church after the Apostles, and therefore not supported by their example.

At this point we have considered two steps of Downame's argument, each of which depended upon a particular use of the past as precedent, the notion of 'first institution', whereby the antiquity of episcopal government was traced to the Apostles, and the elision of divine and Apostolic ordinance. The final stage of the argument concerned a reinterpretation of the Protestant canon to confirm that 'Apostolic' bishops could be found within the reformed tradition. Hence, Downame argued, 'the form of government by bishops is best, as having not only the warrant of scripture for the first institution, but also the perpetual practice of the Church from the Apostles times to our own age'. It remained to show that the episcopal function was defended by the 'best reformed divines', among whom Downame numbered Luther and Melanchthon: 'those Godly and learned men allowed the Episcopal function, and simply desired the continuance thereof, if with it they might have enjoyed the Gospel'.[119] Although Downame attempted to portray Melanchthon and Luther as reformers who supported a revival of Apostolic episcopacy, the argument quickly diverted to the topic of Roman corruption.[120] The title of bishops, he argued, carried a damaging connotation because the Roman church had corrupted the office; Downame therefore maintained that the reformers could be credited with *restoring* episcopacy to sound usage:

Now that the Protestants which subscribed to the Augustaine confession did simply desire the continuation of the Episcopal government; I prove, because so soon as they could, they procured the restitution thereof, though under other names, because the names of B. B. [bishops] and Archbishops, by reason of the corruptions of the Popish prelates, were odious.[121]

While this may have explained how some reformers retained the episcopal *function* – a point with which reformed critics would have agreed, citing Presbyters as embodying that function – it left out the principal issue: episcopal jurisdiction. Downame's *Defence* avoided any sustained

---

[119] Ibid., Bk. IV, ch. 7, p. 150.

[120] The text of the Huntington copy of the *Defence* features corrections of passages cited by Downame. For example, the following sentence: 'I would to God it lay to [in] me, saith *Melancthon*, to restore the government of Bishops.' In this example, 'to' is crossed out and replaced with 'in', an emendation that alters the way in which the passage conveys Melanchthon's intention.

[121] Downame, *Defence of the sermon*, Bk. IV, ch. 7, p. 165.

treatment of the power of bishops over other clergy, and the relation of this power to the King's ecclesiastical sovereignty and the English common law – the exact tensions raised by critics of the governance of the Church of England.

A pointed attack on Downame's position appeared in Henry Jacob's *A declaration and plainer opening*. The tract was written first to acquit Jacob of the charge of being a Separatist, and second to refine and explain the argument that 'Christ is the only author, institutor, and framer of his Visible and Ministeriall Church.'[122] It was in this vein that Jacob addressed the question of Apostolic succession, and how this determined the organisation of the church as an institution:

> Namelie, if Christ and his Apostles in their institution and practise left no Diocesan or Provinciall Church, but such as were each of the one ordinarie Congregation onely, then now still and for ever all true Ministeriall Churches are each of them but one ordinarie Congregation only. This doubtless can not be denied. For it is unlawfull to holde any forme of a Church now which was not then, or hath no pattern for it under the Apostles.[123]

It will be noted that Jacob did not espouse a rigorous connection to the Word, meaning the exact words of Christ; for in emphasising the importance of the 'institution and practice' of the Apostles he implied that such ordinances were on a par with those of Christ. This endorsement of Apostolic practice was aimed squarely at George Downame's *Defence*, references to which saturated Jacob's tract. Indeed, Jacob met Downame on his own scholarly ground – the historical defence of Apostolic succession – and argued that such a defence was untenable when weighed against the doctrine of the church established by the first institution, that is, by Christ and the Apostles. Here again, Jacob condemned the English Church as a political association: 'And so D. *Downame's* dissolute ground of a Church, viz. That it may follow the order of the *civill State* is neerely also quite overthrowne.'[124]

Hierarchy and jurisdiction were the problems around which an explicit answer to Downame's *Defence* was organised. For those who attacked diocesan episcopacy, arguments from antiquity held less authority than the divine law of scripture and the prerogatives of the Crown. Hence an anonymous writer – perhaps the author of the *Answere* of 1609 – argued that Downame 'hath no one place of scripture, under the shadow whereof, he can

---

[122] Henry Jacob, *A declaration and plainer opening of certain pointes, with a sound confirmation of some other, contained in a treatise entitled, The divine beginning and institution of Christes true visible and ministeriall church* ([Middelburg: Printed by Richard Schilders], 1612), sig. A^{2r-3v}.
[123] Ibid., p. 11. [124] Ibid., p. 29.

find any shelter, to shroud his episcopal function, as a divine ordinance'.[125]
This argument seemed all the more effective when we reflect on both the
verse glossed by Downame (Rev. 1: 20 'The seven stars, are the Angels of the
Seven Churches') and his scant use of scripture in either the 1608 sermon or
the later *Defence*. Indeed, it was tenuous to style the bishops as the 'stars' of
the Church, especially when alternate verses (for example 1 Timothy 3: 1–7;
Titus 1: 6–9) were available. Hence, the crucial parts of the argument concerned the relation between matters of doctrine and matters of discipline:

> It is to be noted (saith he) that Our Church Acknowledgeth nothing as a matter of faith,
> which is not contained in God's word, or grounded thereon. And I will note it with him
> that he noteth well for us and against himself; for if the government of the Church by
> such Bishops as he speaketh of, be a matter of faith, why putteth he a difference between
> matters of discipline and the Articles of faith?[126]

The 'difference' noted by the anonymous writer consisted in the gap between
the purity of doctrine – expressed here as the 'Articles' of faith – and the
manner in which that doctrine was administered throughout the Church.
Earlier on, the writer observed that the testimony of the Fathers and the
judgements of the councils could be very easily manipulated. The ultimate
rule of faith was founded on scripture alone, for the scripture was the vessel
of divine doctrine and hence superior to the opinions of men.

Among the most interesting passages of the *Replye* were those which
concerned the problem that Downame had failed to address – the temporal
power that bishops seemed to exercise in the course of what they maintained
were purely spiritual duties. Downame had argued that bishops should be
called 'Lords' owing to their status as Christ's earthly substitutes. Yet, argued
the anonymous writer, to grant this title was 'to bring a confusion into the
Church, and overthrow that difference, which the lawes of God and men
have set between civil and ecclesiastical functions'. The distinction between
lords 'spiritual' and 'temporal' had to be maintained, as did the authority of
those who exercised these powers: 'For if the Bishops be not civil Lords, nor
their Lordship a civil honour, because they are distinguished from the nobles
of the laitie, by the name of Lords spiritual; then it followeth that their
Lordship and honour annexed thereunto, is merely spiritual.'[127] Central to
this case against episcopacy was the idea that it was a 'political' office that
had been directed toward spiritual ends. The solution proposed was that,
since the Lords temporal held political power in the civil sphere, the Lords

---

[125] [Attrib. to Richard Sherwood], *A replye answering a defence of the sermon, preached at the
consecration of the bishop of Bathe and Welles, by George Downame, Doctor of Divinitye.
In defence of an answere to the foresaid sermon imprinted ann 1609* ([Amsterdam: G.
Thorp], 1613 [i.e. 1614]), *4ᵛ.
[126] Ibid., p. 47.   [127] Ibid., pp. 283, 287.

spiritual – the bishops – should confine themselves to their pastoral office, referring matters of deprivation to the proper civil authorities.

The reformist assault on Downame, as well as Thomas Bilson's *Perpetual gouernement*, resumed in another work by Henry Jacob. Here again he displayed the originality of his mind: the Apostolic succession of bishops might be valid, were it not for 'circumstances now evident … against the best sort of Diocesan bishops'. Beginning in the third century after the death of Christ, Jacob noted a departure, and cited Beza in support of the contention that one of the central tenets of the Apostles' doctrine was that 'no Pastor should be obtruded on a flock against their wills'.[128] The reference to the 'will' of the flock is crucial to the argument that Jacob wished to make, that is, the churches during and since the Apostles' times allowed for matters of governance only in accordance with 'the practice of peoples free consent'. Applied to present circumstances, it could be argued that since the 'power of ordination and jurisdiction by right is seated in the whole congregation', the rule of bishops could only be legitimate with the free consent of the 'Body politicke spirituall'.[129] The true church was not a congeries of independent congregations, but rather a single spiritual body, an 'Ordinarie congregation' under the rule of a 'Universall ordinarie pastor'.

Indeed, Jacob employed the argument that ministers should be elected with the free 'consent' of the congregation in order to make the case for an aspect of the doctrine of the Church that emphasised the body of the congregation, acting together and bound together. The Church of England, with its programme of subscription and deprivation, stripped the congregation of the divinely ordained power of ruling itself, and placed the governance of the church 'within private walls by a few men'. For an Aristotelian like Jacob, rule by a few prevented the congregation from ruling itself, the very process of which defined it as a true church, under Christ:

Now, to come nearer. No proper and perfect Diocesan church, or larger, ever did or doth admit the peoples free consent in their ordinarie government. Universally and alwaies it is so: & indeed it can not be otherwise. For where each Ordinarie congregation is an intire and independent Body Politicke Spirituall, and is indeed with power in itselfe immediately under Christ.[130]

With the rise to power of the bishops, this state of affairs was compromised: the Church was sundered within itself, severed from its ancient foundations, and transformed from a spiritual to a civil body.

---

[128] Henry Jacob, *An attestation of many learned, godly, and famous divines … That the Church-gouernement ought to bee always with the peoples free consent* ([Middelburg: Printed by Richard Schilders], 1613), pp. 15–16, 22.
[129] Ibid., pp. 53, 73. [130] Ibid., p. 86.

Howbeit notwithstanding ... though those titles given to Bishops under Constantine and after ... are too glorious and stately for the Ministers of the Gospel, yet none of them implyeth such Lordship or sole authority Spirituall, as which the words Lord Bishop do imply ... Besides, the Apostolic bishops had not any addition of civil co-active power, as ours have.[131]

Jacob's case against the bishops, therefore, consisted of two claims: first, they exercised superiority over the Church that violated the sovereignty of the Crown in parliament, and second, they had departed from the primitive perfection of the ancient church, and had assumed the trappings of civil office.

Yet reformist responses to the temporal jurisdiction of bishops were most often couched in terms of an argument against that jurisdiction as it was exercised in the Church. While they were aware (as was Henry Jacob) of the problem of conflicting temporal and spiritual jurisdiction, they were primarily concerned with the status of the spiritual institution. Hence, in a tract published posthumously by William Ames, the Cambridge divine Paul Baynes argued that 'the common course and practice of our Prelates in their Courts, their urging of subscriptions, with humane superstitious ceremonies, are presumptuous insolencies against God and His Church'.[132] In other words, the bishops trespassed against the laws of God, and hence violated their charge as spiritual officers. Baynes was neither the first nor the last to condemn the worldliness of bishops, but he did so because it aided the broader argument about the High Commission's usurpation of the governance revealed in the Gospel:

What is more dissonant from the revealed will of Christ in the Gospel, even also from the state of the Primitive Church, then that the Church and Kingdom of Christ should be managed as the Kingdoms of the World; by a Lordly Authoritie, with externall pompe, commanding power, contentious courts of judgement, furnished with chancelors, officials, commissaries, advocates, protors, paristors, and all such like humane devices?[133]

This constituted another direct attack on the Church of England as a political institution, seriously corrupted and hence departed from the divinely ordained exemplar. Having no grounding in doctrine, human ordinances could only be enforced by human devices – by politics, rather than by the revealed will of Christ. Christ's kingdom, famously 'not of this world', had been invaded and brought down to the realm of men, from truth to

---

[131] Ibid., pp. 127, 129.
[132] Paul Baynes, *The diocesans tryall. Wherein all the sinnews of d. Downams Defence are brought unto three heads, and orderly dissolved* ([Amsterdam: G. Thorp], 1621), preface; Fincham, *Prelate as pastor*, pp. 21, 122, 218.
[133] Ibid., Pref.

corruption. The result was a 'mediate' power, that is, a power that inserted itself between Christ and His people:

For herein we are like to the people of Israel, who would not have God for their immediate King, but would have such Kings as other Nations: Even so the Papists, and we after them, refuse to have Christ an immediate King in the immediate government of the Church; but must have Lordly rulers with state in ecclesiastical affairs, such as the world hath in civil.[134]

The problem was clear: the governance of the Church should follow the pattern established in the New Testament. Instead, the bishops had assumed the power of civil officers, and had armed themselves with civil modes of enforcing ecclesiastical discipline. In essence, the government of the Church established *iure divino* by scripture had been supplanted by a mode of governance by *iure humano*, and this threatened God's judgement against both the Church and realm of England.

In addition to the authority of scripture, the question came down to a matter of definition: did the glimpses of church governance afforded by the New Testament apply universally, or did they represent the arrangements of a particular congregation? Were the Apostles part of the history of 'custom', and if not when did 'custom' begin? For Baynes, the ancient church did indeed have something resembling 'superintendents', but this office was a plural rather than singular function: 'We deny the assumption viz. That those Presbyteries of Ephesus were Diocesan Bishops. It is most plaine they were such who did *Communi consilio* tend the feeding and government of the Church; such Bishops whereof there might be more than one in one congregation.' Hence, whereas the function of bishops – 'feeding' and government – were evident, hierarchy was not, and this suggested that the ancient form of governance most closely resembled Presbyterian discipline. Yet the definition took on more technical aspects in Baynes' work. We have seen repeated examples of the charge that defenders of diocesan episcopacy provided flawed interpretations of the scriptural and historical evidence that comprised the foundation of their arguments. However, very seldom did they explore this at length, so Baynes' treatment is worth citing in full:

[Downname]: First they ordained James Bishop of Jerusalem presently after Christ's ascension. Ergo. They ordained Bishops. This is testified by Eusebius, Lib 2 Histo. Cap. 1 out of Clement and Hegesippus ...
[Baynes]: First, for James, we deny that he was ordained Bishop, or that it can be proved from antiquitie, that he was more than the other Apostles. That which Eusebius reporteth, is grounded in Clement, whom we know to be a forged magnifier of Romish orders, and in this story he doth seeme to imply, that Christ should have ordained Peter, John and James the greater bishops. Seeing he maketh these to have

---

[134] Ibid., Pref.

ordayned James after they had got of Christ the supreme degree of dignity, which these forged deceitful epistles of Anacletus do plainly affirme.[135]

Faced with the same set of scholarly histories, and much the same textual tradition, Baynes' course against Downame was to argue that his opponent had relied on a forged narrative of the link between civil and spiritual authority. It was a tactic borrowed straight from Catholic/conformist controversies. Moreover, Downame was, in effect, guilty of shoddy historical practice, for he imposed meanings on the Fathers that were not present in the originals. In support of this contention, Baynes pointed out that: 'The fathers use the words of *Apostoli* and *Episcopi* amply, not in their strict and formal proprietie.'[136] In other words, when the Fathers spoke of bishops, one could not infer that they meant to impute to these officers the type of jurisdiction that Downame claimed they possessed. Here Baynes held Downame to the standard of contemporary humanist canons of scholarship, complete with critical philological readings of historical texts.

As we have seen, the debates that occurred in the wake of Hampton Court witnessed tensions between two visions of the Church, and between concepts which defined these visions: spiritual versus political and doctrine versus law. The debate on bishops reflected similar tensions, and was defined too by debate over the Apostolic origins of the early church. Reformists argued that the history of the church found for a Presbyterian model of discipline: pastors rather than prelates, and free congregations rather than a unified church. Conformists argued that diocesan episcopacy and the power of the bishops over the rest of the clergy were 'notes' of a true church; in administering subscription, defenders of episcopacy claimed to be acting according to the scriptural warrant that called for 'order', and also as inferior magistrates charged with the administration of the Crown's ecclesiastical sovereignty. Yet there was a tension in conformist accounts of the origins of episcopacy: did bishops hold their power by divine right, through the Apostles, or merely through the custom of the early church? Thomas Bilson sought to subject episcopacy to the sovereignty of the Crown in parliament, while Carleton and Downame denied that bishops operated under such limitations. In order to diffuse the charge that bishops trespassed on the sovereignty of the Crown in parliament, defenders of the office offered a doctrinal and historical account of its origins and jurisdiction, and established episcopal governance as a core aspect of the practice of the ancient church. In addition to calling this version of history in question, Reformists raised questions about the implications of episcopacy for both the purity of doctrine and the common law. It was thus that bishops were portrayed as usurping the sovereignty of

---

[135] Ibid., pp. 26–8.   [136] Ibid., p. 28.

the Crown in order to promote ceremonies, practice, and doctrine that were neither ancient or reformed, nor true notes of the church.

These debates indicate the way in which the problem of authority persisted and grew more complex as the reign progressed. At issue was both the precise nature of ecclesiastical authority, and the sources from which this authority was derived. Both sides entered the debate armed with contrasting historical narratives of the relationship of civil and spiritual authority. The conformist position linked the legitimacy of episcopal governance with the need to preserve the stability and unity of the church; writers from Bilson to Godwin and Downame predicated their arguments on a reading of the history of Christianity that emphasised both apostolic continuance, and the freedom of the church to rule itself according to custom and historical practice. Their opponents rejected this notion of custom as being based on a misinterpretation of what the proper sources said, and proposed instead a Presbyterian model of governance. It was, they argued, a mode of governance that better reflected the reality of the ancient church, and which fitted better within the English system of ecclesiastical rule by the Crown in parliament. It becomes clear that the debate on episcopacy gave rise to contrasting versions not only of the history of Christian practice, but also how religious institutions cohered with the civil polity – this was governance in both senses of that term. For conformists, episcopal governance formed a central pillar in the settlement that defined the Elizabethan ecclesiastical polity and shaped the way in which they approached, and situated themselves in, the history of Christianity. To establish this version of history as 'authentic' was to establish episcopal governance as also being authentic; they occupied the same tradition and had existed in history. Proponents of Presbyterian discipline said much the same thing, and challenged the historical and political positions of their opponents with a countervailing narrative that linked the purity of doctrine with the mode of governance to be practised in the Church. Rejecting custom and the argument that the stability of the Church depended on the uniformity of public doctrine – and hence obedience to bishops – they argued instead that the only authentic mode of ecclesiastical rule was that which could be found in the practice of the ancient church, a ministry of pastors rather than prelates.

5

Bellum ceremoniale: *scripture, custom, and ceremonial practice*

As was the case with episcopacy, the evidence of scripture and the history of the early church were central to both defences and criticisms of ceremonial practice. Conformists sought to differentiate between the ceremonies of the English Church and the ceremonies described in scripture and the history of early Christianity. In addition to arguing that there was no necessary link between the two, they suggested that the Church held the power to establish ceremonial practices it deemed edifying, but yet were *adiaphora*.[1] These arguments defined a church based partly in scripture and partly on 'custom' and the example of history; the Church was partly spiritual and partly temporal, and in its temporal aspect it could be shaped by the design of human agents.[2] Reformists promoted a view of an institution derived from scripture and emulating it perfectly in all forms of rites and governance – a spiritual association. Hence, they stressed the perfection of the 'first institution' – the church established by Christ and handed to the Apostles. Writers like Henry Ainsworth condemned their opponents for reproaching 'the faith and witnesses' of the true church, and sought reform governed by its example.[3] They maintained that the ceremonial practice of the English Church should be based on that described in scripture, and confirmed by the practice of the Apostolic church. Clearly, then, the reformist stance on ceremonial practice was rooted in a firm sense of historical understanding. This runs counter to what some commentators have suggested about them, and overlooks the simple point that, since it was in historical

---

[1] For a treatment of *adiaphora* in the early Reformation Church, see Bernard J. Verkamp, *The indifferent mean: adiaphorism in the English Reformation to 1554* (Athens, OH, 1977).

[2] Hooker was the forerunner in this line of argument. In addition to Arthur Ferguson, *Clio unbound: perception of the social and cultural past in Renaissance England* (Durham, NC, 1979), p. 216, see Eng-Hang Tan, 'Polemics, persuasion and authority: an investigation of the theological method of Richard Hooker in "The laws of ecclesiastical Polity"', (Ph.D. diss., Trinity Evangelical Divinity School, 1997); William Henry Harrison, 'Prudential method in ecclesiology: authority in Richard Hooker's "Of the laws of ecclesiastical politie"', (Ph.D. diss., Boston College, 2000).

[3] Henry Ainsworth, *Counterpoyson. Considerations touching the points in difference between the godly ministers & people of the Church of England, and the seduced brethren of the separation* ([Amsterdam: G.Thorp], 1608), **2.

argument that conformist defences of ceremonies were rooted, it was on this terrain that they would be met and engaged with.[4]

Here again we recognise the centrality of historical scholarship to the business of religious controversy. In stressing the need to emulate the church of the first institution, reformists made a theological and political point. In one sense, they urged the purity of doctrine and the need to defend this purity. The second and closely related argument promoted a concept of an immemorial church over which Christ and the Word alone were sovereign. This is not to suggest that, like the common law, the church existed 'time out of mind'; merely that there was a point in its early history that represented the brief moment of the existence of the 'true' church as a complete and pure entity, and that its subsequent history was one of decline and corruption. In reprising a vision of this original purity, and in identifying Christ and the Word as its lone and sovereign rulers, reformists provided a strong case against the Church being governed according to 'custom' and human policy.[5] The conformist response to this position, if it was to be effective, had to be profoundly subtle. As we shall see, the argument that emerged stressed a notion of 'custom', which held that ceremonial practice in the early church had not reflected a divine ordination, but rather the habits of worship of a particular time and place. It was along this argumentative line that conformists offered an historical defence of the ceremonies established by the Canons of 1604, a defence that was based upon an interpretation of the Church of the first institution.

What emerges are contrasting views of the character of early Christian history, and hence of the church itself. Conformists saw it as dynamic and changeable, and premised a defence of episcopacy and ceremonial practice on the argument that 'custom' obtained where the governors of the Church judged points of ceremonies and governance to be *adiaphora*. Reformists, in emphasising the purity of the first institution, regarded any departure from it as a decline; in their view the Church was, as it were, immemorial. Yet it was so because it was rooted in a history which they defended as immemorial: not stagnant, but serving as a guide to animate the Church in the present. In ceremonies they found a strong echo of the authentic practice of the ancient church, and if the earthly church were to retain any meaningful connection with this association, then its ceremonial practice must emulate the ancient model without fault or deviation.

---

[4] Indeed, one author has noted that 'Insisting on the rule of Scripture alone, puritan ideology dismissed the value of precedent, tradition, and historical continuity, refusing to privilege any historical time.' See Achsah Guibbory, *Ceremony and community from Herbert to Milton* (Cambridge, 1998), p. 29.

[5] I am acutely conscious of the parallel here with Pocock's notion of sovereignty, immemoriality, and the common law. See J. G. A. Pocock, *The ancient constitution and the feudal law. A reissue with a retrospect* (Cambridge, 1987), p. 51.

SUBSCRIPTION AND AUTHORITY: THE *ABRIDGMENT* CONTROVERSY

The Elizabethan Church was the site of active debates on ceremonies, history, and ecclesiology.[6] The Thirty-nine Articles codified the conformist position on these questions, and introduced a tension between doctrine and law that would be exploited by reformists. Article 19 affirmed that the 'true' church could be found wherever the Word was preached and the sacraments properly administered: 'This visible Church of Christ is a congregation of faithful men, in which the pure Word of God is preached, and the Sacraments be duly administered according to Christ's ordinance.' The wording of the article seemed to imply not only that there was parity among members of the Church, but that the sacraments were patterned exactly on the first institution. Yet Article 23 provided that preaching and ministering of the sacraments could be performed only by those who were 'lawfully called' by 'men who have public authority given unto them in the Congregation, to call and send Ministers into the Lord's vineyard'. This article applied additional elements to the notion of a 'congregation': that is, there were orders of clergy, a select number of whom were authorised by the whole to institute and remove ministers. Finally, Article 34 described a concept of tradition, or 'custom':

It is not necessary that Traditions and Ceremonies be in all places one, or utterly alike ... Whosoever through his private judgement, willingly and purposely, doth openly breach the traditions and ceremonies of the Church, which be not repugnant to the Word of God, and be ordained and approved by common authority, ought to be rebuked openly, (that other may fear to do the like), as he that offendeth against the common order of the Church, and hurteth the authority of the Magistrate, and woundeth the consciences of the weak brethren. Every particular or national Church hath authority to ordain, change and abolish ceremonies, or rites of the Church ordained only by man's authority, so that all things be done to edifying.[7]

Here was the core of the conformist position, which emphasised the concepts of *adiaphora* and public doctrine, and wherein the stability of the Church took precedence over the purity of doctrine. Yet in the text of these articles lay a doctrinal tension: was the Church a congregation of equals governed by the ordinances of God, or was it a national association, a channel for the legal and ecclesiastical sovereignty of the Crown, and guided by 'custom' in the form of human ordinances?[8]

[6] For the Admonition controversy, see Peter Lake, *Anglicans and puritans?: Presbyterianism and English conformist thought from Whitgift to Hooker* (London, 1988), pp. 13–64, and for the Marprelate controversy see Michael Mendle, *Dangerous positions: mixed government, the estates of the realm, and the 'Answer to the xix propositions'* (University, AL, 1985), pp. 80–7. An excellent assessment of Marprelate in the context of seventeenth-century pamphleteering can be found in Joad Raymond's *Pamphlets and pamphleteering in early Modern Britain* (Cambridge, 2003), ch. 2.

[7] *A theological introduction to the Thirty-nine Articles of the Church of England*, ed. E. J. Bicknell, 3rd edition, revised by H. J. Carpenter (London, 1955).

[8] In the Elizabethan setting, these tensions were explored in a number of reformist petitions that sought to attack the doctrinal foundations of the Elizabethan reconstruction.

It has been shown that debates after the Jacobean settlement were defined by a tension between doctrine and law. At the same time as the controversy sparked by the Millenary Petition was underway, a debate over subscription was taking place in the Diocese of Lincoln. A multi-authored petition from this region was presented to the King on 1 December 1604. Although no copy survives, it was epitomised, augmented, and published as the *Abridgment* in 1605.[9] Listed prominently in the opening pages were a multitude of controversial works from the Elizabethan period, patristic texts, and reports of ancient councils. Their inclusion was intended to suggest that there was a broad consensus among past and present theologians that challenged the liturgy set forth in the Book of Common Prayer and the doctrinal foundation of the Canons of 1604.[10] We will recall that at issue in debates among Protestants were the legal aspects of the Jacobean settlement, especially the thirty-sixth Canon which set forth three articles to which all members of the clergy were required to subscribe.[11] One of the articles concerned subscription to the Prayer Book which, argued the petition, did not offer a sound treatment

See [John Field and Thomas Wilcox], *An admonition to the Parliament* ([1572]); [attrib. to Robert Waldegrave], *A lamentable complaint of the commonalty* ([London, 1585]); John Penry, *An humble motion with submission vnto the right Honorable L. L. of Hir Maiesties Priuie Counsell* ([Edinburgh], 1590); for full details see Peter Milward, *Religious controversies of the Elizabethan age: a survey of printed sources* (London, 1977), pp. 25–33, 35–8.

[9]   *An abridgment of that booke which the ministers of Lincoln diocess delivered to his Maiestie upon the first of December last* ([W. Jones' secret press], 1605). For details, see Peter Milward, *Religious controversies of the Jacobean age: a survey of printed sources* (London, 1978), p. 5.

[10] For popular reaction to the Book of Common Prayer, see Judith Maltby, '"By this book": parishioners, the Prayer Book, and the established Church,' in *The Early Stuart Church, 1603–1642*, ed Kenneth Ficham (Stanford, 1993), pp. 115–37. Patterns of local subscription to the liturgy and a treatment of 'prayer book conformity' are further developed in Maltby's *Prayer Book and people in Elizabethan and early Stuart England* (Cambridge, 1998), ch. 6, Appendices 1–2. For 'clerical conformity', see Kenneth Fincham, 'Clerical conformity from Whitgift to Laud', in *Conformity and orthodoxy in the English Church, c. 1560–1660*, ed. Peter Lake and Michael Questier (Woodbridge, Suffolk, 2000), pp. 125–58.

[11] Bancroft's articles were closely modelled on Whitgift's Three Articles, which read:

1. That the Kings Maiestie under God, is the only supreme Governour of this Realm, & of all other his Highnes Dominions & Countreys, as wel in all spiritual or Ecclesiastical things or causes, as Temporall: and that no forreigne Prince, Person, Prelate, State, or Potentate, hath or ought to have any Jurisdiction, Power, Superioritie, Preheminence, or Authoritie Ecclesiasticall or Spirituall, within his Maiesties said Realmes, Dominions, and Countreys.

2. That the Books of Common prayer, and of Ordering of Bishops, Priests and Deacons, containeth in it nothing contrary to the Word of God, and that it may lawfully be used, and that he himselfe will use the forme in the said Booke prescribed in publicke Prayer, and Administration of the Sacraments, and none other.

3. That he alloweth the booke of Articles of Religion agreed upon by the Archbishops & Bishops of both Provinces, and the whole Cleargie in the Convocation holden at London in the yere of our Lord God, one thousand five hundred sixtie and two; and that he acknowledgeth all and every the Articles therein contained being in number nine & thirty, besides the ratification, to be agreeable to the Word of God.

Constitutions and canons ecclesiastical (London, 1604), sig. F[2v].

of the scriptures, omitting some and including apocryphal passages. For the Lincoln ministers, the scripture was the immemorial and immutable revelation of God, pure and perfect in itself and thus not subject to human 'custom'. The Jacobean settlement was thus depicted as a departure from the liturgical traditions of the ancient church and of the best reformed contemporary churches:

> We are confirmed in this our First argument against subscription to the Book of Common Prayer, by the practice of the Church of the Jewes before Christ, of the primitive Church in the ages next succeeding Christ and his Apostles, and of all the best reformed Churches at this day: in none of all was any part of the Canonical scripture ever commanded to be left out of the publicke reading.

In fact, argued the ministers, this apostasy was a sign that: 'Barbarism had invaded the Church of God.'[12] This was a rival concept of tradition, and the reference to the 'practice' of the church amounted to a defence of what the ancient church left in the historical record, and the suggestion that the Word, rather than men, determined the pattern of tradition.

A complex exegesis of the Prayer Book also examined and interpreted the textual authorities often cited by defenders of the Church. In part, the tract reinterpreted this tradition in order to show how the scriptures, the Fathers, and contemporary controversialists offered evidence against the use of cross and surplice, and the retention of kneeling at communion. The *Abridgment* therefore employed 'tradition' in two senses: positively, as shown in the preceding paragraph, and negatively, in order to refute conformist arguments. Hence, the argument was less about the Jacobean Church than about how it compared to the ancient exemplar described by the New Testament, and interpreted by ancient and contemporary writers. As a result of this comparison, the *Abridgment* suggested that the Church of England still embodied the sort of idolatry associated with the Church of Rome, a step which entailed a retreat from reform: 'the retaining of popish ceremonies will certainly be a means to endanger the doctrine that we professe, and to bring the people back again to popery'.[13] For the ministers of Lincoln, the epitome of Roman error lay in the authority vested in the church's human governors and they found a parallel for this in the governance of the English Church: 'The Lord hath given to no creature absolute power in ecclesiasticall matters, soe as they may appoynt or doe therein whatsoever seemeth good unto themselves, but he hath sett down in his word certaine generall rules which contain a perfect direction for such rites and orders, as he will have his Church to observe in his worship.' Although it was affirmed that the King held supreme ecclesiastical authority, the ministers noted that the King was

---

[12] *An abridgment*, pp. 4–5.   [13] Ibid., p. 24.

nevertheless bound by a higher law. This argument was put forth in a
sentence that echoed the language of the Act of Supremacy:

> And although the magistrates authority be very great, and the King within his owne
> Dominions be indeede supreme governor in all causes, and over all persons, as well
> Ecclesiastical and Civil, he may not appoynt to the Church, what rites and orders he
> thinks good, but he is bound to observe therein those rules which God in his word,
> hath prescribed to his Church for her Direction in those Matters.[14]

A similar point on the duty of religious princes appeared in the writings of
Elizabethan reformists, and was echoed too by conformists such as Thomas
Bilson. In general, English reformist thought held that the governance of the
church was ordained by the Word, and could not be altered – even slightly –
by human agents. The same assumption underlay Henry Jacob's statement
that the 'mind of the magistrate' was an insufficient authority when it came
to the ordering of the Church. Common to many reformist writers was the
claim that the doctrine of the Church was established as a matter of divine
law, and this warrant was seen to include liturgy, sacraments, discipline, and
governance.

Despite its qualification, the statement concerning the King's ecclesiastical
supremacy contained more than a hint that, if the King were to stray from his
duty to the Church, such a departure entailed a violation of his oath to
'defend' the faith as delivered by Christ. Since this seemed to justify resistance, defences of the policy of subscription were combined with statements
about the Crown's authority over the Church. In response to a petition
against subscription by a group of ministers in Devon and Cornwall,
Thomas Hutton argued for the 'virtues of obedience', and stressed the need
for uniformity and stability as antidotes to private opinion and faction.[15] The
argument put forth by Hutton emphasised those elements of the Church that
were central to its definition as a political association: order, uniformity,
hierarchy, and sovereignty. In addition, Hutton defended diocesan bishops
as crucial guarantors of 'order' and 'conformitie', and admonished the
ministers for ignoring their duty to superiors, remarking that they 'stand
out against all order, they must reverse all laws, and quite disannul
Ecclesiastical authority, which is most suitable to them in principle, who
deny Christian kings their Royal power in Ecclesiastical causes, contrary to

---

[14] Ibid., pp. 43, 44.

[15] No copy of the petition survives. One of its authors may have been Samuel Hieron, a preacher
in Modbury, Devonshire, whose sermon 'The Doctrine of the Beginning of Christ' (1604)
took the form of a catechism on clerical offices: 'Q. What is the outward meanes by which
Faith commeth? A. The hearing of a Preacher, which is sent[D], Rom. 10, 14, 15.' The text of
the marginal note suggested that clerical subscription was not a sound manner of determining
the fitness of ministers: 'D. That is, who is endued with gifts to teach: for God sends no other.'
See *The sermons of Master Samuel Hieron, formerly collected together by himselfe* (London,
1620), p. 578.

God's law, and the Lawes of our Country'.[16] This argument turned on the assumption that the authority of the visible church was guaranteed by English law, and Hutton pointed out that critics of the Church sought to undermine the political stability of the commonwealth. Hutton did not address the doctrinal case put forth by his opponents, choosing instead to focus on the political implications that seemed to result from the attack on conformity and subscription. Yet this was not a purely secular argument; rather, Hutton sought to promote the ancient pedigree of sovereignty claimed by the English Church. Linking the purity of doctrine with the sovereignty of the visible church, Hutton furnished a doctrinal case for the measures criticised by reformist petitioners: 'the ancient true Catholicke faith we have in peace for seven and forty years continually embraced, and with all the well-established good orders, God hath wrought in the heart of his Church, and which the excellent authoritie of the King's highness requireth, to whom we owe all obedience in greater things'.[17] All measures to ensure conformity were therefore instituted in the name of order and the preservation of true doctrine.

The Devon ministers quickly replied to Hutton's tract and sought to address the doctrinal elements of his case. In particular, they attacked episcopacy with the plea that Hutton 'search the scripture' for evidence of a clerical hierarchy in the earliest churches. With respect to the textual authorities on which Hutton's case was founded, the ministers sought to challenge the implication that the evidence of Fathers and Councils was somehow superior to the testimony of scripture: 'It were no hard manner to produce testimonies out of Ancient Fathers, both mentioning and approving this kind of government. But as that which the Scripture give no warrant to, all the authorities of all the men in the world can not justifie; so that which is grounded upon the word, needs no further confirmation.'[18] The argument was an effective one, for rather than quarrel separately with the political and spiritual elements of Hutton's position, the authors isolated an issue that pointed to a contradiction in the conformist case. Bishops enforced conformity and thus ensured the stability of the Church as a 'political' entity, yet the ministers dismissed this as a political rather than pastoral function. This in turn cast doubt on their spiritual authority which, the ministers argued, was not based in doctrine. The process of subscription and deprivation without a

---

[16] Thomas Hutton, *Reasons for refusal of subscription to the booke of common praier, vnder the hands of certaine ministers of Devon, and Cornwall word for word as they were exhibited by them to the Right Reverend Father in God William Coton Doctor of Diuinitie L. Bishop of Exceter* (Oxford, 1605), p. 65.

[17] Ibid., p. 199.

[18] [Anon], *The remoouall of certaine imputations laid vpon the ministers of Deuon: and Cornwall by one M. T.H., and in them, vpon all other ministers els-ewhere, refusing to subscribe* ([Middelburg], 1606), p. 11.

scriptural warrant was all the more damaging, given that good ministers were being replaced by 'Hirelings and Pluralists', who sundered the Church, 'to the rejoicing of Atheists and Papists'.[19] Subscription, the ministers argued, had no warrant in the ancient church, and like 'the Lordly Primacy of Bishops' was but a 'Politicke Device'. Where Hutton had set aside doctrine in order to make the case for the necessity of 'order', the ministers based their argument on the premise that subscription violated the doctrinal pattern of the first institution.

These ministers made no call for the dissolution of the established Church, nor did they express a need to separate from it. Rather, they sought a reformation of its original governance, 'so that the Primitive beauty of God's Church might be restored'. The same criticism that they had aimed at ceremonies of 'human invention' was now directed at the governance of the English Church, which was seen to supplant 'the Kingly function of Christ'. The ministers also pointed to the doctrinal implications of the Canons of 1604. At the core of this argument was the suggestion that the divine pattern of governance had been supplanted by the will of the King, and its purity compromised by the use of measures like subscription and deprivation:

the Scripture ... have delivered an exact Platforme of policie for the House of God which is the Church, and yet the same be alterable according to the will of Princes, and the forms of civill government there where Religion is established, we hold it as a wrong done to the Magestie of God, that his councels should (without any revealed warrant from himselfe) give place to Men's devices and that order should be forced to yield to Humane Ordinance.[20]

Princes and parliaments were bound to protect the mode of governance commanded by God. Rather than quarrel with the function of the High Commission or assert the authority of the English common law, the ministers emphasised that the scripture was the sole authority by which the rites and governance of the Church should be established. Where the conformist case depended on rites enforced by law, reformists argued that all modes of discipline and governance had to be grounded in doctrinal precept, and confirmed by the practice of the ancient church. The question that this opened up was whether the 'will' of the prince itself amounted to 'custom'. For conformists, the will of the prince was a competent guiding power, a power exercised for the good of the Church; the Act of Supremacy placed this power in the hands of the Crown, yet the problem which emerged among reformists concerned the possibility that this power might be used at the cost of the doctrinal purity of the Church. If the Crown promoted a false standard of doctrine, then what recourse was to be had?

[19] Ibid., p. 15.   [20] Ibid., pp. 23, 25, 39.

Yet reformists were reluctant to ponder this question, and directed their attention instead to the issue of episcopacy and its impact on the purity of doctrine. Hence, a further contribution to the debate made the case that, in addition to the 'platforme of policie' evident in scripture, the bishops had abandoned the ideal of 'reformation'. Samuel Hieron's dialogue between the 'Old Protestant' and the 'New Formalist' surveyed the controversy between John Jewel and Thomas Harding, as well as the Catholic response to Jewel written by Richard Bristow.[21] Hieron maintained that, in enforcing conformity and deprivation, the bishops had abandoned not only the reformed tradition but also the testimonies of the Church's most august defenders: 'lamentable is the case of Christ his church amongst us, that some of her principall watchmen should in this sort patronize lyes, and uphold manifold defects and deformities, striving against all reformation, to the endangering of the substance of itselfe or our religion'.[22] There were two elements to Hieron's case: first, the ceremonies established by the Canons of 1604 were of human devising, and second, they were enforced by diocesan bishops whose power was founded upon a corruption of scripture. Among the contemporary writers whom Hieron singled out was 'T. H.' – Thomas Hutton – whose tracts in defence of subscription and episcopacy were seen to bear the principal hallmark of the Catholic mode of controversy: deception and the corruption of printed authorities.[23] He criticised Hutton's position through an extended discussion of the Jewel–Harding controversy, in the course of which episcopacy *iure divino* was shown to be a mark of 'popery'.[24] Hieron suggested that the alienation of the reformed churches of Europe would be the result of the effort to defend episcopacy as the permanent governance of the English Church:

Old. Prot. – The Romish Harding, but especially Bellarmin that stout champion for popery; striveth to prove by all reasons he can the superioritie of Ministers, to be *iure divino*, that is by the law of God, and from apostolicall institution. But this assertion seemeth to imply most dangerous conclusions. D. Willet hath observed one ... namely, *that hence necessarily will follow, that other reformed Churches without this prescript of Government by Lord Bishoppes, are Churches erronious.*[25]

---

[21] Samuel Hieron, *A short dialogue prouing that the ceremonyes, and some other corruptions now in question, are defended, by none other arguments then such as the papists haue here tofore vsed: and our protestant writers haue long since answered* ([W. Jones' secret press], 1605). For details of the Jewel–Harding controversy – and a list of sources – see Milward, *Religious controversies of the Elizabethan age*, pp. 1–6, 39–46.

[22] Hieron, *A short dialogue*, p. 22.

[23] 'To the same effect also is it now lately published against the Ministers of Devonshire and Cornwall, by T. H. of good wit and paynes, yet over carryed with selfe conceit.' Ibid., p. 26.

[24] For details see Lucy E. C. Wooding, *Rethinking Catholicism in Reformation England* (Oxford, 2000), pp. 193–8.

[25] Hieron, *A short dialogue*, p. 29. Italics in original; Hieron did not cite which of Willet's works he had in mind.

Hieron's use of the Catholic example and citation of Andrew Willet was intended to apply also to the case of the Church of England: to retain episcopal governance was to embrace a doctrinal error that severed the Church from the community of the reformed churches.

Hieron sought to emphasise the argument that the churches of England and Rome presented themselves as exemplars of the 'true' church. The result was that English Protestants had come to accept episcopacy as a mark of the church, which in turn alienated them further from the reformed tradition.[26] That this statement was delivered in the form of a précis of an earlier controversy did not diminish the seriousness of the charge, which Hieron then paired with a discussion of the legal implications of subscription. This took the form of a short essay, 'Certain considerations', which laid out the case for why refusal of subscription should not result in the deprivation of ministers. Where the dialogue itself had examined the problem of subscription against the backdrop of controversies between Catholic and reformed divines, the essay considered its relation to English law. Hence the example of Magna Carta was employed to argue that the deprivations were illegal: 'Let the learned Lawyers judge, whether this be not against the Great Charter. Likewise, whether the Bishops and others of the said Convocation, be not excommunicated *ipso facto*, for infringing the liberties of the sayde Charter.'[27] Here one concept of custom was set against another: conformists defended the customary right of the Church to establish rites and to employ subscription to ensure this custom was followed, while reformists stressed the custom of the common law as a check to the unlimited jurisdiction of bishops over other members of the clergy. Hieron therefore set out both a doctrinal and a legal case against Jacobean conformity; that is, the Church had come to accept a mode of governance supported by the error-ridden Church of Rome, and these governors promoted ecclesiastical discipline that violated the protections granted by the common law.

Although there was no response to Hieron's dialogue, a reply to an unpublished tract by John Burges showed how conformist controversialists sought to make a doctrinal case for diocesan episcopacy while side-stepping the issue of 'popery'.[28] Burges, a minister beneficed in Lincoln diocese, preached a sermon before James I at Greenwich in July of 1604, and used

---

[26] The tensions in Catholic–Protestant debates have been traced as they impacted controversies among English Protestants. See T. H. Wadkins, 'Theological polemic and religious culture in early Stuart England: the Percy / 'Fisher' controversies, 1605–41' (Ph.D. diss., Graduate Theological Union, Berkeley, 1988), pp. 112–76.

[27] Hieron, 'Certaine considerations why the ministers should not be remoued', appended to his *A short dialogue*, p. 56.

[28] Peter Lake has characterised Burges' position on conformity and subscription. See 'Moving the goal posts? modified subscription and the construction of conformity in the early Stuart Church', in *Conformity and orthodoxy*, ed. Lake and Questier, pp. 179–205.

the occasion to launch an attack on the ceremonies enjoined by the Canons of 1604.[29] Burges was subsequently deprived and imprisoned, and the sermon was not published until 1642; however, an 'Apology' setting forth Burges' reasons for refusing subscription must have been circulated as a manuscript, which came into the hands of William Covell.[30] Covell opened his *Briefe answer* with a weary statement to the effect that there was no glamour in defending the *status quo* and continued by observing that Church government was instituted to ensure order: 'God therefore respecting man's weakness hath appointed Magistrates and governors in both [church and commonwealth] to serve as eies to guide and direct what is fit to be done, and so to this end made laws concerning indifferent things, that so the whole body may be governed with comliness, order and edification.'[31] Covell embraced the precept that linked uniform religion with political order, and sought to establish it as a divinely ordained point of doctrine. Since the attainment of 'order' rested on the use of laws to regulate 'things indifferent', the practice could be defended as a matter of political expediency. Moreover, because stability in the church was itself divinely ordained, human governors were free to devise the means by which this stability could be maintained. Covell argued that it was God's will that there be a 'continuance under a new Prince of the olde, ancient and true religion', and sought to link these concepts with uniformity, stability, and sovereignty.

Covell's position also implied that antiquity provided a justification for the kinds of powers that were required to promote religious uniformity. The argument revolved around two themes: first, obedience and the dangers of faction, and second, the ancient roots and modern affirmation of the need for uniformity and religious order. On obedience, Covell wrote that 'the precept of the Superior doth bind more than the conscience of the inferior; for the subject hath the command of his lawful superior, whether King or Bishop'. Like William Wilkes, Covell depicted non-conformity as the result of private 'fancy': 'Where private fancies adventure to interpret the limitations of their own obedience, the wisdom of those that make laws shall be of little use.'[32] The actions of these ecclesiastical lawgivers were justified not only on the ground of political expediency, but also by the practice of the ancient church.

---

[29] For details of Burges' deprivation see Stuart Barton Babbage, *Puritanism and Richard Bancroft* (London, 1962), pp. 166–74; Kenneth Fincham, *Prelate as pastor: the episcopate of James I* (Oxford, 1990), pp. 216, 324.

[30] John Burges, *A sermon preached before the late King Iames His Majesty, at Greenwich, the 19. of July, 1604* (London, 1642). To the sermon were attached two 'Letters by Way of Apology', in which Burges repudiated his earlier position. See Milward, *Religious controversies of the Jacobean age*, p. 5.

[31] William Covell, *A briefe answer vnto certaine reasons by way of an apologie deliuered to the Right Reuerend Father in God, the L. Bishop of Lincolne, by Mr. John Burges* (London, 1606), *4ʳ.

[32] Ibid., pp. 19, 46.

Here, Covell marshalled a battery of ancient sources to prove the presence of bishops in the ancient church:

For if Clement saide true (whom Polidore allegeth to that end) that Peter in every province appointed one Archbishop, whom all other bishops in the same province should obey, if the name of Archbishop and Bishop were not so unusuall that Volusianus was not afraid to say, that Dionysius Areopagatica was by S. Paul made Archbishop of Athens.[33]

In addition to furnishing historical defences of bishops and a clerical hierarchy, Covell also sought to diffuse the doctrinal objections to the ceremonies. He did so in order to downplay the charge that bishops were political agents, enforcing ceremonies of human invention: 'From all antiquitie, it then appearing many things profitable to edification, to be read in the Church, both in the time of the Jewes before Christ, as also since, which the Church did not esteeme Canonical.'[34] In short, Covell provided historical grounds for episcopacy and 'things indifferent' in order to address the charge that the Church's doctrine was primarily of 'human invention'.

Thomas Hutton returned to the theme of the original institution of episcopacy in the second part of his response to the Devon ministers.[35] He argued that the King was the agent best suited to ensure the agreement between the divine pattern of the Church and its visible element. Like Covell, Hutton maintained that hierarchical governance was needed to ensure that 'popery' was kept out of the English Church. Yet, perhaps sensitive to the charge that episcopal government seemed to violate both scripture and the common law, Hutton emphasised the ecclesiastical sovereignty of the Crown, and depicted the King as the guardian of the church that had languished in the wilderness during the period of Roman domination. Given this, Hutton argued, it was unlikely that the King's actions constituted a violation of God's will; quoting a royal proclamation of February 1603, he noted:

The like doth manifest itselfe in that royal care of our dread sovereigne, wherein we may safely repose ourselves knowing from our heart his Magesty, as he holdeth himself obliged both in conscience and wisdome, so hath and will use all good meanes to keep his subjects from being infected with superstitious opinions in matters of religion. This especial divine care, his learned orations, general proclamations, finall determination at the last conference have all solemnly witnessed to the world, in redeeming the state of our Church from all such scandals, as were injuriously brought upon her, and upon that truth, which we do maintaine.[36]

---

[33] Ibid., p. 34.   [34] Ibid., p. 78.

[35] Thomas Hutton, *The second and last part of Reasons for refusall of subscription to the Booke of common prayer, vnder the hands of certaine ministers of Deuon. and Cornwall, as they were exhibited by them to the right Reuerend Father in God William Cotton Doctor of Divinitie, and Lord Bishop of Exceter* (London, 1606).

[36] Ibid., p. 42.

Hutton tried to diffuse the charge that the Crown's ecclesiastical policy and the deprivations that took place in the aftermath of Hampton Court provided evidence of the use of political tools to enforce erroneous doctrine and practices. Rather, he portrayed Jacobean ecclesiastical policy as a restoration of ancient doctrine defined by 'reverence' rather than idolatry. This brought the argument back to the question of custom and the will of the prince, and Hutton affirmed that the duty of the king to his subjects ensured that the purity of doctrine would be protected.

However, the argument that the disputed ceremonies and governance served as a block to popery was disingenuous when aimed at Protestants. Therefore, Hutton argued that the Jacobean settlement *restored* the ceremonies of the ancient church. For example, he defended kneeling as an action that 'reverenced' Christ in his lifetime and recognised his status as a 'prophet of God': 'So that mere kneeling, that is having of the knee, is not worshipping in a divine manner. Children do it to their parents, subjects to their King.'[37] Hutton defended ceremonies as signs of reverence, as aids to the understanding of religious duty, and thus fitting accompaniments to worship. In addition, Hutton employed the concept of 'custom', which identified patterns of worship that were peculiar to individual gathered churches:

therefore we pray, kneele, confesse our sinnes and sing Psalms, and all little enough, no way crossing the practise of Our Saviour more in this, then in the use of leavened bread in the time of the Sacrament, but here in following our Saviour, because he did what the use of his times and Countrie made fit, and decent, and what decencie, and custom of our times, and Countrie hath now made usuall, and convenient.[38]

Hence, re-casting the nature of the first institution defended the liberty of the Church to order ceremonies. The actions of Christ were depicted as expressions of local custom rather than ordinances that had to be obeyed by His Church. 'Custom' therefore served as the justification for the use of ceremonies that were defended as 'indifferent': so long as ceremonial practice was 'decent', then it was immune from the charge of idolatry, as well as the doctrinal objection that the scripture contained a perfect pattern for the ordering of worship. Hutton also toned down his rhetoric, for where in the first instalment of his response to the petitioners he fulminated against non-subscribers as 'traitors' and 'punys', here he urged them to see that 'custom' served as a continuity, binding the English Church to that left on earth by Christ.

Thomas Sparke who, as chaplain in ordinary to the bishop of Lincoln, had a unique vantage point on the controversies over subscription

---

[37] Ibid., p. 51.   [38] Ibid., p. 57.

and ceremonies adopted a similar tone.[39] Sparke had once been a vocal critic of Jacobean conformity, and he was candid enough to admit that he too could not reconcile aspects of the Book of Common Prayer with the Word; this gave his pamphlet something of the feel of a conversion narrative more commonly associated with the Catholic branch of the literature.[40] However, it also included a strong note of endorsement for English ecclesiastical governance against those fomenters of 'domesticall controversies' who, 'both in pulpit and print, have thought they might not onely bitterly seeke the disgrace both of it, and the governors thereof, but also make ... a plain and open schisme therein'.[41] Less concerned with the finer points of the Church's antiquity, Sparke made the case for the sovereignty of the visible Church – channelled through Crown and bishops – to order itself through its Canons and councils:

> therefore we may not deny the Christian supreme magistrate, who by God's ordinance is to be *Esai 49:23* as a nurse father unto his Churches under him, nor the Bishops and others of the clergy by his authority lawfully assembled in a National Synod, authority in such matters as these, for the more orderly government of the Church in their judgements, to prescribe ordinances, alwaies provided that the rites and ceremonies that thereby they impose upon the Churches, be not contrary, but rather consonant to the generall rules left them in the Word, to direct them therein.[42]

The *Abridgment* had also referred to the 'general rules' laid down in scripture, but these rules were identified as a 'perfect' pattern for the ordering of all aspects of doctrine and governance. For conformists, on the other hand, the notion of 'general rules' left a good deal of latitude when it came to matters of doctrine and discipline, and opened the further issue of what contemporaries called the 'sufficiency of scripture'. Could the rites, ceremonies, and discipline appropriate to an institutional Church be found entirely in scripture, or could these matters be left to human agents? Not surprisingly, Sparke argued that the scriptures contained 'all truth, concerning faith and God's worship necessarie to Salvation', but that when it came to the 'outward accidentall and changeable rites and ceremonies ... the Churches of Christ have libertie to ordaine touching them, as the governors thereof shall think fittest'.[43] Once the governors of the Church established such orders, then all had to obey them. Sparke emphasised order and public worship:

---

[39] Thomas Sparke, *A brotherly perswasion to vnitie, and vniformitie in iudgement, and practise touching the receiued, and present ecclesiasticall government* (London, 1607); Babbage, *Puritanism and Richard Bancroft*, pp. 62–3, 135.

[40] For a treatment of Catholic conversion literature see Michael Questier, *Conversion, politics and religion in England, 1580–1625* (Cambridge, 1996), chs. 1–2.

[41] Sparke, *Brotherly perswasion*, sig. B[3v].   [42] Ibid., p. 8.   [43] Ibid., p. 11.

that the Churches of Christ have freedome and libertie according to those generall rules to prescribe orders, rites and ceremonies, and then they having so done, it is not for private men to refuse, for the maintenance of good order and peace therein, to conform themselves thereunto, for that the publicke judgement of the Church in such matters, is always to be preferred before the private opinion of this man or that, and the Church is not to stay from making any constitutions in such things, untill she can be assured that all will be pleased therewith, for then hardly ever should she make any, and so also there would never be an end of brawles, jarres, discords, and dissentions thereabout.[44]

This was an attempt to move the argument away from the controversial concept of custom; 'general rules' answered the need of a church which sought to rule itself, and Sparke was anxious to defend this policy as something evident in the scripture. He therefore employed two types of criteria for identifying the rites of the Church: the spiritual aspects that pertained to salvation – the internal element – and those things designated as 'circumstance' – the external element – which fell under the jurisdiction of the Church's human governors.

Against the charge of 'idolatry' frequently put about by those Protestants who sought further reform in the Church, Sparke replied that the English tradition was unique for having exchanged idolatry for reverence. This assumption lent shape to his defence of the ceremonies enjoined by subscription in the thirty-sixth Canon: kneeling was a sign of people's 'humbling' themselves before God, the surplice a 'decent distinction' like the scholar's cap or lawyer's gown, and the cross in baptism an 'admonitory token' signifying a common faith in the resurrection.[45] At the centre of the case in support of ceremonies, therefore, was the idea that the visible church through the ages had established incidental aspects of ceremonial practice, and that the Hampton Court conference had merely continued this tradition by substituting 'reverence', 'edification', and 'comliness' for superstition and error. Sparke concluded by asking English Protestants to accept this decision in order to preserve the stability of the Church:

our common Mother the Church of England ... is troubled with so dangerous enemies, both on her right hand and left, and so to bury and extinguish for ever the odious name of Puritants, and to put an end to all shewe of schism, distraction and division amongst ourselves [let us] give over contending any more thus amongst ourselves, about these our Mother's outward fashions, trimmings and deckings.[46]

To reformists, well-crafted arguments about 'custom' and *adiaphora* did not sufficiently address the intermingling of divine and human ordinances, doctrine and law. Given their firm commitment to the purity of doctrine, there was little chance that they would accept that *adiaphora* could be defended on doctrinal grounds. Writing in response to Covell, Hutton, and

[44] Ibid., p. 12. [45] Ibid., pp. 17–23. [46] Ibid., p. 81.

Sparke, Samuel Hieron argued that the Word was the only legitimate guide for the ordering of the liturgy.[47] Citing examples from ancient and more recent councils, Hieron argued that the history of the church showed that deprivation of ministers only proceeded after a lengthy period of formal disputation and that Hampton Court did not fulfil this requirement. The bulk of his treatise (the work stretched to 226 pages) was concerned with a line-by-line exegesis of the Prayer Book, and argued that all things necessary to Church polity could be found in the Word. To attack the liturgy in such a detailed manner was to shift the emphasis of the debate back to the axis of the laws of God versus the laws of men. Like Henry Jacob, Hieron argued that it was the purpose of the Church's governors (or 'stewards') simply to maintain and conserve the doctrinal perfection of the Church:

> And surely as God did first (with his own finger) enter and sanctifie the writings of his Word, in the table of stone: so hath he shewed what our care should be, for keeping the fountain of life pure, and as a spring shut up of his own care hereof; made manifest unto us, partly in the charge, he hath given the Church ... to take heed of adding thereto, or detracting therefrom.[48]

Given the immemoriality of the Word, and the fact that it served as a conduit for the law of God, alterations or deviations such as those found in the Book of Common Prayer could not be permitted. For Hieron, this constituted a departure from the divine pattern and entailed a severing of the Church of England from the 'true' church; this Hieron defined in doctrinal rather than institutional terms. In a sermon preached in the same year that his tract in defence of the ministers appeared, Hieron provided a firm statement on the sufficiency of scripture:

> Touching the largenesse and amplenesse of the Word of God, I set downe this point, That all necessary points, either touching faith or manners, are abundantly contained and laid forth in the Scriptures; for proofe whereof, that one saying of the Apostles is sufficient; The whole scripture, is given by inspiration of God, and is profitable to teach, to improve, to correct, and to instruct in righteousness.

Having established this principle, Hieron used it to condemn ceremonies and worship devised by human agents: 'that is called an addition to the Word of God, which being commended unto men as a matter of religion, cannot be justified, nor warranted, nor made good by the written word'.[49] To suggest that aspects of worship and ceremonial practice not sanctioned by scripture could be 'made good' amounted to a rejection of the doctrinal grounds of 'things indifferent'. Moreover, Hieron's reference to 'manners' suggested

---

[47] Samuel Hieron, *A defence of the ministers reasons, for refusall of subscription to the Booke of common prayer, and of conformitie* ([Amsterdam?, 1607–8]), *3.

[48] Ibid., pp. 8, 11.

[49] Samuel Hieron, 'The Dignitie of Scripture', in *The sermons of Master Samuel Hieron*, p. 73.

that the outward form of worship had at all times to receive confirmation from scripture, rather than being derived from 'custom'.

While Hieron's sermons made no specific mention of the controversy over subscription that dominated his other works, they nevertheless offered important insights into the reformist position. Hieron conceived of the Church as an institutional manifestation of the pattern laid out in scripture. Although differing from conformists on crucial issues, he also thought of the Church in corporate terms, but as a corporation made by God and not by men: 'it must needes be an absolute and entire body, without any superfluity or defect, and containe the most necessary and exact form of doctrine, seeing that God is the author of it, who both in his wisdom knew what was convenient'. In a second sermon on scripture, Hieron explained the importance of the Word as a model. The body spiritual could only survive if its fundamental elements were in good order:

> Understand, therefore, that the writing of the Word, was, and is, for the Good of the Church in this respect, even that it may have one certaine and infallible rule, by which all doctrine may be tried, all controversies in religion decided, all doubts resolved, and every conscience firmly grounded and settled in God's truth.

For Hieron, the Word was the conduit that linked the church in his time with its most ancient beginnings; it was through the Word that God spoke to His people. Hieron's argument did not entail a repudiation of the importance of either antiquity or scholarship; rather, he sought to emphasise the testimony that confirmed the practice of the earliest churches. Human commentators were to be set aside: 'for the bookes of Moses are more Ancient than any humane writers, in that they set down a history from the beginning of the world, a thing which other writers knew not of, or else borrowed from Moses, or else, corrupted with many fables, and ridiculous narrations'.[50] For Hieron, the scriptures were more ancient, and thus more accurate than any other writings. Rather than having no sense of or interest in history, then, Hieron can clearly be seen instead to have embraced a different set of historical sources – for him, scripture and history were one and the same.

Shortly after the appearance of Hieron's tract in defence of the ministers, a conformist statement about the 'general rules' of scripture was published. This took the form of a sermon preached in 1605 and published in 1607 by Francis Mason, Archdeacon of Norfolk.[51] Mason's argument was based on the assumption that the Church of England was fundamentally different in nature from the other reformed churches, and that this difference justified its

---

[50] See ibid., p. 77; 'The Second Sermon – the necessity of writing the scripture', in *The sermons of Master Samuel Hieron*, p. 79.

[51] Francis Mason, *The avthoritie of the Chvrch in making canons and constitutions concerning things indifferent, and the obedience thereto required* (London, 1607). A second edition appeared in 1634 and a third in 1705.

ceremonies and the means by which they were enforced. Here again, the argument turned on the notion that 'decent' ceremonial practice promoted order in the Church. Mason defended the disputed ceremonies as 'honest' and 'decent', and the surplice as a 'garment comely in the public administration'. The unifying concept was 'order' and Mason employed it as a prohibition of religious disorder. He thus spoke of bees, cranes, storks, and other classical metaphors associated with the idiom, as well as the figure of the body politic. The result was a reiteration of the definition of the Church as a political association, with an hierarchy of religious offices. It was also a warning against 'private fancy': 'every man must keep his own ranke, and therein proceed according to order'.[52] As we have seen, Presbyterian 'parity' furnished conformists with the opportunity to reaffirm both the sovereignty and hierarchy of the Church. Mason most probably had these debates in mind. Frequently noted in the margins of the sermon was one 'T. C.', presumably Thomas Cartwright, the father of English Presbyterianism. Quoting Cartwright's injunction that the Church of England should seek to emulate the 'best reformed Churches', Mason proffered an argument for the sovereignty of a national church: 'Yet we cannot but marvel that Men will urge us to Conformity with Foreign Churches to which we owe no subjection, and will not conform themselves to their own Mother the Church of England, in whose bosom they live, and whereof they are members.' Instead of offering a pattern to be emulated, the reformed churches reflected a broad variety of practices, and so Mason asked 'whose pattern shall we follow?' It was a rhetorical question, for the Church of England was bound to the state, and the stability of this relationship was more important than were minor departures from the worship of other churches:

> For there is a great difference between a popular State and an absolute Kingdome: Between small Territories and ample Dominions: Between the schoole of Geneva and the renowned Universities of Oxford and Cambridge. Neither is any Man to be offended with the Diversity of Ceremonies in divers Countries: for as Socrates declareth, those ancient Churches which embraced the same Religion had notwithstanding variety of ceremonies.[53]

Mason argued that it was perfectly appropriate for the Church to frame its Canons 'according to the general Canons of Holie Scripture', and while assembled in a 'sacred synod'. Yet this consensus, and by implication the sovereignty of the Church, was endangered by those among the ordinary clergy who attacked the Church and its liturgy, and who opened the door to religious competition that might undermine ecclesiastical polity:

---

[52] Ibid., pp. 9, 11, 15, 21–3.   [53] Ibid., pp. 43, 44.

[The Papist] deviseth and plotteth to undermine both Church and Commonwealth, while we are contending with one another. And as you rejoice the Papists, so you encourage the Brownists, who build their conclusions upon your premises, and put your speculations in practice. For have not your ringleaders proclaimed that our Government by bishops is popish, our liturgie popish, our ministering of baptism with the cross popish, our kneeling at the communion popish; our garments for publicke administration, popish … and almost everything Popish?[54]

Here was a further conformist justification of ceremonial practice based on the premise that stability and order took precedence over the purity of doctrine.

None other than Samuel Hieron quickly answered Mason. Once again, Hieron objected to the laxity with which conformists treated the scriptures and vigorously attacked the proposition that the Word contained 'general rules' which could be embellished by human agents.[55] The scripture glossed by Mason's sermon: 'Let all be done decently and in order', left a degree of latitude for what constituted 'order' and 'decency', and privileged institutional stability above the purity of doctrine.[56] Hieron aimed his rabbinical grasp of the scriptures at this argument, and identified two potential problems stemming from a liturgy made up of a combination of divine and human ordinances: first, the 'simple' would be led to follow 'false' doctrine, splitting the Church from within, and second, this would lead to incursion by sects, whether Protestant or Catholic. With respect to antiquity, Hieron argued that the question was 'not whether it be or hath been used at all, but whether it be or hath been well used'.[57] Yet this was no endorsement of 'decency' or 'comliness', but rather a warning to the ordinary clergy to beware of being led into error and to reject the modes of rites and governance set forth in the Canons of 1604. Hieron urged his readers to disavow the established liturgy in order to protect the peace of the Church:

The Truth is, that these Apocryphal writings contain in them many corruptions and lies; and so taken and proved by the learned in the ages past and present, which howsoever we read to you, for instruction in manners, as we were appointed by our Bishops: *yet you must not beleeve nor receive them*, for in truth they corrupt good manners; we therefore beseech you Bretheren, have care of your own safety, take heed of yourselves, that you beleeve not these lies and corrupt instructions, which for the love we beare for the Peace of the Church.[58]

---

[54] Ibid., p. 67.

[55] Samuel Hieron, *The second parte of the defence of the ministers reasons for refusal of subscription & conformitie to the book of common prayer* ([Amsterdam?, 1608]).

[56] 1 Corinthians 14: 40.

[57] Hieron, *Second parte of the defence*, pp. 13–25 passim, 41.

[58] Ibid., p. 241. In an undated sermon, 'The Platform of Obedience', Hieron proposed another argument for giving obedience only to God: 'In a word, let every man enter secretly between God and his own soule into a vow, that hereafter he will devote all the intention of his minde, all the strength and power of his body, first to the understanding, and next to the practice and execution of those holie duties, which God hath ordained, that we shall walk in them.' *The sermons of Master Samuel Hieron*, p. 340.

Hieron issued the final part of his *Defence* triptych in 1608. His *Dispute* was written in response to Covell, Hutton, and Sparke, and also sought to defend the arguments put forth in the *Abridgment*. Hieron offered a sweeping criticism of the controversial methods employed by his opponents:

To produce scripture and antiquity, for the clearing of questions Theologicall, is an approved course. They have, for them, neither: against them, both the one and the other ... they also have against them the judgement of our moderne writers also, and the custome of the best reformed Churches. Concurrence with them in opinion and practice (some Lutheran churches excepted) they have none, but for the antichrist of Rome, and his devoted Synagogues.[59]

Hieron offered a different reading of the ancient pattern of the church, one that proposed a doctrinal history that was distinct from that claimed by Canterbury and Rome. He therefore conceived of the church as an immemorial body of laws that defined the connection between the church established by Christ and its earthly descendant, and which possessed its own 'custom' in both opinion and practice. As a point of doctrine, kneeling could not be found in the ancient church – hence, it must have been introduced at some later point; that is, it was human, rather than of divine institution. Once again, we see that 'custom' could be employed in several ways, whether being dismissed as the work of men, or celebrated as the divine pattern left in the scripture and emulated by the reformed community. Reformists could therefore exploit the Catholic church as an example of the latter kind of 'custom', and thereby dismiss the conformist case as a similar error:

What hath not the plea of ancienter birth and greater age, then from the term and poynt of 300 or 400 years, is, in cases of divinity and religious exercises, reputed an infant or novelty; rather than an antiquity, and that which is of long standing. If we shall peruse the story of the Church, from Christ to that Antichrist Pope Honorius the 3, and from him to the time wherein the decree of the said Pope for a reverent inclination to the Sacrament ... we shall find that kneeling at the Sacrament, was not intertayned into observation and practise as a received and allowed gesture in the Church, not much above 300 yeares since ... it was not received into use, either at the Institution, or afterwards for the space of 1220 yeares.[60]

To kneel at communion, Hieron noted, was to leave the 'imitable practice of Christ', a departure that represented 'an inconformity to the Lord's will'. The definition of the church offered in Hieron's pages emphasised an immemorial collection of practices, established first by Christ and then passed on to the Apostles. The rise of Roman idolatry represented the nadir of the ancient church, and the initial departure from the first institution. Here was the doctrinal crux of Hieron's argument against kneeling at communion: since it was not known to Christ or the primitive and Apostolic churches, and since the

[59] Samuel Hieron, *A dispute vpon the question of kneeling, in the acte of receiving the sacramentall bread and wine, proving it to be unlawfull* ([London: W. Jones' secret press], 1608), ¶3.
[60] Ibid., p. 139.

Church of England had labelled it 'indifferent', it was no great matter to refuse subscription: 'that upon our lawfull refusal to kneele at the sayd Supper, we may therefore lawfully disobey some commandement of the King and Church under his Government in matters indifferent'.[61] Hieron urged his readers to consider the laws of God and the laws of men, and to obey the former.

The same message – with a crucial departure – was put forth by Thomas Draxe, in the *Lambes spouse*.[62] Following Henry Jacob's conception of a gathered church of free Christians, Draxe sought to portray the Church as contiguous with its divine founder, 'and the Church being ingrafted unto him, draweth and receiveth the same from Him by the hand and instrument of faith'. Here again we find the reformist argument that posited the immemoriality of true doctrine and the first institution. One could recognise the church of the first institution, continued Draxe, if one could detect an agreement between belief and ceremonial practice: 'for then undoubtedly we have that faith [that] engrafteth us unto Christ, and saveth our soules'.[63] The central purpose of Draxe's work was to contribute to the literature on the ceremonial practice of the Church, and so accompanying his tract was an appendix, 'touching the doctrine, nature and use of the Sacraments'. This brief work was modelled after catechisms of the period, and took the form of a dialogue between master and pupil.[64] In one exchange, the discussion turned toward salvation:

Q: Are the Sacraments necessary to Salvation?

Ans: Yes, for first God in his wisdom and mercy hath instituted them to that end, and hath also commanded them to be used. Secondly, by the refusal and contempt of them, we declare ourselves to bee none of Christ's disciples, of whom these sacraments are badges.[65]

This was a seemingly contentious statement, which implied a special place for the Church and its clergy in the process of salvation. It has been argued that this posture toward the doctrine of grace may have contributed to suspicions of Arminianism among the high clergy of the Jacobean Church.[66] Yet

---

[61] Ibid., pp. 43, 165.

[62] In addition to the work considered here, Draxe published scriptural commentaries; a work of devotion in two volumes, *The Christian armourie* (1611); a Latin phrase-book, *Colliepeia* (1607, 1625, 1631); and a book of adages, *Bibliotheca scholastica instructissima* (1616).

[63] Thomas Draxe, *The lambes spouse or the heauenly bride* (London, 1608), sigs. B^{2v}, F^{2v}.

[64] For a study of sacramental catechisms, see Ian Green, *Print and Protestantism in early modern England* (Oxford, 2000), pp. 288–304. This literature suggests that there was potential for a wide-ranging debate over the doctrinal premises of the sacrament, and this supposition is confirmed by catechisms that, claimed their authors, were 'necessary for these times'. See [Anon], *Motives to godly knowledge* (London, 1613), and Charles Richardson, *The doctrine of the Lords supper* (London, 1616).

[65] Draxe, 'An Appendix or necessary addition, touching the doctrine, nature and use of Sacraments', in *The lambes spouse*, n. p.

[66] See Fincham, *Prelate as pastor*, pp. 248–93.

Draxe's tract seems to have passed without notice, although in the Bodleian copy a contemporary hand provided a correction to the passage cited above: 'only generally necessary'.[67] Moreover, Draxe's silence on the issue of what posture should be adopted by communicants seemed to depart from the key issue in the debate on the ceremonial practice of kneeling at communion. Where others suggested that it be received 'with reverence' (and hence kneeling), Draxe simply noted that communion should be received 'very often'.

Draxe's position was rare, but by no means was it unique. Richard Gawton, perhaps a preacher in the county of Hereford, published a single work on the question of ceremonial practice. It took the form of a dialogue between master and pupil, and considered the sacrament of the Lord's Supper within the context of the definition of the true church. Gawton described a gathered church in the manner of Draxe and, while avoiding the issue of kneeling, linked the church and its sacraments with the process of salvation:

Q: What are you taught to believe concerning the Church?

A: I am taught three things. First, that God hath a Church or company of people whom he hath gathered to himselfe by the preaching of the gospel through all the worlde, John 17.64.20. and therefore is called the Catholicke or Universall, and Holy; for that as God himselfe is Holy, so holinesse becommeth his House. 1 Peter 1.16. Secondly, that this Church is the Spouse of Christ, who gave himselfe for it, that he might sanctifie it, &c. Eph. 5.25.26.27. And thirdly, that in this Church there is a communion, or spiritual partaking of all giftes and graces both of soule and body, 1 Cor. 12.4.5.6. And that the onely true members of this Church are assured of the forgiveness of their sinnes by Christ.[68]

Here we find a clear statement that salvation depended on membership in, and communication with, the universal church, which was defined as a gathered spiritual community that preached the Word. This resembled Henry Jacob's dictum that the true church comprised 'one ordinarie congregation (and no more) having power in itselfe (by the free consent of the members thereof) to administer all their spiritual affaires and government'. It was these points of 'matter and forme', Jacob continued, in which 'a visible political Church differeth essentially from a Diocesan, Provincial or Universall Church politicall'.[69] While Gawton noted that the church was 'universal', he defined it as a spiritual preaching association, rather than an hierarchical episcopal church. It would be unwise to impute undue

---

[67] Bodl. Mason AA 54.

[68] Richard Gawton, *A short instruction for all such as are to be admitted to the Lords Supper* (London, 1612), sig. B[3v].

[69] [Henry Jacob], *A collection of sundry matters ... appointed by God for his visible church spiritually politicall* (1616), sig. A[3r].

significance to the works of Draxe and Gawton – neither sought to contribute directly to the debates with which we have been concerned. However,
their work suggests that English Protestants were far from unanimous on the
relation between the Church as an institution and the rites and ceremonies
that defined it. What Draxe and Gawton shared with reformists was the idea
that salvation could be found only through communication: for both writers,
the Lord's Supper constituted a central note of the Church, a commemora-
tion of its founding, and a sure tie to its Founder. However, in emphasising
the place of ceremonies in the process of salvation, they seemed to imply an
enhanced role for the ministry, and thus less to the doctrine of double
predestination.

One of the more important contributions to the debate on ceremonial
practice does not appear to have been written in response to a particular
work. John Gordon, who held his Doctorate of Divinity from Oxford and
who had been present at the Hampton Court conference, was perhaps best
known as the author of a sermon celebrating the Anglo-Scottish union.[70] In
1612 he published *EIPHNOKOINΩNIA*, which argued that the process
of reform that defined English Protestantism was notable for having restored
the ceremonies of worship to their 'originall use'.[71] Indeed, the theme of the
work was the 'conversion' of ceremonies formerly the preserve of pagan
worship, and their restoration to sound usage as revealed by the teaching of
scripture and the example of the ancient church. Gordon posited the 'reform'
of idolatrous ceremonies as part of the historical identity of the church, and
portrayed it as a process sanctioned by divine warrant. For example, he
offered the case of Egypt:

> Seeing that God ordained the ceremonies, with which the Israelites were accustomed
> when they did worship the Idols of Egypt, to be used in His owne worship, it follows,
> that these customs and ceremonies, as also the Material things that were abused to
> Idolatry ... may lawfully be converted to some use in the true worship of God,
> according to these examples of the ceremonial Law.[72]

Gordon sought to establish an historical precedent that provided a sound
doctrinal and historical case for the power of the Church to establish
ceremonies. Sensitive to the charge that kneeling at communion was a
hallmark of Roman idolatry, Gordon presented evidence for the

---

[70] John Gordon, *England and Scotlands happinesse: in being reduced to vnitie of religion, vnder
our invincible monarke King Iames* (London, 1604). In that sermon, Gordon sought to
connect James VI and I with history's greatest Christian emperor: 'Whereby it appeareth
that the religion which your Magesty hath established in your realmes, is conformable to that
of your predecessor Constantine' (p. 27).

[71] John Gordon, *EIPHNOKOINΩNIA. The Peace of the communion of the Church of
England* (London, 1612), sig. Bᵛ.

[72] Ibid., sig. B²ʳ.

'conversion' of pagan modes of worship to sound usage as part of 'true worship'. Here 'custom' took on a new form, as the intervention of human agents was portrayed as something designed for the ultimate benefit of the Church, and the restoration of pure doctrine from a previously corrupt state.

For Gordon, the link between ceremonies and scripture had been temporarily severed by the Church of Rome, the most flagrant example of the conquering of the law of God by the law of man. It was this point that in turn allowed him to portray the English Church as having restored the ceremonial practices of the Apostles to proper use. The Roman Church had corrupted even those ceremonies established by the 'first institution': 'the Externall Ceremonies, as well as cloathing, as others, which are used in the Church of England, were first instituted to be used in the service of the True Religion, but afterward was violently employed by the Popes, after they became Temporal tyrants'.[73] Here Gordon sought to portray the church of the first institution and the Church of England as sharing a mode of ceremonial practice. Against this institutional harmony he contrasted the rise of the corrupt Church of Rome, and blamed the papacy for driving the true church into the wilderness. This represented a reversal of the argument which reformists aimed at their opponents, and vindicated diocesan bishops from the charge that they had corrupted the purity of doctrine. To drive the point home, Gordon offered a defence of the surplice on Apostolic grounds: 'the Apostles did continue in the establishment of the Christian Religion, the use of the white Garment in the Church service; notwithstanding that they knewe well that it was before their time, abused to the service and worship of idols'. Having reformed and converted the wearing of a surplice-like garment to sound usage, the Apostles could be said to have 'instituted' its use under newly prescribed rules. Hence, 'the use of the white garment is an Institution Apostolic ... it followeth, that the use of it in our Church services in England, hath for the warrant thereof the authority of the Holy Apostles of Christ'.[74] Here, the concept of 'custom' was bolstered by the claim that it possessed an Apostolic pedigree.

Gordon organised his second argument, that concerning kneeling, around the concept of 'custom' and cited passages from the New Testament that described Christ's posture at the Last Supper as a guide to the customs of the times in which the Gospels were written. This allowed him to separate what was enjoined by divine command from what could be attributed to 'custom'. For example, when 'lying at table' Christ 'did use the gesture ... which was in use before his time'. Ancient sources affirmed that the recumbent posture had been the custom of the Jews, and the Last Supper signified the moment at

---

[73] Ibid., sig. B³ᵛ.   [74] Ibid., sigs. B³ʳ–B⁴ᵛ, Cᵛ.

which Christians adopted the practice.[75] This moment also happened to coincide with the founding of the faith itself. With the rise of Rome, the custom of lying was exchanged for the custom of kneeling; hence the association of kneeling with the Roman confession meant that it was tainted by idolatry. Like Christ and the Apostles before them, however, the English reformers merely adopted this custom of kneeling and restored it to sound usage:

> The Reformers did well to restore the true Olde masse, which is our Communion, and did well to retaine the gesture of kneeling, as it was in the olde Masse of the Communion, and although the Papists doe abuse kneeling in the Idolatrous adoration of the Sacrament, it is lawfully restored to the invocation of God by Christ ... even as Christ himselfe, and his Apostles, and the Christians in the Primitive Church did use.[76]

The polemical purpose of Gordon's piece was to draw links between the ceremonial practice of the Church of England, and the 'true Olde masse' celebrated by Christ and the Apostolic churches. Gordon suggested that by restoring formerly idolatrous customs to sound usage, the Church of England was partaking in an ongoing process of reformation that linked it to both Christ and the ancient church. Rather than an argument based on an uninterrupted history of ceremonies, Gordon's work presented an analysis of various points in the history of the church when a corrupt ceremony was restored to sound usage. In this scheme, the demise of the Apostolic church paralleled the rise of the papacy and helped to define an era of corrupt rites and ceremonies. Like Christ, the reformers took a corrupt ceremonial practice, restored it to sound usage, and implemented it as part of true worship. Hence, gestures that once stood as badges of idolatry became signs of reverence and edification, rather than arbitrary customs imposed by human agents.

Robert Bruce, one-time moderator of the General Assembly of Scotland and a staunch opponent of episcopacy furnished a further consideration of the doctrinal and historical case of the sacraments of the Church. As we have seen, common to conformist defences of ceremonial practice was the suggestion that the scripture contained only 'general rules' by which rites and worship were to be ordered. *Adiaphora* constituted the gap between what the scripture enjoined and what the Church established by its authority. In sermons that treated 'preparation' for the sacraments, Bruce overturned this

---

[75] So went the narrative. In terms of the substantive aspects of the case, Gordon left room for 'things indifferent': 'Christ exorteth his Disciples [Matt 6: 9; Luke 11] often to pray and teacheth them the form of prayer, which we call the Lord's Prayer: but he doth not prescribe any particular gesture of the body to be used when we pray, so that he did leave the gesture to be observed according to the order and custom of the Church' (sig. E^{4v}).

[76] Ibid., sig. F^{2r}.

argument by suggesting – *pace* Henry Jacob – that there could be no separation of Word and practice:

> Therefore the Word onelie cannot be a Sacrament, nor the Element only, cannot be a sacrament; but the word and element conjunctly, must make a sacrament. And so Augustine said well, let the Word come to the element, and so yee shall have a sacrament. So then, the Word must come to the element: that is, the Word preached distinctly, and all the parts of it opened up, must go before … the sacrament; and the Sacrament as a seale must follow, and so be received accordingly.[77]

Bruce's argument was guided by the assumption that the 'true' church could only be found in the unspoiled 'essential forme' prescribed by scripture, and that it was contiguous with the practice of true doctrine, rites, and ceremonies. Bruce posited the decline of the sacraments within a broader conception of the decline of the church in its Latin and Roman settings. In both cases, the adoption of ceremonies not found in the Word meant the departure of the church from its ancient exemplar. It was this point which led Bruce to offer a definition of the church: 'Then the Scriptures call [Christ] a spiritual head, as they call us a spiritual body: and, as the life which wee get from Him is spiritual … therefore he is called a spiritual head: therefore he is called the head of His Church, because he furnisheth her with spiritual motion and senses, which is the life of the Church.'[78] Here was a further parallel with the work of Henry Jacob: the Church, if it was to be designated as a 'true' church, had to be a literal embodiment of its founder, and had its continued life in the sound practice of pure doctrine and ceremonies.

Christopher Sutton, Canon of Westminster and, from 1618, Canon of Lincoln, furnished similar connections between ceremonial practice and the ancient church. Here was a cleric whose sympathies would seem to have run in the mainstream of conformist opinion, yet in a tract published in 1616 he expressed concern about the implications of the conflict over ceremonies. The controversy whose origins he traced to the *Abridgment* threatened to shatter the uniformity and stability of the Church of England which, he argued, had to align itself with a singular rule of faith, 'that by the old way unto the good way, by the first institution unto the best institution, all that are in doubt, all that erre, may more easily care for to attaine and enjoy the same, which Almighty God promised unto the people of Israel'.[79] Sutton reminded his readers that the Doctors and Councils did not supersede the scripture, which he portrayed as the court of final appeal; hence his

---

[77] Robert Bruce, *The mysterie of the Lords Supper. Cleerly manifested in five sermons; two of preparation, and three of the Sacrament it selfe* (London, 1614), sig. 4^{v-r}.

[78] Ibid., pp. 31^v, 63^v.

[79] Christopher Sutton, *Godly meditations upon the most holy sacrament of the Lords Supper … with a short admonition touching the controuersie about the holie eucharist* (London, 1616), pp. 347–8.

portrait of the church emphasised its continuity in the Word, rather than its visible or scholastic elements: 'By this we see the means of seeking out the truth, which is, how that the Fathers look back to the Apostles, the Apostles to Christ, Christ to the prophets, the Prophets to the Lawes, the Lawe to the first pattern upon the Mount.'[80]

Sutton's call for order, combined with his assertion that the true church had its being in the Word, pointed up a fundamental tension in conformist arguments on ceremonial practice. To be recognised as a true church, the Church of England had to reflect its doctrinal and historical connections with the early Christian and Apostolic institution. Yet it was also a state church, professing a uniformity of doctrine and public worship, and reserving the right to establish means by which both worship and conformity might be promoted. The question was whether these elements of the English confession could be defended on doctrinal and historical grounds, and it was the reformist refusal to accept that they could that continued to drive the debate. In addition, conformists had available to them a limited number of argumentative options, and so, as we have seen thus far, the notion of 'custom' and the question of the interpretation of history and scripture were themes that continued to shape the debate.

COMPETING FOR THE REFORMED TRADITION: THE DEBATE ON MORTON'S *DEFENCE*

Thomas Morton's defence of conformist ceremonial practice touched off the most substantial controversy about ceremonies in the late Jacobean period. Morton's book produced a reaction in England as well as in Scotland. Written as a belated response to the *Abridgment* issued from Lincoln diocese in 1605, the *Defence* made a vigorous attack on 'non-conformists' who denied the Church its 'liberty' to establish its mode of rites and governance. Morton sought to provide a doctrinal and historical defence of those aspects of rites and worship that were peculiar to the Church of England, and which reformists attacked as a corruption of the purity of the Word and the evidence of history. In order to mount a case against the rites and ceremonies established by the Canons of 1604, the *Abridgment* made exhaustive use of scriptural commentaries by the Doctors and Fathers, as well as contemporary works by both critics and defenders of the English Church.[81]

---

[80] Ibid., p. 349.
[81] Among the authors listed were Cyprian, Jerome, Hosius, Bellermine, Jewel, Hooker, Robert Horne, Rainolds, Bullinger, Zwingli, Thomas Cooper, Calvin, and Andrewes – nearly one hundred in all. See *An abridgment*, sigs. A³ʳ–A⁵ᵛ.

In particular, Morton singled out the text's misinterpretation of the Fathers, whose position on scripture he portrayed as justifying the conformist argument concerning 'things indifferent':

All these places of Fathers are taken *a scriptura negente*, that is, from Scripture forbidding the unlawfulness of such things, which are directly contrary to the will of God, revealed in Scripture; and not *a scriptura negata*, that is, from the Silence of the Scripture, in matters called in question only besides and not against Scriptures. Whence no solid argument can be made against Things Indifferent.[82]

Morton sought to defend 'things indifferent' as necessary to establish modes of worship that were neither condemned nor enjoined by scripture. Since the scriptures were 'silent' on kneeling at communion, it was impossible to condemn the practice based on the evidence of scripture.

The argument concerning the enforcement of things 'indifferent' was related to that concerning the sovereignty of the Church, that is, its power as a political body to establish laws where the scriptures were 'silent'. One of the most durable reformist arguments against the Church of England was that subscription and deprivation could not be defended with reference to scripture, the practice of the ancient church, or the example of contemporary reformed churches. Morton sought to dismiss reformist claims that English discipline had no sound doctrinal, historical, or reformed warrant, and so he sought to defend subscription and deprivation as both ancient and reformed:

Concerning the censures of the Church, you cannot be ignorant, that it hath been the common discipline in all Churches ancient, and lately reformed, to impose and challenge of Ecclesiastical persons with subscription to the orders constituted therein; ordaining that in the end such persons should be deposed from their places, that shall factiously oppose thereunto, to the disturbance of the peace of the Church.[83]

Here Morton sought to reinforce the doctrinal case for subscription and deprivation of non-conforming clergy. The implication of the argument was that the authority and laws of the Church were sovereign and complete in themselves, and free from the interference of other bodies. A further aspect of this sovereignty included the power to determine matters of doctrine and discipline, a power that Morton identified as being peculiar to the English Church. Indeed, like John Gordon, he argued that a mark of the Church's authority lay in its ability to 'restore' to sound usage those ceremonies previously corrupted by the Roman church. Although he did not use the

---

[82] Thomas Morton, *A defence of the innocencie of the three ceremonies of the Church of England. viz. the surplice, crosse after baptisme, and kneeling at the receiuing of the blessed Sacrament* (London, 1618), p. 14.
[83] Ibid., p. 45.

term, Morton's notion of 'custom' was defined by what was left behind once idolatrous ceremonies and practices were removed from the Church:

> But our Church, in her singular wisdom, as she hath most religiously dealt with the number of superstitious and Idolatrous rites in the Romish Church, which she hath abandoned; so hath she discretely ordered those ceremonies, which she thought goode to retaine, by removing only the abuses and Superstitions, and reforming them, either by Translation or else by Correction.[84]

As we have seen, reformists decried the disjunction between scripture and practice in the rites and governance of the English Church, and argued that this disjunction represented the evidence of that Church's apostasy, rather than a mark of its sovereignty. William Ames, in the first of two tracts written in response to Morton, argued that this disjunction signalled the departure of the Church of England from the perfection of the ancient model. Morton had claimed that there was an important distinction between matters of doctrine and ceremony: the first he designated as the realm of divine law, while the second was 'not the body, but the garment of religion'.[85] In other words, the ordering of the external element of religion was left to the liberty of the Church. Ames argued that this distinction between doctrine and ceremony was false: matters of ceremonial practice had to be derived from and limited by the 'substantial' form of divine law: 'For doctrinall opposed to ceremoniall in the formed signification of these words, I never heard of before ... Ceremoniall is opposed to Morall, and sometimes to substantiall; but to doctrinal it cannot properly, because there is ceremoniall doctrine as well as morall or substantiall.'[86] For Ames, all aspects of ceremonial practice had to be derived from scripture, but in the case of the Church of England there seemed to be a disjunction between the substantial doctrine of the Word and the outward practice of the Church. Ames' elision of the purity of doctrine with ceremonial practice amounted to an argument that disallowed either 'custom' – whether for edification or as an antidote to idolatry – or the suggestion that scripture contained both specific and general patterns for worship.

Of course, conformists continued to employ the concept of *adiaphora* to diffuse the question of the disjunction between doctrine and ceremony. Morton had taken the argument a little further by suggesting that the New Testament contained two patterns for establishing ceremonies and worship: those things directly enjoined by scripture, and those not so enjoined and hence left to the liberty of the Church. For Ames, this argument applied a

---

[84] Ibid., p. 134.　　[85] Ibid., p. 3.

[86] William Ames, *A reply to Dr. Mortons generall Defence of three nocent ceremonies. viz. the surplice, crosse in baptisme, and kneeling at the receiving of the sacramental elements of bread and wine* ([Amsterdam: Printed by Giles Thorp], 1622), sig. B[3v]; Keith Sprunger, *The learned Doctor William Ames* (Urbana, IL, 1972), esp. pp. 3–101.

false distinction to divine worship. In reality, all actions performed in God's name were sacred, and it was on this ground that Ames rejected the conformist argument about things 'indifferent': 'Beside neither Scripture, nor the Interpreters of Scripture, nor any good reason will allow, that there is any indifferent worship of God.'[87] The debate again returned to the church of the first institution, and the practice of the ancient and Apostolic churches; all confirmed that worship was either true or false. Reformists maintained that there had to be continuity between the church of the first institution and the contemporary institution, for all aspects of doctrine and ceremony were immemorial and could not be established as elements of 'custom'. With respect to this category, Ames argued that concerning the 'custom of the ancient Church', the 'best Writers' and other inheritors of the Apostles' doctrine would have been unwilling to add or subtract anything from divine worship, and it was up to those in later ages to follow this example. Returning to the problem of governance, Ames concluded that the episcopal government of the English Church also severed its link with the ancient church:

But if our ecclesiastical government be considered, and some ceremonies superstitious, we deny utterly, that we have such a reformation therein, as may represent the faith of the Primitive Church. Let the defender tell us ... If there were in the Primitive Church chancellors, commissaries, Officials under the Bishops, which executed the censures of the Church? If he can shew any primitive, pompous Bishops that had sole authoritie of Ordination and excommunication?[88]

Ames isolated two points central to the broader debate over subscription: not only were the ceremonies enjoined by the Canons of 1604 'superstitious', but the means by which they were enforced relied on an hierarchical mode of governance, rather than one defined by pastoral function. Neither practice could be found in the primitive church. The question posed by Ames concerned the identity of the reformed tradition, which he defined as being conspicuously free from an excess of human authority in the spiritual realm. For critics of the Church, the reformed tradition and the New Testament provided a model for the establishment of modes of governance and ceremonial practice, and early commentators and historians confirmed this model. The 'additions' of human agents and the layering of 'custom' on these foundations of belief represented further corruption of the perfection of the primitive church. In the case of the bishops, this corruption was carried on for purely political ends.

This latter point was given further development in the second instalment of Ames' response to Morton. Ames launched an attack on 'popery', a complex concept of great importance to the political understanding of

---

[87] Ames, *A reply to Dr. Morton's generall Defence*, p. 23.   [88] Ibid., pp. 54, 63–4.

Jacobean writers, and widely used in intra-Protestant controversies.[89] In the hands of reformist writers, the term *popery* was employed to denote both an historical corruption of the primitive perfection of the first institution, and the continuation of medieval patterns of worship, discipline, and governance in the reformed Church. Both of these elements appeared in Ames' second work. For the first, Ames revisited the writing of Martin Bucer, the reformed divine and Regius Professor of Divinity at Cambridge, who wished to see religion 'reduced to the first Apostolical simplicitie, as well in things externall as internall'. Ames invited his reader to judge who in the English Church had departed from this ideal: 'Now let any indifferent man judge, whether the Prelates, or we go further with M. Bucer. We follow him at his heeles ... The Prelates on the other side, let him go alone, or rather set themselves against him all the way.'[90] In thus setting themselves against a divine who was emblematic of the reformed tradition in England, the English bishops had, in effect, set themselves against the *entire* reformed tradition. Yet there was no mention of predestination in these works by Ames, nor did they show concern with the doctrinal aspects of the attainment of grace.[91] Rather, the argument turned on the axis of divine institution versus human invention, the mode of worship and governance enjoined by the scriptures and its subsequent corruption by human agents. Ames' response to Morton suggested that English Protestants were fundamentally divided on the historical identity of the church, and the implications of this identity for contemporary questions of ceremonial practice: 'Consider, that the reformed Churches about us can easily judge that this Ministry of the English bishops, by writing so offensive bookes to maintain mens devices in God's worship, is a ready way to bring in Popery.' Subscription leading to the deprivation of sound ministers was thus portrayed as a process not supported by either scripture or English law, but as an attempt by the bishops to defend their usurped sovereignty *within* the Church.

A second controversy over ceremonies was touched off by the publication of John Sprint's *Cassander Anglicanus*.[92] The purpose of the tract was to defend subscription and deprivation as part of the Apostolic heritage. Sprint

---

[89] For treatments of how 'popery' was employed as a political concept, see Peter Lake, 'Antipopery: the structure of a prejudice', in *Conflict in early Stuart England*, ed. Richard Cust and Ann Hughes (London, 1989), pp. 72–106; Mark Goldie, 'Ideology', in *Political innovation and conceptual change*, ed. Terence Ball, James Farr, and Russell Hanson (Cambridge, 1989), pp. 266–89.

[90] William Ames, *A reply to Dr. Mortons particular defence of three nocent ceremonies. viz. The surplice, crosse in baptisme, and kneeling at the receiving of the sacramentall elements of bread and wine* ([Amsterdam], 1623), p. 6.

[91] For a discussion of predestination in Ames' work, see Sprunger, *The learned Doctor William Ames*, pp. 127–52.

[92] There seems to have been no response to a sermon preached at Whitehall by John Buckeridge (*A sermon preached before His Maiestie at Whitehall, March 22. 1617. being Passion-Sunday, touching prostration, and kneeling in the worship of God* [London, 1618]).

departed from the question of the wider reformed tradition, and focussed on the particular problems of the English Church. From the point of view of many controversialists, it was necessary to show that an hierarchical and sovereign church was not merely a 'politicke device', but also in agreement with the doctrine and practice of the ancient church. There was a need for an historical pedigree for the type of church established by the Elizabethan settlement, and further bolstered by the Canons of 1604. Sprint maintained that since the church had been handed to the care of the Apostles, one could assume that the Apostolic office was defined by the ability to take disciplinary action: 'the Apostles by direction of the Holy Ghost, and upon reasons of common and perpetual equitie did freelie practise themselves, and caused others to practice, yea advised and enjoined'.[93] In the context of the debate on episcopacy, examined in the previous chapter, Sprint's contribution portrayed bishops as both pastors and prelates.

To illustrate the point, Sprint published a broadside, 'The Anatomy of the Controverted Ceremonies', which compared the Apostolic church to the Church of England. The purpose of the broadside was to illustrate the parallel conditions of the two churches, each disturbed by faction, and each choosing as a matter of policy to impose worship on a few for: 'the avoyding of offence, and such other conveniences accidentall, not inherent, neither purposed by Ceremonies in their Nature not evill, but merely Indifferent: the one bringing a public good to the whole Church, the inconvenience of the other but private to a few, who take offence, and in this case by their own default'.[94] Sprint portrayed non-conformity to the ceremonies in terms of an offence against the body politic of the Church, and contrasted 'private persons', 'noveltie', 'errors', and 'contentions' with the peace and stability of a uniform public profession.[95] The broadside did not simply offer a parallel history, or an argument for the historical pedigree of the disputed ceremonies. In order to argue that discipline was a 'note' of the church, Sprint furnished a case for the Apostolic pedigree of those measures designed to ensure conformity.

Sprint also included defences of the disputed ceremonies and of the office of bishops, and situated both within a carefully developed account of 'custom'. As had other conformist writers, Sprint sought to offer a distinction between those aspects of doctrine and worship that were enjoined by scripture, and those that were left to the judgement of the church. With respect to ceremonies, he argued that points of doctrine were either 'fundamental' or 'circumstantial': the former were found in scripture, while the latter

---

[93] John Sprint, *Cassander Anglicanus; shewing the necessity of conformitie to the prescribed ceremonies of our church, in case of depriuation* (London, 1618), p. 8.
[94] Ibid., p. 37.   [95] Ibid., pp. 40, 41, 75.

'included under General rules, and are left free to Every Church to bee determined as shall best serve for the edification thereof'. Within the 'general rules' dictated by scripture, sovereign churches could judge which ceremonies served as decent marks of reverence and 'helps' to edification. Sprint also argued that the institution of ceremonial practice should be left entirely in the hands of the bishops, and suggested that there was an ancient precedent for turning customs and traditions into law: 'some of the ancient Bishops, governing at severall times, in divers places, did commend the traditions, which they liked or fancied themselves, to their posteritie for lawes ... And their posteritie were no less superstitiously obsequious in observing, then they in prescribing'.[96] Here, Sprint assembled the examples of bishops in different times and places into a precedent for the English Church.

Sprint posited three types of tradition: those left to the church by Christ and set forth in the scripture; those 'not written, but delivered' (practice); and 'divers observations' particular to a time and place (custom). The first was the core of the first institution, while the second and third represented the additions of sovereign churches either through decisions made by councils or through the absorption and 'conversion' of corrupted practice to sound usage. Like John Gordon, Sprint argued that one of the marks of the Church of England's sovereignty was its ability to restore 'usurped and abused' ceremonies to sound usage and that this ability was part of the glue that held the Church together: 'if disputation bee once admitted on the one side, from the divers custom of some Churches, to condemne others in these Ceremonies, there will arise *interminat a luctatio*, a boundless struggling or contention'.[97] Here again, the uniformity of public doctrine and the stability of the Church as an institution took precedence over the purity of doctrine.

The later stage of the debate on ceremonies reveals the staying power of early Jacobean texts. Where Thomas Morton's *Defence* had looked back to the *Abridgment*, another tract of 1618 took the form of a defence of the Millenary Petition against the *Answere* issued by the Oxbridge divines. The book, 118 pages in length, was anonymous and its author maintained that it had 'laid hid' for twelve years.[98] A dig at John Sprint's *Cassander Anglicanus* (published in 1618) suggests that, whatever the fortunes of the manuscript, it was brought up to date before publication. In spite of this, it reflected earlier concerns and its margins were filled with commentary on books that dominated learned debate in 1606. Among these was *Basilikon doron*, in which

[96] Ibid., pp. 81, 92.   [97] Ibid., pp. 98–9, 100.
[98] Babbage examined a manuscript version of the tract, which was published in 1618 by William Brewster and Thomas Brewer of Leiden. See Babbage, *Puritanism and Richard Bancroft*, pp. 54–6; Keith Sprunger, *Trumpets from the tower: English puritan printing in the Netherlands, 1600–1640* (Leiden, 1994), p. 214.

James VI and I had professed his commitment to reformation, and which reformists cited to prove that this commitment had been undermined. The bulk of the text dealt with the character of reformed doctrine as it applied to the rites and governance of the English Church. Also considered was the problem of 'things indifferent', which, if they truly were *indifferent*, could be set aside without much difficulty: 'Then seeing the removing of these cere- monies will be no offense of conscience to those that hold them indifferent, and yet the retaining of them will grieve the consciences of many good Christians that take them not to be such: we humbly beseech your excellent Magesty to take away these occasions of stumbling.'[99] To address the King in this way was a clever tactical move, for it served to remind the reader that it was the Crown in parliament, rather than the bishops, which constituted the supreme law-giving authority over the Church. It also affirmed a principal tenet of the reformist position on the political aspect of the English Church: the King was a 'nursing father' whose power of censure was legitimate provided that it was employed for the preservation of true doctrine.

This last point served to set the stage for the argument against subscrip- tion, especially to rites not enjoined by the scriptures. There was no attempt on the part of the author to deny that subscription was a mark of the sovereignty of the Church. Rather, the whole process of subscription was described in historical terms, as a policy to ensure conformity to the Word, rather than obedience to the laws of men: 'This forcing of subscription to Ceremonies not warranted by the Word, is contrary to the Scriptures and practice of the Church: In Nehemiah's time Subscription was required, and an oath of the Cheefe of the people; but it was only to walke in God's law: *Neh. 10: 29*, not to keepe any traditions not written.'[100] Hence, the author rejected neither the programme of subscription nor its yoking with a profes- sion of allegiance to the Crown. Rather, he objected to the enforced observa- tion of ceremonies and points of doctrine that had no pedigree in scripture. The argument turned on the pivot of the irrefutable requirements of God versus the traditions of men. Therefore, in a manner common to reformist tracts examined thus far, the sovereignty of the Church was redefined in terms of the preservation of ancient and God-given doctrine, rather than its corruption with traditions, customs, and the trappings of human invention. It was this assumption that guided the argument concerning the *ex officio* oath of subscription enjoined by the thirty-sixth Canon: 'We hope your Majesty seeth, what just cause the Petitioners had to move, that the othe *Ex officio* be more sparingly used.'[101]

---

[99] [Anon], *A true, modest, and iust defence of the petition for reformation, exhibited to the Kings most excellent Maiestie* ([Leiden], 1618), p. 6.
[100] Ibid., p. 137.   [101] Ibid., pp. 225–6.

What united reformist contributions to the debate on ceremonies was a desire to address the separation of the purity of doctrine from the nature of ceremonial practice. Another reformist work of 1618 also took up the cudgels against human traditions. Thomas Dighton, a layman, argued that 'innovation' in religion posed a fundamental violation of the liberties of subjects and maintained itself through corrupt learning. Hence, it was a 'high presumption to tender any innovation by farre-fetcht devices and novelties, or some Old Tradition, or worme-eaten ceremony, full of incertainty, to the direct disabling of all sufficient truth, and offence of tender consciences'.[102] Not only did Dighton portray the disputed ceremonies as indefensible from the point of view of doctrine, but he also emphasised the political nature of subscription, itself a violation of the common law. The core of the argument contained an attack on the clergy who propped up the 'two corruptions [of] Incertaintie and Noveltie' by resort to subscription, which Dighton portrayed as a political device, whereby those who would not subscribe were 'perpetually imprisoned without bail or mainprize, onely because we do not in God's publicke worship conforme unto men's inventions'.

Dighton's treatment of the power of the clergy over one another and the laity explored the doctrinal implications of the defence of ceremonies penned by Draxe and Gawton. He argued that subscription and the ordination of ceremonies constituted a meddling with the free operation of grace – bishops now claimed a role in the salvation of other Christians, a position that violated the tenets of Calvinism. He moved from there to an attack on the bishops:

But is not this I pray you, some small parcel of the voice of the beast, yea is it not an apparent branch of his great blasphemie, to assume authoritie, to ordaine ceremonies and callings for the publicke worship of God, and to appropriate unto them holy and religious uses, and spiritual intentions, which power is onely proper and peculiar unto God himselfe; and yet even this divine authoritie doe they dare to assume, as their *jure divino* hath publicklie proclaimed.[103]

The 'assumed' power of the bishops trespassed on the realm of the divine. For Dighton, this represented both a doctrinal innovation and an assumption of power over sin and salvation – the sole province of God and the doctrinal bedrock of orthodox Calvinism. Dighton brought together, for the first time in the works examined thus far, a range of the issues that would divide English Protestants in the early seventeenth century: ceremonies, subscription, episcopacy, and Arminianism.

---

[102] Thomas Dighton, *Certain reasons of a private Christian against conformitie to kneeling in the very act of receiving the Lords Supper* ([Leiden], 1618), sig. A3v.
[103] Ibid., p. 73.

The link between ceremonial practice, subscription, and the Calvinist doctrine of grace was made in Dighton's *The second parte of a plaine discourse*, published in 1619. Here Dighton argued that the clerical hierarchy of the Church of England had, with 'wisdom, learning, and authority', departed from the 'practice of Apostolical Primitive Churches'. The bishops had erected a new sovereignty maintained by subscription and deprivation, and had enforced conformity to rites not sanctioned by scripture:

for without the warrant and commandment of the Word, subscription to or approbation of anything of divine use cannot be an act of the faith of God's elect, but of some other counterfeit faith, transformed I confesse into the likeness or appearance thereof ... or some other ... having dazzled their sight, or darkened their judgement, will by degrees lead them into the boggs and quagmires of Arminius his inherent grace, free will, or other like deceivable fables, and damnable errors.[104]

Of all the works cited so far in this study, this contained the first overt reference to the problem of Arminianism. The initial debates on ceremonies and subscription had dealt almost exclusively with the questions of antiquity and authority: were there ancient precedents for the sign of the cross, the wearing of the surplice, and kneeling at communion, and were there like precedents for a programme whereby they were enforced? Dighton, however, presented the question in terms of the stability of 'state and Church' – it became a battle for the Church, and a struggle to redeem its historical identity from doctrinal corruption and error. Not only was Dighton one of the first to raise the problem of Arminianism in the context of debates on ceremonies, he was also one of the first to blame the King and bishops for leading the Church into error[105]:

For the prevention whereof, they will teache and maintaine, preserve and defend the substance and foundation sound and sincere from error and corruption: and therefore though the Magistrate and Church do grievously sin in commanding, yet they in conformity to them, are mere patients, and not agents.[106]

This was a clear statement that the vaunted 'defenders' of the faith had abandoned their duties, and had introduced and subsequently defended patterns of rites and governance that were not part of the ancient identity of the church. Central to all of Dighton's works, then, was a definition of a church

---

[104] Thomas Dighton, *The second part of a plain discourse of an vnlettered Christian, wherein by way of demonstration hee sheweth what the reasons be which he doth ground upon, in refusing conformity to kneeling in the act of receiving the Lords Supper* ([Leiden, 1619]), sig. A⁴ʳ.

[105] The two problems were connected. There is little evidence that Dighton actually believed that a doctrinal tilt toward Arminianism was underway; rather, he sought to point to the doctrinal implications of an intrusive programme of conformity. See Fincham, *Prelate as pastor*, pp. 299–300.

[106] Dighton, *The second parte of a plain discourse*, pp. 35–6.

whose doctrine was descended directly from the scripture, and whose mode of governance was pastoral, rather than episcopal. This definition of the church in turn defined the offices and functions of its chief governors to preserve the purity of doctrine, and to guard against practices of human invention and the impostion of 'custom'.

John and Stephen Denison wrote two further works in the controversy over ceremonies. The latter is best known as the author of *The white wolfe*, a sermon preached at Paul's Cross in 1627. In 1621 Denison published *The doctrine of both the Sacraments*, which offered both a defence of sacraments based on the first institution, and an example of how the governors of the Church might justly order 'external' aspects of worship. Ceremonial practice was most pure at the time of the first institution, and the Church of England had departed from this purity:

> if you looke back to the first institution, you shall find your practise not agreeable thereunto, and therefore it is not good nor Christian. And certainly things in their first institution were the purest; Doctrine was most pure in the first preaching, to wit, out of the mouthes, and from the pennes of the Prophets and Apostles: the Sacraments were most free from corruption at their first administration.[107]

Not only were the sacraments examples of unsound doctrine, but the manner in which they were enforced suggested that the bishops had departed from the pastoral function described in the scriptures. Denison asked, '[W]hat hath one Minister authoritie to tyrranise over another, if we looke to the purest original, Christ saith, "It shall not be so among you, for you are brethren, etc"?' This was a clear argument against subscription and deprivation, combined with a definition of the sacraments that emphasised the purity of the first institution – we might hasten to identify Denison as a reformist of the mainstream. That position held that what was enjoined by scripture and the first institution was immemorial and unchangeable, and implied that the Church had no power to establish or alter the divine pattern. Denison suggested otherwise:

> But here it is to be noted, that a Minister is not bound to deliver the whole will of God at all times: hee must observe the circumstances of time and place. Christ delivered the whole will of His Father, but yet sometimes he did forebeare ... Again, the circumstances of place must also be observed: That Doctrine which is fit for one place is not fit for another.

Having offered a defence of 'circumstance' and hence custom, Denison then offered a case for the divinely ordained separation of scripture and practice: 'in matters substantiall and fundamental God hath reserved the power

---

[107] Stephen Denison, *The doctrine of both the Sacraments: to witte, Baptisme and the Supper of the Lord* (London, 1621), p. 53.

particularly to himselfe, as our onely lawgiver ... Yet in matters circum-
stantiall he hath left great power to His Church.'[108] Denison elaborated the
point about 'custom' by looking closely at the Jewish feast of Passover – itself
the model for the Christian celebration of the Eucharist, but clearly one that
the church had seen fit to modify:

> For in the first institution of the Lord's Supper, the Lord Jesus washed the feete of the
> Communicants. John 13.5. But the Church observeth no such ceremonies. In the first
> institution, Christ administered it in an upper chamber, Luke 22.11. but the Church
> administers it in the publicke assembly. At the first institution Christ and His
> Disciples eate and dranke at the Table, Luke 22.21 but succeeding Churches eate
> and drinke in their seates, or in any place of the Synagogue. In the first institution, the
> Sacrament was received sitting, or rather leaning, John 13.12, but in succeeding ages,
> It is received by some Christian Churches standing, or walking, as at Geneva: by some
> sitting as by the Dutch; and some kneeling, as by the English.

Here Denison pronounced on the central ceremonial question in the
Jacobean Church, and defended kneeling at communion as a mode of worship peculiar to the English Church, but nevertheless indifferent. Following
conformists such as William Covell, Denison concluded that the Church was
authorised to establish whatever 'circumstantial' matters of worship it saw
fit, provided this establishment contributed to 'order': '[Christ] hath left
many circumstantial matters unto the discretion of His spouse; alwaies
provided, that She observe the generall rule, that is, that all things be done
honestly, and by order.'[109] Taken as a whole, Denison's work offered a
doctrinal and historical justification for 'custom', *adiaphora*, and the ordering
of external elements of worship.

   The governors of the Church as 'custodians of order' was the theme of a
sermon preached by John Denison.[110] Following the Jacobean dictum
'blessed are the peacemakers', Denison argued that 'Peace is the nurse of
piety; by it Religion thrives and the Church flourishes.' Scripture stressed the
importance of peace in the church and supported those who filled the role of
peacemakers. Denison sought to provide a scriptural warrant for the legal
checks against those who refused to subscribe, and for condemning all those
who disturbed the order of the Church: 'There are some, who like
Salamanders, live in the fire of contention; that are never quiet within
themselves, but when they are at variances with others. Some there are that
are still sowing the seedes, and blowing up the coales of contention.'[111]
Central to the position was that 'order' was divinely ordained, while the
means by which it was established were left to the liberty of the Church.

---

[108] Ibid., pp. 55, 64, 70.   [109] Ibid., p. 72.
[110] The phrase is taken from Fincham, *Prelate as pastor*, p. 304.
[111] John Denison, *Beati pacifici: The blessednes of peace-makers: and the aduancement of Gods
children. In two sermons preached before the King* (London, 1620), pp. 15, 35.

Denison did not seek to examine the controversy in terms of the doctrinal principles of his opponents, and indeed a sermon preached before the King was an unlikely venue for such a discussion. A further contribution to the controversy was purposefully didactic: a sort of catechism on the question of kneeling and its doctrinal context. Like Thomas Morton, James Wats looked back to the *Abridgment* and defended the sovereignty of the Church to establish ceremonies and all other modes of worship: 'I think we should not contend that rites and ceremonies should be anywhere the same, but there must be this proviso, that all come as neere as may to the word of God; and that Edification (with decent order) may be furthered ... herein liberty was left to the choice of every distinct Church.'[112] Following Francis Mason in suggesting that the Church of England's sovereignty was complete and indivisible, Wats argued that it consisted in the establishment of 'circumstances ... for the further gracing and adorning' of the rites of worship. The key concepts here were 'edification' and uniformity: the former an indifferent 'help' to worship, the latter the governing precept of the stability of the Church defined as a political association. In a nod to the reformed tradition, Wats suggested that even Calvin advocated a uniform confession: 'Godly divines would not have contention or opposition, maintained in the Church for things indifferent, or that may be tollerated when they once are growne to be in use. M. Calvin saith, that diversity of rites and usages in one and the same Church well composed or ordered, is not tolerable.'[113] Wats therefore sought to align the ambitions of Jacobean conformity with those of the reformed tradition – order, decency, and edification were the standards by which the circumstantial aspects of rites and ceremonies were to be judged. Yet here too there lingered a tension between doctrine, history, and ceremonial practice. This tension flared up in a collection of works published after the death of James, and demonstrates the continuity of an issue whose history is traceable to the Elizabethan settlement.

THE JACOBEAN CHURCH AFTER 1625

The years following the death of James VI and I saw the publication of tracts that sought to continue the debate instigated by the *Abridgment*. A number of Jacobean tracts on 'things indifferent' formed the subject of a substantial work by Thomas Paybody, who set out to answer a number of texts from the controversies over subscription: the 1606 *Suruey* of the Book of Common Prayer, works by William Bradshaw, and William Ames' criticism of Thomas

---

[112] James Wats, *The controuersie debated about the reuerend gesture of kneeling, in the act of receiuing the holy communion* (London, 1621), sig. C3v–r.
[113] Ibid., sig. Fv.

Morton's *Defence*. Paybody argued that the scriptures contained no direct ordinance concerning gestures used in worship, and suggested that 'occasion' – a modified notion of custom – should be used as a guide:

> Wherefore commandments of gestures in prayer, and in other services much more, be limited to occasions; for like occasion ever happeneth not, and the judgement of such occasion is varied according to circumstances of abilitie, company, time, place, edification … there is no expresse and absolute commandment of any gesture.[114]

Citing with approval Gabriel Powel's tract, *De adiaphoris*, Paybody argued that where the scriptures were silent, then churches were 'free' to establish modes of worship 'without prohibition'.[115] Reformists countered that the enforcement of erroneous doctrine could not be justified. Samuel Hieron's *Dispute on the question of kneeling* had presented the argument that to 'forbeare' modes of worship that could not be found in the Word constituted 'an inconformity to the Lords will: and some derogation also from the wisdome of His spirit'.[116] Seizing on this passage, Paybody argued that the divine institution of scripture descended directly to the governors of the Church, whose ordinances represented an extension of divine law, and were to be obeyed on that ground:

> Constitutions are divine, either simply, or respectively; simply, when God immediately stamps them with his holie authoritie: respectively, when man sets his authority upon them, which God himself hath bestowed upon him in things of libertie, and indifferencie: in this sense all constitutions may be called divine, wherein the general rules of the Word be kept, whether they be of Ecclesiastical things, or civil. Now such constitutions do bind the conscience of men to a necessitie of obedience, as the lawful ordinances of a man in his own house do binde the consciences of his domesticks.[117]

Paybody's work sought to answer both the theological and political implications of the reformist case against 'custom'. In terms of the former, he argued that the 'libertie' of the Church was 'bestowed' by God, and that this implied that the ability to establish modes of worship and 'things indifferent' was a right granted *iure divino*. One aspect of this argument concerned the authority of the Church itself, which Paybody sought to assert against 'certain ignorant people'. Here he emphasised not only public worship, but also a vision of a national church that would be developed in controversies between English and Scottish writers:

---

[114] Thomas Paybody, *A iust apologie for the gesture of kneeling in the act of receiving the Lords Supper. Against the manifold exceptions of all opposers in the Churches of England, and Scotland* (London, 1629), p. 21.
[115] Ibid., pp. 21–6 passim. [116] Hieron, *A dispute vpon the question of kneeling*, p. 43.
[117] Paybody, *A iust apologie*, pp. 223–4.

As for the imputations of Puritans and Schismatics, so farre forth as the same be cast upon you for refusing to kneele, it is because you refuse and oppose the Church in a matter indifferent. For to strive against a National Church, and break the peace of it unjustly (as to break it about such mutable gestures in God's worship, as are truly indifferent both in nature and use is to break them unjustly) was ever held for a Schismatical course. [118]

There was no concession on Paybody's part to the doctrinal objections of his opponents, whom he portrayed as a group bent on toppling the Church. Much the same message was put forth in works by John Burges, an early opponent of Jacobean ceremonies, who nevertheless made peace with the Church and conformed. [119] In two tracts published during 1631, Burges set out to offer a doctrinal justification for the peculiar ceremonies of the Church of England. The first [120] took the form of a defence of Thomas Morton's tract and, in the course of 653 pages, offered a commentary on the controversy over ceremonies that was instigated by the publication of the *Abridgment*. Burges' main opponent in this work was William Ames who, it will be recalled, penned a substantial attack on Morton; Ames was also Burges' son-in-law. Hence, Burges urged conformity: 'for sure I am that God hath made you very capable of a settled station in the Church of England, unless your settled Resolution against her Discipline shall give impediment'. [121]

In a second work published during 1631, Burges set down the doctrinal case for the ceremonies of the Church of England. Like other conformist writers, he was sensitive to the fact that the ceremonial practice of the Church was under continual attack by reformists who argued that there could be no doctrinal case made for *adiaphora*. Moreover, like others among the Church's defenders, Burges sought to establish a link between English ceremonies and governance and the reformed tradition:

Whatsoever therefore in the worship of God, or Government of the Church, is not essential or Divine, but may be varied and disposed of, according to the generall rules of the Word; that wee call Matter of meere order in Contradistinction to matter of simple Necessity, whereunto the Conscience is bound; because in these things, nothing but obedience is left to the Church; but a power of *Disposing* (which is to order) is left to her in those things, to doe (according to the generall rules of the Word) therein,

[118] Ibid., p. 226.   [119] See Fincham, *Prelate as pastor*, p. 223.

[120] John Burges, *An answer reioyned to that much applauded pamphlet of a namelesse author, bearing this title: viz. A reply to Dr. Mortons generall defence of three nocent ceremonies, &c.* (London, 1631). In the epistle to the reader, Burges remarked that the work had been written in 1619; in a Dedication to Charles I, he noted that the time had come to vindicate Morton once and for all. This suggests that Morton's *Defence* was still available in print. Morton published a further tract on ceremonies in 1631: *Of the institution of the sacrament of the blessed bodie and blood of Christ, (by some called) the masse of Christ* (London, 1631).

[121] Burges, *An answer reioyned*, p. 51; Sprunger, *The learned Doctor William Ames*, p. 236.

whatsoever, saith Master Calvin, *The necessity of the Church shall require*, and Advantage in spiritual things. [122]

Here was an attempt to find ancient and reformed warrants for the institution of ceremonial practice in order to bind individual consciences, and thus preserve order in the Church. A number of marginal references testified to the controversies over ceremonies that followed the imposition of the Canons of 1604. But Burges' historical scope did not begin at 1604, which suggests that contemporaries both recognised and sought to promote continuities in the post-Reformation Church of England. Recalling a crucial Elizabethan controversy, Burges noted that:

in the first Admonition to the Parliament, they quarrelled at the frame and forme of our church-Orders; and, set down this rule, *whatsoever* is not commanded of God in his word may not be received in the Church. This, when Master Cartwright undertooke to defend against the late Archbishop, Doctor Whitgift.

Burges recognised that all post-Reformation disputes over doctrine and ceremony had been carried on according to the same precepts, and they defined a fundamental division among English Protestants over where the authority of the spirit ended – if it did at all – and where the customs of men took over. Second, there were the political consequences of continued religious conflict, and here Burges sounded an irenic note, asking 'whether it shall not be better ... to beare the use of those things, rather then to occasion the rending of the Church, the displeasure of our Governors, the stopping of our mouthes, the desolation of our flockes'. [123] Not seeking to defend things indifferent on doctrinal grounds, Burges instead emphasised the need to preserve the stability of the Church, even if this meant embracing elements of doctrine whose purity was not complete.

References to the Elizabethan setting also appeared in John Denison's *Heavenly banquet*. Burges had suggested that Thomas Cartwright affirmed the 'liberty left unto the Church in constituting matters of Order' – a clear attempt to co-opt one of the scions of reform to the support of the doctrine of *adiaphora*. [124] Similarly, Denison maintained that it was a matter of broad agreement that the Church possessed the sovereignty to order its own modes of worship and ceremonies:

The very quotation of learned divines for proofe of this proposition ... would fill many sheets of paper. Yea these things are so general and evident truths, that Master Cartwright himself saith, 'I know no man that ever denied, that the Church may make orders, in such things as are not specified, and precisely determined in the

---

[122] John Burges, *The lawfulnes of kneeling in the act of receiving the Lords Supper* (London, 1631), pp. 8–9. Italics in original.
[123] Ibid., pp. 44–5, 119–20. [124] Ibid., p. 44.

Word.' In which words he intimateth what are things indifferent; namely such things as are not specified, and precisely determined in the Word: and then, that the Church may determine or make orders concerning the same. [125]

Denison engaged in a very close reading of the scriptural evidence that described the posture of Christ at the Last Supper. His purpose was to cast doubt upon the reformist argument that this posture – consistently described as 'sitting' – represented a divine act, and thus constituted the first institution. Denison argued that while Christ may have sat at table to celebrate the Passover, his doing so also signified a break with Jewish custom and the establishment of a new feast of sacrifice:

> Thus Our Saviour might lawfully sit at the passover, as the Evangelists doe shewe he did. But that he sate at the institution of the Supper, they shewe not; Neither can it be by any passage of Scripture proved. Therefore, forasmuch as there is neither precept or precedent, concerning any gesture to be used in the Act of Receiving the Sacrament, and consequently it being a matter indifferent, the disposing thereof is in the power of the Church, who hath made the choise of kneeling, as the fittest and holy action. [126]

Denison's work reveals that at stake was a definitive account of what constituted the moment of the first institution. Moreover, it appeared that in exchanging a Jewish custom for a new practice, Christ Himself set the precedent for both the use and alteration of 'custom'. Similar accounts of the celebration of the Last Supper dominated controversies over kneeling at communion from 1604 onward. Reformists firmly maintained that there could be no separation of doctrine and practice, and hence that sitting at communion was a divinely established point of doctrine that had to be preserved. Conformists sought to locate the Church of England within the broader history of free churches, whose right it was to establish modes of worship. Yet English conformists also emphasised the points at which their Church departed from these historical and contemporary reformed examples – it was an institution both spiritual and political, a national church wherein religious uniformity and political obligation were fused in the public worship:

> For it is not the office of every private man to judge of comlinesse, and dispose of order in the publicke affairs of Church or Commonwealth: but to them it doth belong who have places of government therein … We find it true in experience, even about this particular action, that so many men, so many opinions: One like sitting best, another standing, a third kneeling. Now if everyone shall in this case assume unto

[125] John Denison, *The heauenly banquet: or The doctrine of the Lords Supper, set Forth in seuen sermons* (London, 1631), p. 299. Citations are taken from a tract appended to the edition of sermons: 'A iustification of the gesture of kneeling, in the act of receiuing the sacrament of the Lords Supper' (London, 1631).
[126] Denison, *The heavenly banquet*, p. 309.

himselfe the liberty of choice, what order, what comlinesse shall we see in our assemblies? [127]

Chance references to Arminianism aside, the dispute on ceremonies did not represent the sudden shattering of a Jacobean consensus over Calvinism; rather, it testified to the continuation of a deep-seated conflict over the doctrine and governance of the Church.

This conflict helps to explain an important aspect of the divisions that existed between English Protestants during the reign of James VI and I. It has been argued that definitions of sovereignty did not predominantly turn on a legal axis, but on the question of the 'governance of the Protestant religion'. [128] While ecclesiastical sovereignty was indeed one aspect of the debate, its definition was inseparable from a range of profoundly complex questions about doctrine and history. Moreover, these controversies reached back to the Elizabethan settlement, and were wrapped around a core of interrelated issues: the Canons of 1604, subscription and deprivation, diocesan episcopacy, and the doctrinal case for and against ceremonies. In a response to John Burges' book in defence of kneeling, William Ames was able to draw all of the issues together. Responding to Burges' suggestion that the Church of England constituted an 'association representative', Ames suggested that:

This representative mother, is very seldom extant, viz. when there is a parliament, which we have not had these divers years: And when she appeareth, she can give no milk to her children, further than she have commission from man: None of her children can have accesse unto her, only she appointed many years since, certaine servants of hers ... to dyet them, with drye ceremonies, and scourge them, with silencing, deprivation, excommunication. [129]

Ames described a church that had fallen away from its reformed foundations, and that was also alienated from its legal protectors in parliament. Since 1559, Crown in parliament constituted the sole channel through which ecclesiastical sovereignty flowed; and since 1604 reformists had argued that the High Commission had systematically undermined this sovereignty. Ames dismissed Burges' claim that there was no harm done in urging conformity to 'things indifferent', those 'accidental' aspects of worship not specifically enjoined by the 'substantial' elements of the Word. Instead, it was a cover for the arbitrary exercise of the political power of diocesan bishops:

---

[127] Ibid., p. 312.

[128] D. Alan Orr, 'Sovereignty, supremacy and the origins of the English Civil War', *History*, 87 (2002), 474–90, at 490.

[129] William Ames, *A fresh suit against human ceremonies in Gods Worship. Or a triplication unto. D. Burgesse his rejoinder for D. Morton* ([Amsterdam], 1633), p. 89.

To the Laws of the Land that they doe not duly submit themselves, it appeareth out of that which the parliament ... saith; divers painfull, and learned Pastors ready to performe the legall subscription, have been deprived for refusing canonical subscription: which could not be, if Canons were legall, and their makers Obedient to Law. They charge also the bodies, lands, and goods of subjects further than is lawfull ... So that it is by this plaine how the Convocations may be said to make a faction even against Parliament.[130]

William Bradshaw would have heartily agreed, as would all of those on the reformist side who remained unconvinced about the doctrinal justifications offered in defence of the Canons of 1604, episcopacy, and the ceremonial practice of the Church.

The Thirty-nine Articles introduced a fundamental tension into the post-Reformation Church of England. They defined the Church both as a congregation united in the Word, practising sacraments of 'Christ's ordinance', and as a sovereign 'national church' which could 'ordain' its own ceremonial practice. It was the practice set forth in the Canons of 1604 which served as the impetus for the *Abridgment* controversy, and which Thomas Morton sought to defend in his work of 1618. Driving the debate were competing conceptions of the link between doctrine and ceremony, scripture and 'custom', concepts that defined a rift that involved fundamentally different interpretations of scripture and the history of the early church. The conformist case maintained that there was a difference between scriptural warrant and the 'general rules' whereby the Church might order its own worship and exact its own discipline; worship and discipline were in turn defended by the concept of *adiaphora* and the argument which stressed a scriptural warrant for 'order' and stability in the uniform confession of the Church. Reformists contended that the severing of doctrine and practice represented a departure from the doctrinal purity of the church of the first institution. The ensuing argument concerned competing accounts of the ceremonial practice and governance of the early church, and also trenched upon the topics of the common law and the ecclesiastical sovereignty of the Crown. Where conformists initially sought to defend the Church on doctrinal and historical grounds, as the argument progressed they increasingly emphasised the need for 'order' in the body politic of the Church, and underpinned this with a variety of accounts of how 'custom' figured in the history of Christianity. Here again we discover the elements of a larger debate over authority, and it was a matter of ceaseless dispute over whether scripture alone, scripture augmented with the customs of the church, or custom designed to restore a purer and ancient pattern of worship formed the legitimate basis for the ceremonial practice of the English Church. This drove the two sides further

[130] Ibid., p. 113.

apart: writers such as William Ames began to call for formal separation from the Church, while conformists continued to stress the need for obedience to governors and for the unity of worship, while stressing the Church's place as an institution that existed both in the realm of the scripture, and in the history of human culture.

6

Ceremonies, episcopacy, and the Scottish Kirk

Thus far, the debates that this study has surveyed have been confined to the polemical world of English Protestantism. The present chapter expands this purview to an examination of tensions within 'British' Protestant thought, for common to the debates surveyed thus far has been the sporadic contribution of Scottish writers, against whom some of the principal conformist works were directed. It is to be remembered that James was King of Scotland before he became King of England, and so when he arrived in London in 1603 he also assumed jurisdiction over the Church of England, while retaining jurisdiction over the Kirk.[1] The problem (as the foregoing sentence suggests) was an extremely complex one, and has yet to receive the attention it deserves.[2] One perspective that may prove useful for our understanding of the complexity of 'British' ecclesiology is that of doctrinal dispute. For as we have seen at some length, the Church of England proclaimed itself to be the one 'true' church, both ancient and reformed. However, an examination of polemical debates reveals that the Kirk also claimed to exemplify the 'best reformed' church and, crucially, a *national* Church. The contemporary literature in which these

---

[1] We lack a sound study that links problems in English ecclesiology with those in Scotland, and it must be said that the history of the Church of Scotland is far less developed as a field. On the organisation of the Kirk, its parishes, and its ministry, see Walter Roland Foster, *The Church before the covenants: the Church of Scotland, 1596–1638* (Edinburgh, 1975). The tension between Edinburgh and Canterbury is partially treated by David George Mullan, *Episcopacy in Scotland: the history of an idea, 1560–1638* (Edinburgh, 1986); Mullan has more recently completed a study of reformist ideas, *Scottish Puritanism, 1590–1638* (Oxford, 2000). For political matters, see Jenny Wormald, *Court, Kirk, and community: Scotland, 1470–1625* (Toronto, 1981). One of the principal shortcomings in the field is the lack of minutes for important Assemblies; hence, our understanding of these proceedings must rely on the reports of contemporaries. First among these is David Calderwood, whose *The true history of the Church of Scotland* was apparently written in 1627, but not published until 1678, and then in abridged form.

[2] But see Jenny Wormald, 'James VI and I: two kings or one?', *History*, 68 (1983), 187–209. The article provides an excellent overview of the practical legislative problems of the Union of the Crowns, as well as a summary of the relevant literature. For a detailed study of the Union, see Bruce Galloway, *The Union of England and Scotland, 1603–1608* (Edinburgh, 1986). However, Galloway did not place a great deal of emphasis on religion.

questions were explored illustrates tensions within two of the three kingdoms from the point of view of ecclesiology: either the Kirk would remain sovereign over itself, or it would be comprehended by the jurisdiction of Canterbury. The following discussion focuses on the problem of governance and worship in both churches as presented in the literature of religious controversy.[3] This issue furnishes us with a perspective on a central and long-standing dispute among Protestants in England and Scotland, a dispute that would reach its height in the National Covenant, and which would shape positions on religion and politics in the emerging crisis of the 1640s.

The debate to be surveyed below impinges in a significant way on what scholars have come to call the 'British problem' and the perspective that sees the conflict of the mid seventeenth century as a 'war of religion'.[4] In answering the charge that the Church of England had no sovereignty over the Kirk, English conformists spoke of the Church of 'Great Britain', a phrase that erased the Kirk's claim to national distinction.[5] As Peter Lake has argued, one aspect of the conformist position from Whitgift onward was that the church could vary with 'circumstances', and thereby accommodate itself to the 'structure of the secular state in which it had to exist'.[6] Yet neither state was entirely secular, and this is why aspects of ecclesiology could so readily migrate into the realm of politics; indeed, this book began by suggesting that the two realms were so closely linked that there is little value in attempting to conceive of them as separate entities. As has been shown at length, conformists wished to provide spiritual legitimacy for

---

[3] Adding the perspective of Ireland, John Morrill has called this problem one of 'ecclesial acculturation'. See 'A British patriarchy?: ecclesiastical imperialism under the early Stuarts', in *Religion, culture, and society in early modern Britain: essays in honour of Patrick Collinson* ed. Anthony Fletcher and Peter Roberts (Cambridge, 1994), pp. 209–37, at p. 210. See also Peter Donald, *An uncounselled king: Charles I and the Scottish troubles, 1637–1641* (Cambridge, 1990), chs. 1–2; Conrad Russell, *The causes of the English Civil War* (Oxford, 1990), chs. 3, 5.

[4] *The British problem, c. 1534–1707: state formation in the Atlantic Archipelago*, ed. Brendan Bradshaw and John Morrill (Houndmills, Basingstoke, 1996). One dimension of this problem was addressed in histories of the Reformation Kirk. For a treatment of some of this literature, see Mullan, *Episcopacy in Scotland*, pp. 136–50. See also Russell, *Causes of the English Civil War*, chs. 3–5; *The new British history: founding a modern state, 1603–1715*, ed. Glenn Burgess (London, 1999), pp. 1–22; Conrad Russell, 'The British problem and the English Civil War', *History*, 75 (1987), 395–415; Ian Green, '"England's wars of religion"? Religious conflict and the English Civil Wars', in *Church, change and revolution*, ed. J. van den Burg and P. G. Hoftijzer (Leiden, 1991), pp. 100–21; Glenn Burgess, 'Was the English Civil War a war of religion?: the evidence of political propaganda', *Huntington Library Quarterly*, 61 (2000), 173–201.

[5] This aspect of Church–State relations was not covered in *Protestantism and national identity: Britain and Ireland, c. 1650–c. 1850*, ed. Tony Claydon and Ian McBride (Cambridge, 1998). But see the relevant discussions of Scottish 'identity', pp. 15–22, 51–2, 68–9.

[6] Peter Lake, 'Presbyterianism, the idea of a national Church and the argument from divine right', in *Protestantism and the national Church in sixteenth century England*, ed. Peter Lake and Maria Dowling (London, 1987), pp. 193–224, at p. 207.

an institution that was also conspicuously domiciled within channels of civil sovereignty, and the burden of their case, combined with the attacks of their critics, led them away from the issue of doctrinal purity and toward a conception of a holistic church 'of the realm'. Presbyterians came to oppose the claims of the English Church over them, and they did so by emphasising a Presbyterian mode of governance that was in turn yoked to doctrinal purity and political independence. They stressed the historical authenticity of Presbyterianism in the context of an emerging awareness that the Kirk was in some sense a 'national' institution, a church peculiar to the Scottish historical experience and hence the Scottish historical consciousness.[7]

BANCROFT AND THE PRESBYTERIANS

The Scottish Kirk was reformed on the basis of a legal settlement.[8] The Reformation parliament of 1560 established the foundation of the Kirk: it could examine candidates presented to benefices, it could restrict public office to Protestants, it was fiercely anti-Catholic, and it had exclusive jurisdiction over preaching, aspects of rites and governance, and, crucially, the ordering of its own liturgy.[9] Instead of Convocation, the Kirk was governed by a General Assembly of presbyteries – there were bishops, but not in the English way. For in Scotland bishops could not harness civil power in the process of enforcing conformity, nor could they administer the property of their dioceses. This meant that they could not deprive ministers, but rather that they themselves could be suspended or deprived by the General Assembly.[10] Yet the Union of the Crowns in 1603 challenged this sovereignty by creating a complex problem of royal and ecclesiastical jurisdiction, a conflict of ecclesiastical histories, and, ultimately, a lasting division within

[7] J. G. A. Pocock, 'British history: a plea for a new subject', *Journal of Modern History*, 47 (1975), 601–21, at 610–15.

[8] Alan MacDonald, *The Jacobean Kirk, 1567–1625: sovereignty, polity and liturgy* (Aldershot, 1998), p. 7. MacDonald's book is the first modern study that presents the Jacobean Kirk as a whole; it makes good use of archival sources as well as the standard contemporary accounts, and I have drawn on it for the purposes of establishing the context. The standard contemporary accounts are: David Calderwood, *History of the Kirk of Scotland by Mr. David Calderwood*, ed. T. Thompson, 8 vols. (Edinburgh, 1842–9); James Melville, *The autobiography and diary of Mr James Melvill*, ed. R. Pitcairn (Edinburgh, 1843); and John Spottiswoode, *History of the Church of Scotland ... by the Right Rev. John Spottiswoode*, ed. M. Russell and M. Napier, 3 vols. (Edinburgh, 1847–51).

[9] For the legal aspects of the settlement, see Francis Lyall, *Of presbyters and kings: Church and state in the law of Scotland* (Aberdeen, 1980), pp. 12–18. For basic narratives, see William Ferguson, *Scotland's relations with England: a survey to 1717* (Edinburgh, 1977), ch. 5; Wormald, *Court, Kirk, and community*, chs. 5–8.

[10] Alan MacDonald, 'Ecclesiastical representation in parliament in post-Reformation Scotland: the two kingdoms theory in practice', *Journal of Ecclesiastical History*, 50 (1999), 38–61.

the British reformed tradition. In fact, the Union of the Crowns meant that the English episcopate would seek to extend its jurisdiction, and English doctrine, over the Scottish Kirk. This policy would be resisted on both political and theological grounds.

Richard Bancroft set the tone of ecclesiological debate between Scots and English controversialists. This architect of the Jacobean Church was most active in late-Elizabethan controversies, notably that between conformists and 'Martin Marprelate'. Bancroft's importance to the Scottish context, however, may be attributed to three works published within a period of five years; these set out to challenge reformist attacks on the Church of England, and did so by scrutinising the doctrines of Thomas Cartwright, among others. Yet in the Kirk Bancroft also found a concrete institution, a church that claimed its own doctrinal and historical legitimacy, and hence, independence. Bancroft's writings treated two important aspects of the problem presented by the Scottish Kirk: the continuity and identity of the Apostolic church and its agreement with the reformed tradition, and the mode of governance suited to that church.

The sermon Bancroft preached in February 1588 was important for two related reasons. First, it stood as a reasoned repudiation of the position of the Presbyterians, who offered a mode of governance that, they argued, reflected the law of scripture and the historical pattern of the church in a manner that was superior to episcopacy. Second, Bancroft's sermon was vigorously attacked, and the exchange tells us important things about the assumptions on history and governance that obtained before the accession of James I. Bancroft's sermon provided a sketch of the controversies that had taken place since the Reformation, from the Admonition controversy, the debate between conformists and Marprelate, to complex Catholic/Protestant controversies. Indeed it was unusually driven by an historical narrative, itself designed to explicate the verse on which the sermon was based: 'Stay prophane and vaine bablings, for they will increase unto more ungodliness.'[11] Bancroft organised his attack on the Presbyterians as a history of schism, an identification of the true and ancient church, a history of the need for subscription, and a discussion of the nature of royal authority in the spiritual realm.

According to Bancroft, Presbyterians posed distinct challenges to the English conformists. Above all, they promoted the existence of an alternative form of ecclesiastical governance, and thus an alternative definition of the church:

This forme of government they call the tabernacle which God hath appointed, the glory of God, and of his sonne Jesus Christ, the presence of God, the place which he hath chosen to put his name there, the court of the Lord, and the shining forth of Gods

---

[11] The verse is 2 Timothy 2: 16.

glorie. Where this ecclesiasticall synode is not erected, they say Gods ordinance is not performed: the office of Christ as he is a king is not acknowledged: in effect that without this government we can never attain to a right and true feeling of Christian Religion.[12]

Bancroft's response revealed that Presbyterians emphasised the invisible aspect of the church, stressing the continuity of doctrine, rather than the succession of the institution. This position was hostile to the idea of a sovereign, monarchical Church of England, whose visible element was of equal importance to its continuity with the Word. Bancroft therefore sought to provide a doctrinal defence of the visible element of the Church, particularly its mode of governance; he consulted reformist tracts, examined their evidence, and pronounced on their errors. Drawing on Cyprian, Tertullian, Augustine, and a handful of scriptural references, he suggested that Presbyterian discipline could not be found in the historical record of the 'true' government of the Church established by Christ.[13] Since Presbyterianism had no defensible history, Bancroft saw it as an invention of those seeking to challenge the authority of the Church and its governor. He took pains to point out the way in which this authority was exercised, but did so in a manner that suggested that the Crown governed in conjunction with others:

In this supremacie, these principall points were contained; that the king hath ordinarie authoritie in causes ecclesiasticall: that he is the chiefest in the decision and determination of church causes: that he hath ordinarie authoritie for making all lawes, ceremonies, and constitutions of the church: that without his authoritie, no such lawes, ceremonies or constitutions are or ought to be of force.[14]

Here was a portrait of the Christian prince, who exercised complete sovereignty over all aspects of doctrine and discipline. In writing of the king as the 'chiefest', a word that implied a governing hierarchy and thus the presence of other units that partook in ecclesiastical sovereignty, Bancroft uncovered a second challenge posed by Presbyterian controversialists. While he did not speak of estates, Bancroft clearly had them in mind, for what 'established' the Church of England were the conjoined powers of King, Lords, and Commons – the sovereignty of the Crown in parliament. Presbyteries, argued Bancroft,

---

[12] Richard Bancroft, *A sermon preached at Paules Crosse the 9. of Februarie, being the first Sunday in the Parleament, anno. 1588* (London, 1588), p. 9.

[13] Ibid., pp. 10–33. One scholar has argued that Bancroft's sermon did not equal the programmatic statements on the ancient status of episcopacy that were evident in *A Suruay of the pretended holy discipline* (London, 1593). However, in repudiating the antiquity of Presbyterian discipline, Bancroft's sermon made a detailed historical argument for episcopacy. See W. D. J. Cargill Thompson, 'A reconsideration of Richard Bancroft's Paul's Cross sermon of 9 February 1588/9', *Journal of Ecclesiastical History*, 20 (1969), 253–66, at 265.

[14] Bancroft, *A sermon*, p. 70. On absolute and 'ordinary' powers, see Francis Oakley, 'Jacobean political theology: the absolute and ordinary powers of the King', *Journal of the History of Ideas*, 29 (1968), 323–46.

constituted assemblies not incorporated into the legitimate branches of the state; they were, to employ the Latin appellation, an *imperium in imperio*.[15] The example he employed was the creation of the presbyteries in Scotland in 1581, and the excommunication of ministers who refused to subscribe to the *Book of discipline*:[16]

> The king with the advice of his Estates in Parleament, having resolved upon a certain fact committed by some of his subjects, that it was treason: these men in their assemblie (esteeming their judgement to bee the soverigne judgement of the Realme) did not onely approve the same fact as lawful, but ordained al them to be excommunicated, who woulde not subscribe to their determination therein.

The result, argued Bancroft, was an imposition on the ecclesiastical sovereignty of the Crown in parliament, and it was this point that underlay his attack on the political intentions of the Presbyterians who, 'under the pretence of their presbyteries, they trod upon his scepter, and labored to establish an ecclesiastical tyranny of an infinite jurisdiction, such as neither the law of God or man could tollerate'.[17] In other words, Presbyterians sought to erect a rival confession that undermined both the historical identity of the true confession established in scripture, and the earthly authorities whose task it was to ensure the survival of that confession within the visible association of the Church. On the basis of their claim to a jurisdiction above that of the monarch, Bancroft likened Presbyterians to Roman Catholics: both represented churches 'in error' which moreover sought to subvert the ecclesiastical sovereignty of the Crown in parliament.

Bancroft's sermon was answered by John Davidson, a member of the Edinburgh presbytery, who argued that in charging the ministers of the Kirk with treason, Bancroft was guilty of dissembling: 'Not being able I say, to find any thing against the brethren of England, in this case ... he raungeth abroad making choise, especially of Scotland, hee setteth upon it with al his maine.'[18] Davidson portrayed the conformist bishops as enemies

---

[15] For a discussion of Presbyterian governance in the context of a debate on estates, see Michael Mendle, *Dangerous positions: mixed government, the estates of the realm, and the 'Answer to the xix propositions'* (University, AL, 1985), pp. 63–96.

[16] For details, and for an overview of the patterns of 'dissent' in the Kirk generally, see Michael F. Graham, *The uses of reform: 'godly discipline' and popular behaviour in Scotland and beyond, 1560–1610* (London, 1996), pp. 136–49.

[17] Bancroft, *A sermon*, p. 74. For details of the crisis, see MacDonald, *The Jacobean Kirk*, ch. 1, passim.

[18] John Davidson, *D. Bancrofts rashnes in rayling against the Church of Scotland* (Edinburgh, 1590), sigs. 3ʳ–4ᵛ. The charge was partly accurate: for in the course of the Marprelate controversies with English Presbyterians, Bancroft often looked to Scotland for examples of the dangers which he perceived to attend that mode of governance. See Bryan Spinks, *Sacraments, ceremonies and the Stuart divines: sacramental theology and liturgy in England and Scotland, 1603–1662* (London, 2002), p. 52.

of reform, and hence the real enemies of the Kirk. In addition to Bancroft, Davidson mentioned Patrick Adamson, Archbishop of St Andrews, whom he portrayed as assisting in Whitgift's policy of enforcing clerical conformity via subscription to the Three Articles. The principal rift between the Presbyterians and English conformists would concern the matter of governance. Davidson replied to Bancroft's castigation of the Presbyterians with equal vigour: 'I surely persuade my selfe, that those lordly brethren of DIOTREPHES, who rule or rather tyrannise above their brethren with violence & cruelty, should be quickly charmed from authorising such rashe libertie of public rayling, and defaming of a whole neighbour church, which hath so well deserved of the present state of Englande.' Davidson concluded by arguing that it was up to the Kirk to defend itself against Bancroft and his peers. While it would remain for other writers to depict this defence as a struggle for the liturgical and historical sovereignty of the Kirk, Davidson urged that its doctrine be defended:

we must not leave the just defence of our honest cause of Christian Discipline, which (touching the substance thereof, whiche chiefly is in controversie) hath no lesse warrand to be continued perpetually within the Church, under this precept of Christ, 'feede my sheepe', then hath the preaching of the worde, and ministration of the Sacraments, and so consequently floweth no more from the authoritie of the Civill Magistrate than they doe.[19]

In short, Davidson was claiming that the Kirk was exempt from the authority of the Crown, because its pattern of doctrine and governance came exclusively from the scripture. The argument was more explicit than English reformist treatments of the separation of civil and ecclesiastical authority, perhaps owing to the fact that Davidson's case also exhibited another dimension: a struggle for sovereignty between the possibility of one central ecclesiastical authority and the competing notion of two sovereign churches.

It is little wonder that Bancroft sought to repudiate Presbyterian discipline as both theologically unsound and politically dangerous. In a new work, Bancroft set out to defend the English Church as both 'Apostolic' and 'reformed'. It was in this context that he situated his attack on Presbyterian discipline and the motives of those who promoted it. The Presbyterians, he suggested, 'seeke new platformes of Church government, in this place or that place: when as we have one of our owne, which is in my conscience truly Apostolicall, and so farre to be preferred, before any other that is received this day by any reformed Church in Christendome'.[20] Bancroft sought to establish the Apostolic pedigree of the governance of the Church of England,

---

[19] Davidson, D. *Bancroft's rashnes*, n. p. This tract contains many errors and irregular pagination.
[20] Richard Bancroft, *A Survay of the pretended holy discipline* (London, 1593), *3ʳ.

and also to defend its claim to sovereignty over doctrine and discipline. It was from this point of view that he questioned the legitimacy of Presbyterian synods:

In those Synods they have practiced censures, made lawes of their owne, and disallowed some of those, which the state of this realme hath made. Unto these and such like their private Conventicles, they have appropriated the name of the Church, and having separated themselves in a sorte ... they are become joined into a new brotherhood of the Allobrogicall Discipline.[21]

Bancroft's choice of epithet revealed that he regarded both reformist and Presbyterian critics of the Church of England as members of the same faction: Geneva was, in ancient times, a town of the Allobroges, a Gaulish tribe. Clearly he saw both groups as united in their theological attacks on the Church of England, attacks that also constituted a direct challenge to the ecclesiastical sovereignty of Crown in parliament. In terms of theology and the history of the early church, Bancroft sought to depict his confessional rivals as upstart associations, lacking a sound Apostolic pedigree. This is an important avenue by which the *Suruay* must be interpreted; it was not only a criticism of Presbyterian discipline, but also a defence of the Church of England's claim to an Apostolic mode of governance, itself defined by a clerical hierarchy:

After the death of the apostles, and of their assistants: vz: the Bishops placed by them, as is mentioned, the Ecclesiastical hystories, and the auncient fathers, have kept the register of their names, that succeeded sundry of them, and ruled the Churches after them, as they before had ruled them. Whereupon they were called from all antiquitie: the Apostles and the Apostolicall mens successors. This inequality in the Ministery of the worde, hath been approved and honoured by all the auncient fathers (noe excepted): by all the generall Councells, that ever were held in Christendome.[22]

As we have seen, this argument was central to defences of English episcopacy. Yet Bancroft went further, ranging the reformed tradition and its texts in order to gather an overwhelming fund of evidence to support the claim that episcopacy was both ancient and reformed. The eighth chapter of the *Suruay* was devoted to precisely this task. Bancroft cited writers from the reformed tradition: Luther, Beza, Calvin, and Zanchi. Perhaps the most pointed testimony came from Andreas Osiander:

Osiander writeth: even as though he had spoken of the Church of England. *Although in the Primitive church (when she flourished with myracles) there were divers degrees and orders of Ministers: some Apostles: some Prophets, some Evangelists, and some Pastors and Doctors: yet as now the state of the Church is, the Ministers may be devided into three orders or degrees: vz: Deacons, Pastors, and Superintendents* ...

---

[21] Ibid., p. 57.   [22] Ibid., pp. 106–7.

who are set over all other pastors, that they may visite the state of their Churches, and punishe both the Pastors and the people, if any thing be done amisse: or if any thing fall out that they cannot correct, they referre it unto a higher court, consisting of devines and politick men, who by the civil Magistrates authoritie, or approbation, doe amend such defects, &c.[23]

The issue with episcopal jurisdiction in the English setting concerned the relationship of the High Commission to the common law which, argued writers like William Bradshaw, compromised the sovereignty of the Crown in parliament. Here, Bancroft provided a defence of the High Commission and of episcopal jurisdiction over both individual congregations and the Church writ large as having descended from the Crown. Moreover, he sought to align the mode of governance of the Church of England with that practised by the Apostolic church, and to defend the notion of a clerical hierarchy as ancient, rather than novel. It was this last point that allowed Bancroft, in *Daungerous positions*, to attack Presbyterian discipline as politically subversive. Indeed, where the *Suruay* had drawn upon a wealth of texts from the reformed tradition, *Daungerous positions* examined the writings of John Knox and George Buchanan. The latter has been identified as one of the most articulate proponents of the idea that the 'realm' of Scotland was possessed of an 'ancient Scottish constitution', with its own claims to immemoriality and sovereignty.[24] Bancroft counted Knox and Buchanan among the 'consistorian puritaines' whose barrage of petitions, pamphlets, and other texts comprised the great exegesis carried on in *Daungerous positions*. Among the passages cited there, Bancroft isolated Knox's statement calling for reform of the Kirk: 'if Kings and Princes refused to reform religion, the inferior Magistrates or people, by direction of the ministrie, might lawfullie, and ought (if need required) even by force and arms, to reform it themselves'.[25] Bancroft offered a 'history' of Presbyterianism in Scotland, assessing its doctrines and political implications, and bemoaning the fact that Scots divines furnished the impetus for 'English Genevating' and 'English Scottizing' – that is, the erosion of the doctrine of the Church of England. The peroration to Book One put the case clearly:

---

[23] Ibid., pp. 118–19.

[24] See H. R. Trevor-Roper, 'George Buchanan and the ancient Scottish constitution', *English Historical Review*, Supplement 3 (1966); J. H. Burns, 'The political ideas of George Buchanan', *Scottish Historical Review*, 30 (1951), 60–8; and J. H. Burns, 'George Buchanan and the Anti-Monarchomachs', in *Political discourse in early modern Britain*, ed. Nicholas Phillipson and Quentin Skinner (Cambridge, 1993), pp. 3–22, at pp. 4, 5, 22.

[25] Richard Bancroft, *Daungerous positions and proceedings published and practised within this iland of Brytaine, vnder pretence of Reformation, and for the Presbiteriall discipline* (London, 1593), p. 9

Marry nowe that the chiefest of them, for the excusing of themselves, and that they might shew, whose schollers they are, have presumed to publish (and that in print) such strange & seditious doctrine, as doth tend to the like disturbance, and indeed the utter overthrow of the freest and most absolute Monarchies, that are or can be in Christendome, not omitting withal, to solicite and incourage our pretended reformers in England, to proceed as they have begun, in following their steps, contrary (I am sure) both to the word of God, and to all the lawes and customs of this Realme.[26]

What Knox and Buchanan defended as a mark of the sovereignty of the Kirk, Bancroft claimed as a particular 'custom' of the realm, and by extension the Crown itself. Under Elizabeth, the question of monarchical jurisdiction was less complicated than it would become under James VI and I's attempt to 'reunite' his Christian kingdoms.[27] Indeed, the accession of James VI of Scotland to the English throne created problems of jurisdiction that the Union of the Crowns did not address. As both Catholic and Protestant controversialists divided over the question of who could claim a connection with the ancient and 'true' church, so too did Protestants in both kingdoms compete for, as Bancroft put it, 'possession' of the reformed Church in Britain. Of the two sides, however, the conformists had greater reserves on which to draw: Scottish ecclesiology could boast of no Hooker or Jewel, but writers found themselves having to engage with arguments drawn from these seminal texts. Like English reformists, the Scots came to exploit the tension over civil and spiritual authority that defined the dually established Church, and to defend the independence of the Kirk based upon an alternate narrative of doctrine and authority.

ONE CHURCH, TWO NATIONS?: JURISDICTION AND CONFESSIONAL RIVALRY

After the Union of the Crowns, relations between the Kirk and English conformists began to simmer over the issues of governance and jurisdiction.[28] A series of General Assemblies were announced and then postponed, and protesting clergy were jailed and the rest harangued by official publications calling for order; meanwhile recalcitrant Presbyterians were brought to England to hear sermons extolling the virtues of English ecclesiology.[29] The most serious phase of the conflict concerned the General Assembly held in

---

[26] Ibid., p. 33.
[27] W. B. Patterson, *King James VI and I and the reunion of Christendom* (Cambridge, 1997), pp. 1–30.
[28] MacDonald, *Jacobean Kirk*, p. 107; G. Donaldson, 'The attitude of Whitgift and Bancroft to the Scottish Church', *TRHS*, 4th series, 24 (1942), 95–115; Maurice Lee, 'James I and the revival of episcopacy in Scotland, 1596–1600', *Church History*, 43 (1974), 49–64.
[29] Privy Council of Scotland, *A declaration of the iust causes of his Maiesties proceeding against those ministers, who are now lying in prison, attainted of high treason* (Edinburgh and

Glasgow during June 1610. James established courts of High Commission to put an end to the challenges to his authority that had defined the opening years of the reign; the policy was to be enforced by the bishops, overseen by the arch-episcopal sees of Glasgow and St Andrews.[30] As had been the case in England, protest against the Kirk led to the hardening of those measures designed to combat non-conformity, which in turn ensured that the issue of episcopacy would continue as a source of conflict. The bishops, therefore, could

call before them any person dwelling within their provinces whom they hold to be scandalous. And if they find them guilty and impenitent they shall command the preacher of that parish where they dwell to proceed with excommunication which if their command be not obeyed, they shall conveen [the] minister before them and proceed in censuring him by suspension, deprivation, or warding.[31]

Bancroft's policy of subscription had moved North, and the episcopate gained power as a result. The cleric and historian David Calderwood reported that the Assembly affirmed the right of the King to call General Assemblies, but all meetings were to be moderated by a bishop, rather than an appointed 'constant' moderator preferred by defenders of the Kirk. The General Assembly could not deprive or otherwise censure bishops, but acted as the King's adviser in this task. Clearly, Bancroft's policy was to strip the Kirk of its channels of sovereignty, replacing them with visitations and deprivations after the English style.[32] In December of 1610, the Archbishop of Glasgow was consecrated in London, along with the bishops of Brechin and Galloway. The consecration was presided over by the bishops of London, Bath and Wells, and Ely; Bancroft was present, but not involved in the ceremony, which took place thirteen days before his death.

The waning of the sovereignty of the Kirk under English bishops drove one writer to reflect on Scottish history. A tract published from Edinburgh in 1610 looked back to the Church Jurisdiction Act of 1579 and reiterated the point that, in 1581, the royal household had subscribed to the Negative Confession.[33] This was a powerful reminder that the King himself had previously endorsed the doctrinal and governmental sovereignty of the Kirk, and

London, 1605); Stephen King, '"Your, best and maist faithfull subjects": Andrew and James Melville as James VI and I's "loyal opposition"', *Renaissance and Reformation*, 24 (2000), 17–30.

[30] See Mullan, *Episcopacy in Scotland*, pp. 114–35.

[31] *The register of the Privy Council of Scotland*, ed. J.H. Burton et al., 14 vols. (Edinburgh, 1877–98), vol. VII, pp. 101, 474; vol. VIII, pp. 418–19. See also MacDonald, *The Jacobean Kirk*, p. 144.

[32] David Calderwood, *The true history of the Church of Scotland, from the beginning of the reformation, unto the end of the reigne of King James VI* (London, 1678), pp. 617–44.

[33] See Lyall, *Of presbyters*, pp. 17–18. The Negative Confession, or King's Confession, was a Protestant statement of belief that rejected Catholicism; it was the foundation of the National Covenant (1638) and survived until the Westminster Confession (1648).

its connection with the Scots reformation parliament. Among a number of arguments against episcopacy was the suggestion that the doctrine and discipline of the Kirk was approved by divine warrant and the authority of the Scottish parliament:

This is the only true Christian faith and religion pleasing God, and bringing salvation to man, quilk now is by the mercy of God revealed to the world, by the preaching of the blessed Evangell: and received, believed, & defended, by many and sundrie notable kirkes and Realmes, but chiefly by the Kirk of Scotland, the Kings Majestie, and Three Estates of the Realme, as Gods eternall truth and only ground of our Salvation: as more particularly expressed in the confession of our Faith, established and publicly confirmed by sundrie Actes of Parliament.[34]

Here was a defence of the Kirk on both doctrinal and political grounds. English conformity, which the anonymous writer interpreted as being motivated by the desire to build a uniform church in both realms, was therefore characterised as both an intrusion on the sovereignty of the Scots parliament and a doctrinal error. The same tensions between doctrine and discipline ordained by God and that ordained by man served as the hinge of the argument: as the anonymous writer noted, 'we detest all the vaine allegories, rites, signes and Traditions brought into this Kirke, without or against the Word of God, and doctrine of this true reformed Kirke'. The tract concluded with a promise that the Scots ministers would 'defend' their 'doctrine and discipline' against what one scholar has vividly described as the attempt to graft 'diocesan government on to the Presbyterian briar'.[35]

The General Assembly held at Glasgow was the site of a small but important polemical skirmish. In addition to the accounts of the Assembly given by the historians David Calderwood and John Spottiswoode, a number of shorter works, none of which has yet been noted by modern scholars, also dealt with the proceedings. The first to appear was a narrative of the Assembly itself, published anonymously in Middelburg by Richard Schilders.[36] The author recalled the promise 'made openly in Edinburgh' by James on his departure for England, to the effect that he would 'not hurt or alter' the Kirk.[37] For indeed, a *rapprochement* of sorts had taken place between the King and his Kirk, and it was clearly a matter of contention as

[34] *The confession of faith, subscrived by the Kings Maiestie and his household* (Edinburgh, 1610), pp. 3–4. The tract was republished in Leiden in 1638.
[35] Ibid., pp. 5, 6. Tom Webster, *Godly clergy in early Stuart England* (Cambridge, 1997), p. 313.
[36] The tract is not included in the lists presented in Keith Sprunger, *Trumpets from the tower: English puritan printing in the Netherlands, 1600–1640* (Leiden, 1994), pp. 224–30.
[37] [Anon], *A briefe and plaine narration of proceedings at an assemsemblie [sic] in Glasco. 8 Iun. 1610. anent the innovation of the Kirk-government* ([Middelburg], 1610), sig. A². For James' affirmation to preserve the state of the Kirk, see Spottiswoode, *History of the Church of Scotland*, vol. III, p. 137.

to who had poisoned the relationship.[38] Yet the *Narration* corroborated Spottiswood's account of the major decisions taken at Glasgow, all of which served to enhance the power of the bishops:

> In the afternoone the privie conference met, and make upp their conclusions, viz. 1. The Assemblie at Abirdeen was unlawful. 2. All power of convening, & discharging generall Assemblies, pertayneth only to the King. 3. Ordination, admission, deprivation, & suspention. 4. Visitation of Churches, and 5. Excommunication and absolution be proper to the Bishopps: if they be slacke, the generall Assemblie shall trie & report to his Ma. That he may censure them according to their merit.[39]

A programme of visitation, subscription, and deprivation – the same measures employed by Bancroft to ensure the uniformity of the Church of England – would promote order in the Kirk. The Crown, in essence, had adopted a single ecclesiastical policy to deal with two different churches. The *Narration* confined its exploration of this theme to a short preface, which intimated that the Scottish nobility had supported the King after being 'corrupted by the treasure of Englande', and further pressured by Bancroft's 'hyrelings'.[40] It also told of a number of sermons preached in the course of the Assembly by Spottiswoode; John Law, Bishop of Orkney; and Phineas Hodson, one of the King's Chaplains; there were also sermons by 'the Kings Chaplaines D. Hampton & D. Merdon'. Of all of these, the latter two survive, and offer an excellent insight into how conformist ideas tested in England were applied in the Scottish context.[41]

Christopher Hampton held a Doctorate in Divinity, and the sermon preached before the Glasgow Assembly was his only published work. Its basic message concerned the nature of the King's sovereignty in religious causes, and he presented the case in terms of an historical narrative that blended civil and ecclesiastical authority. Hampton employed the examples of religious princes like Solomon and David, but also sought to assign an ancient British pedigree to the power claimed by James and disputed by the Presbyterians:

> Eleutherius a Bishop of Rome advised Lucius … that was King of Britaine about 150 years after Christ, and giveth this reason of his advice; *Quta Vicarius Des estis in vestro regno*: you (saith the Bishop of Rome to the King) may make Lawes for religion, because you are Gods Lieutenant, Vicar and Deputie within your owne

---

[38] For an account of the consensus that obtained in the Kirk between 1597 and 1602, see MacDonald, *The Jacobean Kirk*, ch. 4, passim.

[39] *Briefe and plaine narration*, sig. A[8r].

[40] There may have been some truth to this charge, for part of James' policy in Scotland involved co-opting nobles to gather the votes he required. For details, see K. M. Brown, 'In search of the godly magistrate in Reformation Scotland', *Journal of Ecclesiastical History*, 40 (1989), 553–81.

[41] *Briefe and plaine narration*, passim, and sig. B[2r].

Kingdome: so the municipal Lawes of our kingdom intendeth: for they account not the Prince a meere Civill or Ecclesiasticall person, as they doe others, but mixt· by reason of the power he hath in both.[42]

English historians had employed the example of Lucius to extend the ecclesiastical supremacy of the English monarchs forward from the arrival of Christianity, but Hampton used this historical pedigree for extending regal sovereignty beyond England to include Britain. This suggested that the problem addressed was not so much James' jurisdiction as King of Scotland, but rather that of extending to the Kirk those means of enforcing religious uniformity used in the Church of England. The purpose was to justify the creation of a uniform mode of doctrine, discipline, and governance for England and Scotland, and hence Hampton stressed the importance of 'publick' worship as a means of maintaining pure doctrine:

there is a reason for publique assemblies: that the puritie of sincere Doctrine might be kept inviolable by that means from the corruption of Gentilitie, the poyson of Heresie, and the rage of Schisme: whilest the worship of God is not left arbitrarie, or voluntarie, but hath a prescript forme from whence it is unlawful to decline … The remedy for these inconveniences [i.e. of schism] is to cut off arbitrarie worship, to restraine and suppresse whispering or corner divinitie.[43]

One of the consequences of defining the Church as a political association was that it had to be governed like a political association, and it was this to which reformists objected most strenuously. Yet the conformist case displayed a great inflexibility: a uniform faith established by law had to be enforced, for to do otherwise would undermine faith, law, and sovereignty. Hampton tried to soften the case for uniformity, in the manner that Bancroft had with subscription, by cloaking it in a reformed genealogy: the precept of a 'settled forme of prayers and Ecclesiastical rites', he argued, 'is not my owne conceit, I learned it from Mr Calvin'.[44] Like many of the conformist writers examined thus far, Hampton argued that the ecclesiastical sovereignty of the Crown was both historically sound, and in agreement with the judgements of the reformed divines.

The second message conveyed by the sermon concerned the historical pedigree of the Church of England, and its claims to partake in the body of Christ. In the main, Hampton presented his case as it related to the debate on the 'notes of the Church' that engaged the attention of English conformists

---

[42] Christopher Hampton, *A sermon preached in the cittie of Glasco in Scotland, on the tenth day of Iune, 1610. At the holding of a generall assembly there* (London, 1611), p. 4.

[43] Ibid., pp. 16–17.

[44] Ibid., p. 17: 'Concerning the forme of prayer (saith he) and Ecclesiastical rites, I doe very well like that they should be certaine in a prescript order, and that the Pastors be not suffered to swerve from it .'

and their Catholic opponents.[45] This was done partly to demonstrate that the Church of England was truly Christian and reformed, but it also served as a way of introducing the argument against Presbyterian discipline. In the same manner as conformists in the debate on ceremonies sought to argue that there was no necessary connection between doctrine and practice, Hampton suggested that there was a difference in kind between belief and action. Freedom of conscience was preserved, so long as clergy conformed by their actions: 'Wherein if brethren will hold but that moderation which true Divinitie teacheth, and retaine this freedome, our Christian libertie in their consciences, which is not infringed; and conforme their actions, that they doe not overthwart good order, to the disturbance of the Church, and offence of the Magistrate'. Finally, Hampton argued, based on a theory of patriarchalism, that since the family was not defined by parity, no case existed for extending that condition 'onely to the Church'.[46] Taken as a whole, the argument sought to assert the authority of diocesan bishops over the 'external' aspects of worship, and also to defend their position in relation to the ordinary clergy.

Hampton's reference to 'conscience' was developed in the second sermon preached at Glasgow. George Meriton – Doctor of Divinity and one of James' chaplains – explored the problem of conscience: its nature, its consolations, its failings, and particularly its tendency to err. In essence, Meriton sought to call into question the reliability of conscience, and to argue that some means were required whereby the conscience received guidance. Hence, 'what a woefull case all Heretickes, Hypocrites, Schismatics, and ignorant men and women are in, whose knowledge is perverted and who live in error. They want the testimony of a good conscience.'[47] Where Bancroft and Hampton's sermons had taken the form of historical or political essays, Meriton's followed the common genre of devotional or instructional sermons one commonly finds published during the period.[48] Frequent sermon-givers such as Anthony Maxey, Lancelot Andrewes, or William Cowper, Bishop of Galloway, often cast their sermons as admonitory primers on scripture, duty, and devotion. A good part of Meriton's sermon obeyed this pattern, but then it abruptly

---

[45] Ibid., pp. 16–28. See also Lucy E. C. Wooding, *Rethinking Catholicism in Reformation England* (Oxford, 2000). T. H. Wadkins, 'Theological polemic and religious culture in early Stuart England: the Percy / "Fisher" controversies, 1605–1641' (Ph.D. diss., Graduate Theological Union, Berkeley, 1988), pp. 25–71.

[46] Hampton, *A sermon*, pp. 28, 29. For patriarchalism in this period, see Gordon Schochet, *Patriarchalism in political thought* (Oxford, 1975).

[47] George Meriton, *A sermon preached before the Generall Assembly at Glascoe in the kingdome of Scotland, the tenth day of iune, 1610* (London, 1611), sig. C[4r].

[48] For this see Mary Morrissey, 'Scripture, style and persuasion in seventeenth-century English theories of preaching', *Journal of Ecclesiastical History*, 53 (2002), 686–706.

changed tack, and under the heading 'Particular Doctrine upon the present occasion', addressed the central issue.

This Meriton identified in terms of the political and religious costs of Presbyterian discipline, which he portrayed as running counter to the law of scripture, the example of history, and the laws of the kingdom. To make the case, Meriton availed himself of the metaphor that likened church and commonwealth to a natural body:

A Commonwealth is fitly resembled to the body of a man; and were it not a mad hearing if the feete should say to the head, we will weare the hatte? If the knees should strive to carry the eyes? Or if the shoulders should claime each of them an eare? But if it were so indeede, what a mis-shapen body would this be?[49]

Employing the metaphor of the body politic allowed Meriton to make a point that the concept of 'estates', employed by Bancroft, did not adequately capture.[50] Estates described a distribution of power among King, Lords, and Commons as the sovereign lawgivers, but Meriton – in the manner of Edward Forset – considered the natural condition of the body and the spiritual body politic. This allowed him to argue that an hierarchical mode of governance was in some sense a natural aspect of the church:

so it must bee in the Church of God, where some are eyes, some eares, some head, some feet, some must be high, some low, some rule, some obey. This comlinesse of order is the beauty of Gods Church, for beauty is the daughter of order, the more seene the more admired; & order is the well disposing of *equall and unequall things*.[51]

Meriton described order as 'coming from God' and infused in all things, a strand of thinking that we might trace to the first book of Corinthians: 'For the body is not one member, but many.'[52] Here was a description of a spiritual body politic wherein all things were divinely proportioned in respect to all other things. Meriton depicted Presbyterian discipline as alien to this order: 'the power which now it exerciseth, and place which now it challengeth ... as farre as ever I could learne is somewhat out of order; and altogether unknowen unto ancient times'. Meriton then offered examples from Augustine, and scriptures from Titus, Corinthians, and Luke, to show that scripture and history confirmed that the 'consent of all Churches in all times, together with the warrantise of Gods word, give precedency in power, and in place to the Bishop'.[53]

---

[49] Meriton, *A sermon*, sig. D^{2v}.
[50] Mendle's contention that talk of estates was a 'royalist ploy' overlooks the crucial relationship between metaphorical language and estates theory. See *Dangerous positions*, pp. 61–2, 101–2, 111–12.
[51] Meriton, *A sermon*, sig. D^{2r}.   [52] 1 Corinthians 12: 14.
[53] Meriton, *A sermon*, sigs. D^{2r}–D^{3v-r}.

The early literature on the question of the Kirk followed Bancroft's example of attacking both the theological and political consequences of Presbyterian discipline. Conformist complaints that the erosion of the 'true' church and the realm itself were close at hand revealed a fundamental assumption: in all cases, the Church of England was seen to constitute the 'best reformed church', a point which served to bolster the claims of diocesan bishops as the legitimate governors of that Church. As was the case in controversies between English Protestants, both propositions would be tested in the course of religious controversy. What began to emerge in debates on episcopacy and ceremonies was a tension between two historical narratives that probed the relationship of civil and ecclesiastical authority, and which did so by variously imputing a Presbyterian or episcopal mode of governance to the ancient church. Central to the conformist programme in both England and Scotland was an emphasis on 'order' in the visible church, a condition that, according to reformist critics, was privileged at the cost of the purity of doctrine.

'SALUS ECCLESIAE SUPREMA LEX ESTO'

The conflict over episcopacy and ceremonies that had defined relations between the Kirk and the Church of England was renewed in an unprecedented scope in the autumn of 1617.[54] As had been the case with previous controversies, the Scots controversy over ceremonies and governance was touched off as the result of the imposition of an unpopular measure on the Kirk, in this case the Articles of Perth.[55] Of particular concern to Presbyterians was the first article, which enjoined that the communion be

---

[54] John D. Ford, 'The lawful bonds of Scottish society: the Five Articles of Perth, the Negative Confession and the National Covenant', *Historical Journal*, 37 (1994), 45–64; John D. Ford, 'Conformity and conscience: the structure of the Perth Articles debate in Scotland, 1618–1638', *Journal of Ecclesiastical History*, 46 (1995), 256–77; Ian Cowan, 'The Five Articles of Perth', in *Reformation and revolution*, ed. Duncan Shaw (Edinburgh, 1967), pp. 160–77. Also useful is *Original letters relating to the ecclesiastical affairs of Scotland … 1603–25*, ed. Beriah Botfield, 2 vols. (Edinburgh, 1851).

[55] These articles were passed by General Assembly at Perth on 25 August 1618. It would not be until 4 August 1621 that Parliament would fully ratify them.

1. The sacrament of the body and blood of Christ should be received kneeling.
2. It might be administered in private to the sick.
3. When infants could not conveniently be baptized in church they might be baptized at home.
4. Children being eight years old, and after being instructed in the Lord's Prayer, Creed, Ten Commandments, and Catechism, should be brought to the bishop on his visitation, to be examined in the religious knowledge, and to receive his blessing.
5. The days commemorative of Christ's birth, passion, resurrection, ascension, and the sending down of the Holy Ghost should be kept in devout observance.

received in a kneeling posture. From a doctrinal point of view, this represented an important parallel with the English experience; Scottish writers
would refer both to this history, and to the literature of controversy published in England in order to address questions of doctrine in the Kirk.[56] In
1617, during a visit by James, a number of Scottish bishops knelt to receive
communion. However, some among the clergy argued that kneeling violated
the pattern of the first institution of the sacrament at the Last Supper; hence,
the Bishop of Galloway could argue: 'I think as yet that the best form of
taking it is, as we do, sitting; because, first, Christ Our Lord did so.'[57]
The debates on ceremonies and episcopacy in Scotland opened up the question of which of the churches of Britain exemplified ancient and reformed
perfection.

The King found himself faced with a schism in the Kirk, and intending to
put an end to the problem summoned an assembly to be held at St Andrews in
November 1617. David Calderwood reported that the clergy refused to accept
the Perth Articles, and described the King's reaction:

Sundrie rumours went in the moneth of January, that the King was highly incensed at
the Bishops, specially at Saint Andrews ... because the five Articles were not yielded
unto: And at the Ministry, for driving of time. But he will let the Kirk of Scotland
know, what it is to have a do with an old King, or to abuse his lenitie: That he would
have no Convention of Ministers to treat in time coming of the matters of the Kirk,
but only the Bishops ... and that there was a warrant set down from the King, to
discharge Presbyteries, and Sessions of Particular Kirks, as mutinous Conventions.[58]

Here it seemed that James was prepared to assert his control over the Kirk via
diocesan bishops. Yet he was also asserting his right to hold jurisdiction over
a united, rather than a 'particular' church – a position that implied that
the decisions of assemblies held without royal sanction were not binding.
A Royal Proclamation issued in Edinburgh on 3 August 1618 called for a
further assembly, and on the twenty-fifth of that month representatives of the
Kirk met at Perth. Calderwood provides a brief list of those who attended;
the small number of delegates suggests that, owing to the short notice given
by the Crown to prospective attendees, very few of them reached Perth in
time for the Assembly. In any case, a letter from the King was read:

Hoping assuredly, that ye will have some better regard of our desires, and not permit
the unrulie and ignorant multitude, after their wonted custome, to oversway the

---

[56] On this point I disagree with Peter Donaldson, who argued that with respect to debate on the
Perth Articles the 'English background helped little'. See *An uncounselled king*, p. 13.

[57] For details of the Proclamations, see Mullen, *Episcopacy in Scotland*, ch. 9; for Galloway, see
Original letters, ed. Botfield, vol. II, pp. 513–14.

[58] Calderwood, *The true history of the Church of Scotland*, p. 691; Keith Sprunger, *Dutch
puritanism: a history of the English and Scottish churches of the Netherlands in the sixteenth
and seventeenth centuries* (Leiden, 1982), pp. 138, 142, 235, 309, 343.

better and more judicious sort; an evil which we have gone about with much pains to have amended in these Assemblies, and for which purpose, according to Gods ordinance, and the constant practice of all well governed Churches in all ages, we have placed you, that are Bishops and Overseers of the rest, in the chiefest Roomes.[59]

Here we find further parallels with the position of English conformists, developed in the proclamation issued to summon the conference at Hampton Court; in that document, the desire to limit the dangers of faction was combined with an affirmation that the worship of the Church of England was 'agreeable to the worde of God, and the forme of the Primitive Church'.[60] Also notable was the King's endorsement of diocesan episcopacy as the legitimate mode of governance over the Kirk, a point which reopened the controversy between episcopacy and presbytery, and which drew together conformist and reformist traditions in the two kingdoms. At stake was the sovereignty of two distinct churches, each boasting its own history and connections with the primitive church, and each calling itself the 'best reformed' church. Since there could only be *one* true church and since the Crown's ecclesiastical sovereignty could be seen as not divisible among 'particular' churches, the Anglo-Scottish debate presented problems unique to the struggle to define the English Church as the true *Protestant* Church.

A short essay by William Cowper, Bishop of Galloway, furnished further insights into similarities in the position of conformists in England and Scotland with respect to the question of ceremonies. Probably written immediately after the Perth Assembly, it was reprinted in the edition of Cowper's works published in 1626. One of the central arguments against kneeling, both in England and Scotland, maintained that it was a practice derived from Rome, and thus inappropriate for reformed worship. As has been shown, English conformists employed three concepts to explain the retention of kneeling: that the Canons of 1604 'restored' it to sound usage; that it was a mark of 'reverence' and 'edification'; and that the scripture enjoined only 'general rules' regarding ceremonial practice. With respect to the first, Bishop Cowper suggested that it was 'hard to condemne a thing lawfull in itself, because it hath been abused'.[61] Clearly, he believed – although he did not offer evidence for this belief – that at some point in the early history of the church kneeling lacked any association with 'idolatry'. Next, he addressed 'reverence', and noted as well that churches reserved authority to establish ceremonies: 'Our Church hath determined, that kneeling seemes the most

[59] Calderwood, *The true history of the Church of Scotland*, pp. 699–700.
[60] *Stuart royal proclamations*, ed. J. F. Larkin and P. L. Hughes, 2 vols. (Oxford, 1973), vol. I, pp. 60–3.
[61] William Cowper, 'The Bishop of Galloway, his answers to such as desire of their scruples against the Acts of the Last Assembly holden at Perth, in the Month of August 1618', in *The workes of Mr Willia[m] Cowper, late Bishop of Galloway* (London, 1626), p. 9.

reverent forme, for receiving so great a benefit: and the rude gesture of so many of our people in many parts of the land, requires that they should be led to a greater reverence of that Holy mystery.' This also reflected a strand of the argument that had remained central to the English conformist position since Gabriel Powel's *De adiaphoris*: ceremonies, if indifferent and edifying, could be justified on the basis of reverence and the fact that they were 'helps' to worship. Bishop Cowper emphasised this last point by suggesting that present usage was 'comely'. This left the matter of scriptural precedence, and reformists had long argued that what Christ had *done* at the Last Supper should obtain in the present worship of the Church of England.

> But here it will be objected to me, that our Lorde and disciples sat at Table. I answeare; The evangelist saith, that as he sate at the Table, hee tooke Breade and gave Thanks. This seemeth to note the time of the institution: to wit, after he had done with the naturall and Paschall Supper, *not the gesture*. For why? S. Paul prescribing all that is *essential* in the Sacrament, makes no mention neither of sitting, standing, or kneeling.[62]

Cowper argued that the essential form of the sacrament was of greater doctrinal import than the posture in which it was received; this entailed a separation of doctrine and practice that drew ceremonies from a strictly doctrinal realm, and situated them within the realm of outward worship and discipline.

Another contribution to the debate came from David Lindsay, the loyalist Bishop of Brechin, whom Calderwood described as having 'harangued' the recalcitrant clergy at Perth. Lindsay began by defending the Crown's juris-diction to 'set down laws and orders', not for any arbitrary purposes, but because 'God is not the author of confusion and unquietnesse, but of order and peace.'[63] Therefore, the King acted as God's agent and ensured the peace of the Church. In terms of the theological and textual questions at issue, Lindsay argued that the scriptures did not specify the nature of the first institution: 'Seeing therefore it is not certaine by the Scripture, that our Saviour did sit or lye, when he did institute this sacrament, the gesture of Sitting should not be esteemed and urged, as necessary to be used thereat.' Although Lindsay admitted that Christ and the Apostles may have been seated at table, he also suggested that such a posture was merely 'accidental' and not intended as an immemorial pattern.[64] This paralleled the position advanced by Cowper and provided a pair of terms useful to disputing the strictly doctrinal case against ceremonies and governance. Those practices

---

[62] Ibid., p. 10.
[63] David Lindsay, *The reasons of a pastors resolution, touching the reuerend receiuing of the holy communion* (London, 1619), pp. 9, 10.
[64] Ibid., pp. 24, 31.

initiated by Christ were 'essential'; practices not so enjoined were 'accidental' and fell under the jurisdiction of ecclesiastical governors. These two terms described the separation of 'belief' and 'practice' bemoaned by Henry Jacob, and lay at the foundation of the argument which sustained the conformist position on the question of ceremonies.[65]

Lindsay was not interested in advancing an historical analysis in order to furnish a pedigree for kneeling in the ceremonies of the true church. Rather, his concern was to argue that the lack of specific direction set forth in the scriptures entailed a freedom on the part of the Kirk to determine the form of its own rites and ceremonies:

And so there is neither in the doctrine of Paul, nor in the doctrine of the Evangelists, so much as mention made of Lying, sitting, standing or kneeling; whereby it is evident, that none of these gestures or positions of body, are recommended as necessary. But that this ceremonie is left to be determined by the Church, as the Time, the Place and the Order, are according to the rule of Charitie and Decencie.[66]

This argument was aimed directly at those who found in scripture the literal form for ordering rites and governance; to them it must have seemed like an almost blasphemous repudiation of the authority of scripture. Moreover, Lindsay's reference to 'Time' was a reference to 'custom', a concept employed, as we have seen, by conformists to defend aspects of worship that were not specifically enjoined by scripture, but were instead adapted from the social context. Reformists dismissed 'custom' as the corruption of the first institution by human ordinance. In short, Lindsay was seeking to demolish the one source of authority on which reformists were accustomed to base their arguments, and to show that, over time and in different historical settings, the 'customs' of churches were subject to change.

Like other conformists examined thus far, Lindsay argued that the restoring of 'idolatrous' customs to sound usage was one of the marks of the reformed church, and thus central to the process of reformation:

As we therefore do not, nor should not condemne or despise the judgement of our Godly Predecessors, who, to root out Idolatry, did interchange kneeling with sitting;

---

[65] In a tract published in 1616, Jacob argued: 'If our practise may follow or depend on the minde of the Magestrate in the nature of Christ's visible church under the Gospell, and the forme of government thereof, then our Faith and belief concerning *the nature of the said church and forme of government* thereof may likewise follow the Magestrate's minde and will. For belief and practise cannot be separated: Faith and obedience do goe together. But our faith and belief may not follow the minde of the Magestrate concerning the nature of Christ's visible church under the gospell, and concerning the forme and government thereof. Therefore our practise may not follow or depend on the minde of the Magistrate in the nature of Christ's visible Church under the Gospel and the forme of government thereof.' See *A collection of sundry matters* ([Amsterdam], 1616), sig. B[8v-r].

[66] Lindsay, *The reasons of a pastors resolution*, p. 41.

so should we not condemne and despise the judgement of our Church at this time, who have again interchanged sitting with kneeling, considering it is an Indifferent ceremonie.

At stake, then, was less the antiquity of doctrine than the sovereignty of a reforming church whose present practices agreed with those of the ancient church. Lindsay's ecclesiology was defined by a mingling of scriptural and canonical elements, and the establishment of the latter both defended and celebrated as marks of a sovereign reformed church. Bringing the argument to a close, Lindsay reminded his reader: 'all this alteration and change hath proceeded from the constant resolution, and the instant desire of a most wise and religious Prince'.[67] In short, Lindsay set the problem down before his opponents, and we might usefully define its propositions. First, the Kirk was a true church, both sufficiently reformed and ancient; second, the King possessed jurisdiction over the Church in his dominions. Yet, what was left out of the argument was the fact that some defined the Kirk as both sovereign and reformed, and also as independent of the jurisdiction of the Crown.

It is not surprising, therefore, that defenders of the Kirk leapt to the latter point. David Calderwood entered the fray with a tract that condemned the Perth Assembly as a 'nullity'. Specifically, Calderwood argued that diocesan episcopacy had a connection with Rome, and was a threat to reformed discipline and the sovereignty of the Kirk:

Since the former government was altered, and the insolent domination of Prelates hath entered in by unlawful means among us; popish rites and ceremonies have followed ... This libertie granted to our Church, to indict and hold general assemblies, from yeare to yeare and oftener ... was the chiefe bulwarke of our discipline. This bulwarke was broken down.[68]

What Calderwood described amounted to an attack on the sovereignty of the Kirk and its assemblies, themselves the 'bulwarks' to reformed doctrine – this was precisely what had taken place in the Kirk since 1603. However, this was not, in the broader context of the two kingdoms, a new argument in religious controversy; for it will be recalled that one consequence of the hardening of positions over clerical subscription was a tendency to aim scorn at the bishops, who were regarded as officers who sought to impose their own patterns of rites and governance on the Church. This contradicted not only the law of scripture, but also, as some English reformists argued, the common law of England. The preface to the 1678 edition of Calderwood's *True history of the Church of Scotland* used the phrase *imperium in imperio* to describe the rise of bishops to positions of civil and ecclesiastical power.

---

[67] Ibid., pp. 180–1, 182.
[68] David Calderwood, *Perth assembly* ([Leiden, 1619]), 'Preface to the Reader'.

However, it did not appear in the manuscript and seems to have been added in the course of preparing Calderwood's massive work for printing.[69]

How – in the absence of the phrase – did Calderwood depict the bishops supplying the condition of *imperium in imperio*? The charge had two essential elements. First, the Articles of Perth were characterised as an imposition on the sovereignty of the Kirk, a sovereignty contained in the directions for rites and governance contained in the first institution, and codified in the *Book of discipline*; hence, argued Calderwood, 'Confessions of faith should not be changeable.'[70] The second branch of the argument concerned the 'reformation parliament', which established the Kirk and guaranteed its reformed liturgy with the authority of law. While the Scots clergy were barred from parliament, there was nevertheless a measure of harmony between the temporal and spiritual aspects of the state, as well as occasions that served to reinforce this harmony between the two kingdoms.[71] In 1560, the English had aided Protestants in the northern kingdom by putting an end to the political fortunes of Mary of Guise, the French, and by extension the papacy. These were the political events that had defined Scotland's Reformation, and Calderwood argued that they had come under threat in the early seventeenth century:

The Articles proposed, if they be concluded, they doe innovate and bring under the slander of change the estate of this Church, so advisedly established by Ecclesiastical constitution, acts of Parliament, approbation of other Kirkes, and good liking of the best reformed Christians without and within this Kingdom, and so evidently blessed with happie successe and sensible experience of God's greatest benefits by space of 58 yeares and above, so that we may boldlie say to the praise of God that no Church hath enjoyed the truth and puritie of religion in larger libertie.[72]

Calderwood treated the Perth Articles as innovations that severed the best reformed Kirk from its historical and reformed foundations.

Many writers for the Kirk addressed themselves to the defence of this Presbyterian interpretation of the foundations of their church. Calderwood was by far the most prolific contributor to these controversies; having had a face-to-face argument with James over the latter's policies concerning the external government of the Kirk, Calderwood was deprived, imprisoned, and then banned from Scotland.[73] Decamping to Holland, where he would remain until the King's death in 1625, Calderwood set himself up as a

---

[69] The original runs to six volumes consisting of 3,136 pp., all held by the British Library (Add MSS 4734–9). I am grateful to J. A. W. Gunn for taking time out of his own work in London to examine the MSS in search of the elusive phrase.

[70] Calderwood, *Perth assembly*, p. 31.

[71] For this, see MacDonald, 'Ecclesiastical representation,' pp. 39–41.

[72] Calderwood, *Perth assembly*, pp. 18–19.

[73] See Calderwood, *The true history of the Church of Scotland*, passim.

professional controversialist, engaged in two of the great Protestant controversies of the age: that concerning the Scottish Kirk, and the Arminian controversy. In many ways, Calderwood furnished a strong element of continuity between the debates in Britain from the first decade of the seventeenth century and those that took place between English controversialists and the Remonstrant side at Dordrecht.

Evidence of these connections appeared in Calderwood's reply to David Lindsay's *Resolutions*, in which Calderwood offered a defence of a Presbyterian interpretation of the Apostolic church against either reform or 'custom'. Here again we find the tension that attended the debate over whether the Church would be conceived as a spiritual association defined solely by scripture, or as a 'mixture' of elements, some enjoined as 'essential' points of doctrine, and others 'accidental' points of discipline. Calderwood's position was clear: 'We ought to take heed, not what any hath done before us, sayth Cyprian, but what Christ who was before all, did: we must not follow the custom of men, but the truth of God.'[74] In a reference to the *Abridgment* controversy, Calderwood praised the 'ministers of Lincoln' for their principled stand on this issue, and condemned the scholarly defenders of the 'customs of men' – Thomas Rogers, Thomas Hutton, William Covell, and Thomas Sparke – all of them prominent in the English controversies over clerical subscription. Despite the support of these conformist writers, Calderwood speculated that the mainstream in the Church of England was compelled to conform: 'As for the Anglican Kirke, I deny that the body of that Kirke doth approve kneeling howsoever they may be compelled by their Kirke representative to practise it.' Calderwood's emphasis on the tension between *iure divino* and *iure humano* in the English confession shared a great deal with the work and ideas of his English forerunners, Josias Nichols, Samuel Hieron, Henry Jacob, and William Bradshaw. Common to all was a kind of instrumental anti-popery, whereby the English confession was lumped together with that of Rome.[75] The case was often made by merely conveying the opinion of a writer well placed to judge: 'For PETRUS CVDSENSIUS, a Jesuit viewing the state of the English Kirke anno 1608 give this judgement ... that the state of religion in England was such, as that it might be easilie changed to the Catholicke religion.'[76] Moreover, the 'terrible inquisition of high commission' was likened to that earlier conflagration whereby the Roman church co-opted lay rulers in the rooting out of heresy.

---

[74] David Calderwood, *A solution of Doctor Resolutus, his resolutions for kneeling* ([Amsterdam, 1619]), p. 20.

[75] For Jacobean 'anti-popery', see Anthony Milton, *Catholic and reformed: the Roman and Protestant churches in English Protestant thought, 1600–1640* (Cambridge, 1995), pp. 31–42.

[76] Calderwood, *A solution*, pp. 19, 55.

Calderwood was attentive to the still smouldering controversy over diocesan episcopacy and the High Commission, and sought to exploit its principal texts.

Other tracts of the time revealed a range of opinion among Scottish writers and a broad interest in adapting works of controversy published in England to questions facing the Kirk. John Michelson, a little-known preacher, penned a tract that elaborated, through a series of maxims, why the practices of the Apostolic church should obtain in all matters of rites and governance. For Michelson, the 'definition' of the Kirk was fixed, and could not be subjected to the tampering of human agents:

> The argument must have this forme; what gesture Christ with his Apostles used in the Institution of the Sacrament of his Supper, the same we are bound to use: But Christ, with His Disciples, used the Gesture of Sitting, and not Kneeling: Ergo, wee are bound to sitt, and ought not to kneele.

The ancient church understood the importance of the first institution and maintained this pattern of observance. Once again, Cyprian became the authority who supported the proposition that the 'auncient church ... was not permitted ... to kneele, as it is clearly witnessed'.[77] Yet Michelson strayed beyond the ancients, and toyed with a mildly conformist interpretation of *adiaphora*. Citing with approval Thomas Morton's defence of ceremonies and John Denison's *Beati pacifici* (1620), he suggested that the peace of the Kirk might take precedence over small matters of practice. Returning to the example of the ancient church, Michelson suggested that 'though it were an infallible truth, that they did not kneele on the Lord's daye; yet it may be they did kneele on other dayes, in the act of receiving the Sacrament'.[78] With respect to doctrine of the sacrament, Michelson was firm that the first institution should prevail; yet the practice of the sacrament might be altered according to custom.

This concession to one of the central positions held by defenders of the English Church drew a quick response from Calderwood, who penned an attack on Michelson, as well as on Morton's book. Kneeling before the sacramental elements was dismissed as 'idolatry', as was any suggestion that, even though the English Church 'was like in shew' to the Roman, it had nevertheless restored kneeling to sound usage, and it now stood for reverence.[79] Here, Calderwood attacked precisely the severing of matters

---

[77] John Michelson, *The lawfulnes of kneeling in the act of receiuing the sacrament of the Lordes supper* (St Andrews, 1620), pp. 5–6, 75.

[78] Ibid., p. 75.

[79] David Calderwood, *A defence of our arguments against kneeling in the act of receiving the sacramentall elements of bread and wine impugned by Mr. Michelsone* ([Amsterdam, 1620]), p. 40.

of doctrine (the Word) and matters of practice (ceremonies) that was the hallmark of the conformist case, and the question on which Michelson had seemed to waver. As for the authority of the Fathers so frequently urged in Morton's work, Calderwood countered that they included not one 'expresse testimony' except that dredged up from 'some counterfeit worke'. Yet the soundness of Morton's scholarship was not Calderwood's principal interest. More important was his insistence that the King be shown the degree to which the Perth Articles – measures defended by the Crown – did serious harm to the Kirk. This argument was connected with the broader theological argument that we have seen developed by reformists in the course of the English controversies: that is, the enforcement of a mode of worship not warranted by scripture through a mode of church governance that was a 'political' rather than spiritual device entailed a departure from the tradition of the true church:

> The commandment of the Magistrate cannot make a thing, which of itselfe is scandalous, and hurtful, not to be hurtful, but rather by the strength of his authoritie maketh it more scandalous and hurtful, then it would be. But none of our Formalists will deale in earnest with the Supreme Magistrate, and tell him that he committeth active scandall in laying a stumbling block before the people, and therefore sinneth against the Lord.[80]

From a political point of view, there was nothing really 'radical' about Calderwood's complaint that the magistrate was bound to enforce the true religion; rather, it reflected a strand of thinking voiced throughout the period.[81] For example, the preface to the Thirty-nine Articles noted the Crown's duty to 'preserve and defend' the established faith, and conformists such as William Covell and Thomas Bilson defined the King's duty by his status as 'defender' of the faith. While English and Scots writers divided over the 'definition' of the Church, they broadly agreed that the Crown had certain inviolable duties toward that institution.

In subsequent tracts, Calderwood departed from a pattern of formal works of controversy with their apparatus of scriptural and patristic references, and turned to more popular forms of argument.[82] In one example, he wrote as the personification of the Kirk, condemning the bishops for their lordly, prelatical, and political ways. Indeed, Calderwood argued that the English bishops had compromised the 'liberty' of the Kirk to make determinations in matters of doctrine by assuming the power to establish points of doctrine.

---

[80] Ibid., p. 57.
[81] Kevin Sharpe, 'Private conscience and public duty in the writings of James VI and I', in his *Remapping early modern England: the culture of seventeenth-century politics* (Cambridge, 2000), pp. 151–71.
[82] For the Scottish roots of popular pamphleteering, see Joad Raymond, *Pamphlets and pamphleteering in early modern Britain* (Cambridge, 2003), ch. 5.

He also employed the standard reformist argument concerning the 'function' of bishops – instead of pastors concerned with spiritual affairs, they had become prelates, endowed with political power: 'By what conscience, reason, or law, they have deserted their flocks and pastorall charges, entered into civil place and pompe ... [they have] taken upon them the power of both swords against the whole subjects of this kingdome'.[83] This civil power had manifested itself in clerical deprivations and the operation of the High Commission, subjects with which Calderwood was intimately familiar. Taking the stance of a defender of reformed traditions and law, Calderwood argued that the Kirk had fallen into the grip of a counter-reformation, and required:

A full deliverance from, and a sufficient defence against all novations and novelties in doctrine, sacraments and discipline, and specially such as by constitutions of the Kirk, confessions of faith, loveable lawes of the countrey, and long continued practise hath been condemned, and casten out as idle rites, and Romish formalities.

Both the civil *and* doctrinal aspects of 1560 needed protection, for the Kirk also was a church 'by law established'. That meant that there could be passage of no law 'in derogation, or prejudice of the Acts already granted in favour of reformation'. Defending a settlement already established in law, Calderwood portrayed the Perth Articles as an illegal challenge to the sovereignty of the Reformation Parliament.[84] Calderwood knew very well that if 'corrupt' modes of rites and governance could be promulgated by law, then their removal would also be a matter of law.

A dialogue published in 1620 saw John Murray pressing the tension between *iure divino* and *iure humano*. Indeed, even his interlocutors, Theophilus and Cosmophilus – a lover of God, and a lover of the world – reflected the division, and in the preface Murray pointed out that the work had been written for the benefit of those 'stollen away from the truth'.[85] Murray took the truth of the scripture to be 'self evident', yet still prone to manipulation and obfuscation by means of learning or law. One advantage of the dialogue form was that it could be adapted to resemble an important branch of devotional literature – the catechism; indeed, these were common, being printed in larger runs than was usual for controversial literature, and served to instruct the laity on the basic tenets of their faith.[86] Murray was able to explain complex

[83] David Calderwood, *The speach of the Kirk of Scotland to her beloved children* ([Amsterdam], 1620), p. 65.

[84] Ibid., p. 71.

[85] [John Murray], *A dialogue betwixt Cosmophilus and Theophilus anent the urging of new ceremonies upon the kirke of Scotland* ([Amsterdam, 1620]), sig. A³.

[86] See Ian Green, *The Christian's ABC: catechisms and catechizing in England, c. 1530–1740* (Oxford, 1996), esp. ch. 2.

points of doctrine in a manner not possible in a traditional work of controversy. Hence, he referred to 'substantial' and 'circumstantial' points of doctrine in order to describe what was implied by the oath enjoining subscription to the Perth Articles:

> *Cosm.* It is true Theophile, that bond and the knots thereof, holds fast upon the substantiall poynts of religion, doctrine and discipline, which are unchangable; but not so upon the changeable rites and ceremonies about them.
>
> *Theoph.* Surely Cosmophile, the matter of the oath, and all the particulars thereof, are like a Holy Tabernacle, so joyntly and soundly compacted, and knit together, that the loosing of one pin, being the perill to shake all loose. So albeit some might seeme to be indifferent in themselves severally and apart considered: yet ye must not think it a thing indifferent, to single, and picke out the small pinnes of it at your pleasure, lest all fall downe about your eares.[87]

Here we find not only a fine encapsulation of the debate on the nature of ceremonies, but a good example of the problem presented in terms of a corporate structure – no element of worship, the argument ran, could be considered inferior or 'indifferent'. The whole point of arguing from the first institution was to show that Christ's sovereignty amounted to a divine *imprimatur*. As Henry Jacob argued, 'We believe that the nature and essence of Christ's true visible (that is political) Church under the Gospel is a free congregation of Christians for the service of God, or a true spiritual body politicke.'[88] Reformist ecclesiology held that a perfect agreement between belief and practice defined the 'true' church, and was one of its central 'notes'.

One of the ways that conformists tried to get around this argument was to suggest that the King himself bore a mandate from Christ to ensure the continued peace of the Church, and retained the liberty to order its ceremonies for 'edification'. Murray set this argument alongside a typical reformist reply:

> *Cosm.* [M]ay not the authority of King and Kirke, lawfully reduce and impose these forms?
>
> *Theoph.* It is true, God hath given authority to both, but with this restriction, and direction (sayes the Apostle Paul 2 Cor. 13:10) *not for the destruction, but for the edification of his Kirke.* For the power of authority, is the power of equity, not of injury.[89]

Note that Murray did not deny that either King or Kirk possessed power *iure divino*, but rather stressed that this power was bound to be used for the

---

[87] Murray, *A dialogue*, p. 6.

[88] Henry Jacob, *Anno Domini 1616. A confession and protestation of the faith of certaine Christians in England* ([Amsterdam, 1616]), sigs. B^r–2v.

[89] Murray, *A dialogue*, p. 22. Emphasis in original.

promotion of true doctrine, governance, and worship, and this meant that all points of discipline and practice that they imposed had to come from the pattern of the Word. This position, in turn, encouraged conformists to argue that their opponents unlawfully assumed to themselves the power to dictate the nature of worship to those ecclesiastical authorities competent to make that determination – hence the frequent charges against 'faction', 'singularity', and 'private conventicles'. A further exchange served to illustrate the point:

> *Cosm.* Ye curbe the power and authority of the King and Church strangely *Theoph*, That denieth it to them even in things indifferent.
> *Theoph.* I have told you *Cosm.* that there is nothing indifferent, that breakes these Apostolicall rules. Mans authority is not absolute in things indifferent; but it is tied to these former scriptures: from the which, if it vary, it wants the warrant of divine authority.

For Murray, 'Apostolical rules' represented the immemorial nature of the church's power over itself. This not only constituted an argument for how its doctrine and governance should be ordered, but implicitly repudiated the authority of human governors. Yet Murray was not interested in attacking the authority of the Crown, but argued instead that the diocesan bishops had compromised ecclesiastical sovereignty. It was they who had enforced rites not warranted by scripture, and it was they who 'have left their formal calling; or pastoral charge, & violently thrust honest men out of their places'.[90] With Theophilus' regular refutations of the positions of his inter-locutor, there was little doubt about Murray's own stance on these issues.

One of David Calderwood's most important works was *The altar of Damascus*, published in Scotland in 1621, and then in Latin on the Continent in 1623.[91] Although Calderwood reverted to the formal mode of controversy, his aim remained didactic; the *Altar* was a primer on the technical aspects of English ecclesiology and the legal apparatus that main-tained it. Calderwood's purpose, therefore, was to explain both the nature of the ecclesiastical supremacy of the Crown and the circumstances under which it might become corrupted. This meant a return to familiar categories: 'For we must not consider things indifferent onely in their generall kinde, but

---

[90] Ibid., pp. 23, 37.
[91] *Altare Damascenum, ceu politia Ecclesiae Anglicanae obtrusa Ecclesiae Scoticanae, studio Edwardi Didoclavii. Cui interserta confutatio Paraeneseos Tileni ad Scotos Genevensis; et adjecta Epistola Hieronymi Philadelphi de regimine Ecclesiae Scoticanae.* The full title of the English edition was *The altar of Damascus or the patern of the English hierarchie, and church- policie obtruded upon the Church of Scotland* ([Amsterdam, 1621]). The Latin edition was thus reissued for a different purpose: the refutation of the positions of the Huguenot Arminian, Daniel Tilenus. Yet this was not the first time Calderwood had written against Tilenus; see Calderwood, *Scoti τοῦ τυχονος paraclesis contra Danielis Tileni Silesii Parænesin, ad Scotos Genevensis disciplinæ zelotas conscriptam, cuius pars prima est, episcopali ecclesiæ regimie* (1622).

in their particular and circumstantial use; which if we permit to Princes, they may abuse indifferent things to the great hurt of the Church.'[92] Calderwood's thinking was motivated by yet another maxim which, slightly modified, would play a large role in English ideas after his death; for, he pointed out, the 'salus ecclesiae suprema lex esto'. In other words, the safety of the Church stood supreme, to be maintained, when necessary, even against those governors who did not uphold the true way. The Church was not dependent on the political fortunes of any particular person or group within the state, but nevertheless could be harmed by improper intrusion or negligence. Calderwood, therefore, described the King's power as 'cumulative' – to defend, promote, and protect – rather than 'privative, to deprive and spoil her of any Power Christ hath granted her'.[93] In other words, the King was to remain a 'nursing father' to his Church.

Having reasserted the theory of kingship that paired sound rule with the promotion of true doctrine, Calderwood turned to consider the other aspect of the English religious hierarchy – diocesan bishops. Here, he delved into a branch of evidence not prominent in his 'popular' writing, arguing on the basis of the New Testament that: 'By divine law, one Pastor is not superior in degree above another, no more than one Apostle or Evangelist above another Apostle or Evangelist. The name of Bishops was not appropriate to any eminent rank of Pastors, but was common to all, as may be seene: Act 20; Philip. 1: 1; Tim. 1: 1; Tit. 1: 1; Pet. 5.' This addressed the notion of scriptural support for the hierarchy of the clergy, but left open the question of sovereignty. Hence, Calderwood continued by noting that the bishops were inferior to the Crown: 'they are not Bishops *iure divino* ... For all their jurisdiction and power is united and annexed to the Crown, from whence it is derived'.[94] Calderwood therefore rejected those arguments that cast the bishops as inferior but independent magistrates, and the High Commission as a legitimate extension of the ecclesiastical sovereignty of the Crown.

In the work of William Wilkes and, in particular, Edward Forset, the commonwealth was likened to a political structure that was maintained by balance, a mode of analysis which made it difficult to speak of anything but a well-ordered interaction of groups. From Calderwood's point of view, the bishops had disrupted this balance by claiming powers that were not rightfully theirs. Despite the testimony of renowned clerics, Calderwood argued, the jurisdiction of English bishops had no justification in English law. In addition to Edward Coke's *Reports*, and titles from the English controversy over episcopacy, therefore, he noted Francis Bacon's tract of 1604,[95] which

---

[92] David Calderwood, *The altar of Damascus*, p. 15.   [93] Ibid., p. 15.   [94] Ibid., p. 75.

[95] [Francis Bacon], *Certaine considerations touching the better pacification, and edification of the Church of England* (London, 1604).

warned the new King of the potential problems of 'jurisdiction'. From these English authorities and debates, he concluded:

> It followeth therefore that all the Jurisdiction properly spiritual, which the English prelates doe exercise; as Prelates, is unlawful, howsoever they have the warrant of men's lawes. It is only but to save their own credit, that they have set Downame, Bilson and other their friends on worke, to pleade that Bishops are above Pastors *iure divino*, by divine institution, which they are not able to prove.[96]

Calderwood closed his tract by returning to the theory of estates, arguing that the bishops sought to usurp the ecclesiastical sovereignty of Crown in parliament. It was as if 'the body of the state of the common-wealth were not an entire and complete body and state, without the body and state of the Prelacie, [and] no laws could be made without their consent'.[97]

A second tract published during 1621 – and reissued during the Bishops' Wars – saw Calderwood attacking the bishops from the point of view of the doctrine of the Church. For, he noted, the Church of England could hardly lay claim to being the true church, owing to its deep religious divisions: 'it is not so universall being intermingled with Papists, Anabaptists, Lutherans'.[98] However, this condemnation of the English Church was peripheral to Calderwood's purpose: to offer a contrast between the Church of England and the Kirk in order to determine which most closely conformed to the ideal of the 'best reformed' church. A second layer to the argument concerned the governance of these institutions and its impact on their reformed character. Hence, with reference to the Kirk, Calderwood asked:

> Doe we not condemne Archbishops, Bishops, Holy Dayes, kneeling, confirmation, private baptisme, seeing all those particular heads were damned by our Church either in the former confession, the First or Second Booke of Discipline, and Acts of the Generall Assemblies, before the said confession was sworne and subscribed, and if they pleased to practise them after they were damned, the censures of the Church was inflicted upon them?

Clearly, Calderwood was not averse to the notion of censuring those who would not conform to his vision of the Kirk: conformity and non-conformity in the Kirk were to be assessed by Scottish clerics referring to Scottish Articles and canonical discipline. It was on this basis that Calderwood maintained that there was no doctrinal justification for the bishops to enjoin conformity to a pattern of worship lacking the crucial divine sanction. What conformists defended as a means to promote 'order', Calderwood condemned as the pursuit of corrupt spiritual ends by illegal political means:

---

[96] Calderwood, *The altar of Damascus*, p. 76.   [97] Ibid., pp. 76, 95.
[98] David Calderwood, *Quaeres concerning the state of the Church of Scotland* ([London?, 1621]), p. 3.

bishops by their own sole authority medling with Testimentarie, and other causes, not belonging to ecclesiastical consistories; the Bishop taking to himselfe the sole administration of spiritual jurisdiction over many hundred Churches, yea deputing the same to civilians, Chancellors and Officials, and meddling with the administration of civil affairs, as best beseeming his grandeur.[99]

The whole system of spiritual courts met with his disapproval; indeed, there was nothing 'godly' or reminiscent with the practice of reformed churches in the way in which English bishops pursued conformity. They used the force of Canon law, and claimed to hold power based on the testimony of a mis-rendered textual tradition. In a wide variety of publications, Calderwood had offered a convincing case against the imposition of ceremonies, a case built upon on a number of texts central to debates on Jacobean ecclesiology. His work showed a developed understanding of the works published by English conformists, as well as those of his own countrymen who wrote in support of episcopacy in the Kirk. For all of this, Calderwood's greatest concern was to defend an idea of a doctrinally 'pure' and politically independent Kirk, whose ceremonies and mode of governance gave testimony to its claims of being Apostolic; no 'reformed' church of Britain, this was a purely Scottish institution, possessed of its own history and sovereignty. Yet the problem mentioned at the outset of this chapter remained: how might one King be sovereign over two churches, each with its own vision of doctrine and governance?

THE CHURCH OF 'GREATE BRITTAINE'

Calderwood's torrent of texts finally received an answer from David Lindsay, whose *True narration* addressed his rival's tract concerning the 'nullity' of the Perth Assembly. More generally, it addressed the Presbyterian concern about the gulf between doctrinal matters of 'substance' and those of 'circumstance', that is, between belief and practice. At stake in this debate was the historical pedigree of the policy of the Kirk with regard to ceremonies: were they, as Calderwood argued, only legitimate if enjoined by scripture, or did a precedent exist for the 'liberty' of the Church to make judgements concerning 'things indifferent'? Lindsay adopted the latter position in his preface:

Albeit all things necessarie to the worship of God, and men's salvation, be eyther expressly, or by necessarie consequence, contayned in the written Word, yet the particular circumstances of persons by whom, place where, time when, and of the forme and order how the worship and worke of the Ministrie should be performed, are neither expressly nor by necessary consequence set downe in the Word: but for the

---

[99] Ibid., pp. 6–11.

determination of these, some general rules are given, according to which the Church has power to define whatsoever is most expedient to be observed, and done for the honour of God, and edification.[100]

This presented the standard English conformist case for the Church's ability to establish 'general rules' of worship which led to edification, and pointed to two developed ecclesiologies. Calderwood wrote defences of the Kirk that drew upon a Genevan model and advocated Presbyterian governance, while Lindsay's defence of the doctrine of the Kirk adopted tenets of the English theory of things indifferent in order to defend the position that the English Church exemplified the 'best reformed' church. Hence, where the English debate had concerned those rites and modes of governance appropriate to a single national Church that yet made claims to antiquity, the debate in Scotland concerned two national churches each with distinct claims to antiquity and the reformed tradition.

This set of precepts informed Lindsay's argument, the burden of which was to show that the Church as it existed in England, and was envisioned for Scotland, was both true to the Word and yet legitimately possessed of its own sovereignty. Lindsay saw the Kirk as capable of defining its own order of worship, so long as it was not contrary to scripture: 'It is certaine, that this power cannot reach to anything essentiall or materiall in the worship of God: but to the decencie, and order only, which is to be observed for edification in the circumstances above specified.'[101] In other words, while the substance of ceremonies was inviolable, the Kirk might alter their external form, so long as this practice was guided by the principles of order and edification. From the point of view of English conformists, 'edification' trumped any charge of idolatry or any suggestion that their pattern of worship departed from the Word – such additions to ceremonies were merely 'indifferent'. Lindsay's final task was to suggest that order, decency, and edification were enjoined by the Word as the means necessary to ensure peace in God's earthly church:

the Canons made by her ... ought to be obeyed so long as they stand unchanged or abrogated: not because they contain in them any substantiall or materiall part of religion, or that they have in them any Divine authority ... but because in them order is established, tending to the unity of peace, whereby confusion, scandall, and schisme is eschewed: and because the Power of the Church, whereby these lawes are made, is the Ordinance of God, and confirmed by the Authoritie of His Word, commanding us to Obey them that are set Over us in the Lord, the Canons of the Church must be obeyed.[102]

---

[100] David Lindsay, *A true narration of all the passages of the proceedings in the generall Assembly of the Church of Scotland, Holden at Perth the 25. of August, anno Dom. 1618* (London, 1621), sig. A[3v].
[101] Ibid., sig. B[3r]. [102] Ibid., sig. B[4v].

Like English conformists, Lindsay argued that ceremonial practice was permissible on the grounds that it promoted order in the institution of the Church.

The linchpin of Lindsay's theory of obedience was based in a similar relationship between social order and individual 'conscience', terms which figured in the sermons preached by Hampton and Meriton, and which would play a large role in subsequent debates on English ecclesiastical polity. Lindsay's injunction to obey the Canons of the Church, and his depiction of those laws as divine ordinances, suggested that he sought to establish order and conformity as points of doctrine. So much was also implied by Thomas Bell's use of 1 Corinthians 14: 40 ('Let all things be done decently and in order') to establish that order and peace in the church were enjoined by scripture. This argument may have been intended to diffuse the reformist charge that the Church was overwhelmingly guided by human agents; for both Bell and Lindsay, the Canons, laws, and injunctions to conform were merely the means by which the condition of order prescribed by scripture was achieved in the visible church. This was not a matter for individuals, and hence one must remember that the aim of conformist ecclesiastical polity was defined by the need to maintain order in the political and spiritual bodies politic:

it is ever more expedient to obey a Law, and keepe a lawfull custom, then to doe a thing thought more expedient, if it cannot be done, but by an open breach of the law: because thereby the Law must be brought in contempt, private opinion preferred to publicke authoritie, and so confusion, contention and schisme brought in.[103]

To do otherwise, argued Lindsay, was to 'disprove and condemne all sorts of Government', a purpose he perceived in Calderwood's assault on the Perth Articles. The widely held political virtues of order and obedience were yoked to 'decency' and 'edification' as their spiritual counterparts. All of these concepts described the operation of God's will that peace and stability prevail in church and commonwealth; these conditions, if violated, also entailed a violation of a divine ordinance. Yet this did not necessarily serve to justify absolutist government according to an inflexible divine warrant. What was important were religious and godly magistrates for, argued Lindsay, history showed that as 'the Church decayed under wicked and idolatrous governors, so did it ever revive and flourish under religious and godly Kings'.[104]

When the all-important dimension of ecclesiastical authority is included in the discussion of the power of kings, some habitual scholarly understandings of divine right break down.[105] For many contemporaries, the church *iure*

---

[103] Ibid., sig. C²ʳ.   [104] Ibid., sig. C³ʳ.
[105] That is, English theories of kingship were fleshed out with reference to ecclesiastical sovereignty, and duties to the Church served as a check against the use of absolute power. See J. P. Sommerville, 'English and European political ideas in the early seventeenth century: revisionism and the case of absolutism', *Journal of British Studies*, 35 (1996), 168–94.

divino took precedence, and the success or failure of a governor turned on the preservation of this condition. At the heart of Calderwood's argument was the allegation that the Crown had stood by while the bishops had imposed their own patterns of rites on a church whose ordinances were ancient and inviolable; this imposition also entailed a departure from the reformed tradition. Lindsay answered Calderwood's attack on episcopacy with an appeal to antiquity: 'The former government is not altered, that is, either corrupted or abolished, as you insinuate, but is perfitted by accession of the ancient order, which has been ever in the House of God since the Apostolicall times, and was embraced at the reformation.'[106] Lindsay continued by linking the sovereignty of the Church with the notion of 'restoration', whereby the corruption of the Church had become so pervasive that a centralised, hierarchical, and coercive power was required.[107]

One of Lindsay's aims was to furnish an account of a unified Protestantism that countered the spectre of corrupt Roman Catholicism. This went some way toward answering the charge, put about by Calderwood and others, that Protestantism had become fractured, with some parts in better doctrinal trim than others. In Lindsay's hands, the notion of a *restored* constitutional perfection of the Church was employed as an argument to call into question those who rejected the English model of Church governance. To portray bishops as the restored third estate of the parliament effectively counteracted the reformist argument, for it obliged the writer truly committed to his position to reject the authority of the parliament: 'That the Church, which has ever represented the Third Estate of the Kingdom, was restored in the persons of Bishops, according to the fundamental laws to have vote in Parliament, could be a griefe to none sincerely affected either to the weale of the Country or Church.'[108] This applied more closely to Scotland, where the bishops had been restored to parliament amid a broad conflict over law and ecclesiology.[109]

Yet Lindsay did not seek to press the unity of Protestantism too far and pointed out that governance by bishops was part of the unique history of the English Church after the Reformation. It was perhaps this tendency, which we have seen in the writings of Francis Mason and others, that led reformists to argue that the Church of England had turned its back on the reformed

[106] Lindsay, *A true narration*, sig. D^{4v}.
[107] Lindsay's position on this point is very similar to that of Marco Antonio de Dominis, in his *De republica ecclesiastica, pars secunda, continens libros quintum et sextum* (London, 1620). De Dominis argued that the Reformation had returned the Church to its ancient profile, and hence confirmed it as the best example of the true church left on earth by Christ. For De Dominis' controversial career, see Patterson, *King James VI and I*, pp. 220–59.
[108] Lindsay, *A true narration*, p. 4.
[109] See MacDonald, 'Ecclesiastical representation', pp. 57–61.

tradition. Lindsay replied by suggesting that models of church governance derived from city states such as Geneva were not appropriate to kingdoms, and that in all cases ancient forms were preferable to 'novelty' – Bancroft's label for Presbyterian discipline:

> That the forme of government meete for a Parochial or Diocesan church, such as Geneva or Berne, is not fit in all respects for the universal or for a National Church: That at the beginning of the reformation, sundrie circumstantial ceremonies were changed, or abolished for Superstition, which now tending to edification, and pre-servation of God's worship from all prophaners, and to make conformitie and unitie, both with the Primitive and reformed Churches, may be lawfully and fruitfully received. That antiquity in such things, and universall consent not subject to veritie, is farre to be preferred to new and recent conceits, and customs of private persons, and Churches.[110]

Here, Lindsay sought to distinguish between the history of the Presbyterian discipline and that of England, and to set forth the unique circumstances that attended the governance of a 'national' Church. Lindsay used 'national' in the senses of a church allied with the political complex, and of a church embodying all of the subjects of that political complex. Against this unity and employing the concept of 'custom' to suit the case, he posited that particular churches that clung to outmoded patterns of worship were not supported by the testimony of scripture or antiquity: 'It is true, that when the Church was governed by a paritie of Ministers, they choosed a Moderator by suffrage, though without any warrant or example, eyther out of Scripture or Antiquitie, but being compelled thereto of Necessitie.' The necessity of establishing a reformed church in Scotland against the wishes of a Roman Catholic regent and monarch severed the link between the ancient church and that of the present. As one scholar has noted, the Kirk was left to 'establish itself', and this meant that a premium would be placed on order and obedience to the ecclesiastical sovereignty of the Crown.[111] The succession of a godly prince led to changes in the governance of the Kirk and compelled members – including those voting in opposition to the Perth Articles – to obey its governors:

> This obedience should ever be performed, where it may stand with the feare of God. These things have not been considered by the negative voters: And evidently shew that their pretext of adhering to the particular judgement of the Church ... is no other, but a fair excuse and spacious vaile to cover their willful opposition to his Magestie's will, and the will of the Church.[112]

As thorough as Lindsay's answer was, it still left open the question of how modes of hierarchical and coercive church governance could be squared with

---

[110] Lindsay, *A true narration*, pp. 6–7.   [111] MacDonald, 'Ecclesiastical representation', p. 41.
[112] Lindsay, *A true narration*, pp. 77, 104–105.

alternative histories of the reformed churches, many of which described pastoral rather than diocesan bishops. Some writers took care to shift the blame for the corruption of the Church away from the King, and toward diocesan bishops. For example, William Scott argued that, by stripping the Kirk of the ability to elect a new moderator for each synod, Lindsay and his coterie sought to assume sole control of the Kirk, and to submit 'the outward forme and circumstance of God's worship' to 'civil statute':

the wall and tower of new Episcopacie, cunningly brought in by that Intrant the constant Moderator, and solemnly set up to remaine the Atlas of their Kingdome, with full power of Lordly dominion to be exercised over the Kirke for the Five Articles, the Fundamental Lawes of that usurped authoritie, and to putt forth and hold forth the lawfull and necessarie assemblies of the Kirk, as enemies to the Power of princes.[113]

The problem, according to Scott, concerned the office of bishops in relation to the standard sources of authority – the Word and history of the Kirk – both of which designated them as 'pastors' not 'prelates'. For example, 1 Timothy 3: 16 was cited in support of the contention that pastors should confine themselves to the preaching of the Word: 'let them see how they may be distracted with civil offices and affairs ... so it is, that the office of Bishoprie confounds the spiritual and civill jurisdictions and callings in the person of one'. As we have seen, this confusion of jurisdictions was pointed out by Francis Bacon and reiterated by Calderwood and others; clearly, Scottish writers found some truth in the suggestion that the causes of both Kirk and Crown were compromised by those appointed to rule the ecclesiastical sphere. Scott noted that the bishops had quitted the spiritual realm and entered that of politics: '[that] the Pastors and Bishops of the Kirke ... set themselves to politicke administration, and court affairs, and be occupied in secular and worldly matters, leaving their flocks and following the puffed up pomp and glory of the world, is against the ancient Canons of the Kirk'.[114] Like English reformists, the Scots Presbyterians distinguished between ancient bishops as 'pastors' and prelatical bishops who exercised temporal power.

Where Lindsay had sought to depict the unique character of the Church of England as a justification of hierarchy and coercion in the Kirk, Scott emphasised the unity of the Protestant confession, and celebrated James as the embodiment of the religious prince. This perfection was made all the more vivid by contrasting it with the corruption of episcopacy, 'one of the greatest errors and corruptions', and a threat to 'that Union of these

---

[113] William Scott, *The course of conformitie, as it hath proceeded, is concluded, should be refused* ([Amsterdam, 1622]), sig. A⁴ʳ.
[114] Ibid., pp. 22, 23, 25.

Kingdoms under one God and Christ, one King, one Faith, one Law, and under His Magestie Advanced'. Not only did Scott celebrate the unity of British Protestantism, he portrayed the united kingdoms as a shining example for other reformed churches: 'affixed as it were on the most high pillar in the great Theatre of Europe, testifying and proclaiming to all, his Magestie's pietie, sincerity and zeal to the Gospel of Christ ... against all corruption and thralldome of the Anti-Christ of Rome'.[115] With reference to the English constitution, Scott argued that to allow the bishops power over the other estates was to admit the equivalent of a Trojan horse within the walls; a fanciful metaphor, perhaps, but one nevertheless suited to conveying the image of episcopacy as *imperium in imperio*. Hence, the bishops stood to compromise not only the laws and religion of Britain, but also the peace of Continental Protestantism.

In 1622, Patrick Scot published the first of two responses to Calderwood and returned the debate to the question of a single, sovereign church. Scot argued that the 'Church of Great Britain' should be maintained in the bonds of unity and peace, and that contentions over 'matters indifferent ... Open a Gap to disorder and scandal'.[116] To speak of a Church of Great Britain went some way toward ironing out the question of the jurisdiction of one church over another, by simply positing the existence of a single, imperial church, itself the spiritual manifestation of the centralised temporal government created by the Union of the Crowns.[117] Yet a national Church was no less vexed by the problems of 'ignorance' and 'opinion' than was the English Church itself, and so Scot sought to defend the reformed character of a Church which comprehended all of the king's subjects:

Our Church in the Isle of Great Britaine (praysed be God) is not to plaint: it is established and settled in the fulnesse of Peace, in the sinceritie of Doctrine, and in the Wisdome of Policie and Discipline. The Word is truly preached ... the Policie and Discipline established by the Civil Magistrat in former times in most parts of this Isle, and now confirmed by a religious and learned King, who from his cradle has laboured to see the Church flourish in unitie and peace.[118]

Of course Scot did not mean that James defended the faith from the comfort of the nursery, but rather that he had been destined to do so since birth as the epitome of the religious prince. From Scot's point of view, government in the Church was necessary to prevent the corruption threatened by 'opinion' and the 'imbezzling [of] the Authority of the Fathers'. Yet the argument had less

---

[115] Ibid., pp. 29, 39, 40.
[116] Patrick Scot, *Calderwoods recantation: or, a tripartite discourse* (London: Bernard Alsop, 1622), p. 2.
[117] See Ferguson, *Scotland's relations with England*, p. 107.
[118] Scot, *Calderwoods recantation*, p. 11.

to do with the political dangers of non-conformity than it did with the dangers of 'parity', the condition that would exist under Presbyterian governance:

First there can be nothing more absurd, more against all Law, Practice and Reason, then the paritie of Church-government, or Parochiall Judicature, which you have so long maintained, and which was upon false grounds broached, to overthrow the Bishops, and avert the ancient Discipline of the Church. To make this cleare, I ask you, if there be any Government without Superioritie and Distinction of places? Can civill and spiritual Estates bee better governed, then by one armed with Power and eminencie over others? Is not God's owne citie, Spiritual Jerusalem, a gathering and uniting of Saints into a Divine Policy, whereof the Forme is Order; which, as in all actions, so in the Government of the Church is most necessary?[119]

Scot offered a defence of a system of ecclesiastical governance, which both had ancient warrant and also fulfilled the scriptural injunction to maintain the peace and order of the church. Where the argument departed from the pattern established in other writings was in the suggestion that the government of the Church was *iure divino*, rather than a peculiar circumstance of the English confession. For, Scot continued, 'God gave magistrates and Lawes to his Church', and established also an hierarchical form of government so that 'Decencie and Order might be preserved and Confusion shunned'. Introducing historical evidence, Scot identified the Apostles as the first bishops, charged with ordination and the censuring of heretics, and therefore sought to establish the office as part of the structure of the ancient church: 'All Records witnesse, that severall Bishops succeeded the Apostles at Rome, Constantinople, Jerusalem, Antioch, Alexandria, and other places: All the Councells give preheminence to Bishops; and to the Councils, the Fathers consent.' Scot then moved to the testimony of the reformers – Melanchthon, Zanchi, Bullinger – in order to align the reformed tradition with the authorities of the ancient church: the result was a universal condemnation of 'parity'.[120] Here were the marks of the true church, as the conformists understood it: Apostolic, diocesan, and in agreement with the reformed tradition. Here we see that conformists urged the full weight of ecclesiastical history against their opponents.

It was little wonder that defenders of Presbyterian discipline came to focus on the question of human authority over the Church. In 1624, David Calderwood re-entered the debate with three new works. The first of these might be included under the heading of 'popular' literature, for it offered a very straightforward explanation of the dangers of subjecting the simplicity of the Word to human 'policie': 'But the wisdom of God ... layeth Christ and puritie of religion for a ground, and sinne closeth her eyes to all events

---

[119] Ibid., p. 32.   [120] Ibid., pp. 33, 34, 35.

whatsoever for Christ, and religion should not be servants to policie, but policie ... should serve Christ, and religion.'[121] For Calderwood repeated that nostrum that the doctrine and governance of the Church were 'self evident' and within the grasp of all reasonable people, and not contingent upon 'curiousities of learning' or 'uncertainties of opinions'. Here again were the concepts – doctrine versus discipline, and substantial versus circumstantial – that underlay much of the controversial literature we have surveyed; at stake was nothing less than the definition of the intellectual foundations of the faith and, as always, a divide was seen to have formed between the laws of God and the laws of men. Hence Calderwood could argue that the present conflict concerned the 'ancient libertie' of the Church, itself threatened by 'the present course of conformitie'.[122]

This tension also formed the basis of a more fully developed work of controversy, written in response to David Lindsay's book on the Perth Assembly, as well as Morton's *Defence* and Downame's sermon defending episcopacy *iure divino*. Calderwood's *A dispute on communicating* represented a return to the controversy over ceremonies that formed the core of the debate in the wake of the Perth Assembly. Calderwood's purpose was to defend the pattern of the 'first institution' as the sole standard by which ceremonies might be established. One might wonder why, after so many years of debate on the topic and so many detailed accounts of the posture of Christ at the Last Supper, it was necessary to contribute yet another work to this body of writing. The reason is as simple as it is crucial for understanding these debates: the pattern of the first institution had to be defended again and again, every conformist tract had to be answered, and the sovereignty of the Church and its foundation *iure divino* in the Word had to be upheld. Calderwood saw the practices established in Presbyterian Scotland as exemplary of the Apostolic heritage, the 'pure seed of the ancient church'. Thus, he supported the contention that sitting at the Eucharist was ordained by the first institution:

Howbeit sitting had not beene the ordinarie table gesture at religious feasts, but a new example of Christ and his Apostles, yet seeing it was an example not occasional; or accidentarie but of free choice in setting down the patterne, it is a direction for our imitation, and the Apostles themselves took it so.[123]

---

[121] David Calderwood, *An exhortation of the particular kirks of Christ in Scotland to their sister kirk in Edinburgh* ([Amsterdam], 1624), pp. 7–8.
[122] Ibid., pp. 10, 15.
[123] David Calderwood, *A dispute vpon communicating at our confused communions* ([Amsterdam], 1624), p. 7.

Here, Christ was the innovator, the deliberate author by 'free choice' of a new pattern of usage chosen and adopted for the core element of the worship in His church.

Calderwood went beyond a mere reiteration of what Henry Jacob called the 'Divine Beginning and Institution' of the church. One of the central problems faced by reformists was the legal aspect of English ecclesiastical polity – the very element that David Lindsay offered as proof of the reformed character of the English confession. For Calderwood, a legally defined pattern of doctrine and discipline went against the law of God, and exerted an influence on the process of salvation that was the preserve of God alone:

> The Magistrate hath not power to abolish this law. Obedience to the Magistrate ought not to be the rule of my love to God's glory, or salvation of my brother ... You will say, that we are bound to obey the Magistrate. It is true, we are bound in conscience to be subject to the magistrate, but not to obey him but in the Lord, that is, we are bound to passive obedience, but not to active, except in things lawful. Further, know you not that the Magistrate may abuse a thing indifferent, as well as a private man ... Know you not that the Magistrate may have his owne private respects, and under colour of things indifferent, bring in a corrupt religion?[124]

This statement departed from similar positions taken in the literature that we have been surveying. That a king who sinned against the Church could 'not justly be called king' was a point put forth by Thomas Bilson, yet Bilson also argued that one had to obey in all cases, leaving it to higher powers to judge the king.[125] Calderwood dispensed with this argument and suggested that active obedience was due only to a king who ruled according to the law of God, and further that the maintenance of the confession based solely on the law of God was at the centre of lawful rule. Most striking, however, was the statement that raised the possibility that the Crown could secretly undermine the reformed character of the Church by introducing or sanctioning an innovation or corruption of the true pattern of rites and governance enjoined by divine law. The argument concerning 'things indifferent' did not resolve the point that errors of doctrine entailed a corruption of the first institution.

An articulate defence of the first institution was presented in Thomas Scott's *Boanerges*, a tract written in defence of the ministry of the Kirk. Scott, a prolific pamphleteer and critic of the Spanish Match who was assassinated in Utrecht, argued that episcopacy represented a corruption of the scripture, itself a far superior source of authority than the Canons: 'If you can but name the orders of government and constitutions of the Church, you are able to stop any disputants mouth, to silence any preacher; but this shall

---

[124] Ibid., p. 30.
[125] Thomas Bilson, *The true difference betweene Christian subiection and unchristian rebellion* (London, 1585), p. 251.

not serve your turn in any cause against the majestie of heaven, but the sentence of our Saviour shall be denounced against any hypocritcall Formalist under the sun.' Rather than a formal work of controversy, Scott's tract was designed to foment anti-episcopal feeling. Yet, in suggesting the bishops undermined the 'spiritual stones of God's building', Scott provided his readers with a definition of the Church whose principal elements were a preaching ministry and sacraments rightly administered.[126]

David Calderwood's understanding of ecclesiastical polity was further defined by a desire to sever the political power of the Crown from any notion of 'religious kingship'. The reverence demanded by kings was a sign of political custom, he argued, rather than any innate spiritual calling; this rejected the tradition whereby kings were lauded as the anointed earthly representatives of God, charged by Him with the maintenance of His church. Instead, Calderwood portrayed kings as all-too-human political actors, and hence prone to error:

the bowing to the chair of estate or to the seale of the Prince, is but a civil worship for a political end, to testifie homage and allegiance … It is thought good by the State, that the magestie of princes be upholden by such meanes, because they are but weake mortal men. But God needeth not any such props to hold up his magestie, neither will he have any worship conveyed to him mediately by anie creature.[127]

On the eve of the Bishops' Wars, royal proclamations instructed subjects to avoid any texts issued from Scotland, and so we might number Calderwood, writing in 1624, among those who prompted this action.[128] He saw all of the ordinances of the Church as *iure divino*, and stemming from an entirely different order than the power of the King. The 'King's seale from the Charter' was of human ordinance and could not apply to a divinely sovereign church. In short, Calderwood rejected the notion of ecclesiastical jurisdiction claimed for the Crown in the Act of Supremacy. The role of the monarch was merely to defend the faith as established by God, rather than introduce innovations and then employ the civil sword to compel subjects to obey them. Calderwood also rejected all claims for the English Church as sovereign over the Kirk for, like the Crown, the influence of other churches violated God's *immediate* power over His church, a power that was direct and not channelled through human agents:

---

[126] Thomas Scott, *Boanerges. Or the humble supplication of the ministers of Scotland, to the High Court of Pariament* [sic] *in England* (London, 1624), pp. 2–3, 7.
[127] Calderwood, *A dispute vpon communicating*, p. 55.
[128] For details, and a treatment of the literature on the royal image in general, see Kevin Sharpe, 'The King's writ: royal authors and royal authority in early modern England', in his *Remapping early modern England*, pp. 127–50.

Farther I have concurring with me, the bodie of the Church of Scotland, at least three
parts of the whole number of particular congregations within the realme standing out
against the decrees of that Assembly, and adhering to their former practice, which is
according to the patterne, and to the confession of faith, wherein this Church
professeth the right use of Ministration of the Sacraments, and a detestation of all
rites, and ceremonies, brought in by anti-Christ, or not warranted by the Word
of God.[129]

For contemporaries, 'anti-Christ' was reserved as a term to describe those
who sought to establish themselves as intercessory powers between God and
His people. We have become accustomed to think of the term as applying
mainly to the Pope, but in the debates among English Protestants themselves
the epithet encompassed elements from ceremonies to bishops.[130]

Calderwood reverted to the popular style for the last of his three works
published during 1624. *An epistle of a Christian brother* was, in essence, a
dialogue dominated by the character of the preceptor, whose purpose was to
show how error in apparently minor points of doctrine portended the dissolution of the 'true' church. The watchword of the tract was 'corruption',
'an affliction [by which] our Mother the Kirke and her mother the Truth are
forsaken'.[131] Defenders of Scottish episcopacy and English conformity
sought, through the Perth Articles, to reverse the trend of reformation:

It is true that your larger course is so cunningly covered, that nothing is permitted to
appear at this time, but a small point, the gesture of kneeling at the communion ...
Yet you must thinke of these particulars, as of members of the gross bodie of
conformitie, obscuring the frame of Reformation delivered unto you by the
Fathers.[132]

Here Calderwood – who by then would have started his massive history of
the Kirk – reverted to the tactic of uncovering the historical identity of the
reformed tradition. Questions of ceremonies could not be separated from the
larger matter of the history of the Church as reformed, pure, and linked by
the uncorrupted Word to the church left on earth by Christ. Ceremonies *iure
divino* were: 'her badges most famous in the world, and most meete for
keeping unity among her members in doctrine, sacraments, kirk-service,
discipline, and in the holie ministrie'. From Calderwood's point of view,
the promise of the Jacobean settlement and the 'royal testimonies of his
Magestie's love for strengthening her jurisdiction and furtherance of all her
causes' ran aground on the corruption of practices that would lead to

[129] Calderwood, *A dispute vpon communicating*, p. 72.
[130] See Paul Christianson, *Reformers and Babylon* (Toronto, 1978), ch. 2.
[131] David Calderwood, *An epistle of a Christian brother exhorting an other to keepe himselfe
vndefiled from the present corruptions brought into the ministration of the Lords Supper*
([Amsterdam], 1624), p. 2.
[132] Ibid., p. 7.

corruption of doctrine. The events surrounding the Perth Assembly witnessed the vilification of those who sought to uphold the Presbyterian traditions of the sixteenth century. Calderwood, a deprived minister and exile, knew at first hand the consequences of defending an unpopular position: 'if you refuse to follow the drove in anie new practice, for to defend your libertie by anie good ancient order or custom, you are summarilie condemned of Brownisme, separation, singularitie, Puritainisme, and of Blinde, fained zeale'.[133]

The final contribution to the controversy surrounding the Perth Assembly came in the second of two works from the pen of Patrick Scot. *Vox vera* seems to have been written primarily as an answer to works by Calderwood and as an attack on reformists in general. Scot reported that, on a recent trip to Amsterdam, he found the bookstalls crammed with Calderwood's works, which were in turn read and exchanged.[134] Both Calderwood and his putative readers were described as those who 'labor to draw sovereignty into contempt, annihilate just lawes, taint superior powers with disgraceful notes, and erect democracie or orderlesse confusion, in both Church and State'.[135] Scot was not interested in any formal engagement with Calderwood's arguments, but sought instead to reaffirm the principal tenets of English conformity: that is, the ecclesiastical sovereignty of Crown and bishops, the ancient pedigree of the English Church, and its agreement with the reformed churches. Scot combined these tenets to account for the liberty of the Church: 'The Apostles and sacred writ have delivered unto us, no other precepts, concerning the externall government of the Church, then that *all things in the Church may be done decently and in order*: But on the contrary, our Didoclavius and his followers charge us ... that we marre all decencie, overturn all order.'[136] Scot's label for Calderwood and his co-religionists confirmed the conformist injunction that division and schism were spiritual and political solvents.

What Scot offered, then, was a defence of the power of the Church to judge in 'things indifferent', a power confirmed by the example of the Apostles, and the scriptural injunction to embrace 'decency' and 'order'. In response to Calderwood's charge that the English hierarchy had led the Kirk into error, Scot offered the alternative explanation that governance by bishops obeyed a range of ancient authorities and provided the best means for avoiding error. For Calderwood, any departure from a Presbyterian interpretation of the

---

[133] Ibid., pp. 8, 9, 10.
[134] For the book trade and printing in Amsterdam, see Sprunger, *Trumpets from the tower*, chs. 3 and 4.
[135] Patrick Scot, *Vox vera: or, Obseruations from Amsterdam* (London, 1625), pp. 2, 3.
[136] Ibid., p. 8.

New Testament constituted error, while for Scot the practice of 'indifferent' ceremonies varied from place to place and age to age, and were to be established by the magistrate to promote order in the state. The power to establish 'custom' was, in short, a mark of sovereignty. Presbyterianism and plurality represented the erosion of this order, and therefore Scot's work dealt with a theory of the role of religion in the state and the political dangers of a Presbyterian system, for: 'a politicke or natural body may not subsist intire without a prime member'. Likewise, 'the frame of good government ... is a chiefe type of God's ordinance', and the destruction of this system is founded upon 'Curiosity, singularitie and faction'.

It will be recalled that writers employed holistic metaphors in order to depict the virtues of uniformity and order, while controversialists allied these concepts with an account for the need for stable public doctrine. *Vox vera* was situated within the conformist tradition, but expanded it to account for the developing conception of a uniform and sovereign Church of 'Great Brittaine'. Scot argued that a uniform confession was crucial to 'supporting the heavy frame of Empire'.[137] Again, the argument turned to tension between English conformity and its Presbyterian critics – what Scot called, following Bancroft, 'secret conventicles'.[138] In the context of the ecclesiastical polity Scot sought to describe, truth was the linchpin of the system, and religion the 'stay' of polity: 'In the whole frame of our externall government God hath his true worship. Princes lawful obedience, the lawes due respect, the Pastors beseeming reverence. All our policy tends to the pure preaching of the Word, right administration of the sacraments, to the lawful vocation of Pastors ... and to the cherishing of Christian unitie.'[139] Here Scot combined reformist concepts of a godly preaching ministry as the key to the stability of a monarchical church of the type envisioned by conformists.

From the point of view of the relation between religion and political ideas, Scot's work lends insight into the problems faced by contemporaries who sought to develop perspectives useful in addressing the problems of an 'imperial' Church. It is difficult to isolate the point at which conformist writers began thinking of the Church in these terms, but from a conceptual point of view it would have been a short step from defining the Church as a unified political and spiritual association attached to a single polity to

---

[137] David Armitage's work on 'empire' has supposed that religion was more relevant to contemporary perspectives on other lands and peoples than it was to the business of conceptualising 'empire' in the first place. Scot's work provides a corrective to this view. See David Armitage, *The ideological origins of the British Empire* (Cambridge, 2000), ch. 3.

[138] '[T]he common people are so tossed betwixt error and trueth, that their harts are layed open, and themselves made naked to receive every impression of corruption and vanity.' Scot, *Vox vera*, p. 38

[139] Ibid., p. 39.

extending that definition to include both realms. To argue that the English Church was descended from antiquity did little to answer the reformist charge that the institution had fallen under the sway of purely political actors. However, comparisons made between James and religious princes of the past assisted those who wished to argue that 'divine and human lawes enable Princes to prevent confusion of opinions and schismes'. Instead of a pure manifestation of doctrine, conformists tended to conceive of the Church as both a spiritual and a political association, and therefore viewed non-conformity as a political problem, rather than the result of a principled theological position. Scot argued that Church, commonwealth, and 'Empire' existed in a state of balance, and the stability of the whole depended on the internal unity of the various parts:

They are bad States-men that unjustly take from the subject to add to the prerogations and revenues of Kings, thereby they weaken sovereignty, deprive it of the love of the people, make the life of it troublesome and subject to diseases: but you like worse Statesmen, touch the string of Sovereignty with too rough a hand, or rather break it in pulling the natural feathers from it, to enlarge popular libertie. In advancing this Anarchy, you open a door to all manner of evils which with licentiousness and disobedience rush into the commonwealth and make the *great frame of sovereign Empire* unproportionable, uncomely, and altogether unserviceable.[140]

When Scot spoke of the sovereignty of the Church, he did so within the context of the sovereignty of the Crown, commonwealth, and 'empire'. Common to the sound rule of all was the notion of balance: uniformity of religion, allegiance to the Crown, and a harmony of churches in both king-doms. In short, since kneeling was the practice of the Church of England, so should it be the practice of the church of Great Britain, for 'if affaires bee not evenly ballanced without approach to extreames, Church or State govern-ment may erre upon either hand, and so fall into an anarchy or tyranny'.[141] Scot's position was based on the assumption that points of theological difference could be overcome, and that the more pressing need was to ensure the continuation of churches allied by modes of governance, comprehending the same group of subjects, and superintended by James VI and I, Britain's Solomon.

However, the aspirations of national church-building ran afoul of issues of doctrine, and so the debates surveyed in this chapter may be situated within the broader problem of the definition of the church. The definition posited by English reformers was largely theological and textual – found in scripture and historical works – only occasionally making systematic reference to the doctrine and governance of other reformed churches. Where the Scots refor-mers departed from their co-religionists was that there was, in the Kirk, a

---

[140] Ibid., p. 53. Emphasis added.   [141] Ibid., p. 54.

living institution whose doctrine and governance was a material reality. The identity of the Kirk emerged first in 1560, and received articulation in the work of John Knox and the Melvilles; for them, the Reformation parliament had restored the *iure divino* perfection of the Presbyterian model, itself patterned upon the authority of scripture and the examples of the Apostles. Most importantly, the Kirk was defined as an autonomous, self-governing association that was independent of the state. Given the centrality of these historical and doctrinal precepts, the reformist argument displayed a strong element of consistency: writers from Davidson to Calderwood maintained that the scriptures found for Presbyterian discipline, and that diocesan episcopacy represented an assault on the sovereignty of the Crown. Familiar with the writings of their English counterparts, they also offered doctrinal and historical arguments against episcopacy, claiming that it violated an Apostolic warrant for a pastoral ministry focussed on preaching and the proper administration of the sacraments. The kind of uniform public worship envisioned by David Lindsay and his peers was nothing to the purpose if it was not grounded on a legitimate doctrinal case.

The attempt to impose a uniform public worship on the Kirk was an ambition conceived by Whitgift and continued under Bancroft, and then Laud as Bishop of London. It was also an ambition of James VI and I to assert his authority once and for all over an institution with which he had struggled for years. While it has not been the business of this chapter to reconstruct the historical context, that context nevertheless bears on the development of the argument it has traced. While Scots reformers defended the Presbyterian position on doctrinal grounds, conformists – notably Bancroft – argued that presbyteries amounted to 'secret conventicles', an assault on the sovereignty of the Kirk's royal governor. Writers such as David Calderwood, drawing upon the evidence of the English controversy over bishops, argued that tracts such as those by George Downame were evidence that it was the bishops who threatened the sovereignty of Crown in parliament. The controversies that we have surveyed, therefore, tipped back and forth on the axis of doctrine versus law: which mode of governance could claim an Apostolic pedigree, and which was more compatible with monarchy. Conformists took care not to suggest that episcopacy was *iure divino*, but situated justifications for it in the context of an argument that extolled the virtues of unity, uniformity, and order in the Church. It was this that led Patrick Scot to conceive of a church of 'Great Britain', possessed of a uniform mode of governance. Where the Church of England had long been described as bound to the commonwealth, this broader church was imagined as an annex of the truly Imperial Crown, the product of the Union of 1603. Clearly, the debate was not resolved, but resulted instead in the hardening of positions: the Scots were anxious to defend the independence of the Kirk, as well as its ecclesiological character, as qualities based on a sound interpretation of doctrinal and historical precept. Defenders of episcopacy made the same claims, but did so using different evidence toward different ends. Yet both sides agreed on one fundamental issue: that sound religion lay at the centre of a stable polity. Here is where we detect the issue capable of generating more serious conflict: for when articulate writers, united in the belief that religion was the stay of polity, divided on the definition of that religion, then the disruption of the ecclesiastical polity was a likely outcome. This is exactly what emerged in the decade and a half following the death of James VI and I.

7

Conclusion: narratives of civil and ecclesiastical authority

We began with Gilbert Burnet's observation that the 'disciplinarian' controversies of the Jacobean period, while not pitched at the level of Whitgift and Hooker, nevertheless occupied a host of writers and served to define the principal ecclesiological divisions of the period. This book has shown that those writers who were concerned with the ecclesiology of the Jacobean Church were indeed deeply divided on fundamental issues of history, theology, law, and the political implications of monarchical sovereignty over a 'national' church. This book has traced these divisions through a series of thematic debates carried on in printed works that scholars of religion have not yet fully exploited. This literature reveals that the chief concern among these writers was not soteriology, but rather issues concerning doctrine, law, rites, and governance, all of which stemmed from the Elizabethan reconstruction and its Jacobean refinement. We commonly conceive of figures like Richard Hooker and John Jewel as part of an elite group of theologians, isolated from other writers, whose purpose was to provide scriptural and historical defences of the Church; yet, the case has been made that the problem of 'defining' the Jacobean Church absorbed a broad sample of writers, and lay at the heart of debates on governance and ceremonial practice that followed the introduction of the Canons of 1604.

Where others have posited conflict between Calvinists and Arminians, or between 'puritans' and a range of conformists, from 'moderate' to 'avant-garde', this study has examined the broadly based theme of conflict over the nature of the visible church. This conflict reveals that debates on the Church are intelligible in the context of exchanges among writers all of whom sought to contribute to the clarification of what the Church of England was, and to comment on the nature of its governance, liturgy, and ceremonial practice. While situated predominantly in England, polemical exchanges spilled over into a conflict between Presbyterians and conformists eager to promote or to dispute a unity of rites and governance between the Kirk and its neighbour church. Hence, not only was there doctrinal and political conflict over the historical identity of the Church and its status in the realm, but there was also conflict over the ecclesiological implications of what has been called 'the British problem'.[1] In both contexts, narratives of civil and ecclesiastical authority were employed in the course of polemical debates that blended political, religious, and historical precept into a language of ecclesiastical polity.[2] Yet while those whom this book has surveyed were broadly agreed that religion was an element of stable polity, and that historical precept served to legitimise present ecclesiological practice, they were divided over the nature of religion in both doctrinal and practical terms, a division which stemmed from disagreement about the soundness of precept offered by scripture and the historical record of Christianity.[3]

This study has aimed to illustrate the process whereby theological positions were related to, and were the generators of, political assumptions. Clearly, those who believed that religious sovereignty was held by Crown and bishops, rather than presbyteries or congregations, defined themselves as adherents to a particular kind of political vision.[4] Among English Protestants, the points of contention were the status of bishops in the ecclesiastical hierarchy, and the use of specific ceremonies and rites, all taken as signs that the Church was, or was not,

---

[1] See Joad Raymond, *Pamphlets and pamphleteering in early modern Britain* (Cambridge, 2003), esp. ch. 5, where the 'explosion' of print that accompanied the National Covenant is placed within a British and European context. Clearly there were audiences for a literature which dealt almost wholly with problems of Church polity, and therefore our view of early Stuart religion and politics needs to be recast to give a central position to print and polemic.

[2] This theme has been noted, but not fully explored. Anthony Milton has remarked that issues of Church polity 'held implications for civil polity', while J. G. A. Pocock has observed that, since the Church of England was 'essential to the structure of national sovereignty', debates on the place of the Church in 'the realm' should be of central interest to historians of political thought. Thus far, however, Pocock's call has not been heeded. See Anthony Milton, *Catholic and reformed: the Roman and Protestant churches in English Protestant thought, 1600–1640* (Cambridge, 1995), p. 449; J. G. A. Pocock, 'The history of British political thought: the creation of a Center', *Journal of British Studies*, 24 (1985), 283–310, at 287, 288.

[3] Arthur Ferguson, *Clio unbound: perception of the social and cultural past in Renaissance England* (Durham, NC, 1979), chs. 5–6; Patrick Collinson, 'If Constantine, then also Theodosius: St Ambrose and the integrity of the Elizabethan *ecclesia anglicana*', *Journal of Ecclesiastical History*, 30 (1979), 205–29. See also Joseph H. Preston, 'English ecclesiastical historians and the problem of bias, 1559–1742', *Journal of the History of Ideas*, 32 (1971), 203–20; Rainier Pineas, 'William Turner's polemical use of ecclesiastical history and his controversy with Stephen Gardiner', *Renaissance Quarterly*, 33 (1980), 599–608; Robert Dodaro and Michael Questier, 'Strategies in Jacobean polemic: the use and abuse of St Augustine in English theological controversy', *Journal of Ecclesiastical History*, 44 (1993), 432–49; M. E. C. Perrott, 'Richard Hooker and the problem of authority in the Elizabethan Church', *Journal of Ecclesiastical History*, 49 (1998), 29–60; and Arthur G. Holder, 'Whitby and all that: the search for Anglican origins', *Anglican Theological Review*, 85 (2003), 231–52.

[4] Aspects of this theme have been treated by William Lamont, *Godly rule: politics and religion, 1603–1660* (London, 1969); J. P. Sommerville, *Royalists and patriots: politics and ideology in England, 1603–1640* (London, 1999); and Glenn Burgess, *The politics of the ancient constitution: an introduction to English political thought, 1603–1642* (University Park, PA, 1992).

'rightly reformed'.[5] Since the Elizabethan Act of Supremacy and the preamble to the Book of Common Prayer designated the Crown as the 'defender' and 'governor' of the Church, an attack on the one institution was perceived by some to be an attack on the other. Catholics, meanwhile, saw the Church of England as a mere invention, and especially deplored and challenged the idea that a monarch could take the place of the Pope.[6] Thomas Stapleton, the Catholic controversialist, put the case succinctly, arguing that the English confession exhibited no links with the church left on earth by Christ, and had fallen instead under the power of the 'temporal law'.[7] Opinions of this type were thick on the ground in the early seventeenth century, yet they did not signal a consensus; instead, conflicts about 'order and discipline' led writers to ponder the relationship of the Church to the state. However, a desire for conformity and its institutional manifestation comprised but one part of the debate that this study has surveyed. Disaffected Protestants felt the pinch of the law, and argued that the High Commission (a prerogative court which assessed ecclesiastical penalties) lacked the authority to deprive them of their benefices.[8] The result was a very complex exchange carried on in controversial and political writings, of a scope not fully appreciated by scholars.

The present work has proposed that a principal link between politics and religion stemmed from the attempt by conformists to posit a necessary coherence between monarchy and episcopacy, and between the uniform observance of the doctrine of the Church and the maintenance of proper order in society. An examination of the literature of religious controversy helps to refine our understanding of Jacobean politics and ecclesiology. Because the Crown was the 'governor' of the Church of England, the debates in question often had a political dimension; yet this study has not treated 'politics' in the conventional sense. Clerics defending or attacking the Church were not concerned with broad statements about the workings of English society, and were far less well equipped than, say, either the civil or common lawyers to engage with the literature of law and reason of state.[9] We have been told that England's

[5] The phrase is taken from the 'First Admonition to the Parliament' (1572), in *The Tudor constitution: documents and commentary*, ed. G. R. Elton, 2nd edn (Cambridge, 1982), doc. 203, p. 449.

[6] Peter Holmes, *Resistance and compromise: the political thought of Elizabethan Catholics* (Cambridge, 1982).

[7] Thomas Stapleton, *A counterblast to M. Hornes vayne blaste against M. Fekenham* ([Louvain, 1567]), pp. 427–8.

[8] An excellent treatment of the first stages of this debate is Ethan H. Shagan, 'The English Inquisition: constitutional conflict and ecclesiastical law in the 1590s', *Historical Journal*, 47 (2004), 541–65.

[9] Glenn Burgess, 'Common law and political theory in early Stuart England', *Political Science*, 40 (1988), 5–17; Paul Christianson, 'Royalist and parliamentary voices on the ancient constitution', in *The mental world of the Jacobean court*, ed. Linda Levy Peck (Cambridge, 1991),

gradual transition from feudalism meant that the dominant language of politics was that which described relationships between owners of property, and the history of the common law.[10] However, those who participated in religious controversies exhibited assumptions about the workings of society, the power of the Crown, and the reach of the law, and therefore should be of considerable interest to the student of politics. Similarly, many scholars of religion have treated their subject as being nearly apolitical; to the extent religion *has* figured in the political narrative of early Stuart England, it has done so almost exclusively in the guise of 'Arminianism' or 'Laudianism'. This overlooks the simple fact that the Church was an institution, and in turn was linked to the Crown. At the beginning of the reign of James VI and I, the Crown's civil authority was used to promote religious conformity in the 'church of the realm', and this meant that religious controversy invited speculation on the use of civil power in conjunction with newly defined channels of ecclesiastical sovereignty.[11] Ecclesiology was central to conceptions of the early modern English state.

Current studies of political thought in the period include religion, but do not fully explore the languages of politics evident in religious discourse.[12] In fact, there is a point at which offering distinctions between religion and politics ceases to be fruitful; political thought as a secular category nearly vanishes – although debates on taxation and quotidian issues of property rights and litigation were necessarily carried on in a secular idiom – and one becomes aware of a language of ecclesiastical polity that erased the distinction between matters of civil and ecclesiastical authority, yet which raised the question of how the two would relate. The dual establishment that defined the Church after 1559 meant that the temporal aspects of a spiritual institution were a source of comment at those points where they came into contact

---

pp. 71–95, and Christianson's work on John Selden, *Discourse on history, law and governance in the public career of John Selden, 1610–1635* (Toronto, 1996). 'History' was central to debates on both law and religion, for in both cases writers found legitimacy for their positions in the ability to align themselves with a given 'tradition', and differed from one another on interpretations of what this tradition implied.

[10] J. G. A. Pocock, 'Working on ideas in time', in *The historian's workshop*, ed. L. P. Curtis (New York, 1970), pp. 153–65, at p. 160; Pocock, *The ancient constitution and the feudal law: a reissue with a retrospect* (Cambridge, 1987), pp. 30–69; William Klein, 'The ancient constitution revisited', in *Political discourse in early modern Britain*, ed. Nicholas Phillipson and Quentin Skinner (Cambridge, 1993), pp. 23–44.

[11] On this point I agree with D. Alan Orr, 'Sovereignty, supremacy and the origins of the English Civil War', *History*, 87 (2002), 474–90.

[12] Sommerville, *Royalists and patriots*, ch. 6; Glenn Burgess, *Absolute monarchy and the Stuart constitution* (New Haven, 1996); Conrad Russell, *The causes of the English Civil War* (Oxford, 1990); John Morrill, 'The religious context of the English Civil War', *Transactions of the Royal Historical Society*, 5th series, 34 (1984), 155–78.

with the temporal aspect of the state.[13] As we have seen, debates over advowsons and the power of High Commission were spurs to the examination of this tension. Likewise, the authority of the Crown in the spiritual realm was defined as a quasi-political activity. Political thinking had therefore to don the guise of religious controversy and to embrace its central evidentiary proofs: scripture, the Fathers of the Church, ecclesiastical and classical history, and the work of divines from Augustine to Hooker.[14] Writers sought a pedigree for religious authority, and in this process there developed a language of ecclesiastical polity.

This book has also attempted to provide a firmer understanding of the nature of religious conflict in Jacobean England. An important perspective lies in the connection between the Elizabethan period and that which was to follow, for in both settings controversialists debated rites and ceremonies, and matters of ecclesiastical organisation, as well as the problems posed by religious non-conformity.[15] Indeed, the Elizabethan debates furnished a crucial context for the religious conflicts of the subsequent period, as was shown by several brief examinations of Elizabethan controversies that illustrate continuities with the Jacobean Church.[16] Yet these links were not merely intellectual: many of the same clergymen (though not many bishops) enjoyed places of influence in both settings, and the controversialists who engaged each other in the opening decade of the reign of James I got their feet wet in late Elizabethan controversies. Similar continuities can be discovered among those Protestants who advocated the reform of the Church: a petition submitted to the King by a group of twenty-two London ministers offers us some sense of the variety that defined Jacobean reformist thought. 'We have bin brought up', the authors of the petition asserted, 'and taken degrees in the universities: we are many of us become greyheaded in the service of God, and of his Church, having preached the gospell, some of us ten years,

---

[13] J. G. A. Pocock, 'Within the margins: the definitions of orthodoxy', in *The margins of orthodoxy: heterodox writing and cultural response, 1660–1750*, ed. Roger Lund (Cambridge, 1995), 33–53.

[14] Charles W. A. Prior, 'Religious conflict and political language in England, 1580–c.1630', unpublished paper.

[15] Peter Lake, *Moderate puritans and the Elizabethan Church* (Cambridge, 1982); Lake, *Anglicans and puritans?: Presbyterianism and English conformist thought from Whitgift to Hooker* (London, 1988); Claire Cross, *The royal supremacy in the Elizabethan Church* (London, 1969); Robert K. Faulkner, *Richard Hooker and the politics of a Christian England* (Berkeley, 1981).

[16] I am in agreement with John Guy's assessment that the generation of bishops – particularly Whitgift and Bancroft – that came to prominence in the 1580s marked the beginning of a new intellectual posture for the English Church. See John Guy, 'The Elizabethan Establishment and the ecclesiastical polity', in *The reign of Elizabeth I: court and culture in the last decade*, ed. John Guy (Cambridge, 1995), pp. 126–49.

some twenty, some thyrty, and some more.'[17] Yet the periods did differ: the new reign opened with the Hampton Court conference, out of which stemmed the far-reaching Canons of 1604 – the legal foundation of the Jacobean Church. However, the Canons did not fulfil James' desire to settle the 'divisions' in the English Church, for they made into matters of law those aspects of the Elizabethan settlement that had generated heated debates. Rather than quell disaffection with the Church, the Canons of 1604 and the institution they defined would shape exchanges between controversialists for the remainder of James' reign. In other words, the governors of the Jacobean Church made a deliberate effort to settle those disputes that defined the post-Reformation; the attempt was not successful, and the drive to promote uniformity fostered increased conflict.

The debate on the nature of religious authority generated further debate on the nature of the Church and its doctrine and discipline. There were those who defended the Church as an 'orthodox' institution, in which all ecclesiological questions had been settled by its realignment with the directions laid out in ancient and reformed sources.[18] But the existence of a thriving heterodoxy also meant that these questions continued to be raised and served as the impetus for others. How was the Church to be governed? What should be done about non-conformity? What was the link between the purity of doctrine and the nature of discipline in the realm of public worship? What was truly *adiaphora*? Were the Church and its ceremonies the products of experience and 'custom' or were they the immemorial creations of God? What implication did the Union of the Crowns have for the creation of a broader British Protestantism? All of these issues intersect in the literature, and in many cases were treated as a group; an 'official' line is evident in royal proclamations, court sermons, and Canons, and in the work of writers like Thomas Bell, Gabriel Powel, and William Covell. Yet there was not a unified system of ideas and, as shown in connection with the debates on episcopacy, there was some variance on the issue among defenders of the Church. Their opponents were similarly diverse in their tactics. Where William Bradshaw employed common-law arguments to protest the deprivation of non-conforming ministers, Henry Jacob followed the doctrine of *sola scriptura* – in the realm of the church, the Word alone was the sovereign will of Christ, but he drew upon Aristotelian doctrines of associations to discuss the need for 'consent' as the mark of legitimacy of ecclesiastical government. This tension over evidence and its relation to ecclesiology is yet another facet of the debate on religious authority, and therefore

---

[17] *To the Kinges most excellent Majestie the humble petition of two and twentie preachers in London and the suburbs thereof* ([London?, 1605?]), non-paginated broadside.
[18] Milton, *Catholic and reformed*, pt. 2.

writers writing ostensibly on matters of faith and doctrine found themselves confronting the mutable and the political, and were obliged to reconcile them.

The disputes in question were carried out in print and resulted in a vast body of literature consisting of sermons, pamphlets, and broadsides, as well as technical treatments of law, theology, and church history. This literature has been partially addressed in the work of historians of English religion, although much remains to be done; thus, Anthony Milton has argued that 'the greater proportion of printed religious literature on the period 1600–40 remains almost wholly unstudied, and much historiographical debate has focused on a tiny sample of surviving material'.[19] Drawing on the literature of religious controversy, this study has addressed two aspects of Jacobean ecclesiology: how English Protestants sought to 'define' the Church of England, and how religious controversy influenced the way in which contemporaries thought about politics, theology, and the history of their church. The book offers a portrait of the intellectual foundations of Jacobean ecclesiology, as well as an account of how elements of these foundations were challenged in the course of debates among defenders of the English Church and their critics.[20]

The book's third aim – which underpins the previous two – has been to contribute to our understanding of a crucial branch of historical thought, and its role in early Stuart religious debates.[21] Religious dispute was shaped by the burden of demonstrating the continuity of all aspects of rites and governance from the Apostolic church to its Jacobean descendant.[22] English conformists continually stressed that their Church was peculiar, in that it had partaken in the broader Reformation, but yet retained power to establish aspects of doctrine and discipline. There was less need to defend the Church on the grounds of 'reform' than there was to address its antiquity and its connection with the Apostolic church.[23] That is, the English Church was a 'true' church, partaking in the spiritual association established on earth by Christ, and hence partaking also in His body. Indeed, as early Christians sought to prove that they were not separated from the covenant of Abraham and the law of Moses – both vessels through which God had spoken to His

---

[19] Ibid., pp. 6–7, 449.

[20] Charles W. A. Prior, 'Ancient *and* reformed?: Thomas Bell and Jacobean conformist thought', *Canadian Journal of History*, 38 (2003), 425–38.

[21] For the common-law tradition, see Pocock, *The ancient constitution*, chs. 1–3, and for history in the broader period, see D. R. Woolf, *The idea of history in early Stuart England: erudition, ideology, and the 'light of truth' from the accession of James I to the Civil War* (Toronto, 1990); and his *Reading history in early modern England* (Cambridge, 2000).

[22] For treatments of this theme, see Paul Avis, *The Church in the theology of the reformers* (London, 1981); Richard Wilmer, *The Doctrine of the Church in the English Reformation* (Evanston, IL, 1952); H. F. Woodhouse, *The doctrine of the Church in Anglican theology, 1547–1603* (London, 1954).

[23] Prior, 'Ancient *and* reformed?', passim.

people – so the defenders of the English Church had to affirm their connection with an ancient faith that had been usurped by the corruption of Rome, and which was now restored.

For conformists, the faith of England had meaningful links with the Apostolic church, and the textual authorities that testified to the historical continuity of that church described an institution that mirrored English doctrine and discipline. It was a commonplace in theological writing to posit certain 'notes of the church' – marks, whether visibility, succession, ceremonies, or governance, which could be found in the early Christian church and hence which served as hallmarks by which earthly churches were judged. English conformists made doctrinal arguments in support of the ceremonial worship set forth in the Thirty-nine Articles and the Canons of 1604, and argued that the liturgy of the Church of England represented a 'restoration' of the ceremonial practices of the ancient church. Conformists also defended 'discipline', that is, the power to order worship and to censure non-conformity, as a note of the Church, which meant in turn that a doctrinal and historical case had to be made for the agents of discipline, the bishops. Finally, the monarchical element of the Church was explained though references to biblical kings and religious princes, all charged with the defence and promotion of the true faith among their people. Taken together, these propositions defined the Church as both a 'political' and a 'spiritual' institution; that is, it was a state church firmly under the control of the Crown, and it also partook – in a way the Roman church did not – in the spiritual association established by Christ.

This interpretation furnished the context for the great works of ecclesiastical history that appeared during the reign of James, as well as those reformist works that sought a scriptural and historical foundation for the notes of the true church.[24] Aimed ostensibly at Catholic controversialists, works such as Richard Field's *Of the Church* (1606) recast the history of Christianity in the West in a manner that favoured the historical claims of the

---

[24] The literature on ecclesiastical history proves to be diverse: one discovers 'popular' anthologies of all of the principal works of the Fathers. Meredith Hanmer's translation of the works of Eusebius first appeared in 1587, and was in its sixth edition in 1663. Hanmer argued that it was necessary for all good Christians to know the history of their church in order that they might also know its true posture: 'We may see bishops how they governed, Ministers how they taught, Synods what they decreed, Ceremonies how they crept into the Church, Heresies how they were rooted out.' See Hanmer, *The auncient ecclesiastical histories of the first six hundred yeares after Christ, by Eusebius, Socrates, and Euagrius. Whereunto is annexed Dorotheus bishop of Tyrus, of the liues of the Prophetes, Apostles and 70 disciples. All which authors are tr. by M. Hanmer* (London, 1650), sig. A⁶ᵛ. On the other end of the scale, we discover a work 'for the private use of a most Noble Lady, to preserve her from the Danger of Popery'. The book included a primer on the basic positions of the Fathers of the Church, as well as a dialogue between a 'Papist' and a 'Protestant' on the ancient pedigree of the 'reformed' Church of England. See John Williams, *A manual: or, Three small and plain treatises* (London, 1672), pp. 63–5.

Church of England.[25] Yet, as conformists used history principally to challenge Rome's claims to being the true church, their critics employed history against the claims of the established Church, whether it was the legitimacy of the institution itself that they challenged, or simply aspects of its doctrine and discipline.[26] Yet a commitment to scholarship was not all that defined these texts. George Carleton's *Directions to know the true church* (1615) was dedicated to Prince Charles and professed to answer 'divers bookes ... that are written in English to seduce the simple who cannot judge'. The work was part of a larger controversy, but was pitched also to a more general audience, whom Carleton identified as the 'unlearned'.[27] In the Scottish context, David Calderwood's *True history of the Church of Scotland* attempted to carve out a unique history for the Kirk, and in turn to employ this work against the claims to episcopal sovereignty advanced by English bishops. Such histories as Josias Nichols' *Abrahams faith* sought to find an historical pedigree for the 'reforming' position: all points of doctrine and discipline, he argued, could be found in the scripture, and it was a sin to disregard these dictates.[28] This too was a durable theme in English ideas, blending providence with a formal conception of how Christians should at all times be bound to the oldest roots of their faith.

The literature of religious controversy constitutes an important channel that helps us to see how the past was understood in this period. Conformists saw the Church as an institution derived from experience, having been slowly shaped by human agents, answering the needs of circumstance, and embracing custom. The reformist vision also regarded the Church as residing in history, but argued that the process of its shaping had taken place in the Christian and Apostolic period: it exemplified perfection in the moments of its founding because it was at this point that it was most intimately connected with the spirit and intentions of its Founder. The burden of its subsequent history, and of those human agents charged with its guidance, was to ensure that this founding spirit continued to have a presence within it. In other words, the Church existed in history in a particular way, and the way in which reformists approached this existence informed the way that they approached history itself. Hence, John Penry, writing in 1590, used the example of the restoration of the ancient temple of the Jews to suggest that the English Church was within sight of the true faith:

[25] Richard Field, *Of the Church five bookes* (London, 1606).
[26] This debate is covered by Milton in *Catholic and reformed*, pp. 128–72.
[27] George Carleton, *Directions to know the true church* (London, 1615), sig. A[5r], p. 111. For a close study of the controversy that furnishes the context for Carleton's work, see T. H. Wadkins, 'Theological polemic and religious culture in early Stuart England: the Percy / "Fisher" controversies, 1605–1641' (Ph.D. diss., Graduate Theological Union, Berkeley, 1988), chs. 1–2.
[28] Josias Nichols, *Abrahams faith: that is, The Olde Religion* (London, 1602).

Very sober and wise were those priests, Levites, chiefe fathers, and auncient men, who having seene the first temple of Solomon, wept in the daies of Ezra, when they saw the foundation of the Temple, which was after the captivity of Babilon ... And in the time of Nehemiah, the people in the daye of their joyfull solemnitye, wept and mourned, and with one consent joyned unto their feast, wherein they covenanted with God to amend their lives, and make statutes for themselves to follow his Lawe.[29]

Penry's reference to the 'foundations' of the temple was intended to invoke the most ancient grounds of faith; these could be lost and also recovered. Since there was only one temple, so too was there only one 'true church'. English ecclesiology, therefore, turned on the question of which definition of the Church was to prevail, and this meant that the historical narratives that underpinned civil and ecclesiastical authority were under constant re-examination.

What elevates this point to relevance for our understanding of religious conflict and the 'British problem' is that, at an early point in their reformed history, both Scotland and England backed up the purity of doctrine which they professed with the body of law that lent legitimacy to other elements of their polities – parliament lay at the root of each reformation by statute.[30] At this point, roughly 1560, they became 'national' churches;[31] the difficulty lay not so much in the jurisdiction of law – although that would become an issue after 1603 – as in the kind of doctrinal settlement that each body of law would be employed to defend. As it happened, they chose modes of ecclesiastical governance – episcopal and Presbyterian – that stood in contrast to one another. Hence, there was a link between law, the purity of doctrine, and the flavour of Protestantism in each state, but a fundamental difference in the nature of the Protestantism that each state embraced. This tension between doctrine and law would animate religious conflict from the time of Bancroft and Marprelate through to the Bishops' Wars at the end of the Personal Rule. This point serves to illustrate the importance of this study to our understanding of the British problem, for not only did defenders of episcopacy and Presbyterian discipline develop competing historical justifications for modes of governance, but they also linked these to discussions of the purity of doctrine and public discipline.[32] In both settings it was

---

[29] John Penry, *An humble motion with submission vnto the right Honorable LL. of Hir Maiesties Priuie Counsell* (1590), p. 9.

[30] Alan MacDonald, *The Jacobean Kirk, 1567–1625: sovereignty, polity and liturgy* (Aldershot, 1998); Norman L. Jones, *Faith by statute: parliament and the settlement of religion, 1559* (London, 1982).

[31] Peter Lake, 'Presbyterianism, the idea of a national Church and the argument from divine right', in *Protestantism and the national Church in sixteenth century England*, ed. Peter Lake and Maria Dowling (London, 1987), pp. 193–224.

[32] John Morrill, 'A British patriarchy?: ecclesiastical imperialism under the early Stuarts', in *Religion, culture, and society in early modern Britain*, ed. Anthony Fletcher and Peter Roberts

argued that doctrine and law agreed, and in both settings there were disputes over the purity of doctrine that in turn called into question claims to the legitimacy of public discipline. It is at this point that we recognise the common ground among disaffected Protestants in both settings: doctrine was linked to the sovereignty and legitimacy of the political and legal organs who professed to be its arbiters. When a rift over doctrine emerged, a rift over discipline, sovereignty, and law was also likely.

The model of a Jacobean ecclesiological consensus suddenly shattered is difficult to sustain in light of this evidence. The debates that took place between Jacobean Protestants continued along rifts opened in the late Elizabethan Church, which would continue to shape conflict in the Church after 1625. We have seen conflicts between Richard Cosin and Dudley Fenner over the use of High Commission to enforce Whitgift's Three Articles, and have noted the continuation of that debate between William Bradshaw and his critics in the Jacobean setting. Similarly, Bancroft's *Daungerous positions* and *Suruay of the pretended holy discipline* figured in English controversies over episcopacy, and also engaged the attention of Presbyterians like the Scot John Davidson. All of Bancroft's works would be republished in both England and Scotland during the 1630s. Further continuities can be found in the question of ceremonialism that, contrary to what Anthony Milton has suggested, was not a mode of churchmanship unique to the Laudians.[33] Instead, tensions over ceremonies sprang forth in the wake of the introduction of the Canons of 1604, and in the *Abridgment* controversy we find that the issue engaged writers until well into the 1630s. Indeed, figures that would become prominent in these debates, among them Thomas Morton, Henry Jacob, and William Ames, were all active in disputes over ceremonialism and governance in the Jacobean setting. Hence, Jacobean religious conflicts should be seen as a proving ground for the development of a literature, and a set of arguments, that would continue to figure prominently in debates on ceremonies and governance in the Church after 1625. Indeed, rather than a model positing disjunction after 1625, this study points to the potential for the continuity of debate over fundamental issues in early Stuart ecclesiology; their significance may lie in the fact that, in 1640, these issues were still unresolved.

It emerges that a number of ecclesiological issues that scholars have associated with 'Laudianism' or 'Carolinism' were, in fact, deeply

---

(Cambridge, 1994), pp. 209–37; John D. Ford, 'The lawful bonds of Scottish society: the Five Articles of Perth, the Negative Confession and the National Covenant', *Historical Journal*, 37 (1994), 45–64; Ford, 'Conformity and conscience: the structure of the Perth Articles debate in Scotland, 1618–1638', *Journal of Ecclesiastical History*, 46 (1995), 256–77.
[33] Milton, *Catholic and reformed*, p. 530.

entrenched in Jacobean religious culture. One of these was an interest in the patristic heritage of the Apostolic church, which, argue Peter Lake and Julian Davies, was a uniquely Laudian phenomenon.[34] That this is not the case is revealed by a number of examples from the preceding pages, from Thomas James' call for new editions of the Fathers, and the exhaustive table of contents contained in the *Abridgment*, to the reformist Paul Baynes' answer to George Downame's defence of episcopacy *iure divino*. What these exchanges reveal is that patristic scholarship was integral to the business of both defending and attacking the Church. Moreover, the publication of 'primers' on the Fathers, such as Meredith Hanmer's anthology of 'auncient ecclesiastical histories', suggests that the 'Laudian style' and 'recatholicisation' were hardly unique to the Caroline setting, but had a long and well-established tenure in the post-Reformation Church. In addition, there is reason to question whether the views associated with 'avant-garde' conformity – that is, ceremonialism, order, uniformity, and public profession within the visible Church – were really so narrowly confined. Those scholars who have sought to advance this view have overlooked the degree to which these aspects of ecclesiology were broadly held among Jacobean conformists, from Bell to William Covell and Gabriel Powel. This study has addressed these oversights by probing into the intellectual nature of Jacobean religious controversy and defining its major themes.

One central contribution made by the present work concerns conformity and its place in Jacobean ecclesiology. Anthony Milton has argued that Jacobean divines were anxious to draw strong links between their Church and the Continental reformed churches. He suggested that, under Laud, clerics began to move away from this position while at the same time softening their opinions on the 'errors of Rome'.[35] Yet, as we have seen with reference to the work of Francis Mason and John Gordon, and the debate on 'custom' and ceremonial practice, there were many who were willing to defend the English Church *as* English. John Hayward's defence of sacerdotal kingship had less in common with Continental Protestantism than it did with classical arguments about the nature of civil polity, many of them issuing from 'pagan' sources. Moreover, in Thomas Bell's approach to the reinterpretation, rather than dismissal, of Rome we find that

[34] See Peter Lake, 'The Laudian style: order, uniformity and the pursuit of the beauty of holiness in the 1630s', in *The early Stuart Church, 1603–1642*, ed. Kenneth Fincham (Stanford, 1993), pp. 161–85; Lake, 'The Laudians and the argument from authority', in *Court, country, and culture: essays on early modern British history in honor of Perez Zagorin*, ed. Bonnelyn Kunze and Dwight Brautigan (Rochester, NY, 1992), pp. 149–75; Julian Davies, *The Caroline captivity of the Church: Charles I and the remoulding of Anglicanism, 1625–1641* (Oxford, 1992), chs. 1–2.

[35] Milton, *Catholic and reformed*, p. 529.

conformists tended to view Catholic Rome as being in the grip of error, and attributed this condition to the corruption of scripture and the works of the Fathers. To dispense with the Roman church as defined by error would also have entailed the setting aside of a vast textual tradition which conformists needed for their own purposes. Milton overlooks what Thomas James knew well enough: the texts themselves could be redeemed from error, even if Rome could not.

In addition, our recovery of the complexity of conformist thought suggests an alternate explanation for the religious conflicts of the Jacobean age. The complexity of English ecclesiastical polity and the arguments employed to defend its central propositions imply that there were more avenues for conflict than can be explained by a consensus over predestination. Tyacke overlooked, as G. W. Bernard and Julian Davies endeavoured to show, that a 'state' church required a number of concessions in order to justify ceremonies and governance, and it was reformist attacks on these concessions that drove the debate and led writers to consider the constitutional and legal implications of the conformist vision of ecclesiastical polity. As we have seen, elements of this problem were aired in the Elizabethan setting. Therefore, the continuity of the debates we have surveyed serves as the principal challenge to models of religious conflict lately proposed by scholars, and furnishes a crucial insight into how religion impacted politics. We have good reason to question Milton's contention that the Jacobean period witnessed a ' "conformist drift" – a growing preoccupation with the visible church and its concerns'.[36] Instead, this preoccupation can be located in the late Elizabethan Church, and can be traced throughout the period. This study has shown that conformist thought shaped and was shaped in debates with reformists; hence, Protestant thought was not consensual, but was driven by its own internal dynamic.[37] This dynamic serves to clarify Peter Lake and Michael Questier's interest in 'polemical struggle' and its implications for understanding competing conceptions of the Church.[38] Rather than a struggle between a welter of groups of the sort identified by Peter Lake and Kenneth Fincham, the Jacobean Church was the site of a contest among writers who were and wished to continue as Churchmen; the principal cleavage was not between 'denominations' but between proponents of rival visions of a single institution, itself defined by a congeries of scriptural, historical, and political elements. The sheer number of controversial works published

---

[36] Ibid., p. 536.
[37] For this see J. G. A. Pocock, 'The history of British political thought', 289.
[38] See 'Introduction' to *Conformity and orthodoxy in the English Church, c. 1560–1660*, ed. Peter Lake and Michael Questier (Woodbridge, Suffolk, 2000), passim.

during the period suggests that conflict was not contained, that positions continued to harden, and that rifts dating back to the 1580s were kept open.

That religion impacted politics is a point noted by writers throughout English history, and there is much truth to Anthony Milton's observation that points of Church government 'inevitably held implications for issues of civil polity'.[39] However, Milton did not make this link between civil polity and ecclesiastical government with sufficient clarity, nor is it evident in Tyacke's notion of a Calvinist consensus concerning the doctrine of salvation. In the work of both scholars, political conflict followed the familiar pattern of the waning of peace at the hands of a coterie of 'Laudians' with influence at court. While tensions over Arminianism were certainly in the air, one has to ask whether these tensions were strong enough to polarise English society in the manner proposed by either the Laudian or Arminian model. Much more suggestive are the debates surveyed by this study. For when writers seeking to respond to the doctrinal implications of the Canons of 1604 are led into a conflict over the common law, the sovereignty of the Crown in parliament, the relationship of bishops to the estates of the realm, and the nature of ecclesiastical polity in two of the three kingdoms, then clearly one is witnessing a debate about the fundamental elements of Jacobean ecclesiastical polity. In fact, it is the ease with which writers could make the transit between subscription and Apostolic doctrine on the one hand, and Magna Carta and the governance of the realm on the other, which testifies to the centrality of the debates surveyed here to the political conflicts of early Stuart England. Models of religious conflict that propose a sudden upheaval in the 1630s must contend with the fact that fundamental political and religious divisions were well established, and would continue to engage writers after 1625. We are in a position to recognise that polemical debates were defined by the construction, criticism, and dismantling of historical and ecclesiological narratives used to define the relationship between civil and spiritual authority. The age of the *philosophes* and *erudits* was still some distance away: what lay on the immediate horizon was a war of religion, made possible by, as Burnet rightly observed, the formation of parties each armed with a set of assumptions concerning the ordering of ecclesiastical polity. The crisis of the 1640s was a war of religion because the effort to define a composite monarchy and a Church 'of the realm' fell afoul of competing, and ultimately fracturing, visions of Protestantism, politics, and history. I hope to illustrate these themes in a future study.

---

[39] Milton, *Catholic and reformed*, p. 449.

BIBLIOGRAPHY

MANUSCRIPTS

Bodleian Library, Carte MS, fol. 77, n. 590. Earl of Huntington Papers.
Bodleian Library, Carte MS, fol. 59, n. 427. Misc. Ormonde Papers.
Lambeth Palace Library, Bancroft's Register, fol. 127a. 'The Council's Letter from Proceeding Against the Non-Conformitans of the Clergy' (1604).
Lambeth Palace Library, Bancroft's Register, fol. 127b. 'The Archbishop of Canterbury's Directions to the Same Purpose' (1604).

PRINTED PRIMARY SOURCES (INCLUDES MODERN EDITIONS)

Abbot, Robert, *The old waye. A sermon preached at Oxford, the eight day of July, being the Act Sunday* (1610).
An abridgment of that booke which the ministers of Lincoln diocess delivered to his Maiestie upon the first of December last (1605).
Ainsworth, Henry, *Counterpoyson. Considerations touching the points in difference between the godly ministers & people of the Church of England, and the seduced brethren of the separation* (1608).
Allen, William, *An apologie and true declaration of the institution and endeuours of the two English colleges, the one in Rome, the other now resident in Rhemes* (1581).
[Ambrose, St, Bishop of Milan], *Sancti Ambrosii . . . opera, ex editione Romana*, 2 vols. (1603).
Ames, William, *A fresh suit against human ceremonies in Gods Worship. Or a triplication unto. D. Burgesse his rejoinder for D. Morton* (1633).
A reply to Dr. Mortons generall Defence of three nocent ceremonies. viz. the surplice, crosse in baptisme, and kneeling at the receiving of the sacramental elements of bread and wine (1622).
A reply to Dr. Mortons particular defence of three nocent ceremonies. viz. The surplice, crosse in baptisme, and kneeling at the receiving of the sacramentall elements of bread and wine (1623).
Andrewes, Lancelot, *A sermon preached before the Kings Maiestie at Hampton Court, concerning the right and power of calling assemblies* (1606).
The answere of the vicechancelour, the doctors, both the proctors, and other the heads of houses in the Vniversity of Oxford . . . To the humble petition of the ministers of the Church of England, desiring reformation of certain ceremonies and abuses of the Church (1603).
Askew, Egeon, *Brotherly reconcilement* (1605).

266

Bacon, Francis, *Essays*, ed. John Strachan (Hertfordshire, 1997).

[Bacon, Francis], *Certaine considerations touching the better pacification, and edification of the Church of England* (1604).

Bancroft, Richard, *A sermon preached at Paules Cross the 9. of Februarie, being the first Sunday in the Parleament, anno. 1588* (1588).

A Suruay of the pretended holy discipline (1593).

Daungerous positions and proceedings published and practised within this iland of Brytaine, vnder pretence of Reformation, and for the Presbiteriall discipline (1593).

Barlow, William, *One of the foure sermons preached before the Kings Maiestie, at Hampton Court in September last. This concerning the antiquitie and superioritie of bishops* (1606).

The summe and substance of the conference . . . at Hampton Court, January 14. 1603 (1604).

Batt, John, *The royall priesthood of Christians* (1605).

Baynes, Paul, *The diocesans tryall. Wherein all the sinnews of d. Downams Defence are brought unto three heads, and orderly dissolved* (1621).

Becanus, Martinus, *The English iarre: or disagreement amongst the ministers of great Brittaine, concerning the Kinges supremacy* (1612).

[Bede], *Ecclesiastical history of the English people*, trans. Leo Shirley-Price, intro. D. H. Farmer (Harmondsworth, 1990).

Bell, Thomas, *The downefall of poperie* (1604).

The golden ballance of tryall (1603).

The popes funerall, containing an exact and pithy reply, to a pretended answere of a shamelesse and foolish libell, called, The forerunner of Bells downfall (1606).

The regiment of the Church: as it is agreeable with Scriptures, all antiquities of the Fathers, and modern Writers, from the Apostles themselves, vnto this present age (1606).

Thomas Bels motiues: concerning Romish faith and religion (1593).

The woefull crie of Rome. Containing a defiance to popery (1605).

Bilson, Thomas, *The perpetual gouernement of Christes Church* (1593).

The true difference betweene Christian subiection and unchristian rebellion (1585).

[Bodin, Jean], *The six bookes of a common-weale. Written by I. Bodin*, trans. Richard Knolles (1606).

Bradshaw, William, *A consideration of certain positions archiepiscopall* (ca. 1604–5).

English puritanisme containening [sic] *The maine opinions of the rigidest sorte of those that are called Puritanes in the realme of England* (1605).

A myld and iust defence of certeyne arguments, at the last session of Parliament directed to that most Honourable High Court, in behalfe of the ministers suspended and deprived (1606).

A proposition. Concerning kneeling in the very act of receiuing howsoever (1605).

A protestation of the Kings supremacie. Made in the name of the afflicted ministers, and opposed to the shamefull calumnations of the prelates (1605).

A short treatise, of the crosse in baptisme (1604).

A treatise of divine worship, tending to prove that the ceremonies imposed vpon the ministers of the Gospell in England, in present controversie, are in their vse vnlawfull (1604).

A treatise of the nature and vse of things indifferent. Tendinge to proue that the ceremonies in present controuersie amongst the ministers of the gospell in the realme of Englande, are neither in nature nor vse indifferent (1605).

Twelve generall arguments, proving that the ceremonies imposed upon the ministers of the gospell in England, by our prelates, are unlawfull (1605).

[Anon], *A briefe and plaine narration of proceedings at an assemsemblie* [sic] *in Glasco. 8 Iun. 1610. anent the innovation of the Kirk-government* (1610).

Broughton, Hugh, *Declaration of general corruption, of religion, Scripture, and all learninge: wrought by D. Bilson* (1604).

Two little workes defensiue of our redemption (1604).

Broughton, Richard, *The first part of Protestants proofes, for Catholickes religion and recusancy* (1607).

A plaine patterne of a perfect Protestant professor (ca. 1608).

Bruce, Robert, *The mysterie of the Lords Supper. Cleerly manifested in five sermons; two of preparation, and three of the Sacrament it selfe* (1614).

Buckeridge, John, *A sermon preached at Hampton Court before the Kings Maiestie, on Tuesday the 23. of Sepember, anno 1606* (1606).

A sermon preached before His Maiestie at Whitehall, March 22. 1617. being Passion-Sunday, touching prostration, and kneeling in the worship of God (1618).

Burges, John, *An answer reioyned to that much applauded pamphlet of a namelesse author, bearing this title: viz. A reply to Dr. Mortons generall defence of three nocent ceremonies, &c.* (1631).

The lawfulnes of kneeling in the act of receiving the Lords Supper (1631).

A sermon preached before the late King Iames His Majesty, at Greenwich, the 19. of July, 1604 (1642).

Burnet, Gilbert, *An exposition of the thirty-nine articles of the Church of England* (1699).

Calderwood, David, *The altar of Damascus or the patern of the English hierarchie, and church- policie obtruded upon the Church of Scotland* (1621).

A defence of our arguments against kneeling in the act of receiving the sacramentall elements of bread and wine impugned by Mr. Michelsone (1620).

A dispute vpon communicating at our confused communions (1624).

An epistle of a Christian brother exhorting an other to keepe himselfe vndefiled from the present corruptions brought into the ministration of the Lords Supper (1624).

An exhortation of the particular kirks of Christ in Scotland to their sister kirk in Edinburgh (1624).

History of the Kirk of Scotland by Mr. David Calderwood, ed. T. Thompson, 8 vols. (Edinburgh, 1842–9).

Perth assembly (1619).

Quaeres concerning the state of the Church of Scotland (1621).

Scoti τού τύχονος *paraclesis contra Danielis Tileni Silesii Parœnesin, ad Scotos Genevensis disciplinœ zelotas conscriptam, cuius pars prima est, episcopali ecclesiœ regimie* (1622).

A solution of Doctor Resolutus, his resolutions for kneeling (1619).

The speach of the Kirk of Scotland to her beloved children (1620).

The true history of the Church of Scotland, from the beginning of the reformation, unto the end of the reigne of King James VI (1678).

Carleton, George, *Directions to know the true church* (1615).

Iurisdiction regall, episcopall, papall (1610).

Certain arguments to perswade and prouoke the most honourable and high court of Parliament now assembled (1606).

Certain demandes with their grounds, drawne out of holy writ, and propounded <u>in soro conscientiae</u> by some religious gentl. (1605).

Certaine considerations drawne from the canons of the last Sinod, and other the Kings ecclesiastical and statue [sic] *law* (1605).

Churchyard, Thomas, *Churchyards good will* (1604).

Clapham, Henoch, *Errour on the left hand, through a frozen securitie* (1608).

Coke, Edward, *The preface to his charge given at the assize holden at Norwich* (1606).

Collins, Samuel, *A sermon preached at Paule's- Crosse, vpon the 1. of Nouember, being All-Saint's Day, anno 1607* (1607).

The confession of faith, subscrived by the Kings Maiestie and his household (1610).

Constitutions and canons ecclesiastical (1604).

Cosin, Richard, *An answer to the two fyrst and principall treatises of a certaine factious libell* (1584).

An apologie for sundrie proceedings by iurisdiction ecclesiastical, of late times by some chalenged, and also diuersly by them impugned (1593).

Covell, William, *A briefe answer vnto certaine reasons by way of an apologie deliuered to the Right Reuerend Father in God, the L. Bishop of Lincolne, by Mr. John Burges* (1606).

A modest and reasonable examination, of some things in vse in the Church of England, sundrie times heretofore misliked (1604).

Polimanteia, or, The meanes lawfull and vnlawfull, to iudge of the fall of a common-wealth (1595).

[Cowper, William], *The workes of Mr Willia[m] Cowper, late Bishop of Galloway* (1626).

Darley, John, *The glory of Chelsey Colledge revived* (1662).

Davidson, John, *D. Bancrofts rashnes in rayling against the Church of Scotland* (1590).

Denison, John, *Beati pacifici: The blessednes of peace-makers: and the aduancement of Gods children. In two sermons preached before the King* (1620).

The heauenly banquet: or The doctrine of the Lords Supper, set Forth in seuen sermons (1631).

Denison, Stephen, *The doctrine of both the Sacraments: to witte, Baptisme and the Supper of the Lord* (1621).

[Anon], *A dialogue, concerning the strife of our churche* (1584).

Dighton, Thomas, *Certain reasons of a private Christian against conformitie to kneeling in the very act of receiving the Lords Supper* (1618).

The second part of a plain discourse of an vnlettered Christian, wherein by way of demonstration hee sheweth what the reasons be which he doth ground upon, in refusing conformity to kneeling in the act of receiving the Lords Supper (1619).

Dominis, Marco Antonio de, *De republica ecclesiastica, pars secunda, continens libros quintum et sextum* (1620).

Dove, John, *A defence of church gouernment. Dedicated to the high Court of Parliament* (1606).

Downame, George, *A defence of the sermon preached at the consecration of the L. Bishop of Bath and Welles, against a confutation thereof by a namelesse author* (1611).

A sermon defending the honourable function of bishops (1608).

Two sermons, the one commending the ministerie in generall: the other defending the office of bishops in particular (1608).

Draxe, Thomas, *The lambes spouse or the heauenly bride* (1608).

Eedes, Richard, *Six learned and godly Sermons* (1604).

England, Church of, *Articles agreed upon by the archbishops and bishops . . . in the convocation holden at London in the year 1562* (1684).

The booke of common prayer, and administration of the sacraments, and other rites and ceremonies of the Church of England (1604).

[Fenner, Dudley], *A counter-poyson, modestly written for the time, to make aunswere to the obiections and reproches, wherewith the aunswerer to the Abstract, would disgrace the holy discipline of Christ* (1584).

[Fenton, John], *King Iames his welcome to London* (1603).

[Field, John, and Wilcox, Thomas], *An admonition to the Parliament* (1572).

Field, Richard, *Of the Church five bookes* (1606).

Floyd, Thomas, *The picture of a perfit common wealth* (1600).

Forset, Edward, *A comparatiue discourse of the bodies natural and politique* (1606).

A defence of the right of kings. Wherein the power of the papacie ouer princes, is refuted; and the Oath of Allegeance iustified (1624).

[Fulke, William; Fenner, Dudley; Travers, Walter?], *A briefe and plaine declaration, concerning the desires of all those faithfull ministers, that haue and do seeke for the discipline and reformation of the Church of Englande* (1584).

Fuller, Nicholas, *The argument of master Nicholas Fuller, in the case of Thomas Lad, and Richard Maunsell, his clients* (1607).

Gardiner, Samuel, *A dialogue or conference betweene Irenaeus and Antimachus, about the rites and ceremonies of the Church of England* (1605).

Gawton, Richard, *A short instruction for all such as are to be admitted to the Lords Supper* (1612).

Godwin, Francis, *A catalogue of the bishops of England, since the first planting of Christian religion in this island* (1601).

Gordon, John, *EIPHNOKOINΩNIA. The Peace of the communion of the Church of England* (1612).

England and Scotlands happinesse: in being reduced to vnitie of religion, vnder our invincible monarke King Iames (1604).

Enotikon or A sermon of the vnion of Great Brittainie (1604).

Hall, Joseph, *A common apologie of the Church of England: against the vnjust challenges of the over-just sect, commonly called Brownists* (1610).

Hampton, Christopher, *A sermon preached in the cittie of Glasco in Scotland, on the tenth day of Iune, 1610. At the holding of a generall assembly there* (1611).

Hanmer, Meredith, *The auncient ecclesiastical histories of the first six hundred yeares after Christ, by Eusebius, Socrates, and Euagrius. Whereunto is annexed Dorotheus bishop of Tyrus, of the liues of the Prophetes, Apostles and 70 disciples. All which authors are tr. by M. Hanmer* (1650).

Hayward, John, *An answer to the first part of a certaine conference, concerning succession* (1603).

A reporte of a discourse concerning supreme power in affairs of religion (1606).

Heylyn, Peter, *Cyprianus anglicus* (1671).

Hide, Thomas, *A consolatorie epistle to the afflicted catholickes, set foorth by Thomas Hide Priest* (1579).

Hieron, Samuel, *A defence of the ministers reasons, for refusall of subscription to the Booke of common prayer, and of conformitie* (ca, 1607).

A dispute vpon the question of kneeling, in the acte of receiving the sacramentall bread and wine, proving it to be unlawfull (1608).

The second parte of the defence of the ministers reasons for refusal of subscription & conformitie to the book of common prayer (1608).

The sermons of Master Samuel Hieron, formerly collected together by himselfe (1620).

A short dialogue prouing that the ceremonyes, and some other corruptions now in question, are defended, by none other arguments then such as the papists haue here tofore vsed: and our protestant writers haue long since answered (1605).

Hobbes, Thomas, *Leviathan, or The matter, forme, & power of a common-wealth ecclesiasticall and civill* (1651).

Holyoake, Francis, *A sermon of obedience especially vnto authoritie ecclesiasticall* (1610).

[Anon], *An homelie against disobedience and wylfull rebellion* (1570?).

Hooke, Henry, *A sermon preached before the king at White-hall, the eight of May 1604* (1604).

Hooker, Richard, *Of the lawes of ecclesiastical politie* (1618).

Hutten, Leonard, *An answere to a certaine treatise of the crosse in baptisme* (1605).

Hutton, Thomas, *Reasons for refusal of subscription to the booke of common praier, vnder the hands of certaine ministers of Devon, and Cornwall word for word as they were exhibited by them to the Right Reverend Father in God William Coton Doctor of Divinitie L. Bishop of Exceter* (1605).

The second and last part of Reasons for refusall of subscription to the Booke of common prayer, vnder the hands of certaine ministers of Deuon. and Cornwall, as they were exhibited by them to the right Reuerend Father in God William Cotton Doctor of Divinitie, and Lord Bishop of Exceter (1606).

Informations, or a protestation, and a treatise from Scotland (1608).

Jacob, Henry, *Anno Domini 1616. A confession and protestation of the faith of certaine Christians in England* (1616).

An attestation of many learned, godly, and famous divines ... That the Church-governement ought to bee alwayes with the peoples free consent (1613).

A Christian and modest offer of a most indifferent conference, or disputation, about the maine and principall controversies betwixt the prelats, and the late silenced and deprived ministers in England (1606).

A declaration and plainer opening of certain pointes, with a sound confirmation of some other, contained in a treatise entitled, The divine beginning and institution of Christes true visible and ministeriall church (1612).

The divine beginning and institution of Christs true visible or ministeriall church (1610).

Reasons taken out of Gods word and the best humane testimonies prouing a necessitie of reforming our churches in England (1604).

To the right high and mightie prince, Iames by the grace of God, King of great Britannie, France, and Irelande defender of the faith, &c. An humble supplication for toleration and libertie to enioy and observe the ordinances of Christ Iesus in th'administration of his churches in lieu of humane constitutions (1609).

[Jacob, Henry], *A collection of sundry matters ... appointed by God for his visible church spiritually politicall* (1616).

A position against vainglorious, and that which is falsly called learned preaching (1604).

James I, King of England, *Basilikon doron. Or, His Maiesties instructions to his dearest sonne, Henrie the prince* (1603).

The true lawe of free monarchies: or The reciprock and mutuall dutie betwixt a free king, and his naturall subiects (1598), in *The political works of James I*, ed. C. H. McIlwain (Cambridge, MA, 1918).

James, Thomas, *The humble supplication of Thomas James student in diuinity, and keeper of the publicke librarie at Oxford, for reformation of the ancient Fathers Workes, by papists sundrie ways depraved* (ca. 1607).

Kellison, Matthew, *A suruey of the new religion, detecting manie grosse absurdities which it implieth* (1603).

King, John, *The fourth sermon preached at Hampton Court on Tuesday the Last of Sept. 1606* (1607).

Laud, William, *A sermon preached on Munday, the sixt of February, at Westminster: at the opening of the Parliament* (1625).

Leigh, William, *Queen Elizabeth paraleld in her princely virtues, with David, Ioshua and Hezekia* (1612).

Lindsay, David, *The reasons of a pastors resolution, touching the reuerend receiuing of the holy communion* (1619).

A true narration of all the passages of the proceedings in the generall Assembly of the Church of Scotland, Holden at Perth the 25. of August, anno Dom. 1618 (1621).

[Lipsius, Justus], *Six bookes of politickes or Ciuil doctrine, written in Latine by Iustus Lipsius*, trans. William Jones (1594).

Maihew, Edward, *A treatise of the groundes of the old and newe religion* (1608).

[Marprelate, Martin (pseud.)], *Theses Martinianae* (1589).

Mason, Francis, *The avthoritie of the Chvrch in making canons and constitutions concerning things indifferent* (1607).

Maunsell, Andrew, *The first part of the catalogue of English printed bookes* (1595).

Maxey, Anthony, *The churches sleepe, expressed in a sermon preached at the court* (1606).

Maynwaring, Roger, *Religion and alegiance: in two sermons preached before the King's Maiestie* (1627).

Melville, James, *The autobiography and diary of Mr James Melvill*, ed. R. Pitcairn (Edinburgh, 1843).

Meriton, George, *A sermon preached before the Generall Assembly at Glascoe in the kingdome of Scotland, the tenth day of iune, 1610* (1611).

Michelson, John, *The lawfulnes of kneeling in the act of receiuing the sacrament of the Lordes supper* (1620).

Morton, Thomas, *A defence of the innocencie of the three ceremonies of the Church of England. viz. the surplice, crosse after baptisme, and kneeling at the receiuing of the blessed Sacrament* (1618).

A direct answer vnto the scandalous exceptions, which Theophilus Higgons hath lately obiected against D. Morton (1609).

Of the institution of the sacrament of the blessed bodie and blood of Christ, (by some called) the masse of Christ (1631).

[Anon], *Motives to godly knowledge* (1613).

[Murray, John], *A dialogue betwixt Cosmophilus and Theophilus anent the urging of new ceremonies upon the kirke of Scotland* (1620).

Nichols, Josias, *Abrahams faith: that is, The Olde Religion* (1602).
   *The plea of the innocent: wherein is auerred; that the ministers and people falslie
   termed puritanes, are iniuriouslie slaundered for enemies or troublers of the state*
   (1602).
Ormerod, Oliver, *Picture of a Puritane: or, a relation of the opinions, qualities, and
   practises of the Anabaptists in Germanie, and of the Puritanes in England*
   (1605).
Panke, John, *A short admonition by way of dialogue, to all those who hitherto . . .
   with-held them-selues from comming to the Lordes table* (1604).
Parker, Matthew, *De antiquitate Britannicae ecclesiae & priuilegiis ecclesiae
   Cantuariensis, cum Archepiscopis eiusdem* (1572).
Parker, Robert, *A scholasticall discourse against symbolizing with Antichrist in
   ceremonies: especially in the signe of the cross* (1607).
Parsons, Robert, *A treatise of the three conuersions of England from paganisme to
   Christian religion* (1603).
Paybody, Thomas, *A iust apologie for the gesture of kneeling in the act of receiuing
   the Lords Supper. Against the manifold exceptions of all opposers in the
   Churches of England, and Scotland* (1629).
Penry, John, *An humble motion with submission vnto the right Honorable L L. of Hir
   Maiesties Priuie Counsell* (1590).
[Penry, John], *A briefe discouery of the vntruths and slanders (against the true
   gouernement of the Church of Christ) contained in a sermon, preached the 8.
   [sic] of Februarie 1588. by D. Bancroft* (1590).
Powel, Gabriel, *A consideration of the depriued and silenced ministers arguments, for
   their restitution to the vse and libertie of their ministerie* (1606).
   *De adiaphoris. Theological and scholastical positions, concerning the nature and
   vse of things indifferent* (1607).
   *A reioynder unto the mild defence, iustifying the consideration of the silenced
   ministers supplication vnto the high court of parliament* (1607).
Prynne, William, *A catalogue of such testimonies in all ages as plainly evidence
   bishops and presbyters to be both one, equall and the same in jurisdiction, office,
   dignity, order, and degree* (1637).
[Rainolds, John], *The summe of the conference betwene Iohn Rainoldes and Iohn
   Hart* (1584).
[Anon], *The remoouall of certaine imputations laid vpon the ministers of Deuon: and
   Cornwall by one M. T. H., and in them, vpon all other ministers els-ewhere,
   refusing to subscribe* (1606).
Richardson, Charles, *The doctrine of the Lords supper* (1616).
Ridley, Thomas, *A view of the ciuile and ecclesiastical law* (1607).
Rogers, Thomas, *The faith, doctrine, and religion, professed, & protected in the
   realme of England, and dominions of the same* (1607), republished by the Parker
   Society, ed. J. J. S. Perowne (London, 1854; 1968).
Rogers, Thomas, *Two dialogues, or conferences . . . Concerning kneeling in the very
   act of receiuing the sacramental bread and wine, in the Supper of the Lord*
   (1608).
Scotland, Privy Council, *A declaration of the iust causes of his Maiesties proceeding
   against those ministers, who are now lying in prison, attainted of high treason*
   (1605).
Scot, Patrick, *Calderwoods recantation: or, a tripartite discourse* (1622).
   Vox vera: or, Obseruations from Amsterdam (1625).

Scott, Thomas, *Boanerges. Or the humble supplication of the ministers of Scotland, to the High Court of Pariament* [sic] *in England* (1624).
　The high-waies of God and the King (1623).
　Vox Dei (1624).
[Scott, Thomas], *The interpreter wherein three principall termes of state much mistaken by the vulgar are clearly unfolded* (1622).
Scott, William, *The course of conformitie, as it hath proceeded, is concluded, should be refused* (1622).
[Sherwood, Richard, (attrib.)], *An answere to a sermon preached the 17 of April anno D. 1608, by George Downame* (1609).
　A replye answering a defence of the sermon, preached at the consecration of the bishop of Bathe and Welles, by George Downame, Doctor of Divinitye. In defence of an answere to the foresaid sermon imprinted ann 1609 (1613).
Smith, Richard, *An answer to Thomas Bels late challeng named by him The downfal of popery* (1605).
Some, Robert, *A godly treatise containing and deciding certaine questions, mouued of late in London and other places, touching the ministerie, sacraments, and Church* (1588).
Southwell, Robert, *An epistle of comfort, to the reverend priestes & to the honorable, worshipful, & other of the laye sort restrayned in durance for the Catholicke fayth* (1587?).
Sparke, Thomas, *A brotherly perswasion to vnitie, and vniformitie in iudgement, and practise touching the receiued, and present ecclesiasticall government* (1607).
[Spottiswoode, John], *History of the Church of Scotland . . . by the Right Rev. John Spottiswoode*, ed. M. Russell and M. Napier, 3 vols. (Edinburgh, 1847–51).
Sprint, John, *Cassander Anglicanus; shewing the necessity of conformitie to the prescribed ceremonies of our church, in case of depriuation* (1618).
Stapleton, Thomas, *A counterblast to M. Hornes vayne blaste against M. Fekenham* (1567).
Stockwood, John, *A verie godlie and profitable sermon of the necessitie, properties, and office of a good magistrate* (1584).
Stoughton, William, *An assertion for true and Christian church-policie* (1604).
[Stoughton, William], *An abstract, of certain acts of parliament: of certaine her Maiesties Iniunctions: of certaine canons, constitutions, and synodalles prouinciall* (1583).
A suruey of the booke of common prayer, by way of 197. quaeres grounded vpon 58. places, ministring iust matter of question, with a view of London ministers exceptions (1606).
Sutton, Christopher, *Godly meditations upon the most holy sacrament of the Lords Supper . . . with a short admonition touching the controuersie about the holie eucharist* (1616).
Thornborough, John, *A discourse plainely prouing the euident vtilitie and vrgent necessitie of the desired happie vnion of the two famous kingdomes of England and Scotland* (1604).
　The ioifull and blessed reuniting of the two mighty & famous kingdomes, England & Scotland into their ancient name of great Brittaine (1604).
Tichborne, John, *A triple antidote, against certaine very common scandals of this time* (1609).
To the Kinges most excellent Majestie the humble petition of two and twentie preachers in London and the suburbs thereof (1605?).

[Trismegistus], *Le Pimandre de Mercure Trismagiste*, trans. François de Foix (1579).

[Anon], *A true, modest, and iust defence of the petition for reformation, exhibited to the Kings most excellent Maiestie* (1618).

[Anon], *The unlawfull practises of prelates against godly ministers, the maintainers of the discipline of God* (1584).

[Waldegrave, Robert, (attrib.)], *A lamentable complaint of the commonalty* (1585).

Walpole, Richard, *A briefe, and cleere confutation, of a new, vaine, and vaunting chalenge, made by O.E.* (1603).

Wats, James, *The controversie debated about the reuerend gesture of kneeling, in the act of receiuing the holy communion* (1621).

Whetenhall, Thomas, *A discourse of the abuses now in question in the churches of Christ* (1606).

Wilkes, William, *Obedience or ecclesiastical vnion. Treatised by William Wilkes Doctor in Theologie, and one of his Maiesties chaplaines in ordinarie* (1605).

Willet, Andrew, *Ecclesia triumphans: that is, The ioy of the English church, for the happie coronation of the most vertuous and pious prince, Iames* (1603).

Williams, John, *A manual: or, Three small and plain treatises* (1672).

Willymat, William, *A loyal subiects looking-glasse* (1604).

Wood, Anthony, *Athenae Oxonienses*, 2 vols. (1691–2).

Woodward, Philip, *The fore-runner of Bels downefall* (1605).

SECONDARY SOURCES

Archer, Stanley, 'Hooker on Apostolic succession: the two voices', *Sixteenth Century Journal*, 24 (1993), 67–74.

Armitage, David, *The ideological origins of the British Empire* (Cambridge, 2000).

Atkinson, Nigel, *Richard Hooker and the authority of scripture, tradition and reason: reformed theologian of the Church of England?* (Carlisle, 1997).

Avis, Paul, *The Church in the theology of the reformers* (London, 1981).

Babbage, Stuart Barton, *Puritanism and Richard Bancroft* (London, 1962).

Bernard, G. W., 'The Church of England c.1529–c.1642', *History*, 75 (1990), 183–206.

Bicknell, E. J., ed., *A theological introduction to the Thirty-nine Articles of the Church of England*, 3rd edn, revised by H. J. Carpenter (London, 1955).

Booty, John, *John Jewel as an apologist for the Church of England* (London, 1963).

Bradshaw, Brendan, and Morrill, John, eds., *The British problem, c. 1534–1707: state formation in the Atlantic Archipelago* (Houndmills, Basingstoke, 1996).

Brown, K. M., 'In search of the godly magistrate in Reformation Scotland', *Journal of Ecclesiastical History*, 40 (1989), 553–81.

Botfield, Beriah, ed., *Original letters relating to the ecclesiastical affairs of Scotland . . . 1603–25*, 2 vols. (Edinburgh, 1851).

Burgess, Glenn, *Absolute monarchy and the Stuart constitution* (New Haven, 1996).

'Common law and political theory in early Stuart England', *Political Science*, 40 (1988), 5–17.

'The divine right of kings reconsidered', *English Historical Review*, 107 (1992), 837–61.

'On revisionism: an analysis of early Stuart historiography in the 1970s and 1980s', *Historical Journal*, 33 (1990), 609–27.

The politics of the ancient constitution: an introduction to English political thought, 1603–1642 (University Park, PA, 1992).

'Was the English Civil War a war of religion?: the evidence of political propaganda', *Huntington Library Quarterly*, 61 (2000), 173–201.

Burgess, Glenn, ed., *The new British history: founding a modern state, 1603–1715* (London, 1999).

Burns, J. H., 'George Buchanan and the anti-Monarchomachs', in *Political discourse in early modern Britain*, ed. Nicholas Phillipson and Quentin Skinner (Cambridge, 1993), pp. 3–22.

'The political ideas of George Buchanan', *Scottish Historical Review*, 30 (1951), 60–8.

Burton, J. H. et al., eds., *The register of the Privy Council of Scotland*, 14 vols. (Edinburgh, 1877–98).

Cardwell, Edward, ed., *Synodalia: a collection of Articles of religion, Canons, and proceedings of convocations in the province of Canterbury*, 2 vols. (Oxford, 1842; repr. 1966).

Cargill Thompson, W. D. J, 'A reconsideration of Richard Bancroft's Paul's Cross sermon of 9 February 1588/9', *Journal of Ecclesiastical History*, 20 (1969), 253–66.

Carlson, Eric Josef, ed., *Religion and the English people, 1500–1640: new voices, new perspectives*, Sixteenth Century Essays and Studies, 45 (Kirksville, MO, 1998).

Chadwick, Henry, *The early church*, vol. I of *The Pelican history of the church*, ed. Owen Chadwick, 6 vols. (London, 1967).

Christianson, Paul, *Discourse on history, law and governance in the public career of John Selden, 1610–1635* (Toronto, 1996).

Reformers and Babylon (Toronto, 1978).

'Reformers and the Church of England under Elizabeth and the early Stuarts', *Journal of Ecclesiastical History*, 31 (1980), 463–82.

'Royalist and parliamentary voices on the ancient constitution', in *The mental world of the Jacobean court*, ed. Linda Levy Peck (Cambridge, 1991), pp. 71–95.

Clancy, T. R., 'Papist-Protestant-Puritan: English religious taxonomy, 1565–1665', *Recusant History*, 13 (1975–6), 227–53.

Clark, J. C. D., *English society, 1660–1832: religion, ideology and politics during the ancien regime* (Cambridge, 2000).

'Protestantism, nationalism and national identity, 1660–1832', *Historical Journal*, 43 (2000), 249–76.

Claydon, Tony, and McBride, Ian, eds., *Protestantism and national identity: Britain and Ireland, c. 1650–c. 1850* (Cambridge, 1998).

Clegg, Cyndia, *Press censorship in Jacobean England* (Cambridge, 2001).

Collinson, Patrick, 'A comment: Concerning the name Puritan', *Journal of Ecclesiastical History*, 31 (1980), 483–8.

'If Constantine, then also Theodosius: St Ambrose and the integrity of the Elizabethan *ecclesia anglicana*', *Journal of Ecclesiastical History*, 30 (1979), 205–29.

'The godly: aspects of popular Protestantism', in *Godly people: essays on English Protestantism and Puritanism* (London, 1983), pp. 1–17.

'The Jacobean religious settlement: the Hampton Court conference', in *Before the English Civil War*, ed. Howard Tomlinson (London, 1983), pp. 27–51.

The religion of Protestants: the Church in English society, 1559–1625 (Oxford, 1982).

'Truth, lies, and fiction in sixteenth-century Protestant historiography', in *The historical imagination in early modern Britain: history, rhetoric, and fiction,*

1500–1800, ed. Donald Kelley and David Harris Sacks (Cambridge, 1997), pp. 37–68.

Como, David, 'Puritans, predestination and the construction of orthodoxy in early seventeenth-century England', in *Conformity and orthodoxy in the English Church, c. 1560–1660*, ed. Peter Lake and Michael Questier (Woodbridge, Suffolk, 2000), pp. 64–87.

Cowan, Ian, 'The Five Articles of Perth', in *Reformation and revolution*, ed. Duncan Shaw (Edinburgh, 1967), pp. 160–77.

Cross, Claire, *The royal supremacy in the Elizabethan Church* (London, 1969).

Cust, Richard, and Hughes, Anne, eds., *Conflict in early Stuart England: studies in religion and politics, 1603–1642* (London, 1989).

Davies, Julian, *The Caroline captivity of the Church: Charles I and the remoulding of Anglicanism, 1625–1641* (Oxford, 1992).

Dodaro, Robert, and Questier, Michael, 'Strategies in Jacobean polemic: the use and abuse of St Augustine in English theological controversy', *Journal of Ecclesiastical History*, 44 (1993), 432–49.

Donald, Peter, *An uncounselled king: Charles I and the Scottish troubles, 1637–1641* (Cambridge, 1990).

Donaldson, G., 'The attitude of Whitgift and Bancroft to the Scottish Church', *TRHS*, 4th series, 24 (1942), 95–115.

Drummond, Andrew, *The Kirk and the Continent* (Edinburgh, 1956).

Duffy, Eamon, *The stripping of the altars: traditional religion in England, c. 1400–c. 1580* (New Haven, 1992).

Eccleshall, Robert, *Order and reason in politics: theories of absolute and limited monarchy in early modern England* (Oxford, 1978).

Elton, G. R., ed., *The Tudor constitution: documents and commentary*, 2nd edn (Cambridge, 1982).

Faulkner, Robert K., *Richard Hooker and the politics of a Christian England* (Berkeley, 1981).

Ferguson, Arthur, *Clio unbound: perception of the social and cultural past in Renaissance England* (Durham, NC, 1979).

Ferguson, William, *Scotland's relations with England: a survey to 1717* (Edinburgh, 1977).

Ferrell, Lori Anne, *Government by polemic: James I, the King's preachers, and the rhetorics of conformity, 1603–25* (Stanford, 1998).

Fincham, Kenneth, 'Clerical conformity from Whitgift to Laud', in *Conformity and orthodoxy in the English Church, c. 1560–1660*, ed. Peter Lake and Michael Questier (Woodbridge, Suffolk, 2000), pp. 125–58.
  Prelate as pastor: the episcopate of James I (Oxford, 1990).
  'Ramifications of the Hampton Court conference in the dioceses, 1603–1609', *Journal of Ecclesiastical History*, 36 (1985), 208–27

Fincham, Kenneth, ed., *The early Stuart Church, 1603–1642* (Stanford, 1993).
  Visitation articles and injunctions of the early Stuart Church, 2 vols. (Woodbridge, Suffolk, 1994–8).

Fincham, Kenneth, and Lake, Peter, 'The ecclesiastical policy of King James I', *Journal of British Studies*, 24 (1985), 169–207.

Finlayson, Michael, *Historians, puritans and the English Revolution* (Toronto, 1983).

Fissel, Mark, *The Bishops' Wars: Charles I's campaigns against Scotland, 1638–49* (Cambridge, 1994).

Ford, John D., 'Conformity and conscience: the structure of the Perth Articles debate in Scotland, 1618–1638', *Journal of Ecclesiastical History*, 46 (1995), 256–77.

'The lawful bonds of Scottish society: the Five Articles of Perth, the Negative Confession and the National Covenant', *Historical Journal*, 37 (1994), 45–64.

Foster, Walter Roland, *The Church before the covenants: the Church of Scotland, 1596–1638* (Edinburgh, 1975).

Galloway, Bruce, *The Union of England and Scotland, 1603–1608* (Edinburgh, 1986).

Gee, Henry, *Documents illustrative of English church history* (London, 1910).

Goldie, Mark, 'Ideology', in *Political innovation and conceptual change*, ed. Terence Ball, James Farr, and Russell Hanson (Cambridge, 1989), pp. 266–89.

Grafton, Anthony, *Forgers and critics: creativity and duplicity in Western scholarship* (London, 1990).

Graham, Michael F., *The uses of reform: 'godly discipline' and popular behaviour in Scotland and beyond, 1560–1610* (London, 1996).

Greaves, Richard, 'Concepts of political obedience in late Tudor England: conflicting perspectives', *Journal of British Studies*, 22 (1982), 23–34.

Green, Ian, 'Career prospects and clerical conformity in the early Stuart Church', *Past and Present*, 90 (1981), 71–115.

The Christian's ABC: catechisms and catechizing in England, c. 1530–1740 (Oxford, 1996).

'"England's wars of religion"? Religious conflict and the English Civil Wars', in *Church, change and revolution*, ed. J. van den Burg and P. G. Hoftijzer (Leiden, 1991), pp. 100–21.

Print and Protestantism in early modern England (Oxford, 2000).

Greenleaf, W. H., *Order, empiricism, and politics: two traditions in English political thought* (Oxford, 1964).

Greenslade, S. L., *The English reformers and the Fathers of the Church* (Oxford, 1960).

Greg, W. W., *Some aspects and problems of London publishing between 1550 and 1650* (Oxford, 1956).

Gregory, Victoria Joy, 'Congregational puritanism and the radical puritan community c. 1585–1625' (Ph.D. diss., University of Cambridge, 2003).

Griffiths, David, *The bibliography of the Book of Common Prayer, 1549–1999* (London, 2002).

Guibbory, Achsah, *Ceremony and community from Herbert to Milton* (Cambridge, 1998).

Guilday, Peter, *English Catholic refugees on the Continent, 1558–1795* (London, 1989).

Gunn, J. A. W., *Politics and the public interest in the seventeenth century* (London, 1969).

Guy, John, 'The Elizabethan Establishment and the ecclesiastical polity', in *The reign of Elizabeth I: court and culture in the last decade*, ed. John Guy (Cambridge, 1995), pp. 126–49.

'The Henrician Age', in *The varieties of British political thought, 1500–1800*, ed. J. G. A. Pocock with the assistance of Gordon J. Schochet and Lois G. Schwoerer (Cambridge, 1993), pp. 13–46.

Harrison, William Henry, 'Prudential method in ecclesiology: authority in Richard Hooker's "Of the laws of ecclesiastical politiy"' (Ph.D. diss., Boston College, 2000).

Haugaard, William, 'Renaissance patristic scholarship and theology in sixteenth-century England', *Sixteenth Century Journal*, 10 (1979), 37–60.

Hill, Christopher, 'Archbishop Laud and the English Revolution', in *Religion, resistance, and civil war*, ed. Gordon Schochet, Proceedings of the Folger Institute Center for the History of British Political Thought, 3 (Washington, DC, 1990), pp. 127–49.

Holder, Arthur G., 'Whitby and all that: the search for Anglican origins', *Anglican Theological Review*, 85 (2003), 231–52.

Holland, Susan, 'Archbishop Abbot and the problem of "Puritanism"', *Historical Journal*, 37 (1994), 23–43.

Holmes, Peter, *Resistance and compromise: the political thought of the Elizabethan Catholics* (Cambridge, 1982).

Hotson, Leslie, 'The library of Elizabeth's embezzling teller', *Studies in Bibliography*, 2 (1949–50), 49–61.

Jones, David Martin, *Conscience and allegiance in seventeenth century England: the political significance of oaths and engagements* (Rochester, NY, 1999).

Jones, Norman L., *Faith by statute: parliament and the settlement of religion, 1559* (London, 1982).

Kalo, Ogbu U., 'Continuity in change: bishops of London and religious dissent in early Stuart England', *Journal of British Studies*, 18 (1978), 28–45.

Kennedy, D. E., 'King James I's College of controversial divinity at Chelsea', in *Grounds of controversy: three studies of late 16th and early 17th century polemics*, ed. D. E. Kennedy (Melbourne, 1989), pp. 91–126.

Kenyon, J. P., ed., *The Stuart constitution: documents and commentary* (Cambridge, 1986).

King, Stephen, '"Your best and maist faithfull subjects": Andrew and James Melville as James VI and I's "loyal opposition"', *Renaissance and Reformation*, 24 (2000), 17–30.

Kirby, W. J. Torrance, *Richard Hooker's doctrine of the royal supremacy* (Leiden and New York, 1990).

Kirk, Kenneth E., *The Apostolic ministry: essays on the history and doctrine of episcopacy* (London, 1946).

Klein, William, 'The ancient constitution revisited', in *Political discourse in early modern Britain*, ed. Nicholas Phillipson and Quentin Skinner (Cambridge, 1993), pp. 23–44.

Konkola, Kari, '"People of the Book": the production of theological texts in early modern England', *PBSA*, 94 (2000), 5–33.

Lake, Peter, *Anglicans and puritans? Presbyterianism and English conformist thought from Whitgift to Hooker* (London, 1988).

'Anti-popery: the structure of a prejudice', in *Conflict in early Stuart England*, ed. Richard Cust and Ann Hughes (London, 1989), pp. 72–106.

The boxmaker's revenge: 'orthodoxy', 'heterodoxy' and the politics of the parish in early Stuart London (Manchester, 2001).

'Calvinism and the English Church, 1570–1635', *Past and Present*, 114 (1987), 32–76.

'Lancelot Andrewes, John Buckeridge, and avant-garde conformity at the court of James I', in *The mental world of the Jacobean court*, ed. Linda Levy Peck (Cambridge, 1991), pp. 113–33.

'The Laudians and the argument from authority', in *Court, country, and culture: essays on early modern British history in honor of Perez Zagorin*, ed. Bonnelyn Kunze and Dwight Brautigan (Rochester, NY, 1992), pp. 149–75.

'The Laudian style: order, uniformity and the pursuit of the beauty of holiness in the 1630s', in *The early Stuart Church, 1603–1642*, ed. Kenneth Fincham (Stanford, 1993), pp. 161–85.

Moderate puritans and the Elizabethan Church (Cambridge, 1982).

'Moving the goal posts?: modified subscription and the construction of conformity in the early Stuart Church', in *Conformity and orthodoxy in the English Church, c. 1560–1660*, ed. Peter Lake and Michael Questier (Woodbridge, Suffolk, 2000), pp. 179–205.

'Presbyterianism, the idea of a national Church and the argument from divine right', in *Protestantism and the national Church in sixteenth century England*, ed. Peter Lake and Maria Dowling (London, 1987), pp. 193–224.

Lake, Peter, and Questier, Michael, *The Antichrist's lewd hat: Protestants, papists & players in post-Reformation England* (New Haven, 2002).

Lake, Peter, and Questier, Michael, eds., *Conformity and orthodoxy in the English Church, c. 1560–1660* (Woodbridge, Suffolk, 2000).

Lambert, Sheila, 'State control of the Press in theory and practice: the role of the Stationers' Company before 1640', in *Censorship and the control of print in England and France, 1600–1900*, ed. Robin Myers and Michael Harris (Winchester, 1992), pp. 1–32.

Lamont, William, 'Comment: The rise of Arminianism reconsidered', *Past and Present*, 107 (1985), 227–31.

Godly rule: politics and religion, 1603–60 (London, 1969).

'The rise and fall of Bishop Bilson', *Journal of British Studies*, 5 (1966), 22–32.

Lange, A., *Weisheit und Prädestination: Weisheitliche Urordnung und Prädestination in den Text funden vom Qumran* (Leiden, 1995).

Langton, Stephanie Mary, 'Bishops as governors: diocesan administration and social organisation among the late Elizabethan and Jacobean episcopacy' (MA diss., University of Alberta, 2002).

Larkin, J. F., and Hughes, P. L., eds., *Stuart royal proclamations*, 2 vols. (Oxford, 1973).

Lee, Maurice, 'James I and the revival of episcopacy in Scotland, 1596–1600', *Church History*, 43 (1974), 49–64.

Levack, Brian, *The civil lawyers in England, 1603–1641* (Oxford, 1973).

Luoma, John K., 'Who owns the Fathers?: Hooker and Cartwright on the authority of the primitive church', *Sixteenth Century Journal*, 3 (1977), 45–59.

Lyall, Francis, *Of presbyters and kings: church and state in the law of Scotland* (Aberdeen, 1980).

MacCullough, Diarmaid, 'Richard Hooker's reputation', *English Historical Review*, 117 (2002), 773–812.

MacDonald, Alan, 'Ecclesiastical representation in parliament in post-Reformation Scotland: the two kingdoms theory in practice', *Journal of Ecclesiastical History*, 50 (1999), 38–61.

The Jacobean Kirk, 1567–1625: sovereignty, polity and liturgy (Aldershot, 1998).

Maltby, Judith. '"By this book": parishioners, the Prayer Book, and the established Church', in *The early Stuart Church, 1603–1642*, ed. Kenneth Fincham (Stanford, 1993), pp. 115–37.

Prayer Book and people in Elizabethan and early Stuart England (Cambridge, 1998).

Mason, A. J., *The Church of England and episcopacy* (Cambridge, 1914).

McCullough, Peter, *Sermons at court: politics and religion in Elizabethan and Jacobean preaching* (Cambridge, 1998).

Mendle, Michael, *Dangerous positions: mixed government, the estates of the realm, and the 'Answer to the xix propositions'* (University, AL, 1985).

Milton, Anthony, *Catholic and reformed: the Roman and Protestant churches in English Protestant thought, 1600–1640* (Cambridge, 1995).

'The Church of England, Rome and the true church: the demise of a Jacobean consensus', in *The early Stuart Church, 1603–1642*, ed. Kenneth Fincham (Stanford, 1993), pp. 187–210.

'The creation of Laudianism: a new approach', in *Politics, religion and popularity in early Stuart Britain*, ed. Thomas Cogswell, Richard Cust, and Peter Lake (Cambridge, 2002), pp. 162–84.

'Licensing, censorship, and religious orthodoxy in early Stuart England', *Historical Journal*, 41 (1998), 625–51.

Milward, Peter, *Religious controversies of the Elizabethan age: a survey of printed sources* (London, 1977).

Religious controversies of the Jacobean age: a survey of printed sources (London, 1978).

Morrill, John, 'The attack on the Church of England in the Long Parliament, 1640–1642', in *History, society and the churches: essays in honour of Owen Chadwick*, ed. Derek Beales and Geoffrey Best (Cambridge, 1985), pp. 105–24.

'A British patriarchy?: ecclesiastical imperialism under the early Stuarts', in *Religion, culture, and society in early modern Britain: essays in honour of Patrick Collinson*, ed. Anthony Fletcher and Peter Roberts (Cambridge, 1994), pp. 209–37.

'The causes of the British Civil Wars', *Journal of Ecclesiastical History*, 43 (1992), 624–33.

The nature of the English Revolution: essays (London and New York, 1993).

'The religious context of the English Civil War', *Transactions of the Royal Historical Society*, 5th series, 34 (1984), 155–78.

Morrill, John, ed., *The Scottish National Covenant in its British context, 1618–1651* (Edinburgh, 1990).

Morrissey, Mary, 'Interdisciplinarity and the study of early modern sermons', *Historical Journal*, 42 (1999), 1111–23.

'Scripture, style and persuasion in seventeenth-century English theories of preaching', *Journal of Ecclesiastical History*, 53 (2002), 686–706.

Mullan, David George, *Episcopacy in Scotland: the history of an idea, 1560–1638* (Edinburgh, 1986).

Scottish puritanism, 1590–1638 (Oxford, 2000).

'Theology in the Church of Scotland 1618–c.1640: a Calvinist consensus?', *Sixteenth Century Journal*, 26 (1995), 595–617.

Oakley, Francis, 'Jacobean political theology: the absolute and ordinary powers of the king', *Journal of the History of Ideas*, 29 (1968), 323–46.

Orr, D. Alan, 'Sovereignty, supremacy, and the origins of the English Civil War', *History*, 87 (2002), 474–90.

Treason and the state: law, politics and ideology in the English Civil War (Cambridge, 2002).

Patterson, W. B., *King James VI and I and the reunion of Christendom* (Cambridge, 1997).

Perrott, M. E. C., 'Richard Hooker and the problem of authority in the Elizabethan Church', *Journal of Ecclesiastical History*, 49 (1998), 29–60.

Pineas, Rainier, 'William Turner's polemical use of ecclesiastical history and his controversy with Stephen Gardiner', *Renaissance Quarterly*, 33 (1980), 599–608.

Pocock, J. G. A., *The ancient constitution and the feudal law: a reissue with a retrospect* (Cambridge, 1987).

Barbarism and religion, 2 vols. (Cambridge, 1999).

'British history: a plea for a new subject', *Journal of Modern History*, 47 (December 1975), 601–28.

'The concept of language and the *métier d'historien*: some considerations on practice', in *The languages of political theory in early modern Europe*, ed. Anthony Pagden (Cambridge, 1987), pp. 19–38.

'The history of British political thought: the creation of a Center', *Journal of British Studies*, 24 (1985), 283–310.

'Languages and their implications: the transformation of the study of political thought', in his *Politics, language and time: essays on political thought and history* (New York, 1971), pp. 3–41.

'Time, history and eschatology in the thought of Thomas Hobbes', in his *Politics, language and time: essays on political thought and history* (New York, 1971), pp. 149–201.

'Within the margins: the definitions of orthodoxy', in *The margins of orthodoxy: heterodox writing and cultural response, 1660–1750*, ed. Roger Lund (Cambridge, 1995), pp. 33–53.

'Working on ideas in time', in *The historian's workshop*, ed. L. P. Curtis (New York, 1970), pp. 153–65.

Preston, Joseph H., 'English ecclesiastical historians and the problem of bias, 1559–1742', *Journal of the History of Ideas*, 32 (1971), 203–20.

Prior, Charles W. A., 'Ancient *and* reformed?: Thomas Bell and Jacobean conformist thought', *Canadian Journal of History*, 38 (2003), 425–38.

'The regiment of the Church: doctrine, discipline and history in Jacobean ecclesiology, 1603–1625' (Ph.D. diss., Queen's University at Kingston, 2003).

'Religious conflict and political language in England, 1580–c.1630', unpublished paper.

'"Then Leave complaints": Mandeville, anti-Catholicism, and English orthodoxy', in *Mandeville and Augustan ideas: new essays*, ed. Charles W. A. Prior, English Literary Studies Monograph Series, 83 (Victoria, BC, 2000), pp. 51–70.

'Trismegistus "his great giant": a source for the title page of Hobbes' *Leviathan*', *Notes and Queries*, 51 (2004), 366–70.

Questier, Michael, *Conversion, politics and religion in England, 1580–1621* (Cambridge, 1996).

'Loyalty, religion and state power in early modern England: English Romanism and the Jacobean Oath of Allegiance', *Historical Journal*, 40 (1997), 311–29.

'The politics of religious conformity and the accession of James I', *Bulletin of the Institute of Historical Research*, 71 (1998), 14–30.

'Practical antipapistry during the reign of Elizabeth I', *Journal of British Studies*, 36 (1997), 371–96.

Raymond, Joad, *Pamphlets and pamphleteering in early modern Britain* (Cambridge, 2003).

Richardson, R. C., 'History and the early modern communications circuit', *Clio*, 31 (2002), 167–77.

Robbins, Caroline, 'Selden's pills: state oaths in England, 1558–1714', *Huntington Library Quarterly*, 35 (1971–2), 303–21.

Russell, Conrad, 'Arguments for religious unity in England, 1530–1650', *Journal of Ecclesiastical History*, 18 (1967), 201–26.

   'The British problem and the English Civil War', *History*, 75 (1987), 395–415.

   The causes of the English Civil War (Oxford, 1990).

   'Divine rights in the early seventeenth century', in *Public duty and private conscience in seventeenth century England: essays presented to G. E. Aylmer*, ed. John Morrill, Paul Slack, and D. R. Woolf (Oxford, 1993), pp. 101–20.

   The fall of the British monarchies, 1637–1642 (Oxford, 1991).

   Unrevolutionary England (London, 1990).

Salmon, J. H. M., 'Catholic resistance theory, ultramontainism, and the royalist response, 1580–1620', in *The Cambridge history of political thought, 1450–1700*, ed. J. H. Burns and Mark Goldie (Cambridge, 1991), pp. 219–53.

Schochet, Gordon, *Patriarchalism in political thought* (Oxford, 1975).

Shagan, Ethan H., 'The English Inquisition: constitutional conflict and ecclesiastical law in the 1590s', *The Historical Journal*, 47 (2004), 541–65.

Sharpe, Kevin, *The personal rule of Charles I* (New Haven, 1992).

   Reading revolutions: the politics of reading in early modern England (New Haven, 2000).

   Remapping early modern England: the culture of seventeenth-century politics (Cambridge, 2000).

   Sir Robert Cotton, 1586–1631: history and politics in early modern England (Oxford, 1979).

Shell, Alison, *Catholicism and the English literary imagination, 1558–1660* (Cambridge, 1999).

Shriver, Frederick, 'Hampton Court revisited: James I and the Puritans', *Journal of Ecclesiastical History*, 33 (1982), 48–71.

Sommerville, J. P., 'English and European political ideas in the early seventeenth century: revisionism and the case of absolutism', *Journal of British Studies*, 35 (1996), 168–94.

   'Jacobean political thought and the controversy over the Oath of Allegiance' (Ph.D. diss., University of Cambridge, 1981).

   Royalists and patriots: politics and ideology in England, 1603–1640 (London, 1999).

   'The royal supremacy and episcopacy "jure divino", 1603–1640', *Journal of Ecclesiastical History*, 34 (1983), 548–58.

Spinks, Bryan, *Sacraments, ceremonies and the Stuart divines: sacramental theology and liturgy in England and Scotland, 1603–1662* (London, 2002).

Springborg, Patricia, 'Leviathan and the problem of ecclesiastical authority', *Political Theory*, 3 (1975), 289–303.

Sprunger, Keith, *Dutch puritanism: a history of the English and Scottish churches of the Netherlands in the sixteenth and seventeenth centuries* (Leiden, 1982).

   The learned Doctor William Ames (Urbana, IL, 1972).

   Trumpets from the tower: English puritan printing in the Netherlands, 1600–1640 (Leiden, 1994).

Spufford, Margaret, *Small books and pleasant histories: popular fiction and its readership in seventeenth-century England* (London, 1981).

Sykes, Norman, *Old priest and new presbyter* (Cambridge, 1956).

Tan, Eng-Hang, 'Polemics, persuasion and authority: an investigation of the theological method of Richard Hooker in "The laws of ecclesiastical polity"' (Ph.D. diss., Trinity Evangelical Divinity School, 1997).

Tolmie, Murray, *The triumph of the saints: the separate churches of London, 1616–1649* (Cambridge, 1977).

Trevor-Roper, H. R., 'George Buchanan and the ancient Scottish constitution', *English Historical Review*, Supplement 3 (1966).

Tyacke, Nicholas, 'Anglican attitudes: some recent writings on English religious history, from the Reformation to the Civil War', *Journal of British Studies*, 35 (April 1996), 139–67.

    Anti-Calvinists: the rise of English Arminianism, c. 1590–1640 (Oxford, 1987; paperback edition, 1990).

    'Archbishop Laud', in *The early Stuart Church, 1603–1642*, ed. Kenneth Fincham (Stanford, 1993), pp. 51–70.

    'Lancelot Andrewes and the myth of Anglicanism', in *Conformity and orthodoxy in the English Church, c. 1560–1660*, ed. Peter Lake and Michael Questier (Woodbridge, Suffolk, 2000), pp. 5–33.

    'Puritanism, Arminianism, and counter-revolution', in *The origins of the English Civil War*, ed. Conrad Russell (London, 1973), pp. 119–43.

Tyacke, Nicholas, and White, Peter, 'Debate: The rise of Arminianism reconsidered', *Past and Present*, 115 (1987), 201–29.

Usher, R. G., 'Nicholas Fuller: a forgotten exponent of English liberty', *American Historical Review*, 12 (1907), 743–60.

    The reconstruction of the English Church, 2 vols. (London, 1910).

    The rise and fall of the High Commission, intro. Philip Tyler (Oxford, 1968 edn).

Verkamp, Bernard J., *The indifferent mean: adiaphorism in the English Reformation to 1554* (Athens, OH, 1977).

Wadkins, T. H., 'Theological polemic and religious culture in early Stuart England: the Percy / "Fisher" controversies, 1605–41' (Ph.D. diss., Graduate Theological Union, Berkeley, CA, 1988).

Walsham, Alexandra, *Church Papists: Catholicism, conformity, and confessional polemic in early modern England* (Woodbridge, Suffolk, 1993).

    Providence in early modern England (Oxford, 1999).

Watt, Tessa, *Cheap print and popular piety, 1550–1640* (Cambridge, 1991).

Webster, Tom, *Godly clergy in early Stuart England* (Cambridge, 1997).

White, Peter, *Predestination, policy, and polemic: conflict and consensus in the English Church from the Reformation to the Civil War* (Cambridge, 1992).

    'The rise of Arminianism reconsidered', *Past and Present*, 101 (1983), 34–54.

    'The *via media* in the early Stuart Church', in *The early Stuart Church, 1603–1642*, ed. Kenneth Fincham (Stanford, 1993), pp. 211–30.

Willson, D. H., 'James I and his literary assistants', *Huntington Library Quarterly*, 8 (1944–5), 35–57.

Wilmer, Richard, *The doctrine of the Church in the English Reformation* (Evanston, IL, 1952).

Woodfield, Denis B., *Surreptitious printing in England, 1550–1640* (New York, 1973).

Woodhouse, H. F., *The doctrine of the Church in Anglican theology, 1547–1603* (London, 1954).

Wooding, Lucy E. C., *Rethinking Catholicism in Reformation England* (Oxford, 2000).

Woolf, D. R., *The idea of history in early Stuart England: erudition, ideology, and the 'light of truth' from the accession of James I to the Civil War* (Toronto, 1990).
  Reading history in early modern England (Cambridge, 2000).
Wormald, Jenny, *Court, Kirk, and community: Scotland, 1470–1625* (Toronto, 1981).
  'James VI and I, *Basilikon doron* and *The trew law of free monarchies*: the Scottish context and the English translation', in *The mental world of the Jacobean court*, ed. Linda Levy Peck (Cambridge, 1991), pp. 36–54.
  'James VI and I: two kings or one?' *History*, 68 (1983), 187–209.

INDEX

Titles in the series